THE BOOK OF THE SOLENT

Including the Isle of Wight Coastal Voyage

Calshot Castle

Old Water Gate and Gaol, Southampton

Hulk off the Gun Wharf, Portsmouth

Round Tower, Portsmouth

The Book of
The Solent

including the
ISLE OF WIGHT COASTAL VOYAGE

Edited by

Maldwin Drummond & Robin McInnes

PUBLISHED BY CROSS PUBLISHING
CHALE, ISLE OF WIGHT

in association with

THOMAS REED PUBLICATIONS

©2001 Cross Publishing

ISBN 0 901281 30 1

ISBN 1 873295 51 0 De luxe limited edition

British Library Cataloguing-in-Publication Data
A catalogue record for this book is available from the British Library

Published by
Cross Publishing, Chale, Isle of Wight PO38 2JE
in association with
Thomas Reed Publications
(a division of the ABR Company Limited)
The Barn, Ford Farm
Bradford Leigh, Bradford on Avon
Wiltshire BA15 2RP
United Kingdom

Compiled by
Peter Cross & Robin McInnes

Design by Amanda Backhouse
Digital Artwork by PM Colour Ltd Isle of Wight

Printed in Spain by Bookprint, S.L, on behalf of Midas Printing (UK) Ltd

THE AUTHORS

Kate Ansell has held the post of Solent Forum Officer since 1997. Her role is to co-ordinate and facilitate the work of the Solent Forum. After graduating from the University of Nottingham she worked on environmental issues in the travel, tourism and marine industries before taking up her current post. (Author of Chapter Eight)

Keith Beken was born in 1914. He first qualified as a chemist in 1937 and started taking photographs at sea until 1939. He joined the Royal Air Force in Marine Area Sea Rescue for the five years of the war and returned to Cowes in 1945 where he continued marine photography until the year 2000. (Author of Chapter Seven)

John Bingeman is an amateur nautical archaeologist and has been a government historical wreck licensee for twenty years. After diving on the Mary Rose he was given responsibility (for eight years) for the wrecks of the Assurance (1753), and the Pomone (1811) off the Needles. In 1980 he identified and achieved designation for the wreck of the Invincible (1758) for which he remains the licensee. By profession a chartered marine engineer he also had a career in the Royal Navy achieving the rank of Commander. (Contributor to Chapter Three)

Andrew Butler has lived and worked on the Isle of Wight all his life. Working for many years as a commercial lobster fisherman and more recently for the National Trust he is also President of the Isle of Wight Natural History and Archaeological Society. He has a keen interest in all aspects of natural history including wildlife photography and has illustrated the whole of Chapter Two with his own photographs. (Author of Chapter Two)

Gilly Drummond is a garden enthusiast and historian who was founder chairman of the Hampshire Gardens Trust. She is a member of the English Heritage Gardens Committee and the Government's Urban Green Spaces Task Force. (Author of Chapter Five (Part One))

Maldwin Drummond is an author who farms part of the north Solent shore. He is a past Commodore of the Royal Yacht Squadron and is now their Honorary Historian. A one time editor of the Royal Cruising Club Journal he has sailed from north-west Norway to Salerno, Italy in his cutter 'Gang Warily' as well as cruising under sail in other parts of the world. (Co-Editor, author of Chapter Five (Part One) and Chapter Six)

Nicola Horsey has been Hampshire County Council's Defence Heritage and Tourism Manager since 1990. Prior to that she was the Tourism Manager for the Isle of Wight and then Winchester. At the County Council, amongst other things, she is responsible for marketing Hampshire's remarkable defence heritage legacy of castles, forts, historic ships, military museums and so on through the Defence of the Realm consortium. (Author of Chapter Four)

Robin McInnes is a Chartered Geologist and Civil Engineer and is Coastal Manager for the Isle of Wight Council. He has worked on the Isle of Wight since 1972 specialising in coastal, geotechnical and environmental issues. He has a particular interest in the history and art of the Isle of Wight and has written books, articles and arranged exhibitions for many years. In 1997 he established the Centre for the Coastal Environment within the Isle of Wight Council and a Coastal Visitors' Centre at Ventnor the following year. (Co-Editor, author of Chapter Five (Part Two), Contributor to Chapter Four)

Peter Sedgley is a director of the R J Mitchell Memorial Museum, which incorporates the Southampton Hall of Aviation. Peter learned to fly with the Hampshire Aeroplane Club and worked for several years in civil aviation. A keen sailor and aircraft historian he lives near Romsey with his wife and daughter. (Contributor to Chapter Four)

Dr David Tomalin is a pre-historian and underwater archaeologist who confesses to a longstanding fascination with "mistress Solent". Prior to his retirement as County Archaeologist for the Isle of Wight he and his colleagues have pursued the history of this ancient seaway through its inter-tidal muds, in the depths of its seabed sediments and from the perspective of aerial reconnaissance. Between 1975-1999 Dr Tomalin collaborated with Commander John Bingeman in the execution of the 'designated' historic shipwrecks - the Assurance and the Pomone. Dr Tomalin is a Fellow of the Society of Antiquaries and a Research Fellow of the University of Southampton. After thirty years David and Carol Tomalin are very happily settled on the Isle of Wight where they share interests in the Vectensian landscape. (Author of Chapters One and Three)

ACKNOWLEDGEMENTS

The authors wish to acknowledge the particular assistance provided by the following individuals and organisations during the preparation of this book : Chris Ball, Beken of Cowes, Dr Binney Buckley, Major Nigel Chamberlayne-Macdonald, Deane and Celish Clark, Lady Cooksey, Dave Etheridge, Jenny Jakeways, Rosalie Hendey, Holyrood Galleries, Gill Jolliff, Gill Lacey, the Royal Yacht Squadron, SCOPAC, the Solent Forum, Steven Marshall, Cheryl Taylor, Captain Henry Wrigley.

In the compilation of chapters 1 and 3 on the archaeology of the Solent, David Tomalin thanks his colleagues Professor Michael Collins, Dr Adonis Velegrakis and Dr Justin Dix of the Southampton School of Earth and Oceanographic Sciences for a variety of contributions on the geomorphology of the ancient Solent River. Thanks are also due Dr Rob Scaife and Dr Anthony Long who have generously shared their own research on the palaeoecology and the changing sea-levels of the Solent. The investigation of the submerged Mesolithic site at Bouldnor has been led Garry Momber and members of the Hampshire and Isle of Wight Trust for Maritime Archaeology. This investigation has followed upon earlier work by members of the Isle of Wight Maritime Heritage Project who, in the 1980's, were generously supported by the Manpower Services Commission, Mr & Mrs Trevor Green and the Isle of Wight (County) Council. Details of recent investigations at Testwood Lakes and Langstone Harbour have been provided by Dr Andrew Fitzpatick and Dr Michael Allen of Wessex Archaeology. Information on prehistoric, Roman and medieval sites in the Southampton region has been kindly provided by Dr Andy Russel of Southampton City Museums and by Kay Ainsworth of the Hampshire County Museum Service. The Roman amphorae from the Solent have been examined and petrologically analysed by Professor David Peacock and Dr David Williams of the University of Southampton, Dept of Archaeology. Identification of a number of items composed of the Binstead and Quarr facies of the Bembridge Limestone Formation has been carried out by Dr Alan Insole of the University of Bristol. The writer thanks Ruth Waller and his past colleagues at the Isle of Wight County Archaeological and Historic Environment Service and David Hopkins and his staff at the Hampshire County Sites and Monuments Service for a variety of valuable additions to this brief archaeological narrative. This text has been enhanced by John Bingeman's account of the designated wreck sites and also by some lines which, with the kind permission of Elsevier of Amsterdam, have been reproduced from Solent Science (2000). An outstanding acknowledgement must go to all fishermen, beachwalkers and field observers in the Solent region whose persistent interest has provided the raw material upon which the prehistory of this seaway is still being built.

Other figure acknowledgements
The earliest map of Portsmouth. Portsmouth Central Reference Library and the Fort Cumberland and Portsmouth Militaria Society. The maps on pages 193 and 196 are based upon maps prepared by the Ordnance Survey with the permission of Her Majesty's Stationary Office; Crown Copyright reserved.
Special thanks to Sylvia McInnes, Peter Cross, Diana Harding and Heather Freeman for their valuable assistance and patience.

Picture Credits (Page Numbers of illustrations) :-
Archaeologia : 19. Chris Ball : 121 (top), 124, 125 (top), 134, 150/151, 154 (top). Beken of Cowes : 99, 162, 166 (bottom), 167, 169, 170, 171, 172, 173, 175, 176, 177, 179, 180, 181, 182, 183, 184, 185, 186, 187, 188, 189, 190, 191. John Bingeman : 78, 79, 80. British Archaeological Reports : 67. Andrew Butler : 33, 37, 38, 39, 41, 42, 43, 44, 45, 46, 47, 49, 50, 51, 52, 53, 54, 55, 56, 148 (top). Poppy Cooksey : 111. Peter Cross : 96, 98, 99, 100, 101. Dover Museum : 28. Maldwin Drummond : 105, 106, 107, 108, 109, 111, 113, 114 (bottom), 116, 157,160, 161, 164/165, 166 (top). English Heritage Photographic Library : 66, 88, 91. Dave Etheridge : 112, 114 (top), 115. Dr Andrew Fitzpatrick : 27 (bottom). Don French : 193, 198, 204. Hampshire and Isle of Wight Trust for Maritime Archaeology : 64 (bottom). Nicola Horsey : 92. Holyrood Galleries : End paper maps. Isle of Wight Council : 27 (top left), 61, 68 (top right), 70 (bottom), 72, 135, 136 (top), 140 (top), 142, 143 (bottom) 144, 146. Institute of Geological Sciences : 21 (left). William Le Fanu : 168. Mary Rose Trust : 87. V W McAndrew : 174. Robin McInnes : Title Page illustrations, 15, 34, 48, 85, 93, 94, 104, 119, 120, 121 (bottom), 122/123, 125 (bottom), 126, 127, 128/129, 130, 131, 132/133, 136, 137, 138, 139, 140, 141, 142, 143, 144/145, 146/147, 148, 149, 152/153, 154 (bottom), 155. National Museum of Wales : 27 (top right). Platt and Coleman-Smith (Leicester University Press) : 73. Portsmouth Museum & Records Office : 89. Quarterly Journal of the Geological Society : 26. Royal Yacht Squadron : 118. A Saunders : 86. Solent Forum : 193, 195, 196, 199, 200, 202, 203. Dr David Tomalin : 13, 18, 21 (right), 22, 23, 24, 25, 26, 28, 29 (bottom), 58, 63, 64 (top), 65, 67, 68 (top left), 70 (top), 71, 76. Trustees of the Fishbourne Palace Museum : 60, 68 (bottom left). Trustees of the Brading Roman Villa : 68 (bottom right). University of Portsmouth : 29 (top).

CONTENTS

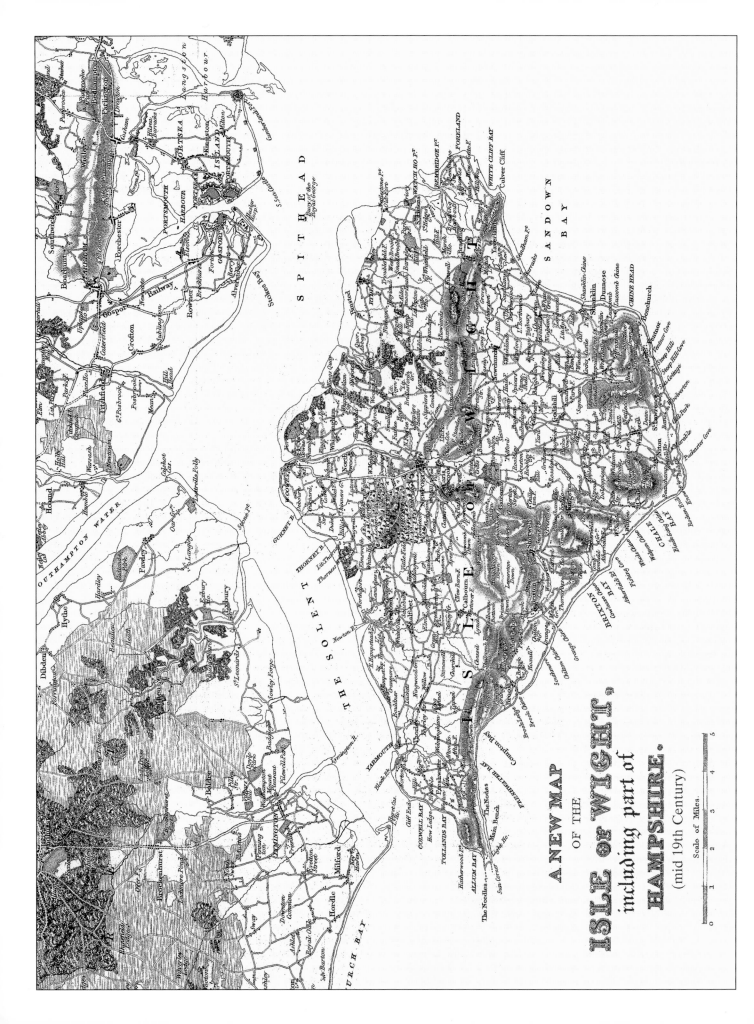

A NEW MAP
OF THE
ISLE OF WIGHT,
including part of
HAMPSHIRE.
(mid 19th Century)

Scale of Miles.

0 1 2 3 4 5

FOREWORD

The Solent and Spithead geographically divide the communities of Hampshire and the Isle of Wight. This sheltered water has, however, brought mainlanders (overners) and Islanders together in a shared history. During the Second World War that great Islander, sailor and yacht designer, Uffa Fox, used to refer to England as "our gallant ally".

There has long been a need for a book that closely examines this unique piece of water with its peculiar tides, ecologically rich shores and shallows.

The book brings together two organisations that are playing an important part in the protection, conservation and understanding of the waters between Hampshire and the Wight. The authors and editors have given their time and their words for free, so adding to and celebrating the work of many in Hampshire and the Island who serve their communities without payment. Their reward is to increase the understanding of the environment of this unique stretch of water and so to enhance and conserve it.

The book is published in August 2001 when many of the most beautiful sailing vessels will be competing in celebration of the schooner *America*'s victory in the race round the Island in 1851 that led, in due time, to the America's Cup. It is hoped this volume will enable visitors and residents alike to understand and enjoy the waters of Hampshire and the Wight.

Mary Fagan
Lord Lieutenant of Hampshire

Christopher Bland
Lord Lieutenant of the Isle of Wight

Cowes

INTRODUCTION

The Solent and its mainland and Island shorelines have a unique and varied character. This has evolved particularly since the end of the last Ice Age, following a steady rise in sea levels. This sea level rise resulted in the drowning of the original Solent river which used to flow eastwards towards the English Channel. Eventually, the chalk ridge between the western end of the Isle of Wight and the mainland was breached resulting in the coastal topography much as we know it today.

For thousands of years the Solent has fulfilled a vital role as a waterway for shipping, trading and other activities such as fishing and more recently recreation. Since Roman times and before, there has been a steady growth in the use of the Solent, particularly as the great ports of Southampton and Portsmouth developed.

The Isle of Wight and the Solent were, from the earliest times, of considerable strategic importance and have been the site of a succession of affrays, invasion attempts and other military activities over the last few thousand years. The proximity of the Solent region to the English Channel has also resulted in the development of a range of skills and crafts which have led, in part, to the economic prosperity of the Solent area as we know it today.

The extensive development along parts of the Solent shoreline, together with recreational and other demands, can cause conflicts with the natural environment which is recognised as being of international importance. A wide range of nature conservation and other designations have been attributed to both the Solent shorelines and to the marine environment itself. There is a need to reconcile the many often conflicting interests that exist in the Solent in order to ensure that activities such as commerce and tourism can continue to exist in harmony with the natural environment. To assist this process, two organisations have played a particular role in the development of an improved understanding of the Solent region and are working to ensure that the Solent can continue to be enjoyed by future generations. In 1985 a two-day conference was held on the Isle of Wight entitled "Problems Associated with the Coastline". The purpose of this event was to highlight a range of issues and conflicts such as possible impacts of aggregate dredging and the knock-on effects of coast protection works on adjacent lengths of coastline. This conference led to the establishment of SCOPAC (the Standing Conference on Problems Associated with the Coastline) which has developed steadily over the last sixteen years and now brings together some thirty organisations with an interest in the management of the shoreline and in particular coastal defence issues. It is important for such an organisation to be in place to achieve a co-ordinated approach to coastal defence and to meet the challenges of predicted climate change which could result in significant alterations to the Solent shoreline as we know it today.

A second organisation, the Solent Forum, was founded in 1992. The aim of the Solent Forum is to assist the co-ordination of a very wide range of activities that take place within the Solent to ensure, as far as possible, that wide-ranging activities such as port operations and shipping, tourism and the natural environment can exist alongside one another. The Solent Forum aims to raise awareness of coastal issues, to seek to resolve conflicts through an understanding of the broad range of activities that take place in the Solent and to commission research and disseminate information. This "Book of the Solent" provides a taste of the wide-range of activities and interests - physical, human and natural that exist in this outstanding part of the British coastline. The book attempts to capture the fascinating history of the Solent and to introduce the reader to some of the special qualities of the area including its historical, environmental and recreational and commercial activities. Both SCOPAC and the Solent Forum commission research to improve knowledge and understanding of a wide-range of physical and other aspects in order to facilitate better management of the area in the future. This book could not have been produced without the assistance of various expert contributors, who, without exception, have written their respective chapters free of charge allowing the proceeds from the sale of this book to be donated equally to the research funds of SCOPAC and the Solent Forum.

Robin McInnes
Chairman of the Officers' Working Group
SCOPAC

Maldwin Drummond
Chairman of the Solent Forum

Chapter One

THE SOLENT IN PREHISTORY

Identifying the Solent

What is the Solent? This simple question has long been fraught with ambiguities. For many, the definition of the Solent has been that strait of water which separates the Isle of Wight from the mainland but many geographers will point to an array of historic maps which are more specific in distinguishing a *Western Solent* and an *Eastern Solent* while omitting reference to a single entity. For mariners however, it seems that the one entity is their accepted definition and this is reflected in the modern admiralty charts which identify a single Solent seaway albeit one with eastern and western arms.

A further complication in the definition of the Solent is presented by the historic anchorage known as *Spithead*. On many charts this name seems to be a substitute for the Eastern Solent while identifying an off-shore location lying between Portsmouth and Ryde. The name Spithead appears to derive from Spit Sand, a shoal which has historically impeded the approach of ships to Portsmouth Harbour. Spit Sand is a naturally accreting sub-tidal deposit and since medieval times it has edged anchoring craft towards a mid-channel position in the Eastern Solent. Increased demand for anchorage at the *head of the spit* was particularly notable in the 19th century when anchorage in the Eastern Solent generally expanded until, at times, moored craft could occupy most of the area from Stokes Bay to St Helens Roads. Once widespread anchorage had been established in this area it is easy to see how mariners could commonly adopt the name Spithead for virtually any anchorage within this eastern approach.

If the term *Solent* is accepted as the collective name for both the eastern and western arms of the seaway north of the Isle of Wight, there arises the complication of Southampton Water. For sailors, this long northern inlet of some 16km may appear to be a distinct and separate entity but geomorphologists are quick to point out that Southampton Water is also an integral arm of a single drowned valley system or *ria*. This entire complex has been properly described as the *Solent estuarine system* and its past and present structure has been well defined in a study produced by the National Environmental Research Council in 1980. Moreover, the integral nature of Southampton Water is confirmed by the presence of an ancient Pleistocene river channel, termed the *Solent River*. The *palaeochannel* of this river has been detected beneath Calshot Spit where it passes northwards through the bed of Southampton Water to drain the rivers Itchen, Test and Hamble. This hidden feature confirms an ancient union between Southampton Water and the Eastern Solent.

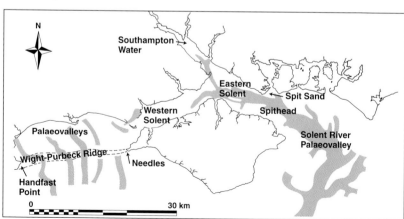

The components of the Solent.

The naming of the Solent

Given the prompting of the geologists and geomorphologists we would be ill advised to spend too much time pursuing the historical definitions of the Solent but it is interesting to observe that the first known use of the name *(Soluente)* was that which was scribed on to a goatskin document of the early 8th century AD. This document was the work of the Northumbrian monk *Bede* who was completing his *Ecclesiastical History of Britain* around the year. AD 730. It is difficult to gauge whether Bede was personally familiar with the geographic setting of the Solent and the Isle of Wight or whether he drew all of his information from others. Elsewhere, while penning his brief account of the Roman history of Britain, Bede helpfully adds that the Isle of Wight *'is about 30 miles in length from east to west and twelve miles from north to south..., being six miles distant from the southern coast of Britain at the east end and three only at the west'*. In its next historical reference we find the Solent described as *Solentan* when cited in a Saxon document of AD 948. The word Solent is not mentioned in Domesday and its next rendering appears as *Le Soland* when cited in a patent roll of AD 1395 (Ekwall, 1960).

For most, the origin of the word Solent has seemed uncertain, although a British source has been proposed by Ekwall in his study of English place-names. Elsewhere, this writer associates the Old English word *sol* with 'a muddy place for animals' but he also recognises the word *sul* or *sol* in the name of the Solway Firth which was written *Sulwad* in AD 1229. This name he attributes to the congregating of the Northern Gannet which is otherwise known as the Solan Goose *(Morus bassanus)*. Here, perhaps, we may find an appealing explanation for the name of the Solent for despite an apparent diminution in its number, this bird has always been found in significant groups in the near-shore waters of the Solent. Solent gannets are annual visitors and they are especially active in spring when their numbers substantially increase as they congregate in flocks.

The use of bird place-names is certainly a common feature of the Solent region, the more obvious examples being *Bitterne* (in Southampton) *Swanmore* and *Swanwick* (Wight and Hamble area), *Goose Rock* (Needles), *Kite Hill* and *Crane moor* (Isle of Wight) and *Hawkhill* (New Forest). In Saxon times Wootton Creek was known as the *'Fugelflete'*, the bird lake.

The archaeological record is also able to identify another vanquished occupant of the historic Solent. Before succumbing to the fatal accuracy of the longbow, it seems that the trusting stork was a common visitor to the region. It is well represented in the faunal remains which archaeologists have recovered within the Saxon town of Southampton (Coy, pers comm). The occasional sighting of vagrant white and red storks are still reported in the Isle of Wight and Tichfield Haven. For British observers these rare movements seem to represent the remnant gestures of this noble and formerly indigenous bird. Today, the congregating of birds in the Solent is a fascinating and leisurely spectacle but for our forebears these annual patterns of migratory and reproductive behaviour were of more practical and culinary interest. The population of wildfowl in the Solent has been ever dependent on a complex sub-tidal and intertidal ecology in which fish, crustaceans and marine plants have played a critical part (Tubbs. 1991 & 1999).

A brief review of the archaeology and palaeoecology of the Solent shows that the present human population has grown from earlier communities who won their subsistence from a rich array of natural resources which they found above and below the tidal zone. Names like Gurnard Bay, Whale Island, Whale Chine, Dolphin Bank and the lost seals of Selsey tell of some of the larger creatures which once could be readily found on our local shores and it should not be overlooked that the waste products abandoned by the occupants of the Newport Roman villa included at least one portion of a whale.

Today, this wheel of natural good fortune has been alarmingly reversed, for with the departure of the cranes, dolphins, porpoises and whales, the diminution of intertidal eel-grasses and a decline in the stocks of edible molluscs, we can see that the dependance of man upon the Solent has been transformed into a dependance of the Solent upon the idiosyncratic decisions of man. A tattered patchwork of statutory and non-statutory planning policies and some grey regulations for the management of the off-shore zone now stand as an uninspiring substitute for the natural colour and vitality which has been progressively drained from this historic seaway.

In search of truth in the 19th century

The first scientific enquiries into the configuration of the Solent began in the early 19th century. The geologist Thomas Webster opened the discussion in 1816 when he compared the chalk stacks at the Needles with those at Handfast Point, on the Purbeck coast. Here he observed that *'the chalk at Handfast Point which being in a line with that of the Isle of Wight appeared like the continuation of the same strata'* (Englefield 1816). Webster considered that these stacks *'like those of the Needles had resisted, longer than the rest, the destroying effects of the waves'* and he concluded that *'these two places were once united'*.

Disquieted by a contemporary regard for biblical timescales, Webster demurred over the means by which the intervening chalk ridge had been lost or submerged. By the mid 1830's, however, all such reservations were confidently dispelled when Charles Lyell turned his attention to the Solent in his new discourse on the *'Principles of Geology'*. Prior to this date, grasp of the Earth's history had been primitive indeed and it had not been helped by the well-meaning calculations of Dr James Ussher, the Bishop of Omagh. In 1597 this ecclesiastical scholar had counted the number of generations contained within the Israelite genealogy of the Old Testament. From this he had concluded that the passage of at least 4004 years was inferred within the ambit of the recorded biblical life-spans. Soon, this figure was being enthusiastically offered by his clerical colleagues as the date of the Earth's genesis and it was not long before it was being appended to printed editions of the Bible.

The Wight-Purbeck ridge formerly extended from the Isle of Wight westwards to Handfast Point (in the distance).

The period 1840 to 1870 finally brought a loss of naivety to mankind for this was a time when a new rationale was applied to the study of earth's history and the origins of human life. The publication of Charles Lyell's *'Principles'* in 1830-33 was followed in 1845 by Alexander von Humbolt's *Cosmos*. These two works presented an entirely new scientific perspective of the nature of the world and its place within the universe. Prior to this date, the discovery of extinct animal remains had been attributed to Divine intervention in the form of sudden and gigantic floods or *'diluvial'* events. It is interesting to see that in 1816, such a simple explanation had been readily accepted by the inhabitants of Brook, on the coast of the Isle of Wight. When prehistoric hazel nuts of the Mesolithic period were uncovered in the neighbouring cliffs, these were popularly acclaimed to be *'Noah's Nuts'* (Webster 1816).

The new light shed by Charles Lyell was able to demonstrate that the past creation of ancient geological deposits was exactly the same as the slow and natural processes of erosion, transportation and deposition which could be witnessed today. The breadth of Lyell's new vision was truly remarkable and it is, perhaps, not surprising to find that his search for examples of *processual* geological phenomena soon came to focus on the Solent.

Turning his attention to the severance of the Wight-Purbeck chalk ridge, Charles Lyell concluded that the present shape of the Isle of Wight, was due to the encroachment and continued action of the sea. Lyell cited Hurst Spit as proof and product of long incremental coastal processes and he drew persuasive comparisons with other British examples including Chesil Beach. In each case he argued that the beach shingle was derived from the slow and on-going erosion of flint-bearing cliffs. This argument was reinforced in 1852 when it was recognised that the deep cutting of Hurst Channel was further evidence of protracted coastal processes (Redman 1852).

The mid 19th century was a time when the processual history of the earth and the antiquity of man were subjects of hot contention in drawing room, public bar and pulpit. In 1859 the publication Charles Darwin's *Origins of Species* was released to an amazed and disquieted public. Darwin's new principles of evolution were promptly endorsed by Edouard Lartet who, in 1860, was quick to point out that these were consistent with his own study *'on the co-existence of Man with certain extinct quadrupeds proved by fossil bones from various Pleistocene deposits bearing incisions made by sharp instruments'* (Lartet, 1860). This evidence comprised carefully fashioned flint implements which had been recovered from great spreads of Pleistocene gravel in the valleys of the Seine and the Somme. Here, his colleague, Boucher de Perthes, had been enthusiastically reporting discoveries since 1836. In his new work *De L'homme antediluvien et ses oeuvres*, published in 1860, his companion readily embraced Lyell's new vision with the words:-

'Who can put limits on the past? Is it not infinite as is the future? Where then is the man who has seen the beginning of any one thing? Where is he who will see the end? ..Let us not bargain over the duration of ages'.

Meanwhile, Lartet was bringing the implications of these new French discoveries to bear on a topic which was highly pertinent to the prehistory of the Solent. This concerned the idea that a submerged landscape might be concealed on the floor of the sea between England and France. As early as 1605 the English scholar Richard Rowlands had considered a hypothetical 'land bridge' between the two countries when seeking to account for the former population of native British wolves. As *'no one would willingly import these wicked creatures into England'* Rowlands concluded that there must once have been a time when dry land in the region of the English Channel had permitted these animals to *'pass over'*.

Lartet was prompt to consolidate this early vision of a lost or drowned landscape. Having compared the character of flint hand-axes found on both sides of the Channel he argued that a similar route had also been followed by other extinct animals as well as groups he described as *'primitive people'*. He also recognised that the animal remains and the hand-axes found on both sides of the Channel were embedded in valley gravels of a similar type. Unfortunately, he remained uncertain as to how these gravel deposits might be linked.

It is slightly surprising find that the issues raised by these new French and English discoveries of the mid 19th century were readily absorbed into hot topical debate in the rural solitude of the Isle of Wight. The venue was the rectory at Brighstone where evidence concerning the submergence of the English Channel was soon applied to the ancient river systems in the region of the Solent. These arguments were assembled by the rector and amateur paleon-tologist, William Fox. Tea-parties and fossil studies at the rectory were a common event and distinguished visitors included Sir Charles Lyell, the palaeontologists Gideon Mantell and John Owen and the poet Alfred Lord Tennyson.

By 1881 ideas on the configuration of ancient rivers and valley gravels in Britain and the Continent had been woven into a single explanatory model concerning the submergence of a continental land shelf. A principal exponent was James Geike who had boldly set out to produce an early conjectural map of this lost landscape. While the scale of this map was too general to convey the ancient configuration of the rivers in our area, Geike had no hesitation in asserting that:-

The Solent is an old land valley. At what particular point the ancient river discharged into the sea, or whether or not it really joined the Seine can only be conjectured.

Geike's ensuing comment confirmed that he largely supposed the drowning of the Solent to be a post-Glacial event for he also remarked that:-

'But that Palaeolithic man saw the Isle of Wight as part of the mainland, there cannot be any reasonable doubt'.

Part of James Geike's reconstruction of the submerged landscape of Europe (1881).

Ictis/Vectis and the drowning of the Solent; some dates old and new

It was more than 400 years ago when the first historians and geographers began to enquire into the nature and origins of the Solent as an open east-west seaway. The first recorded questions are those of William Camden whose first edition of *Britannia*, published in 1586, included the casual speculation that the Isle of Wight with its Roman name of *Vectis* might perhaps be equated with a prehistoric island otherwise known as *Ictis*.

A British island called *Ictis* had been cited in the 1st century BC by the classical writer Diodorus Siculus while describing the land of Britain or *'Prettanike'*. The style of this classical historian commonly included expressions like 'we are told' or 'they say'. This suggests that Diodorus was using the accounts of others and was unable to offer any experience of his own. His gatherings told of an island close to the shore of southern Britain where the natives could cross at low tide whilst drawing waggons loaded with tin ore or ingots. These consignments were loaded into visiting ships bound for the Atlantic seaboard of Gaul (Rivet & Smith 1979, 62-3). Diodorus added that it was people dwelling near the promontory of *Belerion* (Land's End) who prepared this tin and transported it to the tied island of *Ictis*.

Archaeologists are generally agreed that the most credible claimant for the island of Diodorus is St Michaels Mount, near Penzance. This granite islet is accessible at low tide and is very close to the tin stream deposits at Marazion Marsh. The Mount has even yielded scattered fragments of tin ore (Skinner 1797; Hencken 1932; Maxwell 1972; Herring 1992; Penhallurick 1997). A less convincing contender has been the rock promontory of Mount Batten, in Plymouth Sound. This once served as an Iron Age port and it is sited not far from the spot where a prehistoric tin ingot has been found on the sea bed (Cunliffe 1988, 103).

Since Camden's day, the Ictis-Vectis theory has claimed many champions, but it has remained a specious argument, readily flawed by the restriction of tin lodes to the Cornish peninsula. The best that might be postulated is that while Diodorus was gathering descriptions of all islands on the south coast of Britain, he applied the name used in Wight to a trading post in Cornwall. Indeed, he reminds us that he is speaking of more than one place when he attributes his description to *'the neighbouring islands lying between Europe and Prettanike'*. Such a fusion of accounts may permit *Ictis* to mean Vectis whilst excluding the impracticalities of a Vectensian tin trade.

A very different attempt to pursue historical explanations for the severance of Wight was made in the 18th century by Dr Thomas Short, a physician of Sheffield. He produced an extraordinary and unsubstantiated classical reference to a great earthquake which had allegedly severed the Isle of Wight from the mainland in the year AD 68 (Short 1749, 165). The source of this claim has never been substantiated. It has been observed, however, by Charles Thomas (1985) that where the creation of near-shore islands has been discussed, folklore and credulity have always favoured a catastrophic event rather than a slow processual one.

Early protagonists of the Solent River

It was the Rector of Brighstone, William Fox, who was first to pose the direct question *"when and how was the Isle of Wight separated from the mainland?"* This was the title of his perceptive paper published in the *Geologist* in 1862. Fox first considered the old historical *Ictis-Vectis* explanation currently championed by his non-conformist contemporary, the Reverend Edmund Kell of Newport. He then applied his geological knowledge to calculate where the Island's last overland connection or umbilical may have been. Kell, meanwhile, was postulating a fanciful overland staging route which could enable Iron Age people to carry Cornish tin to the Isle of Wight so that it might be laden on to ships which would return past the Cornish coast en route for the Atlantic seaboard of Gaul (Kell 1866). The flaws in this argument were readily recognised by Fox but they were to remain irresistible to many romantic imaginations in the Isle of Wight.

For William Fox, the Wight-Purbeck ridge had been a protective wall of chalk, sheltering the Dorset and Hampshire lowlands from the sea. This meant that an earlier seaward exit seemed necessary to allow the Dorset rivers of Frome, Stour, Piddle and Avon to reach the ocean. Fox developed the ingenious idea of a lost *Solent River* which might formerly pass behind the land of Wight. In post-Glacial times the exit of this river might lie somewhere off the Selsey and the West Sussex coast whilst its inland tributaries, including the floor of Southampton Water, the Test, Itchen, Hamble and Medina, could also include a feature which we might describe as a great westward arm. For Fox, this arm seemed to pass beneath the present Western Solent to serve the east Dorset catchment.

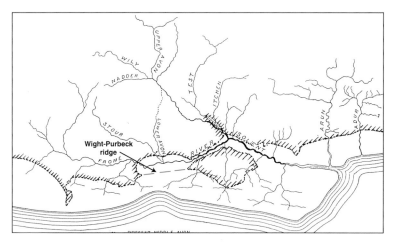

The Solent River and the Wight peninsula as conjectured by Fox and Reid, 1861 - 1905. The Wight-Purbeck chalk ridge is also shown.

Despite Fox's predictions, the presence of buried river channels or *palaeovalleys* gained little interest during the 19th century. When engineers and investors gathered in the year 1900 to propose a plan for an sub-Solent railway tunnel the dangers of encountering a buried channel seem to have been entirely disregarded. Civil engineering experiences gained during the cutting

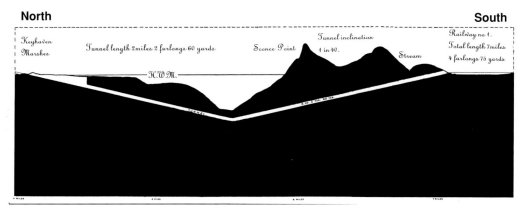

The Solent Tunnel Plan 1900. The designers made little allowance for concealed palaeovalleys in the seafloor.

18

of the Severn Tunnel in 1879 should have rung a cautionary bell yet when a more modest Medina tunnel was planned between East and West Cowes in 1892 a clearance of a mere eleven feet below the seabed was considered to be quite adequate.

Clement Reid's causeway or isthmus

In 1905 William Fox's model for the severance of Wight was taken up by the geologist Clement Reid. Reid first pursued the old and perennial antiquarian hare let loose by Camden, considering how the island of Ictis/Vectis had remained connected to the mainland as late as the 1st century BC. Camden had observed that *"we may well think this Vecta* [Vectis] *to be that Icta which as Diodorus Siculus writteth, seemed at every tide to be an island but when it was ebbe, the ancient Britaines were wont that way to carry tinne thither by carts"*..(Camden [English ed] 1637, 273). With this idea installed there was much printers' ink to be wasted.

Clement Reid wished to consider how the land of Wight might remain connected to the mainland after the sea had breached the Wight-Purbeck ridge. For this he was prepared to accept the date and events offered by Diodorus. Reid rightly dismissed Hurst Spit as a possible isthmus or causeway leading to the Isle of Wight. He now required firmer ground on which to set his groaning carts, the heaped tin ingots and the sweating Britons. He also questioned the feasibility of the great western arm proposed by Fox, observing that after the breaching of the Wight-Purbeck ridge *'there would be two streams in the valley of the* [Western] *Solent flowing in opposite directions from a low watershed or divide'.*

Reid identified his potential causeway or umbilical in the region of the Hamstead – Yarmouth coastline where hard outcrops of the Bembridge Limestone Formation led off-shore in the direction of Lymington. On the Hampshire shore no trace of the limestone could be found but Reid ingeniously suggested that such an outcrop had since been eradicated by coastal erosion prior to the formation of the Pennington-Lymington salt marshes.

Unfortunately, more recent geological mapping in the Western Solent (Hamblin & Harrison 1989) has demonstrated that the Yarmouth-Hamstead limestone outcrop reaches no more than 1.8 km from the Isle of Wight shore. Moreover, Reid neglected to consult Admiralty charts and these would have shown him that the centre of his isthmus was now more than 40m below sea-level. Even if we were to accept Reid's postulation that a greater area of marshland had once extended from the Lymington shore, this is a gulf which is difficult to overcome. Just one year after Reid's publication of his proposed *Ictis* causeway the Reverend E. Green was rightly scathing of these allusions the island of *Ictis.*

'The great puzzle has been the whereabouts of this island; a puzzle which has caused much doubt and wild guess-work.... Most absurd of all - it has been supposed and asserted to be the Isle of Wight, solely because its name is somewhat like Vectis... To make this argument possible requires a capacious imagination indeed. The sea - a deep sea - must be made to dry up - in imagination. The necessary accommodation must be found on the island side - by imagination; and then the tin must be found and dragged to it overland - a further piece of imagination; and all this without a tittle of evidence to suggest the thought, and with the fine port and depot of Clausentum (Bittern, our Southampton) actually in use close to hand. If history can be satisfied

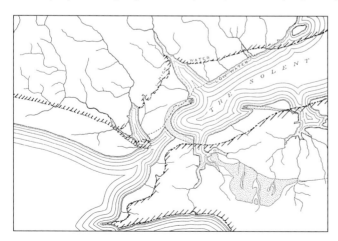

with such work, it must be a waste of time to seek the facts. Archaeology and geography have been so ruthlessly violated on this subject.... from the continued, persistent endeavour of writers to accept or adopt old theories and statements'. E. Green 1906

Clement-Reid's conjectured limestone causeway (1905).

Fathoming the origins of the Solent; some later revelations

During the 1970's the first marine sub-bottom geophysical surveys were conducted by the University of Southampton over the site of William Fox's lost Solent River (Dyer 1972 & 1975). These produced gratifying evidence of the course of Fox's deep and elusive channel as it passed beneath the Eastern Solent. Deep beneath Calshot Spit a substantial channel was also detected leading northward through the floor of Southampton Water. In the Western Solent, results were less rewarding and the supposed 'great western arm' of the lost Solent River could not be found. Here, however, the seismic signal had been dissipated by a blanket of sand and shingle and this left the matter unresolved (Dyer, 1975).

In 1972 the results of a series of bore-hole and sonar studies were published after new engineering operations had been completed at Fawley power station (Hodson & West 1972). These works produced a cross-section through the floor of Southampton Water showing the bedrock of an ancient valley lying 24 metres below Ordnance Datum. Here, the floor was lined with a covering of some 5 metres of Pleistocene gravel. In post-glacial times, the western side of this valley had been infilled with marine silts and saltmarsh sediments. These, it seemed, had steadily accumulated in dynamic equilibrium with a rising and encroaching sea.

On a line between Gosport and Ryde sub-bottom sonar was used to obtain a further transect. This traced the lost Solent valley to a depth of -30 metres OD. A lining of Pleistocene gravel was also detected here and this was capped with a thick mass of post-glacial shingle and sand. These two transects confirmed that the Solent valley had begun life as a deep flat-bottomed river valley and that it had been partially infilled by gravels before it was eventually invaded by the sea.

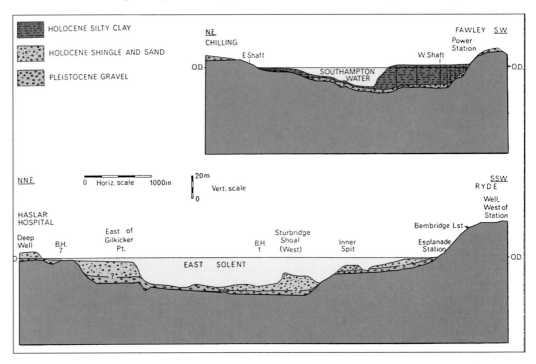

Cross-sections through the East Solent and Southampton Water showing the submerged fills of Pleistocene gravel and Holocene sediment - after Hodson and West (1972).

The next reports on the Solent river valley came from further off-shore. It was soon realised that some 25 km south of Isle of Wight, the course of the lost Solent River could still be traced to the point where it entered a larger complex of palaeovalleys which were associated with the former course of the Seine (Larsonneur *et al.* 1982; Hamblin & Harrison 1989). As Geikie had predicted in 1881, between the French and English coasts lay a drowned riverine landscape capable of accommodating populations of Pleistocene animals and hunters.

During the 1990's a fresh generation of sub-bottom profilers was deployed in the Western Solent and off the bay coast of Christchurch and Bournemouth. These surveys soon discredited Fox's case for a 'great western arm' to the Solent river in post-Glacial times. In its stead came new evidence showing an array of palaeovalleys draining the Dorset and west

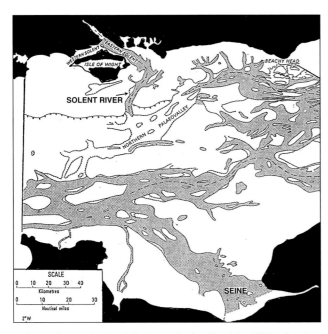

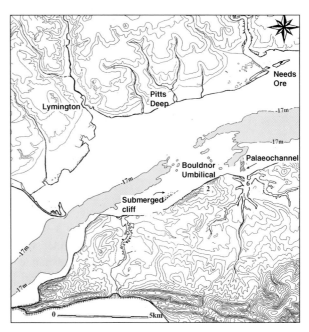

Palaeovalleys in the English Channel, after Hamblin (1972) showing the exit of the Solent River.

A submerged watershed at 17 metres OD marks the last potential land bridge or umbilical between Wight and the mainland (after Tomalin 2000a).

Hampshire coastline and cutting through the Wight-Purbeck ridge (Velegrakis & Collins 1998; Velegrakis 2000; Dix pers comm.). In 1994 a complementary land-based study of the gravel terraces of the Solent region was also completed (Allen & Gibbard 1994). This demonstrated how an earlier Pleistocene valley or lowland had formed in the area which was destined to accommodate the Western Solent. This study concurred with much of the original drainage pattern conjectured by Fox but it failed to embrace the new seismographic evidence which the Southampton oceanographers had gathered off-shore.

The most recent addition to the jigsaw puzzle of the Western Solent comes from archaeological and palaeo-environmental investigations at Yarmouth, Bouldnor and Newtown. At all these sites deep cores have been recovered from sediments on the southern margin of the present seaway. At Yarmouth and Newtown the sedimentology of two feeder river systems has been investigated and this has produced evidence of two differing histories. In general, these differences suggest that Clement Reid was right in supposing that, before post-Glacial inundation, there would have been two streams on the floor of the Western Solent lowland and that these would have been *flowing in opposite directions from a low watershed'*. The favoured position for this watershed or final umbilical is now in the region of Bouldnor Cliff and Pitt's Deep (Tomalin, 2000a). The severing of this umbilical certainly seems to post-date the mid 7th millennium BC for this was a time when an early deciduous forest was flourishing at Bouldnor at depth of 12m below Ordnance Datum (Tomalin, *ibid;* Member 2000). Roots from this submerged forest have been dated at 6430-6120 calendar years BC (GU–5420).

The first people of the Solent valley

When the lost Pleistocene landscape of Solent was earnestly discussed by William Fox's 'Brighstone Circle' in the 1860's there undoubtedly arose the hope that Palaeolithic hand-axes, like those found by Boucher de Perthes, would be discovered in the gravels of the Solent. Since Fox's day, notable assemblages of these tools have, indeed, been found at Red Barns near Fareham and on the Isle of Wight coast at Priory Bay. (Preece & Scourse, 1987; Wenban-Smith *et al.* 2000). At Red Barns, freshly flaked flint hand-axes, cores, flake tools and waste flakes of Lower Palaeolithic date were strewn in a slope deposit on the southern face of Portsdown Hill.

It seems that the occupants of this hill were subsisting in a grassland environment which offered the hunter a fine view over a Solent river which meandered beyond a southern skyline to eventually converge with the valley systems of northern France. Bone fragments recovered from this site show that this was a habitat which was grazed by herds of wild horses. Pleistocene pollen grains and snails were very poorly preserved at Red Barns but a few surviving remains showed some evidence of a temperate climate in which oak, alder and hazel were growing on the valley floor. A prolific scatter of tiny flint chips or spalls showed that the Red Barns site had once been occupied by an industrious group of tool-makers. It seems that the lives of these hunters had been spent in a landscape was probably part of the British peninsular of Europe (White & Schreve, 2000).

At Priory Bay more than 300 hand-axes of somewhat similar character have been recovered from a gravel deposit disturbed by cliff erosion. It seems likely that these implements were produced during a rather different phase in the history of the Solent valley. Possibly, this may be contemporary with the ancient shore-side site at Boxgrove near Chichester. At this latter site the hominid species *Homo erectus* was actively producing hand-axes around 425,000 – 300,000 BC. Here, archaeologists were startled to find that the flint-knappers' workplace had remained undisturbed. At Priory Bay the conditions for survival and preservation have been less favourable because the natural movement of the Solent's ancient gravels seems to have disturbed and destroyed the original living site.

The estimated age of these two sites is now so old that they must be equated with a terrestrial landscape which is far removed from the coastline of Europe as we know it. Some similar axes have even been dredged from the floor of the Solent but, so far, the manner of their recovery and their heavily rolled condition has denied fruitful study. There is clearly a need for far greater scientific vigilance over modern disturbances to the 'sediment archives' which make up the submerged landscape of the Solent This is especially important to coastal managers and planning authorities where the archaeological and palaeo-environmental record is able to impart specific information which tells of the long-term timetable of sea-level rise and coastal change (Tomalin, 1997 & 2000b).

A palaeolithic hand axe dredged from the floor of the Western Solent.

Mesolithic and Neolithic communities were drawn to the rich natural resources of the Solent shore.

Prior to the 1990's the peopling of the Solent floor and its estuarine margins had been a topic which was not well supported by archaeological evidence. In 1889, during the construction of the great Graving Dock at Southampton, some significant discoveries drew brief attention when navvies labouring in their coffered caisson encountered a deep buried shore line overlain by freshwater terrestrial peat (Shore & Elwes, 1889). Later, it was realised that flint implements in this peat signified the activities of Middle Stone Age communities who had ventured out on a land surface which was now some 6.7 metres below present highest astronomical tide and 1.8 metres below Ordnance Datum (Godwin 1940; Oakley 1943).

During the 1930's one particularly active fieldworker on the Isle of Wight drew attention to some similar scatters of Mesolithic flint implements on the southern shore of the Solent. These, he was quick to observe, were mostly clustered around the mouths of creeks where the natural habitat may have been particularly favourable to early human habitation (Poole 1936). At Werrar in the Medina estuary one such site was found on a forested land-surface which had been clearly overwhelmed by the sediments of a rising sea (Poole, *ibid*). During the 1950's a scatter of Palaeolithic implements was found at low tide at Rainbow Bar near the mouth of the Hamble River (Draper, 1951; Hack, 1999) and this drew further attention to the submerged dimension of the ancient Solent valley. These finds were followed by more Palaeolithic implements recovered from the shore and minor islands within Langstone Harbour (Draper, 1962; Rudkin, 1980). The most startling find comes from the deeply submerged forest at Bouldnor. During a recent underwater survey at a depth of -11m, divers of the Hampshire and Wight Trust for Maritime

Archaeology found that a burrowing colony of lobsters had up-cast flint implements and waste flakes. These had been struck by Mesolithic hunters in the mid 7th millennium BC (Momber 2000).

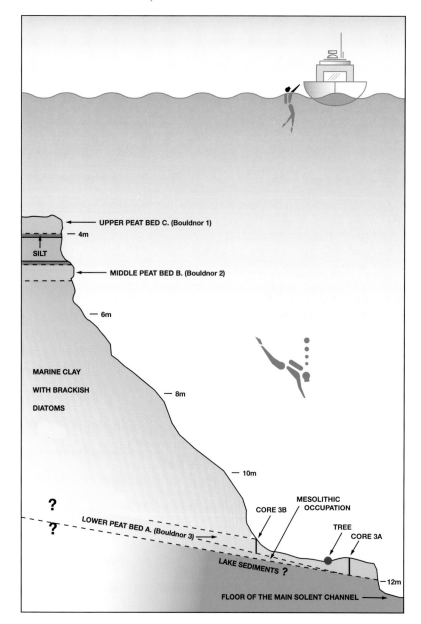

UPPER PEAT BED C. (Bouldnor 1)
— 4m
SILT
MIDDLE PEAT BED B. (Bouldnor 2)
— 6m
MARINE CLAY
WITH BRACKISH
DIATOMS
— 8m
— 10m
MESOLITHIC
OCCUPATION
CORE 3B
TREE
CORE 3A
?
?
LOWER PEAT BED A. (Bouldnor 3)
LAKE SEDIMENTS ?
— 12m
FLOOR OF THE MAIN SOLENT CHANNEL

(above) A tranchet axe from the submerged land surface beneath the Solent.

(left) The discovery of the submerged forest and Mesolithic site on the seabed off Bouldnor near Yarmouth, Isle of Wight (2000).

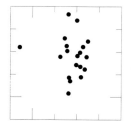

Plan of a fishtrap of circa 3000 BC surveyed within a 5 metre square on Quarr Beach near Wootton, Isle of Wight.

At all of these sites the tools and flint waste recovered from the intertidal and sub-tidal muds appeared to be those produced by hunter-gathers but there has since arisen the possibility that some of these sites may also be linked with the activities of the first farming communities in our region. Many of these sites have yielded crude tranchet axes or picks. On the Wootton-Quarr coast of the Isle of Wight these have numbered over 100. At this location some of these axes seem to be loosely associated with inundated cooking places where large quantities of burnt flint were produced. About 7% of the axes were composed of Greensand chert from the southern sector of the Isle of Wight. This has suggested that the cooking sites may have been associated with seasonal visits to the Solent shore by communities who were exploiting particular opportunities for fishing and fowling on these occasions. Some of these sites may be contemporary with wooden fish-traps which are known to have been in use in the opening years of the 3rd millennium BC. One trap at Quarr has been dated at 4040-3780 calendar years BC (GU-5251).

In search of the first seafarers

The dual role of the Solent as a moat and a means of communication is an ambivalence which has always fascinated both residents and visitors of the Isle of Wight. The earliest cultural perception of the life of Islanders can be glimpsed during the New Stone Age when the first potters were at work and the first communal burial mounds were being raised. The free plasticity of potting clay has always offered infinite opportunity for variety and experimentation yet Island potters of the Neolithic period seem to have shown unquestioning conformity with the styles of their mainland counterparts. This evidence is far from disappointing for it suggests that even in the 3rd millennium BC the Solent was already becoming a ready means of communication on and off the Isle of Wight as well extending ties to trade-friends further afield. Such contact is indicated by the matching of a Neolithic pot from Downton in the Avon valley near Salisbury with an Island pot found at Redcliff near Sandown (Sofranoff, 1975). Both are composed of the same clay and they attest effective cross-Solent transport in Neolithic times. Another Neolithic pot, composed of Isle of Wight clay, can be matched with two exported examples found in the Test valley in the neighbourhood of Winchester (Sofranoff, *ibid;* Tomalin, forthcoming).

A more poignant reminder of Neolithic seafaring is provided by a number of imported stone axes which have been found in and around the Isle of Wight. Several of these have been recovered on the Solent coastline where ancient beach-head bartering or gift transactions may be suspected. Some of the most interesting axes are those composed of Cornish greenstone. These suggest that a coast-hugging route from the boot of Cornwall may have been known to certain seafaring crews. One axe from the Island has undeniably made a very substantial sea crossing. This is composed of a volcanic tuff obtained from the an isolated stone outcrop on the northern coast of County Antrim. The most tantalising body of evidence is offered by a notable number finely polished stone axes composed of lustrous green jadeite (Smith, 1963 & 1965). This alluring material is of continental origin and its occurrence around our shores evokes an untold history of cross-Channel adventures and the homecomings of intrepid Stone Age navigators.

While seafaring activities in the Neolithic period have been largely inferential, evidence during the Bronze Age is quite explicit. An outstanding item of Early Bronze Age date comes from a burial mound on Gallibury Down in the Isle of Wight. This is a finely fashioned handled jar or *vase a anse* which was found with the cremated remains of an adult male (Tomalin, 1988). This vessel displays a warm burnished red sheen and it is certainly quite unlike anything

A 'Group 1' axe of Cornish greenstone shipped to the Isle of Wight in the 3rd Millenium BC. (right) Neolithic man was able to navigate the Solent in dugouts such as these. Perhaps they were also fitted with out-riggers and a simple sail.

produced by British potters of the period. The home of this exotic item lies amongst the great chambered burial mounds of Armorica. This elite French pedigree is clearly endorsed by the golden platelets of Breton mica that glisten on the glossy surface of this vessel. Sometime during the mid 2nd millennium BC this pot made the Channel crossing on the floor of an ocean-going boat. Much-loved, it continued in use even after its broken handle had been skilfully replaced by a suspension thong. Had it continued in further domestic service it would surely have been lost and we must be thankful to the unknown Bronze Age family who finally chose it for the grave.

The idea of Bronze Age sea-going craft setting sail from the Solent has been surprisingly stimulated in recent years. The first strand of new evidence comes from an Early Bronze burial mound on the West Dorset coast at Puncknowle, near the Chesil Beach (Greenfield, 1984). Heaped over the central cremation within this mound was a neat dump of stones which seems to have amounted to about 1.5 tonnes (Tomalin, 1984 & 1988). These stones seemed unremarkable until their petrology was investigated. This analysis revealed that all were composed of Bembridge limestone, a material which could only be obtained in the Isle of Wight. The estimated weight of the dump is significant because this suggests the ballasting of a sea-going vessel capable of making a voyage of at least 120km.

The second strand of evidence concerns a remarkable boat-shaped bowl which was recovered from a peat bog at Caergwrle in North Wales in the late 19th century (Denford & Farell, 1980; Green, 1985). Housed in the National Museum of Wales, this gold-inlaid object had long been thought to be composed of ancient bog oak but in 1985 it was submitted for chemical analysis. The result of this examination was startling because the wood-like composition of this boat model proved to be Kimmeridge shale of the type found in the cliffs of the Isle of Purbeck (Green 1985). While the date of this object remains unproven its style suggests that here we seeing a ribbed and composite craft of the type which was cruising off the Dorset and Solent coast at the close of the 2nd millennium BC.

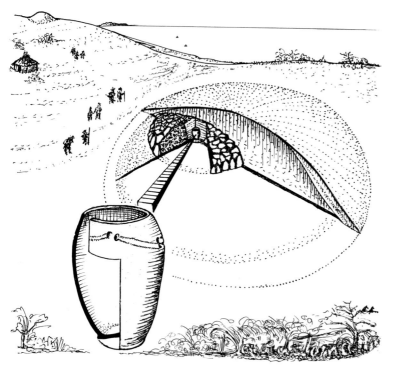

The Puncknowle cairn, Dorset.
The heaped Bembridge Limestone beneath the Bronze Age burial mound represents boat ballast and a sea voyage from the Isle of Wight.

In miniaturised representations of the Caergwrle kind, specific interpretation must always be tempered with caution. Nevertheless it is interesting to observe that if the slender inset gold triangles are indeed images of oars then a minimum crew of 24 would be needed if each man operated a pair of oars. This seems excessive and we might suspect artistic licence. It might, perhaps, be compared with a nine-a-side arrangement which is evident in a gold model sailing boat of Iron Age date which was found in a peat bog at Broighter in County Derry. Other sections of gold-inlay on the hull of the Caergwrle boat convey the ubiquitous convention for lapping water while the underside seems to bear a representation of ribs or frames. In the manner of many of the modern fishing boats of southern Europe, this craft was also equipped with magic eyes. In this instance they were applied to both the bow and stern. This a very unusual arrangement which is now unknown in Europe.

An invaluable source of evidence is the remains of substantial plank-built boats found on the coast of Bronze Age Britain. The first of these was found in 1937 on the shore of the Humber estuary, at North Ferriby, in Yorkshire. Fragments of further carvel boats of this type have since been recovered from Dover and the coast of the Severn estuary. All have been tantalisingly incomplete but the general evidence suggests that these vessels could be some 16m long and, if fitted with a simple sail, they might require stone ballast similar to the weight of the Puncknowle dump (Tomalin, 1988; Wright, 1990). Composite boats of this type all share a number of common

(above) The Caergwrle bowl imitates the features of a Bronze Age boat. Inlaid gold sheet denotes tiny oars and the lapping waves.

(left) The beautifully burnished vase from Gallibury Down provides evidence of a Bronze Age voyage from the Breton coast.

features. These include the use of rebated oak planks stitched together with yew withies, and the threading of ashen cross-members through large carved wooden cleats.

The finding of certain imported French bronze goods has long suggested that significant cross-Channel traffic had been established to and from the Solent region before the close of the 2nd millennium BC (Fox, 1932; Rowlands 1976; O'Connor, 1981). The problem has always been a lack of identifiable boat remains on this sector of the Channel coast. During recent archaeological investigations by Southern Water and Wessex Archaeology at Testwood Lakes near Southampton, these ideas were drastically changed when the substantial remains of two Middle Bronze Age causeways or bridges were discovered in the alluvium of the river Test. Dr Andrew Fitzpatrick reports that these constructions projected from the west bank of the river valley and that a fine bronze rapier had been dropped between the timber piers of one of these structures. The tree ring evidence obtained from the Bronze Age posts has suggested that one structure had possibly replaced the other, perhaps after an operating life of about a century. Amongst the surviving wooden components at Testwood was a large cleat of the type ubiquitously associated with the construction of plank-built boats of the Ferriby type. This find brings us one step closer to the true nature of those elusive craft which were once seen by the Caergwrle modeller when they were cutting through Solent and Purbeck waters.

For the course of some of these early cross-Channel journeys we can look to certain imported continental goods which were being carried across the wet shingle of the Solent. One group of cross-Channel seafarers seems to have distinguished itself by the wearing of finely decorated bronze arm-rings and neck-rings. These are a type which were otherwise made and worn in the valleys of the Seine and the Somme (Rowlands, 1971). Similar arm-rings have been

Bronze arm-rings of the Liss type.

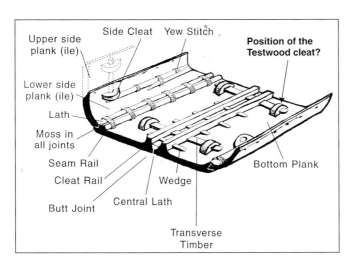

Upper side plank (ile)
Side Cleat
Yew Stitch
Position of the Testwood cleat?
Lower side plank (ile)
Lath
Moss in all joints
Seam Rail
Cleat Rail
Butt Joint
Wedge
Central Lath
Bottom Plank
Transverse Timber

(left) The conjectured position of the Testwood cleat in a bronze Age boat of the Ferriby-Dover type.

(below) The fine bronze rapier lost beneath the Testwood Bronze Age bridge.

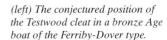

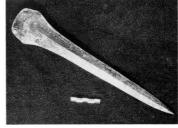

Some complete Dressel 1 amphorae in a princely grave in Hertfordshire and one of the fragments from an Iron Age cargo at Yarmouth Roads.

found at Portsmouth, Hayling Island and Liss while a neck-ring of the same style has been found in the Isle of Wight. All of these items speak to us of ancient seasonal voyages between the Bronze Age maritime communities of the Solent, those of the Somme and the Seine.

By looking at the pottery of the later 2nd millennium we can also detect how out-marriage to distant maritime communities could cement trade friendships while introducing home-made ceramic styles of distinctly foreign types into a maritime region such as the Solent. One Bronze Age potter living in the vicinity of Week Down on the Isle of Wight was faithfully producing vessels in the image of those used in her family home in the distant tip of Cornwall (Tomalin, 1988). Another seems to have learnt her craft somewhere in the region of the Vosges or Upper Rhine. Finally, a Bronze Age potter on Hayling Island busied herself by reproducing large globular pots with distinct Cornish characteristics (ApSimon, 2001). Perhaps each of these potters had once arrived in the Solent as an apprehensive young girl staring through the morning mist while the boat edged towards a distinctly foreign shore.

Havens, markets and the Iron Age 'emporion'

While the discovery of prehistoric maritime objects in our region has presented a certain inevitability, it has not been uncommon for archaeologists to question the relative importance of the Solent in relation to the rest of the English Channel seaboard. The particular importance of the Solent region is certainly evident in the closing years of the 1st millennium BC when the first consignments of imported Italian wine were arriving in southern Britain. In Christchurch Harbour generous quantities of this wine were carried ashore for consumption within the great fortified settlement at Hengistbury Head (Peacock 1971; Williams 1987). In due course innumerable broken wine jars were scattered on this site and these have since encouraged archaeologists to consider the promontory fort at Hengistbury Head to be a port of exceptional importance during the Late Iron Age (Cunliffe, 1987 & 1990).

The amphorae discarded at Hengistbury were mostly of a distinctive type. These were classified as 'type 1' by Heinrich Dressel in his study published in 1899. The production of these particular containers began in the late 2nd century BC and ceased before the close of the 1st century BC (Peacock & Williams, 1986; Williams 1987). While these provide undeniable evidence of the importance of this landing place in the pre-Conquest period it is worth reminding ourselves that there are several other local Iron Age coastal settlements which have yet to benefit from the same level of archaeological investigation. This means that our knowledge of the full regional distribution of these amphorae is still far from clear. At Ampress on the Lymington River; at Exbury on the Beaulieu River; and at Tournerbury on Hayling Island, other substantial fortified settlements of Iron Age type are to found on the shores of natural havens. All of these locations are equally attractive to the mariner. A further coastal settlement of considerable importance once stood at the tip of the Selsey peninsular in a position which has since been drastically eroded by the sea. Selsey was still the 'Island of the Seals' in early medieval times and it was separated from the mainland by the an ancient channel which was probably capable of offering good anchorage to the modest wooden craft of the Iron Age.

Scattered across the landscape of the Isle of Wight are the find-spots of further fragments of Dressel 1 amphorae (Isle of Wight, Sites and Monuments Record (SMR) Trott, pers comm). These suggest that Islanders may have played a particularly active maritime role in the Late Iron Age history of the Solent. Perhaps such a role is mirrored in the events of the medieval period when the king was regularly petitioned with the complaints of continental traders whose vessels had been boarded and robbed by privateering crews from the Isle of Wight (Hockey, 1982). The recovery of fragments of Dressel 1 amphorae and other Roman sherds from an ancient anchorage at Yarmouth Roads suggests that Vectensian voyaging continued well into the Roman period (Tomalin, 1987).

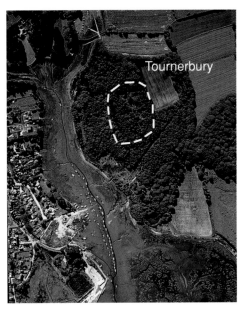

One explanation for the development of early maritime traffic in the Solent could involve a variety of modest coastal trading centres based upon a loose and variable choice of landing sites. A glance at the navigational hazards in the natural creeks and harbours of the Solent is sufficient to show that, at any one time, the mariner's choice could be so readily predetermined by the ever-changing constraints of wind, tide and current (Coles, 1933). The coastline of the Solent estuarine system is so generously endowed with natural havens that we might be wrong to assume that any one location could secure and sustain a primary advantage. An example of a modest yet successful haven of the prehistoric period is Wootton Creek where a significant strew of Late Iron Age and

Now concealed by woodland, the fortified Iron Age settlement of Tournerbury is ideally sited beside a navigable creek on the east shore of Langstone Harbour.

Roman maritime goods has been recently found in the intertidal zone (Loader, *et al.*, 1997; Tomalin, *et al.*, forthcoming). A salutary lesson at this site has been provided by the onshore archaeology. Despite strong evidence of ancient landings and unloadings in the intertidal zone there is virtually no trace of contemporary occupation above high water mark.

Some meagre yet vital comments by classical writers provide vital clues to maritime activities in the Solent in Late Iron Age and Roman times. The first is provided by Strabo who describes the voyages of the *Veneti* during the mid 1st century BC. This Armorican tribe was certainly trading with the Iron Age port at Hengistbury because many of its graphite-coated pots have been found there. In AD 57 the *Julius Caesar* destroyed the Venetic fleet and this disrupted trade with the British coast. Here, Strabo tells us, these Armorican seafarers were commonly landing to trade with a market or *'emporion'* (Mays, 1981). The settlement at Hengistbury has been cited as the possible location of this trading place but a more pragmatic interpretation could see this site as part of a larger conglomeration of favoured landing places in both the Solent and the Isle of Wight (Tomalin *et al.* forthcoming).

It is unfortunate that our present evidence comes from such sparse sources as a few lines

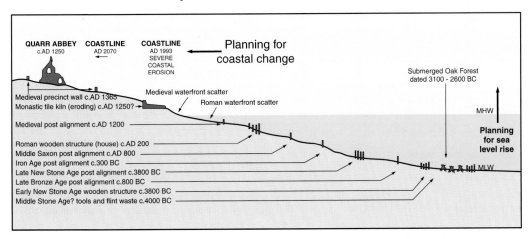

Cross-section of the Wootton-Quarr coastal zone demonstrating how archaeology and palaeo-environmental studies can assist in understanding coastal change (after Tomalin, 1997).

of classical text and some rare imports found on-shore. Once up the gang plank, imports were inevitably dispersed into the countryside and it not surprising that so few can be traced by archaeologists. Nevertheless, some rotary querns of West Country sandstone and Bembridge limestone have been found in a Late Iron Age settlement at Little Somborne near Basingstoke (Neal, 1980) and these certainly demonstrate that the quarrying and shipping of certain products of Isle of Wight stone had already begun in the Middle Iron Age. Viewed collectively, this petrological evidence provides a clear indication that local Solent mariners were very much at home in the near-shore sea lanes of the English Channel and that the West Country coast was easily within their reach. This was valuable navigational expertise which could be readily exploited with the coming of new opportunities under the *Pax Romana*.

Bibliography

Allen, L G, & Gibbard, P L, 1994. 'Pleistocene evolution of the Solent River in southern England', *Quaternary Science Review* 12, 503-538.

ApSimon, A.M., 2001. 'The Creek Field Middle Bronze Age site', in M. J. Allen & J. Gardiner (eds.), *Our changing coast; an interdisciplinary survey of Langstone Harbour, Hampshire.* Council for British Archaeology, monograph series. London.

Boucher de Perthes., 1860. De l'homme antediluvien et ses oeuvres. Paris. translated in R. F. Heizer (ed), *Man's Discovery of his past; landmarks in archaeology,* Prentice Hall 1962.

Camden, W., 1586, 1587 Latin editions, 1610 & 1637 English editions. *Britannia, a chorographicall description of the most flourishing kingdomes, England, Scotland & Ireland..* London.

Coles, K. A., 1933. *Creeks and harbours of the Solent.* London.

Cunliffe, B., 1987. *Hengistbury Head, Dorset; vol 1, the prehistoric and Roman settlement, 3500BC - AD 500.* Oxford University Committee for Archaeology. Monog 13. Oxford.

Cunliffe, B.W., 1988, *Mountbatten, Plymouth, a prehistoric and Roman Fort.* Oxford Committee for Archaeology. monog. 13.

Cunliffe, B., 1990. 'Hengistbury Head: a late prehistoric haven', in S. McGrail (ed.), *Maritime Celts, Frisians and Saxons,* CBA Research Report no 71, 27-31.

Denford, G. T. & Farrell, A. W., 1980. 'The Caergwrle bowl - possible boat model', *International Journal of Nautical Archaeology* 9, (3), 183-192.

Draper, J. C., 1951. 'Stone industries from Rainbow Bar, Hants', *Archaeological Newsletter* 3, (9), 147-149.

Draper, J. C., 1962. 'Upper Palaeolithic flint types from Long Island, Langstone Harbour, Portsmouth', *Proceedings Hampshire Field Club & Archaeological Society* 22, 10506.

Dressel, H., 1899. *Corpus Inscriptionum Latinarium,* XV, Pars 1, Berlin.

Dyer, K.R., 1972. 'Recent sedimentation in the Solent Area'. *Memoire du Bureaux des Recherches des Mines* (BRGM) no 79, 271-280.

Dyer, K .R., 1975. 'The buried channels of the Solent River, Southern England', *Proceedings of the Geological Society,* 86, 239-245.

Ekwall, E., 1960. *The concise Oxford dictionary of English place-names.* 4th ed. Oxford.

Englefield, H. C., 1816. *A description of the principle picturesque beauties, antiquities and geological phenomena of the Isle of Wight.* London..

Fox, W. D., 1862. 'How and when was the Isle of Wight separated from the mainland', The Geologist 4, 452-454.

Fox, C., 1932. *Personality of Britain.* Cardiff.

Geike J., 1881. *Prehistoric Europe; a geological sketch.* London.

Godwin, H. 1940. 'Pollen analysis and forest history of England and Wales'. *New Phytologist,* 39-270-400.

Godwin H. & M. E, 1945. 'Submerged peat at Southampton; data for the study of Postglacial history', *New Phytologist,* 39, 303-307.

Green E., 1906. 'The Isle of Wight and the early tin trade'. *Journal British Archaeological Association* 145-160.

Green, H. S., 1985. 'The Caergwrle bowl - not oak but shale', *Antiquity* 59, 116-7, pl 22 & 23.

Greenfield, E., 1984. 'The excavation of three round barrows at Puncknowle, Dorset 1959', *Proceedings Dorset Natural history & Archaeological Society* 106, 63-76.

Hack, B., 1999. 'More stone tools from Rainbow Bar, Hillhead', *Proceedings Hampshire Field Club & Archaeological Society* 54, 163-171.

Hamblin, R. J .O & Harrison, D. J., 1989. *Marine aggregate survey, Phase 2: South Coast.* British Geological Survey. Kidworth, Nottingham, 30 pp.

Hencken, H.O'N., 1932. *An archaeology of Cornwall and Scilly.* Methuen. London.

Herring, P.C. 1992. *St Michael's Mount.* National Trust archaeological report. Cornwall Archaeological Unit. Truro.

Hockey, S. F., 1982. *Insula Vecta; the Isle of Wight in the Middle Ages,* Phillimore, Chichester.

Hodson, F. & West, I.M. 1972. 'Holocene deposits at Fawley, Hampshire and the development of Southampton Water', *Proceedings of the Geological Association* 83, 421-444.

Kell, E. 1866. 'An account of a Roman building at Gurnard Bay in the Isle of Wight, and its relation to the ancient British tin trade in the Island', *Journal of the British Archaeological Association* 22, 351-368.

Larsonneur, C. Bouysee, P. & Auffret, J-P. 1982. 'The superficial sediments of the English Channel and its Western Approaches', *Sedimentology* 29, 851-864.

Lartet E., 1860. 'On the co-existence of Man with certain extinct quadrupeds proved by fossil bones from various Pleistocene deposits bearing incisions made by sharp instruments', *Quarterly Journal of the Geological Society* 16, 471.

Loader R., Westmore I. & Tomalin D. J., 1997. *Time and tide; a archaeological survey of the Wootton-Quarr coast.* Isle of Wight Council.

Lyell C., P 1830-3 & 1840. *Principles of geology or the modern changes to the earth and its inhabitants considered as illustrative of geology.* 1st ed. Murray, London and 6th ed.

Mays, M., 1981. 'Strabo IV, 4.1: a reference to Hengistbury Head?', *Antiquity* 55, 55-57.

Maxwell, I. S. 1972. 'The location of Ictis'. *Journal of the Royal Institute of Cornwall,* 6 (4): 293-319.

Momber, G., 2000. 'Drowned and deserted: a submerged prehistoric landscape in the Solent, England', *International Journal of Nautical Archaeology* 29, (1), 86-99.

Neal, D. S. 1980. 'Bronze Age, Iron Age and Roman settlement sites at Little Somborne and Ashley, Hampshire', *Proceedings Hampshire Field Club & Archaeological Society* 36, 91-143.

NERC,. 1980. *The Solent Estuarine System; an assessment of present knowledge.* N.E.R.C. Publications. Series C. No 22. 6-19.

Oakley, K. P., 1943. `A note on the post-glacial submergence of the Solent margin'. *Proceedings Prehistoric Society,* 9, 56-59.

O'Connor, B., 1981. *Cross-Channel relations in the Later Bronze Age.* British Archaeological Reports, International Series, 91. 2 vols. Oxford.

Peacock, D. P. S., 1971. 'Roman amphorae in pre-Roman Britain', in M. Jesson & D. Hill (eds), *The Iron Age and its hill-forts.* Southampton University Archaeological Society. 161-188.

Peacock, D.P.S. and Williams, D.F. 1986. *Amphorae and the Roman Economy,* London

Penhallurick, R. D. 1997. 'The evidence for prehistoric mining in Cornwall' in P. Budd, & D. Gale (eds). *Prehistoric extractive metallurgy in Cornwall,* Cornwall Archaeological Unit. Truro.

Poole, H. F. 1936. 'An outline of the Mesolithic flint cultures of the Isle of Wight'. Proceedings Isle Wight Natural history & Archaeological Society 2, (7), 551-581.

Preece, R. C. & Scourse, J. D., 1987. Pleistocene sea-level history in the Bembridge area of the Isle of Wight', in K. E., Barber (ed.), *Wessex and the Isle of Wight;* field guide. Quaternary Research Association. Cambridge.

Redman, J. B., 1852. The alluvial formations and local changes in the south coast of England, *Proceedings of the Institute of. Civil Engineering* 11, 162-223.

Reid, C., 1905. 'The island of Ictis' *Archaeologia* 59, 218-288.

Rivet, A. L .F. & Smith, C., 1979. *The place names of Roman Britain.* Batsford, London..

Rowlands, M. J., 1971. 'A group of incised decorated arm-rings and their significance for the Middle Bronze Age in southern England', in G de D Sieveking (ed.), *Prehistoric and Roman Studies; commemorating the opening of the Department of Prehistoric and Romano-British Antiquities.* British Museum. London. 183-199.

Rowlands, M. J., 1976. *The organisation of Middle Bronze Age metalworking.* British Archaeological Reports 31. (2 vols). Oxford.

Rowlands, R., 1605. (pseud. Verstegen R.), *A restitution of decayed intelligence. Antiquities concerning the English nation.* R. Brusney. Antwerp.

Rudkin, D. J., 1980. *Early man in Portsmouth and south-east Hampshire.* Portsmouth papers no 31. Portsmouth City Council.

Shore, T. W. & Elwes J. W. 1889. 'The New Dock excavations at Southampton', *Proceeding Hampshire Field Club & Archaeological Society* 1, 43-56.

Short, T., 1749. *A general chronological history of the air, weather, seasons, meteors etc in sundry places and different times more particularly for the space of 250 years.* Longman, London.

Skinner, J., 1797. This diarist cites tin ore on St Michael's Mount in his ms journal of a West Country tour through Somerset, Devon and Cornwall. Reproduced in Jones, R. (ed) 1985, *West Country Tour,* p.60. Bradford on Avon.

Smith, W. C., 1963. 'Jade axes from sites in the British Isles', *Proceedings Prehistoric Society* 29, 133-172.

Smith, W. C., 1965. 'The distribution of jade axes in Europe with a supplement to the catalogue of those from the British Isles', *Proceeding Prehistoric Society* 31, 25-33.

Sofranoff, S. E., 1975. 'A petrological study of certain ceramics of the Windmill Hill and Perborough traditions in Wessex'. University of Southampton, Dept of Archaeology, Unpub. M.Sc.thesis.

Thomas, C. 1985. *Exploration of a drowned landscape; archaeology and history of the Isle of Scilly.* Batsford. London..

Tomalin, D. J., 1984. 'The pottery; it character and implications and the evidence for sea transport' in E. Greenfield, 'The excavation of three Bronze Age round barrows at Pucknowle, Dorset, 1959', *Proceedings Dorset Natural History and Archaeological Society* 106, 63-76.

Tomalin, D. J., 1987. *Roman Wight; a guide catalogue.* Isle of Wight County Council. Newport.

Tomalin, D. J., 1988. 'Armorican *vases à anses* and their occurrence in Southern England', *Proceedings Prehistoric Society* 54, 203-221.

Tomalin, D. J. 1997. `Bargaining with nature; considering the sustainability of archaeological sites in the dynamic environment of the intertidal zone', Preserving archaeological remains in situ; *Proceedings of the conference of 1st-3rd April 1996 at the Museum of London.* Museum of London/Univertsity of Bradford, 144-158.

Tomalin, D. J., 2000a. 'Geomorphological evolution of the Solent seaway and the severance of Wight: a review', in M. Collins & K. Ansell (eds.), *Solent Science-a review.* Elsevier. Amsterdam. 9-20.

Tomalin, D. J., 2000b. 'Wisdom of hindsight: palaeo-environmental and archaeological evidence of long-term processual changes and coastline sustainability', in M. Collins & K. Ansell (eds.), *Solent Science-a review.* Elsevier. Amsterdam. 71-84.

Tomalin D. J. & Insole, I. N., 1977. Ms notes on an examination of building blocks recovered from excavations at Romsey Abbey.

Tomalin, D. J., Loader, R. & Scaife, R. G., forthcoming. *'Coastal archaeology in a dynamic environment; a Solent case study',* English Heritage monograph.

Tubbs, C. R., 1991. *The Solent, a changing wild-life habitat.* Hampshire & Isle of Wight Wildlife Trust. Romsey.

Tubbs C.R., 1999. *The ecology, conservation and history of the Solent.* Packard. Chichester.

Velegrakis A., 2000. 'Geology, geomorphology and sediments of the Solent System', in M. Collins & K. Ansell (eds.), *Solent Science-a review.* Elsevier. Amsterdam. 21-44.

Velegrakis, A. F., Dix, J. K. & Collins, M. B., 1999. 'Late Quaternary evolution of the upper reaches of the Solent River, Southern England, based upon marine geophysical evidence', *Journal of the Geological Society,* 156, 73-87. London..

Webster, T., 1816. 'Letters on geology', in Englefield, H. C., *A description of the principle picturesque beauties, antiquities and geological phenomena of the Isle of Wight.* London.

Wenban-Smith, F., Gamble C. & ApSimon, A., 2000. The Lower Palaeolithic site at Red Barns, Porchester, Hampshire: bifacial technology, raw material quality and the organisation of archaic behaviour', *Proceedings Prehistoric Society* 66, 209-255.

White, M. J. & Schreve, D. C., 2000. 'Island Britain -Peninsular Britain: palaeogeography, colonisation and the Lower Palaeolithic settlement of the British Isles', *Proceeding Prehistoric Society* 66, 1-28.

Williams, D. W., 1987. 'Amphorae', in Cunliffe, B., 1987. 271-277.

Wright, E. V., 1990. *The Ferriby boats; seacraft in the Bronze Age.* London.

Bearded Reedling (Panurus biarmieus)

Chapter Two

NATURAL HISTORY

When considering the Solent as a total area it is vast and complex, including as it does not only natural features but also the coastal limits of cities, towns and villages, an oil refinery, marinas, major ports, and ferry terminals. In a natural history context it can best be thought of as a single huge estuarine system which contains in excess of 9,000 hectares of inter-tidal sediment and includes over 6,000 hectares of mud flats, over 7,000 hectares of sand flats, 400 hectares of ancient salt marsh and nearly 1,800 hectares of Spartina marsh. The mud flats are extremely rich in invertebrates and consequently are important feeding grounds for winter waders and wild fowl. In fact they are internationally important for 8 species and nationally important for a further 17 species.

All the sites in the Solent with high nature conservation value have designations ranging from Sites of Special Scientific Interest (SSSI) to Special Protection Areas (SPA's), a European designation to assist the protection of wild birds, and RAMSAR sites which is again an international designation for the protection of wetlands. The Solent, as a result, is thought to be the third most important estuary in the United Kingdom.

To discuss the natural history of the Solent in one chapter is virtually impossible and would be an injustice to the high ornithological, botanical and other wildlife value of these important sites. It is proposed therefore to look at just one area in particular. Newtown in the Isle of Wight, its estuary, meadows and woodland, is an ideal choice as it encompasses something of all of the other sites in the Solent to a lesser or greater degree. A discussion of Newtown does, therefore, reflect to a considerable degree the common features - history, threats, pressures and the subsequent successful management of these special locations.

Situated on the north-west coast of the Isle of Wight, Newtown has an interesting archaeological aspect. It has also faced a potentially devastating environmental threat and it has a proportion of most of the species seen throughout the rest of the Solent. Most important of all is that its surroundings have never been developed so it gives an idea of how the landscape in similar parts of the Solent used to be. Newtown estuary is a National Nature Reserve (NNR), a RAMSAR site, a SSSI and a Special Area of Conservation (SAC) - a designation aimed to protect such locations of European importance under the EC Habitats Directive. Most of Newtown and its environs are owned and managed by the National Trust and thus have the protection of the Trust's Inalienability Clause, the lynchpin of the Trust's constitution.

The Townhall Newtown

The pre-history of the area is fairly well documented as Newtown is particularly rich in fossils and well-preserved remains of animals, plants and insects that have lived there in the past. Situated on a tributary of the old 'Solent River' this small site has seen many different species flourish and subsequently decline over thousands of years of glacial and inter-glacial periods. The scenery will have changed as well, perhaps open flat grasslands with horse, bison and straight-tusked elephants to be seen and hippopotamus wallowing in the rivers; much later wild boar and red squirrel would be living in the woods of oak, birch and hazel. Once rising sea levels severed Britain from the Continent and subsequently the Island from the mainland the scene was set for the estuary to develop into what it is today. One thing that must not be forgotten though is the influence of man and his impact on the area as this is very relevant to the present day importance of Newtown estuary and indeed other Solent estuaries and harbours in relation to nature conservation value.

Although there is ample evidence of early man with numbers of stone tools and other implements being found locally, the story of Newtown really begins in the mid-13th century. The settlement was the last of six boroughs or 'free towns' established by the Bishop of Winchester and the village was laid out by Aymer de Valence, Bishop-elect, in 1254-55. This was part of a long established medieval tradition of such 'new towns' aimed at establishing and encouraging economic activity, in otherwise relatively unproductive feudal manors. They were 'free towns' in as much the people who took up burgages within them were freed of manorial dues and ties that would normally have kept them bound to the land. Instead they paid rent and carried out a trade or following, thus giving them an opportunity to prosper both financially and socially. One of the trades carried on at Newtown was the production of salt and there is evidence of at least seven salt works in the area. Newtown main marsh was reclaimed from the sea between 1656 and 1768 and surrounded by a clay bank; the reason was either to increase the salt production of the area or to gain extra grazing land. In November 1954 the sea wall was breached and the reclaimed land reverted to mud flats that were later colonised by Spartina and other plants to give the marsh very much the appearance that it has today.

Newtown's early economy was based on its sheltered harbour where boats of up to 500 tons burthen were reputed to trade but its full potential was never realised and subsequently the town was overshadowed by the rise of Yarmouth and Newport on the Island and Southampton and Portsmouth on the mainland. The settlement was badly affected following raids by the French and the last one in 1377 was probably the final blow to a project that never really came of age. Over the following centuries the town gradually dwindled away to leave a village, as it is today. In that time also the adjacent woodlands have increased so that some now join the marsh, creating another nationally scarce habitat; Holme and Bishop (1980) described the estuary in their review of the sediment shores of the south coast as 'a superb example of an undeveloped and unpolluted marine inlet'. It is hard to believe now that in 1958 the estuary and surrounding hinterland faced a devastating threat that would have changed the area forever. The Central Electricity Generating Board (as it was then) wanted to build a nuclear power station on the Hamstead side, which forms the north-western part of the harbour. Local residents had heard of the plans and formed a local committee to fight the proposals. Support was initiated from the Isle of Wight Natural History and Archaeological Society (IWNHAS), The Royal Solent Yacht Club (RSYC) and further momentum was added by help from the newly-formed Solent Protection Society. Sailing enthusiasts, including the Royal Yacht Squadron, also added support. Initially the former Isle of Wight County Council, as owners, supported the idea, no doubt thinking of the economic and employment prospects that could arise from such a development. However, the ground swell of public opinion against the scheme resulted in a change of mind by the Council. A prominent Newport businessman used his influence with the National Trust and the Council for the Protection of Rural England for them to work with the IWNHAS to seek to establish a nature reserve instead of a power station. All these representations were successful and the eventual outcome was to see the application withdrawn and Newtown Nature Reserve becoming a reality.

Over the years the National Trust was either gifted or bought most of the estuary and now manages it for nature conservation purposes and also for the enjoyment of the public. It is the only National Trust property in the country that has a harbour master.

Whilst the Newtown estuary is important for a wide range of species, it is the bird life for which this location and indeed much of the Solent has recently been designated by the European Union. The Special Protection Area in fact extends from Hurst Spit to Lee-on-Solent along the south coast of Hampshire as well as along the north coast of the Isle of Wight. The site comprises a series of estuaries and adjacent coastal habitats important for breeding gulls and terns and wintering waders and water fowl. The diversity of habitats within the SPA include intertidal flats, shingle beaches, salt marsh, reed beds, saline lagoons, grazing marsh and other coastal grassland. The proposed SPA includes the Sites of Special Scientific Interest boardering the Solent that had previously been notified under the Wildlife and Countryside Act 1981. These include such important locations as Lymington River reed beds, Hythe to Calshot marshes, the lower Test Valley, Titchfield Haven and the Yar estuary. In addition parts of other Sites of Special Scientific Interest are included within the Special Protection Area, such as Hurst Castle and Lymington River estuary, Lee-on-Solent to the Itchen estuary, Thorness Bay and the Medina estuary on the Isle of Wight as well as Kings Quay shore, Ryde sands, Brading marshes to St Helens ledges, Whitecliff Bay and Bembridge Ledges and other areas of woodland, cliffs and coastal land.

The Solent has received this important designation because the location regularly supports nationally important breeding populations of key species including the Little Tern (Sterna albifrons), the Sandwich Tern (S.sandvicensis), the Common Tern (S.hirundo), and the Roseate Tern (S.douganni) which bred in small numbers between 1990 and 1993. The site qualifies also under the directive as a wetland of international importance by regularly supporting over 20,000 water fowl in the winter. The five year winter peak mean for the period 1988-89 to 1992-93 was 35,910 birds comprising an average of 17,960 waders, and 17,950 water fowl. The site is also important for the internationally important number of wintering migratory water fowl including in particular Dark Bellied Brent geese (Branta bernicula), the Black-tailed Godwit (Limosa limosa), the Shelduck (Tadorna tadorna) Widgeon (Anas penelope), Teal (A.crecca), Shoveller (A.clypeata), Gadwall (A.strepera) and waders including the Grey Plover (Pluvialis squatarola), Dunlin (Calidris alpina) and Curlew (Numenius arquata). In addition Black-headed Gulls (Larus ridibundus) breed in the Solent in numbers approaching international importance. Also an outstanding assemblage of wintering and passage birds are dependent on wetland habitats within the Solent area, including species such as the Red-throated Diver (Gavia stellata), Black-throated Diver (G.arctica) and the Great Northern Diver (G.immer), the Slavonian Grebe (Podiceps auritus), the Red-necked Grebe (P.grisegena), the Black-necked Grebe (P.nigricollis), the Great Crested Grebe (P.cristatus) the Red-breasted Merganser (Mergus serrator), the Little Egret (Egretta garzetta), the Hen Harrier (Circus cyaneus), the Greenshank (Tringa nebularia) as well as a range of other species. This clearly illustrates the diversity and importance of the Solent for ornithological reasons.

'The Black Hut'
Newtown, IW

Recording and monitoring of the natural history of the Solent has been extensive and thorough. It also covers a very long time span with records from the early part of the 19th century to the present day. Not surprisingly, birds are the most studied species and many groups, organisations and individuals over the years have amassed a wealth of information on their numbers and distribution. One of the most important surveys is the Wetland Bird Survey (WEBS) (Waters and Cramswick 1993.5) that was started in October 1993. It combined two previous surveys of wild fowl and waders, the National Water Fowl counts (NWC) and the Birds of Estuaries Inquiry (BOEE). All past data gathered by these two surveys are now treated as WEBS data, the counting methods are the same, but additional species were included. WEBS is administered jointly by the British Trust for Ornithology (BTO) and the Wildlife and Wetlands Trust (WWT). Counts are carried out monthly, on or near dates specified by the organisers, chosen to correspond with spring tides at the coastal sites; the recorders are local amateur ornithologists.

In 1994 an organisation was set up called the Solent Shorebirds Study Group, (SSSG) that brought together wader counters, bird ringers, bird watchers, professional conservationists and local authorities to focus solely on the Solent and its birds. Another group doing sterling work is the Farlington Ringing Group (FRG). In addition to these, there are also the Hampshire Ornithological Society, the Isle of Wight Natural History and Archaeological Society and the Isle of Wight Ornithological Group, all busy recording and monitoring.

Black-headed Gull (Larus ridibundus) colony

The black-headed Gull nests at a number of sites similar to this throughout the Solent area. This one at Newtown contains up to 800 pairs of birds.

Black-headed Gull nest and chicks

Spoonbill (Platalea leucorodia)

*Another recent colonist of Great Britain, the Spoonbill now breeds in this country, and
it is seen regularly in the Solent area.*

Although the avian fauna of the Solent is considered to be the most important aspect of its natural history, and indeed accounts for most of the various designations, the woods, fields, marshes and shingle spits that make up the shore line also have many interesting and rare species inhabiting them. Unusual plants, butterflies, dragonflies and other insects are to be found, and, with our climate apparently changing so rapidly, new examples are being recorded virtually every year. There are, of course, many of the commoner species that are found in southern Britain resident in the Solent region and these have all been well documented and studied. The following descriptions are a representative selection of species found at Newtown and in the Solent, and provides an indication of the interest and diversity of this area.

BIRDS

Red-breasted Merganser *(Mergus serrator)*

This colourful bird *(opposite above)* is one of the species known as 'sawbills' so named because their bills have a series of small, sharp projections along the inside edge that help them grip slippery fish; an unusual food for a duck. They also feed on crustaceans, small molluscs and worms. Known as 'Dutch Widgeon' by the early wild fowlers, or punt gunners of the Solent, the first arrivals are usually in October and the last birds have departed by early spring at the latest, flying north to their breeding grounds.

This is a bird of ancient origin known to have occurred in Britain in the Pleistocene at intervals from the Cromerian Interglacial to the Devensian and as a human food resource from the Mesolithic to the Bronze and Iron Ages. Heavily persecuted because of its fishing ability and supposed effect on fish stocks (much as the similar Goosander is today) it has however remained a very successful bird and numbers are quite stable. In 1999 the peak count at Newtown was 51 on 23 November.

Brent Goose *(Branta Bernicla)*

This small, dark goose is one of the birds for which the Solent is so important. It over-winters in considerable numbers throughout the estuaries and waterways and is the most numerous species of wild fowl to be found. The two principal sites are Langstone Harbour and Chichester Harbour, but Newtown is considered to hold nationally important numbers as well. In 1999, the peak count at Newtown was on 19 December with 1399 being observed.

The Brent Goose breeds on the tundra of Arctic Siberia, west of the Taymyr Peninsular and is thought to have been extremely numerous in the past. However in the 1920s and 1930s the population declined severely, probably due to a shortage of its food plant, Eel grass (Zostera marina). It has since recovered and numbers are now most likely to exceed any previous population peaks. Its feeding habits have also changed and it now eats agricultural crops late in the winter when its normal food is difficult to obtain; this may explain the increase in numbers.

Red-breasted Merganser (Mergus serrator)

*Brent Goose
(Branta Bernicla)*

Little Egret *(Egretta garzetta)*

Up to 1957 there had only been about 25 Little Egrets seen in Britain and the bird was deemed to be a great rarity. In the spring of 1970 an influx took place of unprecedented proportions with over 150 seen in that year. By the beginning of the 1990s birds were over-wintering in the south of England and by the end of that decade they were breeding at Poole Harbour, Dorset with the first pair raising three young at Brownsea Island in 1996. Such is their success rate at colonising Britain that only 4 years after this first event there were 40 nests by the year 2000, with probably a total of 1000 birds in Britain, mostly along the south coast.

Nest sites have been found in Cornwall, Hampshire, Somerset and Essex. The Solent has its share of this conspicuous bird and it is now a common sight anywhere suitable along the Solent shores. It has not, as yet, bred at Newtown but there is a good chance that it will eventually; the largest number seen there in 1999 was 46 on 12 September. A certain number of birds use the Isle of Wight as a night roosting site as they have been seen leaving places such as Keyhaven to fly across the Solent for the night and presumably returning the next day. Night roosting sites along the north side of the Solent have high numbers, for example, in excess of 200 at Tournerbury Woods on Hayling Island and in excess of 95 at Hornsea Island in Portsmouth Harbour in October 2000.

Purple Sandpiper *(Calidras maritima)*

This small wader is found in the Solent only in the winter. A few roost at high tide in the Portsmouth area and then fly across the Solent at low tide to feed on the reefs and shoreline of the Isle of Wight around Bembridge and St Helens.

Little Egret (Egretta garzetta)

*Purple Sandpiper
(Calidras maritima)*

42

BUTTERFLIES

These delicate insects have surprisingly ancient origins with fossil records dating back to the Oligocene era. It is reasonable to suppose that some time after the last Ice Age butterflies started to colonise southern Britain but the earliest written records are only about 200 years old. As Hampshire was considered to be one of the premier counties in Britain for butterflies and moths we are fortunate in having a great deal of information available from the early 1800s to the present day, and indeed, the Hampshire and Isle of Wight Branch of Butterfly Conservation is the largest in the country.

The area around the Solent consists of low-lying cliffs, salt marsh, coastal heath and sand dunes as well as other unusual habitats such as the compacted shingle at Needs Ore Point. Behind the salt marshes are areas of grazing marshes which support quite large populations of

particular species such as the Wall Brown (Lasiommata megera). The Solent coast of the Isle of Wight is much more varied than the mainland side and species such as the Silver-washed Fritillary (Argynnis paphia) can be found in the woods at Newtown and the Small Pearl-bordered Fritillary (Boloria selene) at Cranmore. Butterfly populations in towns and cities must not be overlooked and on either side of the Solent these provide quite safe habitats for many varieties, for example 35 different species have been recorded in and around Southampton (Barker and Budd 1997).

Due to the geographical location of Hampshire and the Isle of Wight it is no surprise that the counties see their fair share of incoming migrant butterflies. One of the most striking is the Camberwell Beauty *(Nymphalis antiopa)* from Scandinavia and one of these butterflies was seen in Southampton on three occasions in 1995.

Another large and distinctive migrant is the Monarch *(danaus plexippus)* that comes all the way from the USA; one was seen at Needs Ore in 1995.

White-Letter Hairstreak
(Satyrium w-album)

White-Letter Hairstreak *(Satyrium w-album)*

Emerging in July this is not an easy butterfly to see as most of its life is spent at or near the tops of trees and it only rarely descends to ground level to feed on the nectar of bramble or thistle flowers. The interesting aspect of this insect is its dependence on Elm (Ulmus spp) and the forecast of a total collapse of the population due to Dutch Elm Disease which in fact did not happen. It was probably under-recorded in the past and much overlooked but after the loss of mature Elms in 1976 and the increase in the number of butterfly enthusiasts it was found that good numbers were making use of young Elm and were present in quite high numbers.

Clouded Yellow (*Colias croceus*)

An immigrant butterfly that in some years will be very scarce and in others extremely abundant. In the good years it may be seen virtually anywhere from coastal marshes to city parks. It recently has overwintered in Great Britain for the first time and may eventually become a resident species.

Silver-washed Fritillary (*Argynnis paphia*)

This is the largest of our native British butterflies, and it is predominately a woodland species. In the Solent area it is not common as few estuaries or waterways have woodland adjoining them, but at Newtown the marsh leads directly into the woods at Town Copse and Walters Copse where a small colony exists. It is usually seen on the wing in July or August flying high over the tree tops before swooping down to feed on bramble flowers. These butterflies are unmistakable, with their bright orange upper sides with dark black ridges, showing up well on the male and the delicate green silver undersides that look as though they were painted in water colour. The females are darker and muddier on the upper wing but the same as the males on the under wing.

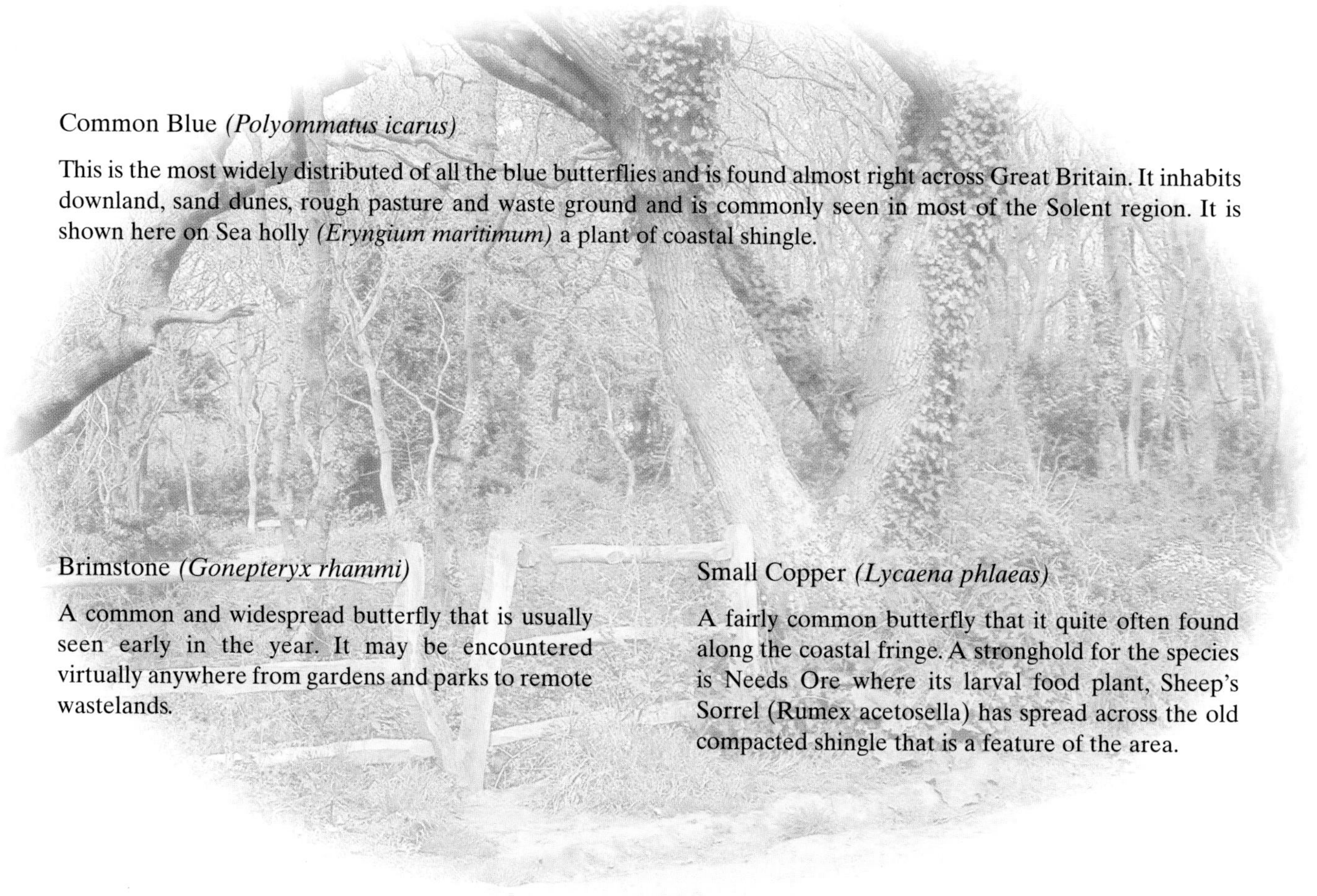

Common Blue (*Polyommatus icarus*)

This is the most widely distributed of all the blue butterflies and is found almost right across Great Britain. It inhabits downland, sand dunes, rough pasture and waste ground and is commonly seen in most of the Solent region. It is shown here on Sea holly (*Eryngium maritimum*) a plant of coastal shingle.

Brimstone (*Gonepteryx rhammi*)

A common and widespread butterfly that is usually seen early in the year. It may be encountered virtually anywhere from gardens and parks to remote wastelands.

Small Copper (*Lycaena phlaeas*)

A fairly common butterfly that it quite often found along the coastal fringe. A stronghold for the species is Needs Ore where its larval food plant, Sheep's Sorrel (Rumex acetosella) has spread across the old compacted shingle that is a feature of the area.

Clouded Yellow (Colias croceus)

Silver-washed Fritillary (Argynnis paphia)

Common Blue (Polyommatus icarus)

Brimstone (Gonepteryx rhammi)

*Small Copper
(Lycaena phlaeas)*

OTHER INSECTS

This is a huge Order with something like 100,000 different kinds of insect to be found in western Europe. In the Solent it is impossible to say how many different species there are but it will most certainly be many as there are a wide range of varying different habitats. A recent survey at Newtown by Adam Wright produced some interesting records and no doubt if other parts of the Solent were surveyed specifically for insects (other than butterflies, moths and dragonflies) then equally unusual and rare species would be discovered. His description of finding and recording some particular species is worth including here verbatim :

"Haematopota grandis. (Diptera : Tabanidae) RDB3. This Horsefly (cleg) is known from coastal marshes and tidal rivers. I have found it in August on the Newtown Harbour Marsh, and one found me in Walter's Copse (a bad choice of "victim")! Falk gives 5 UK post 1960 sites and the possibility of some Welsh records. A new record for the Island, as far as I can establish. Other notables from the Marsh include Long winged conehead (Conocephalus discolor), Lasioglossum malachurus (bee) and Ogcodes pallipes (Acrocerid fly). This was taken together with Acrocera globulus (local) in the same sweep! Taken from drainage ditch adjacent to the Hay meadows, which is probably where they really live. Adults have really humped backs, strange wings and a tiny head. Larvae develop as internal parasites of Wolf spiders (eggs are laid on twigs, but the young larvae are very active and seek out their own hosts). The adults do not feed at all, and have no signs of mouthparts at all. No wonder they're scarce. Very odd beasts!'

Wasp Spider *(Argiope bruennichi)*

A large spider from the Continent that has been expanding its range in Britain over the last 20 years. Commonly found throughout the Solent region from gardens to the edges of salt marshes.

Bee-Wolf *(Philanthus triangulum)*

This once rare insect was confined to St Helens Duver on the Isle of Wight but in recent years has undergone an astonishing range expansion and is now common throughout southern England. It is a digger wasp and stocks its nest with honey bees.

Red-veined Darter *(Sympetrum fonscolombii)*

This is a dragonfly that from being a regular migrant to Britain has now become a resident with breeding populations along the southern coast. Whether they will survive into the future is a matter of conjecture.

Beautiful Demoiselle *(Calopteryx virgo)*

This large damselfly actually resembles a butterfly in flight and is a spectacular insect to see. It is found locally in the Solent area and has a preference for clear, fast-flowing streams.

Wasp Spider (Argiope bruennichi)

Bee-Wolf (Philanthus triangulum)

Red-veined Darter (Sympetrum fonscolombii)

Beautiful Demoiselle (Calopteryx virgo)

Southern Hawker (Aeshna cyanea)

Broad-bodied chaser (Libellula depressa)

MAMMALS

The mammals of western Europe is not a particularly large Order with almost 200 species in total but it does include some very interesting animals, from bats to whales and hedgehogs to foxes as well as deer, seals, squirrels, rabbits, hares and even Red-necked Wallaby! Around the Solent area a good number of different species live and thrive either in the towns and cities or in the marshes and woods as well as in the sea.

Whales and Dolphins

Although there are no modern records available of Cetaceans in the Solent there is one well documented instance from the 19th century. In September 1888 a specimen of either a Sei Whale (Bulaenoptera borealis) or, as some think, a Blue Whale (B.musculus), was seen from the Ryde to Portsmouth steamer quite close to Ryde Pier. It was then hunted by about a dozen small boats for 3-4 hours before being killed by shooting and lancing. It was then towed to Seaview and beached. The illustration is from the 'Illustrated London News' of 29 September 1888. There is also a record of a Bottle-nose Whale (Hyperoodon ampullatus) killed in Southampton water on 8 September 1798.

Red Fox *(Vulpes vulpes)*

One of the most intelligent and successful animals of all, the fox is widespread and numerous throughout the Solent region; it is also in a wider context, the most abundant wild carnivore in the northern hemisphere. It will live virtually anywhere that provides food, shelter and safety, so it can be found not only in woods, meadows and along the shore, but in built up areas throughout the Solent, be it suburban or commercial. This is one of the animals that would have spread up through to Britain after the last Ice Age but for some unknown reason there is no evidence to show it was ever a resident on the Isle of Wight. This is strange but we first hear of it only in the early part of the 19th century and only as a curiosity, it was later brought over from the mainland and released for hunting purposes much the same as the hare (lepus europaeus) in the 16th century.

The effect of the fox on other wild life in the region is probably only minor as it will eat almost anything including earthworms, fruit and refuse, but will cause considerable mortality to nesting gulls, for example when it invades a colony many of which are situated on the Solent shoreline. The fox can live for a maximum of 9 years in the wild given good conditions, but generally their life span is very much less. Between 50,000 - 100,000 are thought to be killed on the roads of Britain each year and therefore a more realistic figure for their life span is probably only 3 years.

Red Fox (Vulpes vulpes)

Red Squirrel (*Sciureus vulgaris*)

Although an animal very similar to the present day Red Squirrel lived in the coniferous forests that covered Britain 12 million years ago the origins of our modern day squirrel date back only to the end of the last Ice Age. As the climate warmed up and the ice retreated so many species moved up from the south to colonise the newly available land and the Red Squirrel was one of them.

Grey squirrels (S.carolinensis) came along much later when the first were brought over from North America and released into Britain in 1876. They eventually outnumbered the Red Squirrel in many parts of the UK and became the most numerous of the genre.

The Isle of Wight is now one of the few strongholds for the Red Squirrel and there are no greys on the Island at all. On the adjacent mainland, across the Solent, the reverse is true. The Red Squirrel is found in suitable habitats right along the Island's Solent shoreline with good numbers at Bouldnor, Cranmore, Parkhurst Forest and around Quarr near Ryde.

Red Squirrel (Sciureus vulgaris)

Stoat (*Mustela erminea*)

These fearless hunters are far more common than is thought, they are just not observed very often. The stoat can kill prey such as a rabbit (Oryctolagus cuniculus) which is more than twice its size and weight. Stoats are found in marshes, near woodland, shorelines and downland. Sometimes a family group may be encountered with the female leading and up to eight cubs following behind in single file.

Stoat (Mustela erminea)

Wood Mouse (*Apodemus sylvaticus*)

A much overlooked and charming little creature, it is widespread and common throughout the Solent region. It is found in many different habitats that include woodland, arable farmland, gardens and sand dunes. It eats, amongst other things, fruit, nuts, snails, earthworms, fungi and sweetcorn but it also provides food for predators such as the kestrel (Falco tinnunculus), all the Owl species as well as the Red Fox (Vulpes vulpes), the Badger (Meles meles) and the Stoat (Mustela erminea).

Wood Mouse (Apodemus sylvaticus)

FLORA

The mixture of habitats found along the Solent shore and hinterland supports a very high number of diverse and interesting plants. For example, at St Helens Duver on the north east coast of the Isle of Wight in the eastern Solent there are about 200 different species in that one area alone. It is obviously impossible to include and illustrate all the examples found throughout the region so therefore a representative selection only follows :

Marsh Mallow (Althaea officinalis)

Marsh Mallow
(Althaea officinalis)

Marsh Mallow is found in most of the salt marshes and estuaries but it is usually only seen in small numbers.

Sea-Holly *(Eryngium maritimum)*

    A plant that has decreased generally in the Solent area. It is found on sandy and shingle beaches, the flowers being a great attraction to insects of all types.

Early-Purple Orchid (Orchis mascula)

Sea-Purslane *(Halimione portulacoides)*

Flowering in mid to late summer this is a typical and common plant of the salt marshes and estuaries of the Solent.

Early-Purple Orchid *(Orchis mascula)*

Flowering in April through to June this is one of the commonest orchids to be seen in the Solent area. It grows along banks and especially in woodland and thickets.

Dog Rose (Rosa canina)

Dog Rose *(Rosa canina)*

Although a very common plant and found throughout the Solent region it is nevertheless an extremely attractive sight when growing through hedges or across waste ground.

Sea-Purslane (Halimione portulacoides)

Sea Kale *(Crambe maritima)*

Sea Kale *(Crambe maritima)*

Found sparingly along the Solent shores the Sea Kale has been a rarity until recent years. Some sites are now showing an increase which is a welcome trend.

Sea Rocket *(Cabile maritima)*

Sea Rocket *(Cabile maritima)*

A typical plant of the drift line on sandy shorelines Sea Rocket is much less common than it was in the past.

Marsh Orchid *(Dactylorchis praetermissa)*

Found, as its name suggests, growing in marshland this is probably the commonest Orchid in the Solent region. *(opposite page)*

Yellow Horned - Poppy
(Glaucium flavum)

A common but striking plant found on the Solent shingle beaches, cliffs and waste ground.

Yellow Horned - Poppy (Glaucium flavum)

References
Aspinall S, Tasiler M. 1992, *'Birds of the Solent'*, JNCC, Aberdeen
Bevis J, Kettell R, Shepard B. 1978, *'Flora of the Isle of Wight,'* Yelf Bros, Newport, IW
Chinnery M. 1986, *'Insects of Britain and W. Europe,'* Collins, London
Cox J. 1996, *'Newtown Management Plan,'* National Trust
MacDonald D, Barrett P. 1993, *'Mammals of Britain and Europe,'* Harper Collins, London
Morey F (Ed). 1909, *'A Guide to the Natural History of the Isle of Wight,'*
County Press, Newport, IW
Oates M, Taverner J, Green D. 2000, *'The Butterflies of Hampshire,'* Pisces Publications
Reid-Henry D. 1988, *'The History of the Birds of Britain,'* Collins, London
Svensson L, Grant P. 1999, *'Bird Guide,'* Harper Collins, London

Chapter Three

FOOTHOLDS ON THE SHORE:
A brief archaeology of some early historic activities on the Solent coast

Early territories and politics of the coastland

It seems that during the opening decades of the 1st century AD political changes in western Europe were exerting considerable influence over the coastal populations of the Solent region. The politics of Late Iron Age Britain have always offered fascination and they have often led to earnest debates over the tribal names and the crude territorial boundaries which can be perceived on Britain's earliest map. The world map of Claudaius Ptolemaeus (Ptolemy) was drawn in the early 2nd century AD and its British section is commonly believed to contain details which had been transcribed from one or more earlier documents of the 1st century AD. The map is also believed to embody an earlier image of the known world as prepared by a Greek scholar, Agathedaemon of Tyre. It is tantalising to find that Ptolemy's original works have long been lost. This is probably due to the sacking of Constantinople. Fortunately, during the Crusades, originals or copies were brought back to Europe and from these a legacy of some fifty-two different copies have survived through the painstaking works of various medieval monks.

In the Solent region Ptolemy's map identifies three named tribes. To the west lies the land of the *Durotriges*. These people generally occupied the area which is now the modern county of Dorset. North of Wight lay the *Atrebates* of the Hampshire region. In Ptolemy's day, this tribe had been generally identified as part of the larger ethnic group known as the *Belgae*. During the late pre-Conquest period the *Atrebates* seem to have been riven with internal disagreement. This may have arisen from the antagonism of pro-Roman and anti-Roman factions. We should not be too surprised, to find that the pro-Roman stance seems to have been adopted amongst the coastal population. It would not be difficult for this section of the tribe to be swayed by the acquisition of Roman commodities through cross-Channel trade. The outcome of this rift was the progressive isolation of the southern *Atrebates* and the eventual forming of a separate tribal entity. Finally, we find these people withdrawn to the eastern margin of the Solent coast. By the time of the Roman conquest they are consolidated in the Chichester-Selsey region where they seem to be known as the *Regni* or *Regnenses* (Cunliffe, 1973).

Since the days of William Camden (1587) scholars have studied and mapped the gold and silver coins of the British Iron Age in attempts to identify the territories actually occupied by Ptolemy's tribes. The purposes for which these coins or *staters* were used is not clearly understood but there is certainly good

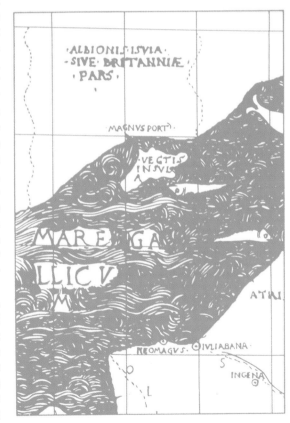

A section of one of the medieval copies of Ptolemy's 2nd century map. This shows the Magnus Portus *and the island of* Vectis *in an ocean alive with fish, the* Mare Gallicum.

evidence to suggest that their circulation was largely contained within each tribal area.

Although archaeologists have done much to refine the cultural characteristics of these tribes, the defining of boundaries is still fraught with difficulties. In the Solent region the eastern boundary of the *Durotriges* is poorly understood because virtually no coins and little evidence of Iron Age activity has been found between the Hampshire Avon and the coast of Southampton Water. The boundary between the *Atrebates* and the *Regni* is also illusive yet this is hardly surprising given that the division seems to have been political rather than ethnic. The Meon river has been suggested as a notional boundary in this quarter but any truce or treaty line such as this could readily waver and change given the eternal human vices of brinkmanship and acquisitiveness.

The tribal situation on the Solent's southern shore has long been an enigma. Ptolemy identifies the Isle of Wight by its common Roman name of *Vecta or Vectis* but this seems to identify the land rather than its people. Nevertheless, it is interesting to observe that some 600 years later Bede reiterates that the island is called *Vectis* while helpfully adding that its occupants call themselves the *Victuarii*. This name makes an interesting comparison with the *Wihtgara* who are cited in an Anglo-Saxon document listing the *Tribal Hidage* in the 7th or 8th century (Hinton, 1979 & 1981).

For many years the evidence offered by Iron Age coins on the island has been generally unhelpful, being too small in number, but the general deployment of metal-detecting machines has made some notable changes. *Durotrigian* silver staters have been commonly found on the island and it might be assumed that these represent at least frequent maritime traffic with Hengistbury and, presumably, a cultural tie with Dorset. Coins of the *Atrebates* have certainly been less common in the island yet the 'saucepan pot' ceramic style of southern Hampshire seems to be well represented in Vectensian sites of the Middle Iron Age.

(a)

(b)

(c)

(d)

(e)

Some tribal coins from the Solent region, (not to scale).

(a) A highly schematic horse characterizes the silver staters of the Durotriges *of Dorset.*

(b) The baleful Medusa *glares from a quarter stater of the southern* Attrebates *of Hampshire/Sussex.*

(c) & (d) The CRAB coins with their Roman eagles may mark the Iron Age coinage of the Isle of Wight.

(e) Molten Gallic silver staters may mark late Iron Age coin production in the Isle of Wight.

Perhaps the most intriguing aspect of Vectensian identity concerns the recent discovery in the Island of wafer thin silver coins inscribed with the letters *CRAB*. Seven of these coins come from a single site discovered by Alan Rowe and they now numerically outweigh a tiny smattering of mainland examples which have mostly been found near the northern shore of the Solent. The discovery of these coins in the Isle of Wight was accompanied by evidence of metalworking and some fine 1st and 2nd century enamelled brooches. At a second site in the Isle of Wight plough-scattered evidence of another Late Iron Age metalworking industry has recently been found. This included scattered fragments of Dressel 1 amphorae. Here, a clutch of Gallic silver coins had been consigned to the melting pot. It seems that the craftsman at this site was an accomplished worker of precious metals for his equipment apparently included a small set of gold-plated scales. Viewed together, these recent finds evoke a new picture of an industrious and prosperous Vectensian community which had the means and resources to produce its own distinctive silver coinage in the closing years before the Claudian conquest.

Roman Solent and the *Magnus Portus*

One of the most tantalising features on Ptolemy's map is his identification of his 'great port', the *Magnus Portus*. Archaeologists and cartographers are now generally agreed that this is not the name of a specific coastal settlement but the technical description of a section of coastline which was suitable for anchorage. This interpretation accords with the descriptive names of certain other anchorages which Ptolemy recorded in some other coastal areas on his maps. This distinction seems to be confirmed by Ptolemy's preparation of a special maritime inventory in which he lists all of these coastal descriptions while omitting any mention of the known coastal towns or settlements which he has otherwise plotted (Rivet & Smith, 1979).

Ptolemy's cartographic rendering of the island of *Vectis* is a poor and shapeless thing. This seems to confirm that he had no real knowledge of the Solent coastline or the precise position of his 'great port'. These shortcomings should not be disheartening because, given that we are not searching for a specific coastal settlement, we have only to apply the eye of the mariner to the Solent to discover where the great anchorage might be. A most helpful source is the advice given to the navigators of wooden sailing ships in the mid-19th century (Hobbs,1959; Tomalin *et al.* forthcoming). This reminds us that..

Between Sturbridge and the buoy of the Middle [Bank] is good anchorage everywhere and merchant vessels generally lie in 4, 5, 6, and 7 fathoms safely sheltered from the southerly winds on good clean ground..... Vessels may stop a tide anywhere between West Cowes and Yarmouth, the nearer to the island the more they will be out of the strength of the tide; but the places most used are Cowes and Yarmouth.

One of the more surprising archaeological discoveries in recent years has been the recovery of Roman 'anchorage debris' from the floor of the Solent. The first finds were made in Yarmouth Roads during the 1980's and they were soon followed by the recovery of fragments of amphorae and other Roman ceramics from the floor of the Eastern Solent; notably in the vicinity of Cowes and the 'Middle Bank' off Ryde. There are even some fragments of Palestinian amphorae.

The pottery found in each of these seabed scatters generally covers much of the Roman period and this implies that in these instances we are not dealing with wrecked cargoes or sunken ships but with accumulations of jettisoned or 'gash' items discarded by ships at anchor. The occurrence of these scatters at precisely the favoured anchorages cited in the British Channel Pilot of 1859 is surely no coincidence and it provides us with new and persuasive archaeological evidence that the *Magnus Portus* of the Roman period was essentially the *Soluente* or *Le Soland* of Saxon and medieval times.

Courting Neptune's bounty

It seems that both politics and practicalities led to the prompt development of a great anchorage in the Solent in the early Roman period. The evidence from Yarmouth Roads shows that ships laden with Roman goods were already arriving in Solent waters before the Claudian invasion of AD 43. This is confirmed by a variety of early high quality Roman table-wares which have turned up in certain coastal settlements in our region. Some of these wares reflect the eating and drinking receptacles which were fashionable in Rome and its provinces during the reigns of Tiberius and Augustus. They also include elegant white or buff-coloured jars and flagons designed for generous servings of wine. These trappings of the good life were so loved by some of their owners that they were readily chosen for the grave and the after-life.

On the eve of the Roman invasion the Roman army required sound intelligence of safe-landing places and potential supply depots on the Channel coast of Britain. It seems that word had arrived that one point of assured safety might be found in Chichester harbour. Here the local king, Cogidubnus, and his Regnensian compatriots were well-favoured towards the Roman

The creek-head Roman Palace at Fishbourne on the Chichester Channel represents the success of new European trade links in the Solent in the first century AD. Courtesy of the Trustees of the Fishbourne Palace Museum.

cause. The collaboration of the Regni in the Roman conquest of Britain was well rewarded and the result for the king and his family seems to have been the construction of a truly magnificent palace at the head of the of the Chichester Channel at Fishbourne (Cunliffe, 1971; Cunliffe & Down 1996).

The principal architectural works at Fishbourne took place around 75AD and they tell us much about contemporary maritime activities in the Solent region. By this date the stone resources of the Isle of Wight had been well prospected and local ships were now ferrying substantial supplies of Bembridge Limestone to masons' workshops on the Chichester shore. It seems that some of these boats were also engaged in long distance coastal trade and that these included trips to the Cornish peninsular. These journeys are betrayed by the presence of discarded ballast stones of Cornish or Devon origin (Cunliffe, 1971). On the Wootton-Quarr coast of the Isle of Wight where intertidal outcrops of Bembridge Limestone were accessible to the Romano-British quarry teams, fragments of 1st pottery have been found which contain gabbro from the Cornish peninsular.

Prior to the Roman Conquest we have seen that cross-Channel trade had already become an important opportune occupation for certain Solent communities. The military organisation of Roman Britain brought some perceptible changes to these *ad hoc* arrangements. The development of Roman cities at London and Colchester placed new emphasis on a Thames-Rhine trade route yet at the same time the construction of the Foss Way from Exeter to York brought a notable demand for the shipments of military supplies to the head of navigation in the river Exe.

Set midway between the mouths of the Thames and the Exe, the Solent was ideally placed to offer a great anchorage on a long coast route which was notable short of safe and sheltered landing places. One craft, up from the Dorset coast, lost its anchor in the Western Solent. We are unable to identify its cargo but the limestone used for its anchor was quarried in the Purbeck region. Perhaps its home port was Poole Harbour where substantial quantities of black coarseware pottery (BB1) were being made for military and civilian consumption (Williams, 1977). Vectensians generally dismissed this product, being satisfied with their own brown ware variant (Vectis ware), but some supplies were brought ashore at Wootton Haven where a contract in beef provisioning seems to have been operating with ships in the *Magnus Portus* (Tomalin *et al.* forthcoming).

(a)

(b)

(c)

(a) Up from the west. A Roman anchor of Purbeck Limestone found on the floor of the Western Solent.

(b) 'RR' marks the ownership of a black-burnished bowl found on the shore at Wootton Haven.

(c) Vectensians generally preferred their own brown-burnished Vectis ware.

It seems that one aspect of the Solent's new role in the 1st century AD was the provisioning of the Roman army. There can be little doubt that the obliging *Regni* would be quick to seize this opportunity by making full use of their pastoral and arable landholdings on the highly fertile West Sussex plain. The early development of Roman villas in this region has been generally attributed to the favoured status of the *Regni* and it has not been overlooked that at least one of these sites seems to have been built to a plan which might be comparable with Fishbourne. West of the palace, between Emsworth and Southampton the situation is less clear but there seems good reason to suspect that early prosperity was similarly grasped. This is certainly evident on Hayling Island where a Late Iron Age religious site was soon up-graded to become a substantial

Seen from the air the Roman Temple on Hayling Island reveals itself beneath a ripening cereal crop.

Romano-British temple. It is interesting to observe that the Iron Age coins recovered from this site betray cross-Channel contact with northern France in the pre-conquest period. On the Isle of Wight recent archaeological investigations suggest that occupation on the Roman villas sites of Newport, Combley and Brading was rapidly developing in the 1st century AD and this may be the result of a strong tribal or political connection which secured an early share of the Regnensian prosperity.

Some Roman occupation sites on the Solent coast may have begun life as small salt-working communities. These could exploit the substantial tidal range of the Solent to retrieve a commodity which was so important for the curing and storage of winter food. Sites of this nature have been investigated in Langstone and Portsmouth Harbours, at Brownwich Farm near the mouth of Tichfield Haven and on the Wootton-Quarr coast of the Isle of Wight (Bradley 1975; Hughes, 1973; Tomalin et al, forthcoming). Some of these activities began in Middle Iron Age times and this is attested by a find from Portsdown Hill (Bradley, *ibid*). This activity can also be traced throughout much of the Roman period. At most of these sites evidence of salt-working is attested by the remains of simple kilns and generous scatters of broken evaporating dishes and troughs. All of this material is composed of weakly-fired clay which archaeologists have termed *briquetage*.

Briquetage clay was normally tempered with liberal quantities of chopped chaff which would expire during firing to produce a porous fabric. An examination of the chaff cavities in surviving fragments of *briquetage* shows that the predominant tempering was winter-sown cereals which would have been cropped during the month of August (Bradley, *ibid*). This indicates that Iron Age and Roman salt production in the Solent was a specific seasonal activity and it has led archaeologists to question what activities may have been taking place at other times of the year. Summer grazing on coastal lowlands has been cited as a distinct possibility as has the gathering of edible seaweed for cattle fodder. The recovery of edible shell fish was important, particularly the oyster *Ostrea edulis* for which the Solent is rightly renowned (Tomalin, forthcoming). Seasonal fishing from boats could be extended into off-shore voyaging and trading during the summer months while inshore fishing and fish-trapping could be cautiously pursued at virtually all times of the year in the more sheltered waters.

Regulation, organisation, exploitation

The course of the Roman road from Chichester to Bitterne bears a most interesting relationship with the Solent coast. The road cuts or clips the heads of six navigable creeks and at each of these we find evidence of substantial Roman buildings (Cunliffe, 1973). The outstanding site is, of course, Fishbourne yet at Bosham, Southbourne, Emsworth, Langstone and Havant traces of Roman buildings have also been found and we may question whether at least some of these owe their origins to precursive maritime settlements of the Late Iron Age. Such pre-Roman settlement might be suspected, for instance, on the banks of the Itchen at Southampton where a certain number Iron Age features and small finds have been found beneath the modern city.

At Havant the Roman road veers to the north-west towards Wickham, by-passing the 3rd-4th century Roman coastal installations at Portchester and passing through a sub-rectangular enclosure on the bank of a major tributary to the Wallington River (Soffe & Johnston, 1974). Here, at Southwick, 'Roman remains' were observed and poorly recorded many years ago (Haverfield, 1900). This site marks the halfway point between Chichester and Clausentum and it has been proposed as a putative Roman station or *mansio*. At Curbridge the road intercepts the upper Hamble estuary around the point of the river's navigable limit. Here we find some weakly investigated evidence of Roman buildings and pottery production in the adjacent fields as well

Principal settlements, communications, ports and anchorages in the Solent region in Roman times.

as the structure composed of limestone blocks engulfed within the river bed (Soffe & Johnston, 1974). It seems that the nature of the road crossing at Curbridge has yet to be fully investigated as, indeed, has the possibility of a Roman quay at this location. There can be no doubt that the archaeological significance of this estuary has been greatly under-investigated and that the entire environs including the banks and riverbed are in need of both survey and monitoring.

The particular importance of the Hamble estuary, during the Roman period, is clearly marked by the discovery of an inscribed lead sheet, or *defixio* on the margins of the lower river. This bears an elaborate message addressed to the twin deities of a local shrine. The writer, one Muconius, is incensed at the theft of his money comprising one gold and six silver coins. '*Whether male or female, boy or girl*', Muconius wants revenge and this he considers should be '*the life, health and blood of him who has been privy to that taking-away'*. Muconius is leaving nothing to chance because he suspects that a second person could have been party to this theft. In this case he calls upon the second diety to make sure that '*the mind that stole this and which has been privy to this'* should also be taken away (Tomlin, 1997).

The cursive writing scratched on this metal sheet is characteristic of the 4th century (Tomlin, *ibid*) and it is particularly interesting to see that Muconius has addressed his fearsome curse to two distinct deities. The principal deity is named as '*Lord Neptune'* and from this we might deduce that this shrine on the lower Hamble was essentially associated with that great superintendent of the maritime world. This is precisely the type of shrine or temple which would serve a coastal community and we cannot but wonder whether the temple on Hayling Island performed a very similar function. The second deity cited by Muconius is an obscure god called *Niskus* who is most probably associated with the properties of water. Elsewhere, in the Pyrenean foothills of southwestern France, water nymphs called *Niske* have been named on cursive texts thrown into a hot spring at Amelie-les-Bains. It seems that this name still survives as *Neski* meaning girl in modern Basque (Tomlin, *ibid*).

It is particularly disappointing to find that so little is known of the Roman activities around the head of the Southampton Water. The coastal settlement at Bitterne stood within the arm of a large meander in the course of the lower Itchen. This has made the site naturally vulnerable to erosion. Later, at the opening of the 20th century, the site was recklessly marred by an uncompromising grid of drear urban houses, a tradition of heritage degradation which has been long sustained in the city of Southampton. Some small opportune excavations have indicated that

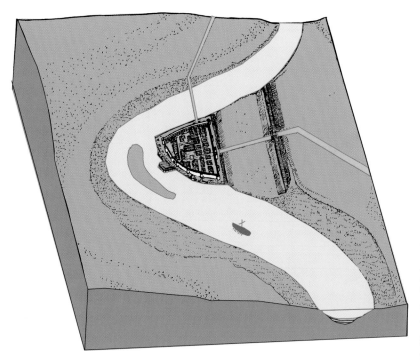

The location of the walled Roman riverside settlement at Bitterne. Its walls were erected in the late 3rd Century AD.

Roman settlement on the flood plain peninsular developed in an *ad hoc* manner during the second half of the 1st century. This may have been a time when the road from Chichester first brought travellers and goods to a fording point on this section of the Itchen. It seems that maritime traffic was also arriving on this shore and there is reason to suspect the construction of an early wooden waterfront. Some fragments of this structure seem to have been glimpsed during building works in the late 19th century (Smith, 1883).

The early use of a quayside at Bitterne seems to be corroborated by the finding of two lead 'pigs' or ingots on the old shoreline. Both of these were found to be inscribed with the name of the emperor Vespasian. This provides forthright evidence that these products had been officially despatched from the smelting shop between the years AD 69 and AD 79. The inclusion of the letters VEB in these cast inscriptions *(IMP VESPASIAN AVG BRIT EXARG VEB)* suggests that the lead was the product of the new mines which had been opened in the heart of the Mendip Hills (Tylecote, 1962). These cumbersome items have persuaded scholars that the Bitterne waterfront was a significant Roman port and that its early development, within some 30 years of the Roman conquest, coincided with the construction of an effective road network which could convey exportable goods from the interior of the new province.

An important arm of this network was the road from Bitterne to Winchester *(Venta Belgarum)*. It seems that the line of this road led to the western or far bank of Itchen at Bitterne. Unfortunately its precise course has yet to be traced south of Eastleigh (Margary, 1955). A second road serving this region crossed the lower Test not far from the Testwood Bronze Age causeway. This was the road which ostensibly connected Poole Harbour with Winchester. Its

One of the 1st century Roman lead 'pigs' or ingots lost in the Itchen mud at Bitterne.

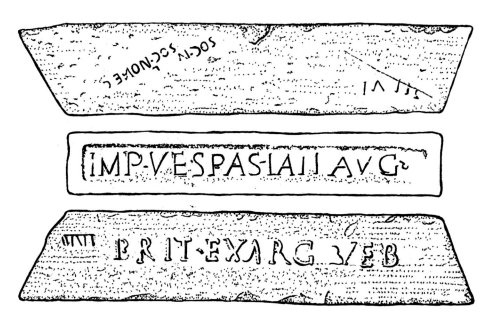

consistent alignment has been reliably traced on both banks of the river yet its course through the valley alluvium to a precise crossing point is still illusive. An intriguing new strand of evidence may be found just 5km upstream at Romsey where excavations have been conducted on the Late Saxon abbey. From the 10th century foundations of this building come some large re-used blocks of Binstead stone (Scott, 1996). This is a facies of the Bembridge Limestone Formation which was generally quarried in the Isle of Wight in Roman times. Each displays an ashlar face bearing tooled pits or rustication. While it is difficult to explain the export and use of this stone in Anglo-Saxon times (Tomalin, 1987) there is little difficulty in matching this kind of decorated block with those employed in Roman bridge abutments (Tomalin & Insole 1977).

The problem of roads, *Clausentum* and the *Portus Adurni*

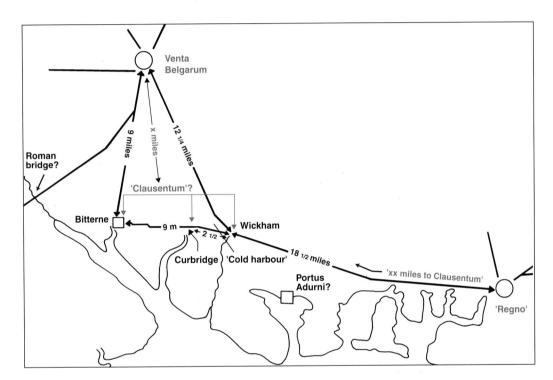

Diagram showing the Clausentum problem. Details given the Antonine Itinery are shown in red.

An appealing conjecture is the identification of the Bitterne settlement with a Roman station which is named *Clausentum* in *Iter VII* of the *Antonine Itinerary*. The *Itinerary* is a written description of some 225 road routes in the Roman Empire and it seems to have been drawn up from a large number of disparate documents assembled during the 2nd and 3rd centuries (Rivet & Smith, 1979). This guide was primarily intended to provide military commanders with precise marching distances for deploying their troops and it includes a route from Chichester to Winchester via a place called *Clausentum*. Since William Camden first ventured the idea in 1586, this place has been commonly accepted to be Bitterne, a settlement which seems to have acquired significant new status as a walled coastal community during the unsettled years of the late 3rd and the 4th centuries.

The marching distances given the *Itinerary* are quoted in Roman miles (1,480m) yet several scholars have wrestled with the problem that an error or shortfall of some 10 Roman miles can be detected in the distance of 20 miles which the Itinerary gives from Chichester to *Clausentum* (Smith, 1883; Haverfield, 1900; Margary, 1955; Johnston & Reed, 1968; Rivet, 1970). The actual distance to Bitterne is some 30 Roman miles and this has thrown into question the geographical placing of *Clausentum*. Some have argued that this might be partially resolved if the name really applied to a stopping point at the junction of the Roman road at Wickham but apart from the old place-name of 'Coldharbour', just west of Wickham and some minor Roman discoveries within the town (Hughes, 1976) there is little firm field evidence here. Nevertheless, the presence of a minor urban settlement or road station *(mansio)* has been postulated (Cunliffe, 1973). It is perhaps surprising that the enigmatic Roman settlement at Curbridge has not been advanced in this search for explanation, for this, too, lies close to the 20 mile distance from Chichester.

Other explanations have settled on the anomaly that Chichester is not identified in the *Itinerary* under its slightly more familiar name of *Noviomagus* or *Navimago Regentium* but is cited simply as *'Regno'*. Professor Rivet has observed that, given that the tribal name of the people of this region seems to have been the *Regni* or 'kingdom', the quoted distance of 20 miles, may have been taken from the tribal boundary which could have been situated some 10 Roman miles west of the tribal town. A further argument has proposed that this particular journey had not been measured in Roman miles but in Gaulish *leuga* which were equal to 1.5 Roman miles. For those adhering to the most favoured attribution at Bitterne, Professor Rivet has offered the solution that the requisite X in the Roman enumeration had simply 'fallen out of the text'. This, he remarks, has at least the virtue of simplicity and it is not without analogy elsewhere.

On the western shore of Southampton Water a further conundrum arises where a Roman road of somewhat doubtful nature has been postulated over a distance of 7 miles between Dibden and the Solent shore at Stone Point, near Lepe. An ''agger' or embanked course for this road has been perceived on Beaulieu Heath and Blackwell Common while in some other places a compatible alignment seems to be taken up by lanes and hedgerows (Sanders, 1927; Margary, 1955). It has been observed however that the cross-profile of this road is more akin to a bank and

Portus Adurni? The Roman and Norman defences at Porchester. Moored yachts now rest in a tidal channel which was once occupied by Roman ships. Courtesy: English Heritage.

ditch and until confirmation is obtained the possibility cannot be excluded that it is no more than a ditched estate boundary of medieval date (Hants SMR note). The existence of a Roman road has also been suggested on the Isle of Wight, leading southward from a coastal building at Gurnard, but despite the enthusiasm of local Victorian antiquaries the idea is quite without foundation.

The construction of walled Roman forts on the shores of the English Channel and the North Sea has been a fascination of antiquaries. The British shore forts are strung out between the Solent and the Wash where they were strategically placed to harbour garrisons which could readily supply and support the defending fleet, the *Classis Britannica*. A Roman military handbook of the late 4th century, the *Notitia Dignitatum*, helpfully lists a total of nine forts all of which were under the command of a 'Count of the Saxon Shore' *(Comes Litoris Saxonici per Britannias)*.

The *Notitia* survives as a 15th century copy and in this we find that last of the listed forts is named *Portus Adurni*. Here, 'a unit of scouts' *(exploratores)* seems to have been operating . It is interesting to see that the list makes no mention of *Clausentum*. Those who have assumed that the list runs consistently from east to west have been persuaded that *Portus Adurni* can be identified as the fine Roman fort which stands at the rear of Portsmouth Harbour at Portchester. Unfortunately there remains some uncertainty as to whether the *Notitia* has named the full number of shore forts and whether, indeed, they are reliably listed in order.

Green sails, grey men

The fort at Porchester is perhaps the finest of the British shore forts and its mellow flint and stone walls still safely enclose a secure area of almost 4 hectares. It seems that building activities began here in the late 3rd century around the time when the corrupt naval commander Carausius seized independent power in Britain. After some seven years of personal rule, this man was eventually murdered and succeeded by a second usurper, Allectus. Both of these men have been attributed with the initiative of constructing at least some of the forts of the Saxon shore. They also issued coins which helpfully display images of some of the ships of their fleet.

(a)

(b)

(c)

(d)

The boats and ships of Allectus *as depicted on his bronze coins.*

The coins of Allectus are particularly interesting because some show vessels belonging to a special naval force of scouts such as the *exploratores* who are cited by the *Notitia* at *Portus Adurni*. Some coins show small single-masted vessels equipped with 5 to 7 oars per side. One issue shows a vessel which is no more than a rowing boat equipped with three oars per side. Four oarsmen and a steersman are depicted above the gunwale, their bulky torsos emphasising that their modest craft is little more than a skiff (Dove, 1970). Other boats are shown with a high swan-like bow and stem-post yet even here we see the heads of oarsmen protruding above the rail and there is good reason to suspect that the largest of these craft is no more than some 7-8 metres (Dove, *ibid*). Writing in the late 4th century AD Vegetius seems to be describing vessels somewhat similar to these when he describes light scouting boats ..

'which the Britons call picatos...With these it is customary to surprise and sometimes intercept the supplies of hostile ships, reconnoitre and discover their plans. But as their whiteness would show up at a distance their sails and ropes are tinged a green colour which is like the colour of the waves and even the composition the ships are painted with is similarly coloured. The seamen and soldiers are also clothed in the same colour for better concealment on scouting duty, not only at night but also in the day'.

This image provided by the Allectan coins is the closest we come to the colourful sight of green Roman sails, strangely uniformed crews and dappled hulls cutting through Solent waters or riding at anchor in the harbour of Portchester.

(a)

(b)

(c)

(d)

Maritime activity and exports from the Isle of Wight:

(a) Altar of the 'three mothers' found at Winchester.

(b) Medieval mortar of Quarr stone recovered from the Eastern Solent.

(c) Orion rides the waves with a dolphin at Fishbourne Courtesy: Trustees of the Fishbourne Palace Museum.

(d) The maritime panel at Brading Villa, Isle of Wight. Courtesy: Trustees of the Brading Roman Villa.

There has been much discussion as to whether Portchester and some of its well fortified counterparts were built to repel Saxon invaders or to exclude avenging troops sent by the imperial masters of Carausius and Allectus. The size and quality of the work at Porchester suggest sound military planning and it is interesting to see from the fabric of the walls that Solent or Vectensian boatmen were heavily engaged ferrying notable quantities of Binstead stone from the quarry pits of the Isle of Wight. The same ancient walls were well respected in Norman times when a new body of labourers and masons set to work on repairs and conversions which were to produce a highly secure castle.

A pictorial message from a master mariner

For our final view of Roman Solent we can do no better than to turn to the images left by a contemporary witness. The name of the artist is unknown yet we do know a little of his patron. We may suspect that this patron was the kind of man who was able to draw ready benefit from military contracts such as those which sought building supplies and food provisions for the operations at Portchester. In his villa at the head of Brading Haven this *Vectensian* or *Victuarian* entrepreneur was well placed to supply both ships and stone supplies and it seems that he was even able provide or share specialist craftsmen such as tilemakers. One of his men stamped his hand-made tiles with the impression of his own right hand as well as his initial 'R'. It is certainly interesting to find this 'handiwork' at both Portchester and Brading (Tomalin, 1987; Soffe, pers comm).

For our vignette of this lost Roman world of Solent shipping and trade we must turn to the fine and complex mosaic floor which is on view at Brading. In commissioning their mosaic artists, other villa-owners in the Solent region had either knowingly or unknowingly revealed their nautical inclinations when choosing scenes of dolphins or scallop shells as depicted at Fishbourne, Combley and Carisbrooke (Tomalin, forthcoming). At Brading, however, the choice was truly exquisite for in choosing popular scenes from classical mythology it seems that the patron also engaged in a metaphor for his own Vectensian home and the bounty of its neighbouring shores (Tomalin & Hanworth, 1998). The panels in room 12 are cleverly arranged to present ideas and stories at several different levels. In a panel at the head of the lower floor we are reminded of the heavens and we are shown the image of a natural philosopher who is capable of explaining and perhaps navigating his way beneath the night sky. Below him we are shown four images of the earth in which ploughing, shepherding, vine-growing and defence are depicted in classical allegorical scenes. These are accompanied by the four winds whose capricious temperaments can be disastrous to a family which seeks prosperity on land and sea.

In the basal panel set below the land we are shown the sea itself. This is the realm of violent forces. The power of the sea is embodied in the images of monstrous writhing sea-beasts or *tritons*. Fortunately, it seems that our family is well experienced in taming and exploiting these dangerous forces because the artist has turned these into agreeable creatures who are helpfully transporting a pair of nymphs across the compliant waves. One beast is even carrying a crook to remind us that the sea can be benign to sailors and may even shepherd the fleet to the safety of port. Finally, in the midst of the tamed ocean, it seems that we are shown an allegory of the patron and Solent adventurer himself. Here, the artist shows us a young man who has learnt from the astronomer at the top of the mosaic and is now cheerfully returning from his voyage carrying his steersman's oar. His journey has undoubtedly been a success for in his other hand he carries the fruits of the sea and the symbols of his carefree life. These he displays as a well heaped basket of Solent oysters.

The Solent in post-Roman history

It is difficult to fix the precise time when the Romano-British population of the Solent region found that the good life had truly come to an end. A general sea-borne raid by barbarians in AD 367 sent many villa owners scurrying to security of the walled Roman towns such as those of Winchester and Chichester. Not all were too anxious to return. In the years leading to official

Roman withdrawal in AD 410 a number of Solent residents took to burying their money in secluded places. It seems that these people, too, were unable to return.

Despite the problem of raids there are some tantalising hints of continued prosperity. Some of this may have been sustained by successful Solent sea power. From the floor of the 'great anchorage' in the Eastern Solent comes a complete vessel which is suspected to have come from the Black Sea (Williams & Peacock, pers comm). Sometime in the 5th century one Islander was buried in a favourite spot in an old Bronze Age round barrow on Ashey Down. The pot chosen as the cremation receptacle was a jar of distinctive dirty white clay which archaeologists have named 'E ware'. This pot had been had been shipped from Eastern Mediterranean shores when the Atlantic sea lanes to western Britain were still providing a fragile link with Rome's eastern empire. Such imports were accessible to a few communities in Ireland and the west coast of Britain until about AD700 but penetration up-Channel is virtually unknown. This pot provides some evidence to suggest that a few Vectensian seafarers were still capable of making the westward haul to the Cornish coast.

Black sea amphorae recovered from the Western Solent.

The arrival of Saxon raiders and colonisers on the Solent coast has been documented by *Bede* who set down his account some two hundred years after the event at a time when reality had already been distorted by hearsay. The first colonising raids occurred around 530AD when the invaders were probably met by at least some who spoke their mother Germanic tongue. This arose because the Romano-British inhabitants had long made the mistake of co-opting Germanic warriors or *foederati* to help defend the coast from others of their kind. The extent to which policy was pursued has always challenged archaeologists who have tried to resolve the question by seeking out particularly early types of dress fittings which may have been worn by Germanic mercenaries prior to the invasion of AD 530. It has been suggested that the Meon valley and the Portchester district was an area which was specifically settled under treaty by irregular Germanic groups of the 5th century (Cunliffe, 1973). This is an area where the inhabitants are identified by Bede as the *Meonwara* who are linked by him with the Jutish inhabitants of Wight. The identification of pre-invasion mercenaries and post-invasion settlements is a tall order for the archaeologist and David Hinton (1981) rightly warns us that a 'mercenary does not necessarily lurk behind every belt fitting'.

Bede tells us that the invaders of the early 6th century were *'the three great nations of*

The Roman villa at Newport, Isle of Wight was sited conveniently near the head of the navigable river Medina.

The fine late Saxon church at Sompting near Worthing is embellished with Quarr stone shipped from the Isle of Wight.

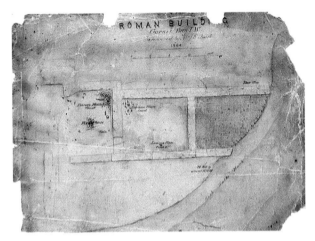

The lost Roman building at Gurnard, Isle of Wight recorded shortly before its loss due to coastal erosion in 1864.

Germany, the Angles, the Saxons and the Jutes'. The seizing of Solent territory seems to have followed a rogues, agreement in which the West Saxons acquired the land of the *West Saex* (Wessex) and the South Saxons established themselves in the land of the *South Saex* (Sussex). Bede tells us that the participating Jutes established themselves on the Isle of Wight and also on that part of the mainland which is opposite the Isle of Wight.

The invaders brought only carnage, death and slavery to the indigenous inhabitants of the region. The *Anglo-Saxon Chronicle* tells of several beach-head landings and desperate battles including those of *Cerdices ora, Cerdicesford,* (Curbridge/Curdridge?), *Natan Lea* (Netley) and *Portes mutha* (Portsmouth). The location of *Cerdices ora* (the landing place of Cerdic) is unknown although the possible analogy with Curdridge suggests that the Hamble might be this haven. (The Anglo-Saxon name of *Ora* stills survives in Needs Ore at the mouth of Beaulieu River).

The *Chronicle* also tells of horrific massacres including that of the men of Wight who tried to defend themselves and their families at a place called *Witgarasbyrig*. This is generally thought to be Carisbrooke where a rectangular stone enclosure of Roman character survives beneath the Norman castle (Rigold, 1969; Johnson, 1976). This 'lower enclosure' has been claimed as a Late Saxon fortified settlement or *burh* (Young, 1983a & b & 2000) but although the site was clearly an important one in the 11th century this argument cannot be convincingly applied to the construction of its stone walls. Significantly, these are devoid of Quarr stone which was, otherwise, so exclusively favoured by the Late Saxon stoneworkers of Wight. The design and siting of the first Norman motte and bailey castle also shows complete disregard for the config-uration of the rectangular enclosure and the motte even engulfs a portion of the walls. This can only mean that, unlike the situation at Porchester, the Norman builders found these to be ancient walls, too delapidated to offer practical defence in the mid 11th century. This situation could hardly fit the walls of a *burh* which was seemingly functioning in the 10th century.

For the nature of the Germanic invaders we can look to the pagan contents of their graves. These have been excavated in varying numbers in cemeteries such as Chessell Down, Bowcombe Down, Droxford, Meonstoke and Bedhampton. The latter may take its name from the Saxon warrior Bieda. In these graves we may find the warlord buried with a sword and shield and a buckle which, sometimes, can be plated with gold or inlaid with silver. His compatriots are often buried with spears and long iron knives (*saxes*). The latter were often fitted with blood grooves for rapid stabbing at close quarters. A few men were buried with a *francisca* or throwing axe which no doubt reflected their particular type of fighting skill.

The burial of pagan Saxon women reveals wide-ranging social status. Silver jewellery and amber beads are commonly favoured and matronly status seems to have been conveyed by a set

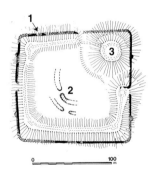

The lower enclosure and early Norman modifi-cation at Carisbrooke Castle showing:
1. Bembridge limestone walling of Roman character.
2. Traces of the first Norman defensive ditch or bailey.
3. The Norman motte.

of elaborate false keys which were worn at the waist and termed a *chatelaine*. Women were often buried with a small iron knife, perhaps reflecting some expectation of self-defence in the afterlife. All of these social groups are particularly well represented in the graves at Chessell Down and Droxford (Arnold, 1982; Aldsworth, 1978). Here we come face to face with the fearsome folk whose successors were destined to stalk the English shopping malls of the 21st century. By the 8th century some of the more violent predilections of the Saxon inhabitants of the Solent region had ameliorated with the spread of Christianity. This meant that a panoply of weapons was no longer required in the grave. In future, the old savagery would have to be satisfied by laws providing for gruesome punishments and executions.

The growth of a Saxon community on the west bank of Itchen river was to have profound implications for the future complexion of the Solent. There is some evidence of Saxon activity here in the 7th century but it is not until the 8th century AD that clear evidence of maritime trade can be detected. Much of this is betrayed by the arrival of imported table wares from the Carolingian empire. Particularly popular were those wares which could be acquired in Rouen and exported out of the mouth of the Seine (Hodges, 1981). Dr Williamson (1998) treats us to a contemporary description of such a voyage when St Willibrand sailed from the mouth of the Hamble in the year AD 721.

They sailed with the north-west wind blowing and a high sea running, amidst the shouting sailors and the creaking oars. When they had braved the dangers at sea and the perils of the mountainous waves, a swift course brought them with full sails and following winds, safely to dry land. At once they gave thanks and disembarked and pitching their tents on the banks of the River Seine they encamped near the city which is called Rouen, where there is a market.

Up-Channel, other traders were busy plying the sea lanes to the Low Countries, returning with goods from the waterfronts of the Rhine at Domberg and Dorestad.

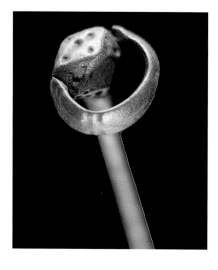

This bronze ring-headed pin betrays Viking landings at Wootton Haven.

The coins found at Southampton suggests that prosperity in the coastal settlement of *Hamwic* really began in the mid 8th century but the same source of evidence also shows a notable decline in the late 9th century when trade and confidence was undermined. It was around this time that the Viking raids began in the Solent and this made the undefended settlement at *Hamwic* a ready victim of its own success. Specific raids on the town are chronicled in the years AD 837, 839 and 860. Isolated and weakly defended, the Islanders of Wight were also sorely tested, having to endure occupation by the Vikings during some of their winter stop-overs. One of the hallmarks of Norse contact has been the appearance of mica-schist whetstones which can be traced to a stone source in the Eidsborg region of central Norway. A notable number of these stones found in the Isle of Wight may reflect a Viking presence which might, arguably, be equated with entries in the *Anglo-Saxon Chronicle* which record raids or occupation in the years AD 999, 1001-6 and 1047. This evidence is not, however, infallible because the use and dissemination of Norwegian whetstones is known to persist into the Norman period and there seems little doubt that some of these items arrived in Britain as a result of North Sea trade.

The remedy for *Hamwic's* vulnerability was eventually found in the 10th century when this settlement was re-established on higher and more defendable ground to the west. It was this site which was destined to become the walled medieval town of *Hamptun* . The new siting transferred human energies to the eastern shoreline of Southampton Water where a fresh threshold would be established for maritime trade. It was after the expansion of Saxon *Hamwic* that we find new evidence of cross-Solent traffic with the Isle of Wight. This is betrayed by deliveries of Bembridge

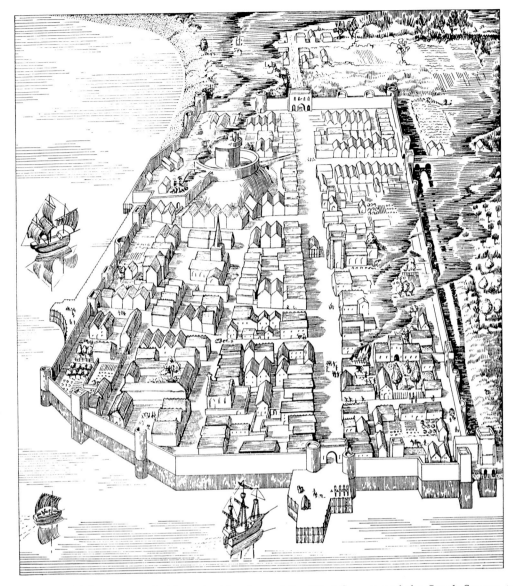

A reconstruction of the walled medieval city of Southampton. The broad main street leading straight to the Quay emphasizes the central role of maritime trade. (Compare with the aerial view of Francheville (Newtown) on page 76).

limestone which were carried into the kingdom of the West Saxons and the South Saxons to provide finishings and embellishments in a burgeoning array of new stone churches. The chosen source of these supplies was a specific facies of the limestone outcrop which is only to be found in one particular quarry on the Solent. By the 12th century these stone pits had been appropriately named *Quarrea, Quarere* or *Quarraria*. By the 13th century this had been simply abbreviated to *Quarr*.

Quarr stone is distinguished by a profusion of tiny fossil mollusc shells which have often dissolved to give the stone a light 'featherbed' quality (Tomalin, 1987). This stone is hard-weathering and it was often selected for the jambs of windows and doors, for external pilasters and for the 'long and short' quoins which were so favoured by Anglo-Saxon stonemasons. In Hampshire and the Solent basin, this Late Saxon export from the Isle of Wight can be traced in the Saxon churches of Little Somborne, Headbourne Worthy; Laverstoke, Tichborne; Hinton, Ampnor, Corhampton, Boarhunt, Fareham and Tichfield (Jope, 1964). It may be more than coincidence that the principal recipients of this exported stone lay in the territory or district of the *Meonwara* where, according to Bede close blood ties were claimed with the Jutes of Wight. Archaeologists have also been able to detect easterly deliveries to the Sussex coast where the magnificent Saxon church at Sompting was embellished with Quarr stone.

One of the most impressive exports of Quarr stone is a mighty tomb slab or sarcophagus lid which made a long journey to the church of Stratfield Mortimer near Reading. The date of this stone is unknown but it seems that it might be an export of the Norman period. This was a time when the Island stone pits were ringing with activity and ships were pressing eastwards from the mouth of the Solent to deliver stone to the new priory at Lewes and to those who were engaged in castle-building at Canterbury and London (Tatton-Brown, 1980). The cost of boat transport was infinitely cheaper than cartage by land and once Vectensian stone supplies were in the Thames estuary, the upstream journey to Reading was no more than a simple matter of paying crane dues and arranging transhipment to barges in London.

At Southampton, the burgesses of the city were quick to secure their own Vectensian supplies when, in AD 1338, they agreed a commitment to King Edward III to provide *'for enclosing the town of Southampton and the neighbouring parts with a wall of stone and lime'* (Platt, 1973). By now however, the thin and elusive band of Quarr featherbed limestone had dwindled to virtual extinction and Islanders had reverted to the working of the Binstead facies. The inclusion of gastropod cavities in this parchment-coloured stone gave a less pleasing image which might be likened to weeviled ships's biscuit. Vectensian stoneworkers were now more innovative in their work and were offering their clients complete sculpted works such as stone mixing bowls or mortars. The export of mortars was remarkably popular and shipments were carried up the North Sea coast as far as Kings Lynn. A lost cargo of mortars, recovered off the Dutch coast by a dredging vessel, is suspected to come from the workshops at Quarr.

Prosperity and anxiety on a beleaguered shore

For the present observer, the spectacle of the historic city of Southampton is an unedifying sight. Its fine medieval walls have now succumbed to the grotesque tyranny of 20th century development. Where sails, towers and battlements once greeted the visitor's eye, we are confronted with the uncompromising concrete statement that the enemy at the gate is now the enemy within. Where the ballista and the falling bomb had failed to break the spirit of this proud city, lame acquiescence has silently conceded the day with a show of tired hands and a stroke of a pen.

The marring of medieval Southampton inevitably evokes interest in less ignoble days yet it is important to remember that the maritime history of the Solent was not confined to this city. Evidence from the 12th century shows that Southampton shared its role with a number of other Solent ports. In many respects these may have functioned in much the same way as the maritime communities of the late prehistoric period. The reasons for Southampton's ascendancy are not difficult to recognise. The long northward reach of Southampton Water made the town a natural entrepot for Winchester and the seat of the Saxons kings.

The Norman invasion reinforced the royal importance of this city and so the interdependence of the two historic communities of Winchester and Southampton was destined to grow. Moreover, the road route from Winchester to London had become very well established in early medieval times and this offered a link with the capital which could not be matched at any other point on the Solent shore. During the early 13th century Southampton expanded its control over Solent maritime trade by way of a royal *fee-ferm* concession obtained from the King (Quinn, 1937). By AD 1324 this had nurtured a collective custom system embracing ports from Langstone Harbour to Hurst Spit.

The emergence of the Solent's other great port followed a very different course. Portsmouth Harbour had gained status in the 4th century when the shore fort at Portchester had served the needs of the Roman fleet (Cunliffe, 1975). The Saxon invasion brought further strategic interest in the harbour and we find that the *Anglo-Saxon Chronicle* does its best to record and explain this event. Unfortunately the *Chronicle* was written more than three centuries later, in the time of King Alfred, and there are strong suggestions that much of this history is allegorical. The *Chronicle* tells us that in AD 501 *'Port and his two sons, Bieda and Maegla came to Britain in two ships and landed at a place which is called Portes mutha and here they killed a young British man of very high rank'*. This yarn must be treated with the greatest caution, especially the account of the man called 'Port'. This character seems no more credible than the man called Whitgar to whom the *Chronicle* attributes the conquest of the Isle of Wight

More interesting is the account of the young British nobleman whom we may interpret as an important leader of an armed defence force. This draws our attention to the apparent use of the shore-fort at Portchester as a continued means of protection in the early 6th century. Once appropriated by the Saxons, the value of the fort seems to have been readily recognised for later, in the 8th and 9th centuries, we find it to be the site of an important settlement (Cunliffe, 1976). During the early 10th century we find that the old stone walls are in use once more when, in AD 904, King Alfred choses Portchester as one of his fortified *burhs*. Here, he hopes, his subjects will be able to resist the Danes. In the 11th century the King still held Portchester but by this time it had been divided into three manors. The archaeological evidence suggests that one of these manors was sited inside the fort but the evidence also shows that by the eve of the Norman conquest much was in decay.

The conversion of the Roman fort at Porchester into an effective Norman castle took place around AD 1100 under the direction of William Maudit. When Henry II came to the throne in AD 1154 however, he decided to retain the castle at Portchester for his own purposes and it seems that the King was now becoming increasing aware of the strategic importance of the harbour. This course of action may also tell us much about contemporary anchoring and unloading arrangements in Portsmouth Harbour in the 11th and early 12th centuries. Portsmouth is not mentioned in the Domesday survey of AD 1086 and this seems to confirm that the Normans were slow to take interest in the east bank of the natural harbour. At this time we are told that both Portsea Island and Hayling Island are joined to the mainland by causeways and that Hayling is the more populous of the two (Hoad & Webb, 1989).

While Porchester was favoured for major defence works at the opening of the 12th century its importance was certainly short-lived. Before the close of this century the role of Portchester is eclipsed by the rise of the new town of Portsmouth. When and why did this change take place? One possibility is that tidal behaviour and sedimentation in the harbour may have altered and these processes shifted maritime activities to the mouth of the port. The Norman Conquest generally coincides with the onset of the medieval warm period and this could be a time when reduced flow in the Wallington river and variation in channel patterns induced significant changes along the Portchester shoreline of the harbour.

On the Portsmouth shore, building activity was well underway in AD 1180 when John de Gisor (or Gison) was busy pioneering the laying out of new streets and tenement plots for the town he proposed to call Portsmouth. Having acquired the manor of Buckland on Portsea Island, some ten years earlier, its seems that John had taken a long term view of this property, especially the excellent natural harbour at the Camber inlet. This Norman enterprise can be compared with similar entrepreneurial ventures in other parts of the Solent where the building of new towns and ports had been pursued in much the same way. At Newport and Newtown and Lymington similar opportunities had been seized by members of the de Redvers family.

The success of John de Gisor was assured in AD 1194 when Richard I assembled 100 ships at Portsmouth as part of a planned expedition to France. The large number of ships cited on this occasion seems to reflect the growing importance of Portsmouth Harbour as a mustering point and haven for military craft. The new town was well-placed to exploit this role and this usefulness is reflected in the granting of the first charter in the very same year. This entitled the townsfolk to

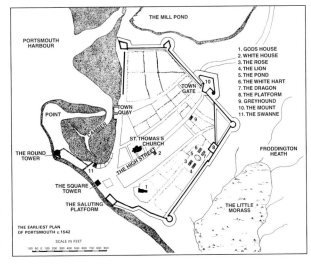

The location of medieval Portsmouth as shown in Tudor times.

Hedges and burgage plots mark the lost Solent town and port of Franchville (Newtown), Isle of Wight. The townhall lies in the middle distance on the right. Grassy streets lead straight to the quay.

impose *pontage* and petty customs on visiting ships but it left the collection of the greater port custom to the *ferm* system in Southampton. This anomaly was to lead to considerable friction in later years.

The role of Portsmouth as an early naval base was consolidated in AD 1212 when King John ordered the *'docks at Portsmouth to be enclosed by a good and strong wall'*. It was around this time that Portsbridge was constructed to provide unimpeded military communications on and off Portsea Island. The early defences seem to have been of poor quality because the town was burnt by French invaders on at least three occasions during the Hundred Years War. Goaded by these humiliations the King ordered a survey of Portsmouth's defences in AD 1386. It was shortly after this date that an earth and timber rampart seems to have been raised. By AD 1538 the defences were in such a sorry state that Bishop Fox of Winchester wryly remarked that the Isle of Wight and Portsmouth were *'too feeble for defence'* and it seemed to him that *'our manner is never to prepare for war even though our enemies be light at our door'* (Patterson, 1987).

In 1539 some new fortifications were well under way at Portsmouth but within two years these were reported to be *'clean fallen down'*. One wonders whether these fell victim to a poor understanding of coastal processes. This was certainly the case in 1631 when a fort was constructed too close to the shore of Sandown Bay (Jones, 1968). The Sandham fort was built no more than 80 feet from the sea. A wall-collapse and fresh cracks were reported even before the work was completed in 1634. Unfortunately the King's engineer dismissed local advice as *'the tongues of men and devilles'*. A victim of his time, he, like others, was fully prepared to disregard the processes which had eroded and destroyed the previous fort, trusting instead in *'a god of truth'*.

Tramping the streets of Portsmouth and Southampton it is not particularly easy to re-discover the ambience of the old medieval towns which engendered these coastal cities. The medieval town of Lymington retains much of its historic character yet the nature of its ancient waterfront has been totally transformed by a burgeoning leisure culture. This would certainly have been incomprehensible to William de Redvers when he nurtured his new or expanded town of *Liminton* or *Lementun* in the early years of the 13th century. The marinas have secured the prosperity of Lymington, an ingenuity that William would surely admire.

There is just one magic place where a medieval port, market and town of the Solent has been transfixed in time. At Francheville (Newtown), on the Isle of Wight coast, *'some five hundred souls'* were pursuing a growing maritime trade when the town was sacked by French invaders during the 14th century. The last raid seems to have been in AD 1377 after which the town never regained its vitality. Nevertheless, a handful of 'citizens' and two Members of Parliament still clung to its status. An incongruous town hall is now surrounded by fields but peeping amongst the hedgerows we discover that the shapes of Silver Street, Gold Street, and the ghost-like burgage plots of the long-lost houses are still followed by the bushy lines of hazel and blackthorn. When the enemy's firebrand was hurled, the ancient burghers of Francheville knew that both their livelihoods and their property were as good as gone as wood and thatch were hungrily consumed. Their townhall was nevertheless rebuilt and today the burghers have bequeathed us just one other valuable property which has been securely constructed in stone. This is the town tavern which also exudes the ancient air of defeat. Its facade welcomes us with the town's brightly painted coat of arms yet behind its bolted door the bar is eternally dry.

Mud, bones and stones

It would be all too easy to scan the on-shore landscape in search of an abbreviated history of the Solent. A book of the Solent should primarily address the components of the estuarine system itself and this must inevitably focus upon the rich cultural and palaeo-environmental legacy which lies within the seabed. On 11 October 1982 our awareness of this hidden resource was truly raised to a new horizon when the gribbled timbers of the *Mary Rose* broke the grey surface of the Eastern Solent. The recovery of this magnificent Tudor warship has been very well told elsewhere, (McKee, 1982; Rule, 1983;) yet we would be quite wrong to suppose that the seabed of the Solent has now given up its prime cultural wealth. The full legacy of historic shipwrecks on the Solent floor is still unknown yet the records assembled from historic manuscripts, fishermens' finds and diver's logs already number some 800 sites. To these must be added the remarkable spreads of discarded artifacts which attest the anchorage of past visitors. These vessels have been the silent purveyors who, for the past five millennia, have quietly delivered fine polished stone axes, gleaming bronze arm-rings, elegant Roman wine jars and robust stone mortars to the ingenious and industrious communities of the Solent shore.

This account has briefly surveyed a little of what has been found and reported yet it can never encompass the true cultural and scientific wealth which is concealed within the fragile and vulnerable environment of the seabed. Glimpsed by a fortunate few, this precious legacy is trawled, dredged and crushed while that which remains is picked over for diving trophies and salvage auctions. The museums and the Sites and Monuments Records of Hampshire, West Sussex and the Isle of Wight offer a slender means of recording and protecting just a little of this diminishing cultural resource (Tomalin, 1996 & 2001). Unfortunately, none of these particular public services enjoy statutory status and this makes them ever vulnerable to an exhausted system of local government which has become bound to ' improve the delivery of front line services' while it has been subtly sentenced to cannibalise its cultural and strategic services which are crumpling unseen in the ranks behind. Until the local authorities of the Solent are directly supported by Government in the day to day task of monitoring and curating the historic environment of the coast, there can be no doubt that bite of the digger's teeth, the cut of the trawler blade and the grasp of the dredger bucket will shred and eradicate the rich cultural legacy which has been preserved in the intertidal and sub-tidal zones. As economic dependency on 'green' and 'historic' tourism expands within our region, this is a mode of blindness and expediency that posterity will not forgive.

One minor concession to the protection of the nation's underwater heritage was secured by a Private Members Bill in 1973. This Act achieved a small measure of regulation over the disturbance of certain historic shipwrecks although their long term sustainability cannot be claimed (Tomalin, Simpson and Bingeman 2000). Fortunately, this 'Book of the Solent' is able to draw upon the experience of Commader John Bingeman whose personal knowledge and diving experience covers the principal shipwrecks which are contained within the 'designated areas' of the Solent seabed.

SOLENT PROTECTED WRECK SITES (reviewed by John Bingeman).

In 1973, a Protection of Wrecks Act was passed to save our underwater heritage. Around our coastline surprisingly few sites have been protected but pleasingly this has not been the case in the greater Solent area. Besides the *Mary Rose*, the following less well known ship wrecks have been protected under the Act.

Hazardous

Off the Witterings in Bracklesham Bay, the *Hazardous* was lost in a storm on the 19 November 1706 when under the command of Lieutenant John Hares. She had been built at Fort Louis,

France in 1698 as a 50 gun 3rd Rate *Le Hazardeux*, and was captured in 1703 by the Channel Squadron under the command of Admiral Sir Claudsley Shovell after :

"she resisted in the most determined way for six hours and struck her colours only after she had been reduced to a perfect wreck."

Towed into Portsmouth, she was rebuilt, enlarged, and a year later commissioned using the same name anglicized. Now with 54 guns she was a 4th Rate armed with a mix of French and British ordnance. At the time of her loss she had been in company and under the orders of Captain John Lowan in the Advice. At the court martial Lowan and his Master Robert Banner were blamed for the loss of the *Hazardous*, and Hares acquitted. Lowan was convicted of disobeying instructions - he should not have been in the Solent waters at all - leading the two ships into shoal waters, and "that he did not make the proper signals" to *Hazardous* when altering course in the dark.

After dragging her anchors across the shoal waters on this dangerous lee shore and touching bottom, Lieutenant Hares realised that *Hazardous* was doomed. He ordered the masts to be cut down, which lightened and stabilised the ship, before slipping her anchors at high water and successfully running her ashore saving all his crew. Today after nearly 300 years of coastal erosion and sea level rise, the wreck will be found some 800 metres out to sea.

Salvage took place at the time and the last recorded report was 9 years later, when the Chichester Customs House Officer reported six bronze guns taken out of her in July 1715. Local divers came across her in the mid-1970s, and over the years brought up any exposed artefacts until in 1984 when severe erosion suddenly revealed well preserved hull timbers and more cannon, it prompted the divers to carry out a detailed archaeological survey. A Government designation order was issued in 1986, the 32nd site to be protected under the 1973 Act.

The site continued to be worked from time to time depending on the amount of wreck exposed. A new aim was set in 2000 to design a 'diver trail' to present the site's archaeology coupled with the abundant marine habitat living on this natural reef. Information boards will be placed and the decision to allow visitor access will be a first on any protected British historic wreck site. In Western Australia similar sites have been a most popular attraction.

Assurance

On the approaches to the Western Solent, many ships have come to grief in the vicinity of the Needles where a shallow underwater ridge continues to the west. Close to the present day lighthouse completed in 1859, a government protected area contains the remains of two naval

A Silver scent bottle recovered from the Needles wreck site - the dipstick is screwed into the top.

ships. The first was the *Assurance* stranded on 24 April 1753; she was a 44-gun 5th Rate that had been built locally at the Richard Heather Yard at Bursledon and launched in 1747. Taking passage was Edward Trelawny, the fourth son of the late Bishop of Winchester who had been Governor of Jamaica for the past 16 years. With his wife, he was bringing home all their belongings and some 60,000 pounds in coins - in those days this was the usual means of transferring one's wealth. Admiralty records say *Assurance* hit an uncharted rock some distance from the Needles Point. However, Charnock, a naval historian tells a rather different story when, on that beautiful spring morning the

Governor, striding the quarterdeck spoke to the Master, David Patterson:

"... he asked a question, suggested by mere curiosity, what depth of water there were around it and how near the ship would pass to that part of the rock appearing above the water. Patterson answered, they should pass so close that the fly of the ensign might touch the rock."

Patterson had plenty of time to contemplate his error of judgement for he was held responsible and sentenced by court martial to three months in Marshalsea Prison, the debtor's prison in London. His short sentence was mitigated in view of the *"obscurity of the rock"*.

Pomone

Fifty-eight years later on 11 October 1811, *Pomone* another 5th Rate of 38 guns was wrecked on the same spot after mistaking the Needles light for Hurst Castle in the mist. In those days the Needles light was situated on top of the cliffs, near the site of the recently closed coastguard

32 lb Carronades recovered from the Pomone wreck site at the Needles - showing guns before and after restoration.

station. The Captain, Robert Barrie, was a hero having undertaken a number of successful actions against the French in the Mediterranean. Taking passage home was the retiring Ambassador from Persia, Sir Harford Jones, complete with a gift of Arab stallions from the Shah of Persia for King George III. It is pleasing to record that no lives were lost from either of the two vessels; Trelawny's money and the Arab stallions were all saved including most of the ship's guns and stores.

Divers have excavated the site for the past 25 years and their conclusions have recently been published (Tomalin *et al.* 2000). A whole variety of artefacts have been recovered including cannon. These recoveries from the two ships are currently on display in the Royal Naval Museum at Portsmouth; and on the Isle of Wight, at Bembridge Maritime Museum and Fort Victoria near Yarmouth. Orientation underwater is difficult and to make it possible for divers to tour the site, a jackstay has been set up between boards attached to sinkers providing salient information. The intention is for managed groups to visit this protected wreck site during slack periods on neaps, since currents can reach 4 knots during spring tides.

Invincible

In the Eastern Solent shortly after the loss of the *Assurance*, a much larger ship became stranded on the Horse Tail sand bank when the Navy had what can only be described as a bad Sunday morning on 19 February in 1758. The fleet had been ordered by Admiral Boscawen in the Namur to weigh anchor at 0230 destined as a second expedition sent to oust the French from the Fortress of Louisbourg in Nova Scotia, Canada. In the previous year, disaster caused by gales had ended the first expedition; *Invincible* had nearly been one of the casualties after losing her rigging and being partly flooded. She was towed off a lee shore by the 60 gun Windsor and sailed home under jury rig for repairs at Portsmouth.

Weighing anchor in this 74 gun ship-of-the-line normally took around two hours but on this occasion there were problems; the anchor refused to break free from the seabed. The 23 inch circumference cable was bar taut with nearly four hundred men on the four capstans breaking capstan bars in their efforts to raise the anchor. The Master, Henry Adkins connected a triplepurchase on the upperdeck manned with a further hundred men. Success! The anchor

Invincible stranded on the Horse Tail with stores being hoisted into hoys.

Artist: John Terry

broke free and catapulted to the surface snagging itself on the ship's cutwater and defied all attempts to free it. Now underway in an east-south-east wind, she headed north-east towards the Horse Tail shallows, went to go about but at this critical moment the rudder jammed - Adkins, the ship's master rushed below to sort out the problem while Captain John Bentley ordered the sails to be backed to slow the ship. With the rudder freed, the ship went into 'irons' as she had lost too much speed to wear ship. Drawing twenty-three feet by the stern, she grounded on the Horse as it was popularly known.

At the court martial, it was hotly disputed that she had "bilged herself" with the trapped anchor still below water; certainly there was no dispute that her hold became flooded to a depth of twelve feet and despite all four chain pumps working continuously the ship's hold remained flooded. It was claimed that four fresh men could shift a ton of water in 45 seconds with a chain pump, so flooding must have been very rapid if four of these pumps could not stem the flooding. At high water she actually floated but had dug herself a 'grave' in the sand bank and kedge anchors failed to extradite her. Attempts to sail her off under full sail also failed while the chain pumps worked continuously. First one pump then a second failed as the winds increased and by Wednesday she fell over on her beam ends. Her fate was now sealed.

Bentley continued to supervise the removal of stores including all the guns except for the 9 pounder quarterdeck guns which had previously been jettisoned. A surprise verdict at the court martial held onboard the *Royal George* acquitted Bentley and his officers of blame for the loss of *Invincible*. Correspondence records that their Lordships at the Admiralty could not believe that a 74 gun ship could be lost outside Portsmouth Harbour with no one "blameable".

The French built *l'Invincible* had been captured off Cape Finistère in 1747 when only three years old. The French had designed a new generation of 74 gun ships that were far superior to anything in the Royal Navy. Capable of over 13 knots she was faster than British ships of the line and could even outsail the fastest of our frigates. Such was her size that her gunports were six feet above the waterline making her broadsides equal to British 1st Rates whose lower gun ports could be as low as three feet above the waterline and were seldom operable except in the calmest of seas. After capture she was commissioned in the Royal Navy as a flagship and was, in 1758, about to convey the military commander, General Amburst to North America for the action against Louisbourg.

Forgotten, her remains were re-discovered and excavated under a Government licence by a group of divers between 1980-90. The main collection of artefacts forms part of the display in 'Wooden Walls' at Chatham Historic Dockyard. A much larger reserve collection is also held by the Historic Dockyard.

A1 Submarine
In 1999, the *A1* submarine lying two miles south of Chichester Harbour was added to the list of local protected wreck sites. Built at Vickers, she was launched in 1902 and had a chequered career. During exercises to the east of the Isle of Wight in 1904 she was run down and sunk with the loss of all her 14 crew when close to the Nab Lightship. The Lightship was replaced by the Nab Tower at the end of the First World War when the Tower built to support the submarine barrier across the Dover Strait was no longer required. The *A1* was salvaged, repaired and recommissioned, serving until 1910 when an internal explosion while alongside at Haslar ended her operational career. Fortunately, on this occasion no one was killed and the injured crew members, including Petty Officer Drury who had been blown out of the conning tower into the sea, were taken to the Royal Naval Hospital, Haslar. At the time, submarines were powered by petrol engines and petrol vapour was given as the cause. She was modified as an unmanned target for the Admiralty Anti-Submarine Committee. A year later she vanished while submerged under automatic control, and searches failed to locate her.
Re-located by divers in the mid-1980s, the site was officially designated to prevent further pillaging. The *A1* was the first all-British designed submarine.

Bibliography - Footholds on the shore.

Aldsworth, F. G., 1978. 'The Droxford Anglo-Saxon cemetery, Soberton, Hampshire', *Proceedings Hampshire Field Club & Archaeological Society* 35, 93-182.

Arnold, C. J.,1982. The Anglo-Saxon cemeteries of the Isle of Wight, British Museum. London.

Bede. C. 730. *The Venerable Bede's ecclesiastical History of England and the Anglo-Saxon Chronicle*. F. A. Giles (ed). London.

Bradley R., 1975. 'Salt and settlement in the Hampshire-Sussex borderland' in K. W. de Brisay & K. Evans (eds), *Salt, the study of an ancient industry, report on the salt weekend held at the University of Essex, 20-23 September, 1974'*, 20-25. Colchester Archaeological Group.

Camden, W., 1586, 1587 - Latin editions, 1610 & 1637- English editions. Britannia, a chorographicall description of the most flourishing kingdomes, England, Scotland & Ireland. London.

Cunliffe, B., 1971. *Excavations at Fishbourne*. Society of Antiquaries Research Report no 26. 2 vols. London.

Cunliffe, B., 1973. *The Regni*. Duckworth. London.

Cunliffe, B., 1975. *Excavations at Portchester Castle Vol. 1: Roman,* Society of Antiquaries Research Report No. 32

Cunliffe, B., 1976. *Excavations at Portchester Castle vol. 2: Saxon,* Society of Antiquaries Research Report No. 33.

Cunliffe, B., & Down, A., 1996. *Excavations at Fishbourne 1969-1988. Chichester excavations* 9. Phillimore. Chichester.

Dove, C. E., 1971. 'The first British navy'. *Antiquity* 45, 15-20 & plate VII.
Haverfield, F., 1900. 'Romano-British remains' in H. A. Doubleday (ed.), *Victoria County History of Hampshire and the Isle of Wight* 1, 265-249.

Hinton, D. A., 1979. *Alfred's kingdom: Wessex and the south 800-1500.* Dent. London.

Hinton, D. A., 1981. 'Hampshire's Anglo-Saxon origins', in S. J. Shennan & R. T. Schadla-Hall (eds), *The archaeology of Hampshire; palaeolithic to the industrial revolution*, Hampshire Field Club & Archaeological Society, monog 1.

Hoad, M. & Webb, J., 1989. 'From the Norman conquest to the Civil War', in B. Stapleton & J. H. Thomas (eds), *The Portsmouth region*. Alan Sutton. Gloucester.

Hobbs, J. S., 1859. *British Channel pilot*. Wilson. London. Reprinted. Barton Truro. 1972.

Hodges, R., 1981. *'The Hamwih pottery: the local and imported wares from 30 years' excavations at Middle Saxon Southampton and their European context'*. Southampton Archaeological Research Committee report no 2; CBA research report no 37.

Hughes, M., 1973. 'Excavations at Brownwich Farm, Tichfield, 1971', *Rescue Archaeology in Hampshire* 1, 5-28.
Hughes, M. 1976. *The small towns of Hampshire*. Hampshire Archaeological Committee. Southampton.
Humbolt, A. von., 1845. *Cosmos*.

Johnson, S., 1976. *The Roman forts of the Saxon shore*. Elek. London.

Johnston, D. E. & Reed, R., 1968. 'The Roman road (route 421) to Bitterne', *Proceedings*

Hampshire Field Club & Archaeological Society 25, 19-26.

Jones, J. D., 1968. 'The building of a fort at Sandown, Isle of Wight'. *Proceedings Isle of Wight Natural History & Archaeological Society* 6, 166-188.

Jope, E. M., 1964. 'The Saxon building stone industry in southern and midland England', *Medieval Archaeology* 8, 91-118.

Margary, I. D., 1955. *Roman roads in Britain : 1, south of the Fosse Way.* Phoenix. london.

McKee, A., 1982. *How we found the Mary Rose.* London.

Patterson, B. H., 1987. *A military heritage; a history of Portsmouth and Portsea town fortifications.* Fort Cumberland Militaria Society. Portsmouth.

Platt, C., 1973. *Medieval Southampton; the port and trading community,* AD 1000-1600. London.

Quinn, D. B., 1937. *The port books or local customs accounts of Southampton in the reign of Edward IV.* Vol 1, 1469-71. Southampton Record Society.

Rigold, S., 1969. 'Recent investigations into the earliest defences at Carisbrooke Castle'. *Chateau Gaillard; European castle studies* 3, 128-138.

Rivet, A. L. F., 1970. 'The British section of the Antonine Itinerary'. *Britannia* 1, 34-82.

Rivet, A. L. F. & Smith, C., 1979. *The place-names of Roman Britain.* Batsford. London.

Rule, M., 1983. *The Mary Rose; the excavation and raising of Henry VIII's flagship.* Leicester.

Sanders, I., 1927 'Ancient road from Purlieu to Lepe', *Proceedings Hampshire Field Club & Archaeological Society* 10, (1), 35-39.

Scott, I. R., 1996. *Romsey Abbey; report on the excavations 1973-1991.* Test Valley Archaeological Trust. Hampshire Field Club monog. no 8.

Smith, C. R., 1883. 'Notes on Clausentum; now Bittern Manor', The *Antiquary* 7, 79.

Soffe, G., & Johnston, D., 1973. 'Route 421 and other Roman roads in South Hampshire'. *Rescue Archaeology in Hampshire* 2, 99-120.

Tatton-Brown, T., 1980. 'The use of Quarr stone in London and East Kent', *Medieval Archaeology* 24, 213-215.

Tomalin D. J., 1996. 'Towards a new strategy for curating the Bronze Age landscape of Hampshire and the Solent region', in D. A. Hinton & M. Hughes (eds.), *Archaeology in Hampshire; a framework for the future.* Hampshire County Council. Winchester. 13-25.

Tomalin, D. J., 1987. *Roman Wight: A guide catalogue,* Isle of Wight County Council. Newport.

Tomalin, D. J., 2001. 'Stress at the seams: assessing the terrestrial and submerged archaeological landscape on the shore of the *Magnus Portus*', in A. Aberg & C. Lewis (eds), *The rising tide; archaeology and coastal landscapes.* Oxbow. Oxford.

Tomalin, D. J, forthcoming. 'Coastal villas; maritime villas; a perspective from the island of Vectis', in *Britannia; the maritime links.* Council for British Archaeology monograph.

Tomalin, D. J, & Hanworth, R., 1998. *House for all seasons; a guide to the Roman villa at Brading,* Isle of Wight. Oglander Roman Trust. Brading.

Tomalin, D. J, & Insole I. N., 1978. Ms notes on Isle of Wight limestone components from the excavations at Romsey Abbey.

Tomalin, D.J, Simpson, P & Bingeman J.M., 2000. 'Excavation versus sustainability *in situ*: a conclusion of 25 years of archaeological investigations at Goose Rock, a designated historic wreck site at the Needles, Isle of Wight, England.' *International Journal of Nautical Archaeology* 29, 3-42.

Tomlin, R. S. O., 1997. 'Roman Britain in 1996, (2) Inscriptions; Hamble estuary'. *Britannia* 28, 455-7.

Tylecote, R.F., 1962. *Metallurgy in archaeology*. London.

Williams, D. F., 1977. 'The Romano-British black-burnished industry; an essay on the characterisation by heavy mineral analysis', in D.P.S. Peacock (ed.), *Pottery and early commerce; characterisation and trade in Roman and later ceramics.* Academic Press. London/

Williamson , D., 1998. *The mariners of ancient Wessex*. Southampton.

Young, C. J., 1983a. 'The Lower Enclosure' at Carisbrooke Castle, Isle of Wight', in B. R. Hartley & J. S. Wacher (eds.), *Papers presented to S.S. Frere.* Gloucester.

Young, C. J., 1983b. 'Carisbrooke Castle to 1100', *Chateau Gaillard; European castle studies* 11, 281-288.

Young, C. J., 2000. 'Excavations at Carisbrooke Castle, Isle of Wight 1921-1996', Wessex Archaeology report no.18. Salisbury.

Bibliography - 'Solent protected wreck sites' by John Bingeman

Owen, N.C, 1987, HMS Hazardous, pre-disturbance survey report. *International Journal of Nautical Archaeology*. 17.4:285.

PRO, 1706, Public Records Office, London, ADM 1/5266 - Court Martial transcript.

Charnock, J, 1798, *Biographia Navalis*, 6:101-102.

PRO, 1753, Public Records Office, London, ADM 1/5294 - Court Martial transcript.

NC, 1811, Loss of the Pomone. *Naval Chronicle*, 26:320-321. London.

PRO, 1958a, Public Records Office, London, ADM 1/5297 - Court Martial transcript.

PRO, 1758b, Public Records Office, London, ADM 2/522 - letter to Admiral Holbourne, the Port Admiral at Portsmouth.

PRO, 1752, Public Records Office, London, ADM 95/25 folio 67 - "*Invicible's* Sailing Report".

'West view of Cowes Castle' *c1730*

Chapter Four

THE SOLENT AS A NAVAL AND MILITARY WATERWAY

Over the last 1,000 years, the Solent has had a unique and vitally important strategic role in the defence of the realm. Much of England's strength derived from the growth in the Middle Ages of Portsmouth as a naval base and of Southampton as a major commercial port which helped to make the Solent a logical place for potential invaders to launch an attack on England. The attackers normally made a direct approach from the east through the waters of Spithead - (see map on the next page). The other alternative was the Needles Passage, to the west of the Isle of Wight, where the approaches to the sheltered waters of the Solent were, and still are, only 1500 yards (1,372m) wide at their narrowest point, with particularly strong tides. This is why the growth of fortifications around the Solent was initially concentrated in these two areas before developments in technology in Victorian times led to fortifications being built further inland.

As far as the development of fortifications around the Solent is concerned, 1495 is a particularly significant date because that is when Henry VII built the world's first dry dock in Portsmouth after choosing Portsmouth as his Royal Dockyard. At the same time Southampton was the third largest port in England and a major exporter of wool, England's staple industry then.

Henry VIII came to the throne in 1509. He was an ambitious man and the England he inherited was a minor country in a Europe dominated by France, Spain and the Holy Roman Empire. Henry established a permanent navy and Portsmouth became the only exclusively naval harbour and Royal Dockyard in the country.

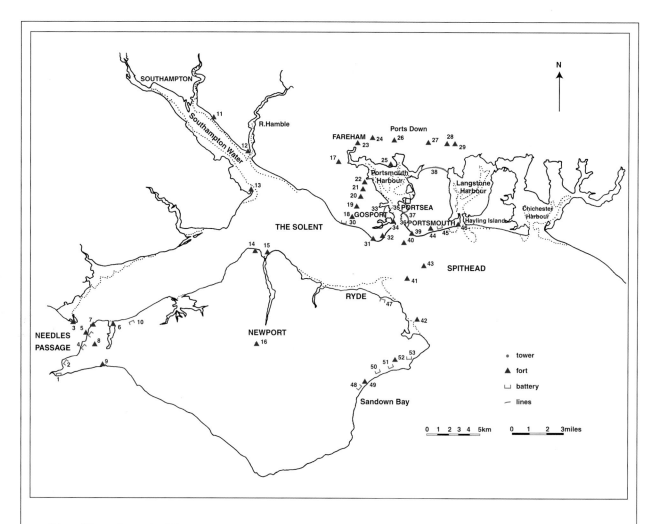

List of Locations: 1 - 53

1 Needles Battery and New Needles Battery	17 Fort Fareham	36 Round Tower and Point Battery
2 Hatherwood Point Battery	18 Fort Gomer	37 Portsmouth Lines
3 Hurst Castle	19 Fort Grange	38 Hilsea Lines
4 Warden Point Battery	20 Fort Rowner	39 Southsea Castle
5 Fort Albert and Cliff End Battery	21 Fort Brockhurst	40 Spitbank Fort
6 Yarmouth Castle	22 Fort Elson	41 No Man's Land Fort
7 Fort Victoria	23 Fort Wallington	42 St Helen's Fort
8 Golden Hill Fort	24 Fort Nelson	43 Horse Sand Fort
9 Freshwater Bay Redoubt	25 Portchester Castle	44 Lumps Fort
10 Bouldner Battery	26 Fort Southwick	45 Eastney Batteries
11 Netley Castle	27 Fort Widley	46 Fort Cumberland
12 St Andrew's Point	28 Fort Purbrook	47 Puckpool Mortar Battery
13 Calshot Castle	29 Farlington Redoubt	48 Barrack Battery
14 West Cowes Castle	30 Brown Down Battery	49 Sandown Fort
15 East Cowes Castle	31 Fort Gilkicker	50 Yaverland Battery
16 Carisbrooke Castle	32 Fort Monckton	51 Redcliffe Battery
	33 Gosport Lines	52 Bembridge Fort
	34 Fort Blockhouse	53 Steynewood Battery
	35 Portsea Lines	

Taken from 'Fortress Britain' by A. Saunders

86

Henry VIII alienated Emperor Charles V of Spain in 1533 by announcing the annulment of his marriage to Catherine of Aragon, who was also Charles' aunt. In 1538 Francis I, King of France, and Charles signed a peace treaty and, at the same time, Henry was excommunicated by Pope Paul III when Henry took the title of Supreme Head of the Church of England. The Pope encouraged Francis and Charles to lead an army against Henry which created an invasion crisis in England.

In response to this crisis, Henry reviewed the condition of the navy, ordered musters of men fit to serve in the army and named commissioners to 'speak and defend' portions of the English coast, shire by shire. This lead to a national defence programme on a massive scale throughout the south coast, including around the Solent. Rather than preventing an actual landing by invaders, Henry's strategy was to prevent the invaders gaining a harbour. Without a harbour the invaders would be unable to land reinforcements and supplies and would therefore find it impossible to back up an advancing army.

Individual forts were built to protect harbour entrances and in between, where necessary, castles and blockhouses (small forts at strategic points) were located. The major castles were designed to be self contained and self defensible, based on the Italian style of bastions which was to become the recognised system of defence for the next 300 years. The bastions were projections from the general outline of a fortress which allowed the guns to fire along the fortress' long walls.

In 1539 the Earl of Southampton and Lord St John went on a boat around the Solent to examine the effects of the wind and the tide; this resulted in castles at Calshot and Hurst and two blockhouses at East and West Cowes. At the same time small improvements were made to Portsmouth's defences. Henry continued his work on fortification, adding Southsea Castle at Portsmouth, Sandown and Yarmouth Castles on the Isle of Wight along with Netley Castle and St Andrew's Castle on the Hamble to protect the entrance to Southampton Water and the River Hamble. This was because of the recurring French threat, which resulted from the French landing on the Isle of Wight in 1545 and a more serious invasion threat later on in 1545 when a major naval battle threatened, but never occurred. The last single incident of the campaign was the sinking of the Mary Rose in 1545 in sight of the King in Portsmouth Harbour, with the loss of up to 700 men.

Cowdray engraving of the sinking of the Mary Rose in 1545 - showing the fortifications in Gosport and Portsmouth at the time. The Mary Rose was built in Portsmouth Dockyard in 1509.

Queen Elizabeth I's reign from 1558-1603 saw England almost constantly under threat from invasions or coastal raiding by the French, Spanish or Spanish Netherlands. Elizabeth's defence policy was mainly based on opposing any threat at sea, culminating in the defeat of the Spanish Armada in 1588, rather than improving or updating the existing coastal defences. However, her father, Henry VIII's work on reconstructing Portsmouth's ramparts was continued and Carisbrooke Castle, a Norman castle on the Isle of Wight, was brought up to date.

Calshot Castle was built to guard the entrance to Southampton Water, using stone from Beaulieu Abbey. Considerable repairs and alterations were made in 1584, during both the American War of Independence and the Napoleonic Wars and at the beginning of the 20th century. It was manned in both world wars and, in 1913, it became the nucleus for one of the first RAF stations and one of the best vantage points for the famous Schneider Trophy air races. In the 1960s the Castle became a coastguard station with a new radar tower alongside.

Calshot Castle   1539-1540

Following the Restoration of Charles II in 1660, there began an expansive programme of fortifications on a scale not seen since Henry VIII's programme over 100 years earlier. This new programme resulted from:
- maritime conflicts with the Dutch, culminating in a humiliation for the English in 1667 when the Dutch sailed up the Medway and burnt a number of English ships, including the *Royal Charles*
- the King's enthusiasm for the navy, resulting in the need to strengthen the naval ports and dockyards
- the standing down of Cromwell's efficient New Model Army at the Restoration. The army was now much smaller, putting more emphasis on the need to build defences and protect the dockyards and naval stores.

Sir Bernard de Gomme, a Dutchman who had loyally served the Royalists during the Civil War, was made Engineer-in-Chief of all the King's Castles in England and Wales in 1661. In 1665 de Gomme commenced a major programme to reform the defences around Portsmouth Harbour over a 20 year period, using Dutch prisoners for the labour force.

De Gomme brought Portsmouth's Elizabethan town defences up to date and strengthened Southsea Castle. The developing dockyard, to the north of the town, was enclosed with a rampart. On the other side of the harbour in Gosport a rampart and a moat, known as the Gosport Lines, were built to protect Gosport and a gun battery (the forerunner of Fort Blockhouse) was built at the entrance to Portsmouth Harbour. Fort Charles was constructed just north of Gosport Hard and Fort James on Rat Island in Portsmouth Harbour. By the 1690s, Portsmouth had become England's strongest fortress.

When William III came to the throne in 1688, Britain became involved in a long contest with France for commercial and colonial supremacy which was not fully resolved until 1815. The increased demands on the navy had a profound effect on Portsmouth, which was the country's chief naval centre. The Dockyard was considerably enlarged with the building of a new dry dock and two wet docks by reclaiming the mud lands of the harbour. By 1710, ten and a half acres had been added to the Dockyard. The old timber dock buildings were replaced with brick-built offices, houses, ropewalks and workshops. The dockyard expanded in size and importance until the increasing number of employees could no longer fit within the walled town. A new town, Portsea, grew up around the dockyard in the early 18th century, separated from Portsmouth by the mill pond. Meanwhile the defences of Gosport were considerably strengthened by rebuilding de Gomme's blockhouse which dominated the western side of the Harbour entrance.

Southsea Castle   *1544*

Southsea Castle was built by Henry VIII to protect the deep channel approaches to Portsmouth. It was held by the Royalists in the Civil War, captured by the Parliamentarians, re-equipped in the 19th century and remained a military establishment until 1956.

The national strategic importance of Portsmouth Harbour was confirmed when Portsmouth and Gosport became the only towns to be newly fortified on a large scale during the 18th century. In particular, the Jacobite Rebellion of 1745 caused much alarm plus the fear that the French would raid the south coast to help the Jacobite Rebellion in Scotland. In 1745-46 the precursor to Fort Cumberland was built on the south east corner of Portsea Island to control the entrance to Langstone Harbour. The fort was later rebuilt in 1794 by convicts using bricks made on site and faced with Portland stone. It is now the country's last and best preserved bastioned fortress.

In 1747 a continuous rampart and moat were constructed right across the northern part of Portsea Island from Portsmouth to Langston Harbour, the first Hilsea Lines. In 1770 work on new fortifications began to enclose Portsea, linking up with the smaller walls of the old Portsmouth defences and sweeping round to the north of the Dockyard.

In 1748 the rebuilding of de Gomme's Gosport Lines began and in 1757 the Lines were extended to enclose an area in Gosport known as Priddy's Hard. In 1777 Portsmouth's magazine was removed for safety from the Square Tower and transferred to a new building in Priddy's Hard. The gunpowder magazine and most of the rampart and moat survive today and are open to the public.

During 1779 there was an invasion attempt by France and Spain and 66 ships reached the Solent, intending to land at Stokes Bay in Gosport. Whilst the ships were forced to retreat because of severe sickness amongst the crews and a lack of planning, the invasion attempt caused considerable concern. This resulted in the building of Fort Monckton at Gilkicker Point in Gosport in 1780, which was then re-built as a stronger fort in 1790.

The need for a larger fleet at this time kept the Portsmouth Dockyard busy and three large storehouses were built here in the 1760s to house the ships' stores and equipment needed for Britain's rapidly expanding fleet. The storehouses are still standing today and form part of the Royal Naval Museum.

There was also a growth in commercial shipyards all round the Solent, notably in the River Hamble and at Buckler's Hard, on the Beaulieu River in the New Forest. This particular shipyard provided three of Nelson's Trafalgar fleet, including one of his favourite ships *Agamemnon*. During the French Revolutionary and Napoleonic Wars (1793 – 1815) the British Navy maintained a presence practically all over the world and Portsmouth's role as the principal naval port was intensified. By 1800 the Royal Navy had 684 ships and the Dockyard was the largest industrial complex in the world.

In 1797 the first steam engine was installed in the Dockyard to pump water from the dry docks and a few years later, the great Marc Isambard Brunel introduced a revolutionary system for the speedier manufacture of ships' pulley blocks. It was not until 1803 that the full potential of the steam engine was realised to power the sawmills and blockmills, turning out thousands of ship pulley blocks. This was the first large scale mass production method in the world.

During the 1840s steps were taken to enlarge the Dockyard with the facilities to deal with the large iron and steam vessels that were being built at that time which needed even more space to be dry docked. From 1868-1876 the Dockyard was extended to enclose 180 acres of mudland and part of Portsea Island, almost doubling the size of the Dockyard. In the late 1880s two more large dry docks were built to cope with the new classes of battleships.

In 1854 Britain and France fought the Crimean War against Russia. Serious deficiencies were found in the supply and organisation of the British Army, which resulted in developments to make it more efficient. Whilst the Royal Navy had traditionally protected Britain from invasion, it had increasing commitments all over the world and many believed that it could not be relied on as the first line of defence. It was decided that the army would have to deal with invaders which it could do more effectively if it was housed in powerful fortifications, which were located in such a way so as to prevent the capture of naval dockyards.

The alliance with France, following the Crimean War, did not last long and there were French invasion scares in 1847, 1851-2 and 1859. Meanwhile, in 1858, Sir William Armstrong produced the new rifled breech-loading cannon. This revolutionised gunnery by greatly increasing the range and accuracy of heavy guns which meant that fortifications could be constructed further apart.

The other equally important technological advance at this time was in warships with the building of the first steam driven iron-clad French frigate *La Gloire* which was launched in 1859. Britain's answer was to launch HMS Warrior in 1860 which was made entirely of iron, though backed with teak to prevent splinters, with additional armour plate. However, by 1861, France had 15 sea-going ironclad ships built or under construction to Britain's seven.

After the invasion panic of 1852, Fort Albert and Fort Victoria were built on the Isle of Wight and new batteries constructed on either side of Hurst Castle, whilst Fort Gomer and Fort Elson were built in Gosport. In 1857 three new forts (Grange, Rowner and Brockhurst) were built between Fort Gomer and Fort Elson, with each fort providing mutual fire support at approximately 1,000 yard intervals. Collectively the forts were known as the Gosport Line, and their purpose was to protect Portsmouth Dockyard from assault and bombardment from a landing to the west. But the Gosport Line was obsolete almost as soon as it was built due to the development of more powerful guns which meant that an enemy based on Portsdown Hill could easily fire into the Dockyard without worrying about the fortifications of the Gosport Line.

In 1859 a Royal Commission was set up under Major (later Sir) William Drummond Jervois to make recommendations for the defences of the country. The Commission's most detailed recommendations were for the Solent area, involving the building of a massive Ring Fortress to protect Portsmouth and the Isle of Wight. The Commission's findings were enthusi-

Hurst Castle was built on the edge of a shingle spit to guard the western entry to the Solent through the Needles passage. Charles I was held here briefly in 1648 and in 1795 two six-gun batteries were built. In the 1860s, the Tudor fort was retained as a keep and magazine, the external batteries demolished and a west battery, with 37 casements, and an east battery, with 24 casements, were built. The cost was estimated at £108,000, the actual cost was £140,000 plus £80,000 for wrought iron shields for the casements fronts.

astically adopted by Lord Palmerston, but the findings had to be substantially trimmed due to political opposition, with Gladstone threatening to resign as Chancellor. Palmerston said to Queen Victoria, 'it would be better to lose Mr Gladstone than to lose Portsmouth.' The result was a massive fortification construction project to protect Portsmouth and the Isle of Wight, consisting of a ring of fortress, the only example ever built in this country.

For the defence of the mouth of Portsmouth Harbour, Fort Cumberland, Southsea Castle, and Fort Blockhouse and Fort Monckton were all strengthened and Fort Gilkicker was constructed in Gosport. Five land forts were built along the ridge of Portsdown Hill (Forts Widley, Southwick, Nelson, Purbrook and Wallington) and Fort Fareham was built to protect the outer defences of Gosport. All of these forts faced outwards, away from the harbour, to protect the naval base from being taken from the landward side. In 1863 it was agreed to build five steel and granite sea forts to protect Spithead (Horsesand Fort, Spit Bank Fort, No Man's Land Fort, Rye Sand Fort and St Helen's Fort) of which four are still standing today.

The Isle of Wight was incorporated into the scheme of defences for Portsmouth Harbour for the first time since Tudor times with the construction of a number of batteries including ones at Cliff End and the Needles, and the building of Golden Hill and Bembridge Forts. Golden Hill was named after the yellow laburnam bushes that grew there.

This huge programme of fortifications marked the completion of permanent self-contained fortifications in this country when, for few years, English military engineering led the field.

By 1895 artillery had improved so dramatically that the whole system of defence of the country's dockyards had changed. The latest breech-loading guns, with an even greater range and accuracy, could be fired rapidly and were easy to conceal in field batteries. The landward facing forts and batteries could therefore no longer protect the dockyard from bombardment and were declared obsolete and, by 1907, most of the forts were disarmed. That many of them never fired a gun in anger can either be taken as a sign of their success as a deterrent, or as a measure of 'Palmerston's Folly.'

By the beginning of the 20th century, Portsmouth Dockyard had begun to build the revolutionary Dreadnought battleships. These were so large that they made most of the docks in the dockyard obsolete so more basins and locks were constructed. By 1914, Portsmouth Dockyard could dock five Dreadnoughts at any one time. During the First World War the Dockyard worked flat out to refit 1,200 vessels and build two battleships and five submarines and by 1918, 23,000 men and women were working in the Dockyard on day and nightshifts.

The Dockyard was also especially busy during the Second World War when the workforce grew to 25,000 people. Although Portsmouth was heavily bombed by the Germans, which resulted in the large ships being sent to safer yards in the north of the country, by the end of the war the Dockyard had repaired or refitted 2,548 vessels. Armies and fleets gathered in and around Portsmouth in the build up to D-Day and engineers in the Dockyard worked on the construction of the floating Mulberry Harbours. Other Mulberry Harbours were built on the mainland shore at Lepe, within the Beaulieu River and on Hayling Island. Fort Southwick, with nearby Southwick House, became the operations centre for the D-Day invasion of Normandy. During the two World Wars the forts in the Solent were maintained and re-armed with modern weapons and searchlights. The sea forts were equipped with anti-aircraft guns and the forts on Portsdown Hill and in Gosport were used as barracks to accommodate the Portsmouth garrison, anti-aircraft magazines and radar centres. Temporary 6" gun implacements were constructed at Lepe with ack-ack (anti-aircraft) defences in Stanswood Bay.

Pickett-Hamilton fort outside the D-Day Museum in Portsmouth

During the Second World War three Pickett-Hamilton forts were constructed on the airfield at Portsmouth. These were really pillboxes which could be raised to bring them into action, or lowered to prevent obstruction to the airfield. Each could be raised or lowered in 12 minutes.

After the Second World War fixed shore batteries became obsolete and Coastal Defence was abolished in 1956.

The development of coastal defence for over 450 years can be traced throughout the coastline of Hampshire and the Isle of Wight, reflecting the on-going importance of the Solent to the rest of the country. Whilst many of the fortifications have now disappeared, some, such as Fort Nelson and Fort Purbrook and Calshot, Southsea and Hurst Castles, have survived and found new roles as places of historic interest, museums and activity centres. Others, such as Fort Southwick, remain in the ownership of the Ministry of Defence and are either being used or, sadly, are being allowed to gradually fall into disrepair. The fortifications that are left serve as a reminder of the importance of having an effective deterrent during the times when this country felt threatened by her European neighbours.

Those that remain today should not be allowed to disappear. They should be conserved for future generations to learn from and enjoy.

The Place of Cowes in the Military History of the Solent

On the River Medina, Cowes   *attributed to E W Cooke*

The waterfront of the River Medina at Cowes has developed gradually over the last 400 years encroaching on the mudflats and marshes with a hotch-potch of timber warehouses, factories, wharves and jetties. Here a range of skilled craftsmen were engaged in the construction of men of war in addition to a diverse range of pleasure, commercial and other military craft.

In view of the strategic importance of the Solent the presence of a skilled workforce in close proximity to the naval dockyards must have been an advantage and this was reflected in a gradual evolution of the shipbuilding industry to include production of destroyers and torpedo boats as well as aircraft, sea planes and, more recently, the hovercraft.

View of Cowes Castle   *Charles Raye 1825*

The military role of Cowes Castle ceased when it was decommissioned in 1854 and it later became the clubhouse of the Royal Yacht Squadron. In the First World War the castle was made available for the use of convalescent naval officers but it was not until the Second World War that the Castle once again assumed an important role as one of the D-Day headquarters of the Solent.

Famous Island names such as Ratsey are associated with the history of Cowes as a shipbuilding centre, but probably the best known name is that of J Samuel White. His grandfather Thomas White, a member of a noted Kent shipbuilding family, moved across the Solent from Gosport to Cowes to establish a merchant shipbuilding and repair yard in 1814. From Thetis Dock, built to the north of what is now Medina Road, Thomas and his sons expanded the business on both sides of the River Medina. They also expanded into yacht and lifeboat construction and, later, into work for foreign and British navies and eventually into building aircraft, becoming a thriving business employing hundreds of men. At East Cowes Joseph White occupied the best yard in the port of Cowes where Joseph Nye had built two "ships of the line" for the Navy in the 1690s. Through their naval contracts the Whites ensured that Cowes has produced ships for the British Navy in each of the last four centuries.

John Samuel White consolidated and reorganised the businesses in 1884 and the firm's work and reputation continued to grow and the industry to flourish until, like other companies hit by cutbacks after the Second World War and the worldwide recession in shipbuilding in the 1960s, it ran into difficulties and started laying off workers. The main shipbuilding yard at East Cowes was closed in 1965 with substantial job losses; it was subsequently sold to the British Hovercraft Corporation. Other parts of the business were closed in later years and J Samuel White became part of an American company, losing its proud name in 1977. Elliott Turbomachinery Limited eventually closed the business in 1981. Part of the site was subsequently acquired by the Isle of Wight County Council as a local regeneration measure and renamed Samuel White Estate. Across the road at Thetis Wharf, site of White's first yard, Harry Spencer (another famous Cowes name) became renowned for making rigging and undertaking restoration work on a number of historic warships including HMS Warrior.

Another company name well known in Cowes and in defence circles is that of Westland. This business was first established in Cowes in the early years of the twentieth century by Samuel

Edgar Saunders who was building boats on the Thames at Streatley and Goring. He set up in West Cowes but later moved across the river into the former LIFU works at East Cowes which was renamed Columbine Yard. The company went on to build lifeboats and craft for the Admiralty,

but Sam's particular interest was in fast motor boats. In 1909 the company began its expansion into aircraft work and twenty years later the company name was changed to Saunders-Roe Limited when A V Roe, an important pioneer in aviation, became the major shareholder. Over the years the firm has expanded so that its sites now cover much of the old town of East Cowes. Other sites have since gone, including the Solent Works at West Cowes and Cornubia Yard at East Cowes which were destroyed in the May 1942 air raid. After the war a familiar sight was the Saunders-Roe Princess Flying Boat which could be seen undergoing trials in the vicinity.

In 1957 Saunders-Roe was chosen to develop Christopher Cockerell's invention and constructed the first hovercraft two years later, the same year in which the company became part of Westland. Although the Westland name is more associated with helicopters the hovercraft proved to be of considerable importance to the economy of East Cowes and of the Island as a whole; it has been used worldwide in both civil and military situations. The giant union flag visible as one enters Cowes Harbour is a reminder of the British Hovercraft Corporation, but the company's buildings now carry the logo of GKN Westland.

Solent Aviation

In 1909 Bleriot flew the Channel. This short flight helped fire the imagination of a generation of young men and inspired them to retreat into outhouses or barns and using what skills they had, attempt to build a machine that flew. Most failed, but a few succeeded and some even went on to paint "Aeroplane Company" over their doorway and start hiring hands. A golden triangle grew between Farnborough in Hampshire, where Cody first flew in 1908, Brooklands in Surrey and the Solent within which the cradle of British aviation was formed. Being an island nation, laced with lakes and rivers, there would be a certain logic for a would be aeronaut to build an aeroplane with floats. The Solent was one vast sheltered runway for seaplanes, its banks were teeming with craftsmen; any shipwright worth his salt could turn out a wooden fuselage or carve a propeller, the sailmaker would trim the fabric and the mechanic could tweak the engine. Twenty-six aeroplane factories sprang up around the Solent; most quickly vanished into obscurity, but others lingered and flourished.

Noel Pemberton Billing was amongst other things a wealthy yacht broker. Together with his young assistant Hubert Scott-Payne they had been inspired by this new adventure, bought a riverside yard near the old floating bridge at Woolston, Southampton and started work building a flying boat. At this time the navy were introducing their latest wonder, the submarine, so it was logical to name their craft that travelled above the waves a "Super Marine". The genesis of the Supermarine dynasty was the PB1, a flying boat that found much praise at the 1914 Olympia Aero Show, which was quite unwarranted since it would not fly. One of Billing's aeroplanes took a full seven days from first design to its first flight on Netley Common, illustrating the belief that building a flying machine rated as much consideration as, say, assembling a good carriage. The start of the First World War was the nadir for Supermarine. With his designs ignored and frustrated by the Government, Billing quickly lost interest in the firm and looked to a career in politics, eventually selling Supermarine to Scott-Payne.

The war was the turning point for Supermarine with Scott-Payne emerging as a successful and respected government contractor, having amassed a fortune building amphibians for the navy. With the coming of peace Scott-Payne set about converting some of these amphibians into spartan post-war airliners for his British Marine Air Navigation Services. Totland Bay was now accessible by flying boat, petrol was urgently delivered to Ventnor, Cowes Week was able to be viewed from the air and a scheduled service was started to the Channel Islands. To accommodate the passengers a terminal was built at Woolston where the amphibians would taxi down a slipway and into the Itchen for take off. An hour and a half later the machine would be hopefully riding at its buoy in St Peter Port Harbour. The Itchen base was called an "Air Port", a name that seemed appropriate and has stayed in the English language ever since.

Although the company only possessed three Supermarine "Sea Eagle" amphibians, they were regarded as Britain's premier flying boat operator. As such they were invited to amalgamate with three larger airlines to become the new Government sponsored airline, Imperial Airways, which later became BOAC, and joined with BEA in 1974 to become British Airways. During the thirties there was a pressing need for Britain to improve its communications with its Empire and the Government embarked upon an ambitious plan to provide the cheapest air mail service in the world, with a rate of one half old pence per half ounce (about 1p per 31.25g). In a bold stroke 28 four engine Short C-Class or "Empire Class" flying boats were ordered straight off the drawing board to implement the scheme. Each aircraft could accommodate 24 passengers in unprecedented luxury together with one and a half tons (1500 kg) of mail. Southampton Water was chosen as the UK terminal, with an area off Netley as a licensed aerodrome and maintenance facilities at Hythe. Services commenced in the closing days of 1936 and within three years Southampton was linked by air to Australia, Asia and South Africa.

Short S-23 Empire, or C-class flying boat "Canopus", the first and probably the most famous of her class.

Communication with the Empire would now be counted in days rather than weeks.

Trials conducted above the Solent using an RAF bomber as a tanker enabled modified C-Class flying boats to be refuelled through their tail. By using this technique Imperial Airways were able to inaugurate a weekly mail service to New York in August 1939, whilst Pan American Airways, using giant Boeing 314 flying boats, commenced a weekly passenger service to Southampton. From this meagre beginning was to grow a vast modern industry that would within two decades see more passengers crossing the Atlantic by air than by sea. This was to bring about the demise of Southampton as a great passenger port and turn the classic transoceanic liners into dinosaurs within a generation.

At the outbreak of war Imperial Airways transferred their operations to Poole Harbour for safety, although following the fall of France services were severely restricted. Some of the flying boats were impressed into RAF service whilst others were sent to operate the "horseshoe" service between Durban and Australia, circumnavigating the Indian Ocean. The Imperial Airways routes produced some intrepid airmen who pioneered the wartime "Atlantic Ferry", flying thousands of lease/lend aircraft from North America to Britain. From the C-Class flying boat Short Bros Aircraft of Rochester, Kent, developed the famous Sunderland long range flying boat. This patrol aircraft played a major role in winning the war against the U-Boat in the Atlantic and Calshot became a major maintenance base for Sunderland and other flying boats.

Returning to the banks of the Itchen, Scott-Payne sought the prestige found in the Schneider Trophy contest. Although the terms for winning included various tests, one aspect alone captured the world's imagination; speed. The winning nation would be the host nation for the subsequent venue and to win the contest three times in five years meant perpetual possession of the accolade. By 1923 the contest had arrived at Cowes. Supermarine had snatched the Trophy from the Italians with a "Sea Lion II" flying boat, the creation of their brilliant young chief designer R J Mitchell. Flushed with success, he redesigned the "Sea Lion" with a larger Napier "Lion" engine and looked forward to a second victory. Cowes was something of a watershed. Until now the event had taken on the ambience of a "gentleman's sport", however the American Government viewed the contest as a showpiece for American aviation, from which commercial orders would follow. Resolving to win at all cost the U.S. Navy entered Curtiss float planes, which were sleeker and potentially faster than flying boats. The investment paid dividends; over the five lap course that lay between Cowes and Selsey Bill, they beat their closest rival, Supermarine, by a hefty 20 mph, with an average speed of 177 mph.

Another four years were to pass before the Trophy returned to Britain and the Solent. To recapture the Trophy, Mitchell designed not only a float plane but also a monoplane, the S4. Although not a success in terms of winning the Trophy, in fact it crashed, the S4 pointed the way to the S5 which was a winner. The S5 heralded a change in Government attitude, which acknowledged the American sponsorship philosophy, took over the purse and supplied pilots from an elite cadre of airmen in the RAF High Speed Flight. In 1927 at Venice a Napier powered S5 beat the Italians with a speed of 281 mph and Calshot was nominated as the venue for the 1929 contest. For this contest Mitchell matched the advanced Rolls Royce "R" (racing) engine with a new enlarged airframe and called it the S6. For the contest the Solent had become a hippodrome alive with one and a half million spectators, all suffering from "Trophy fever". The course was a seven lap 50 kms circuit around the eastern Solent, with four turning points and the start/finish line off Ryde Pier. Although one of the British S6s was disqualified for cutting inside a mark, this did not matter since the other S6 won convincingly at an average speed of 328 mph.

To win the coveted Trophy in 1931 would entitle Britain to retain it forever, but with the nation deep in recession the Prime Minister, Ramsay MacDonald, refused to authorise the £100,000 to sponsor the contest. Salvation arrived at the eleventh hour when the widowed millionairess Lady Lucy Houston announced that she would privately finance the entry to "prevent the Socialist Government being spoilsports". Mitchell meanwhile returned to his drawing board and redesigned the S6 to accept an uprated engine. Just when everything was coming together the French and Italians petitioned to have a year's postponement, stating they were not ready to compete. Britain made a difficult decision and waived the petition. Unsporting perhaps, but Britain too had also endured more than her fair share of difficulties on the road to Calshot, including having two pilots killed. The result was of course inevitable with Flt Lt. John Boothman completing the triangular course around Spithead in an S6B at an average speed of 340 mph and the crowds went home jubilant. Despite having two million unemployed and the nation in poverty, it was money, albeit not their money, well spent and for a few hours they could raise their heads high and Britain was Great again. It is only in hindsight that we can appreciate the full significance of the Schneider Trophy contest. Between 1929 and 1931 about ten years research and development had been condensed into two years to produce a winning entry and without this technology neither the Spitfire nor the Hurricane would have been ready to face the German onslaught during the Battle of Britain.

Supermarine S6B at Calshot, signed by Flt Lt G H Stainforth who took the world air speed record at 407 mph in 1931 and Flt Lt J N Boothman who won the Schneider Trophy that year.

In 1928 Supermarine was absorbed into the Vickers group but Mitchell and his team still continued producing flying boats and amphibians, the most famous being the Walrus. Although appearing as something of an anachronism, being a single engine pusher biplane, its strength and sea worthiness enabled it to recover hundreds of wartime "ditched" aircrew. Mitchell's masterpiece was the Spitfire fighter, which was designed and built on the banks of the Itchen at Woolston and first flew from Southampton (Eastleigh) Airport on the 5 March 1936. Accepted by the RAF, production of the Spitfire at Woolston continued until September 1940, when German bombers found the riverside factory an easy target and it was destroyed. Undaunted Spitfires were still mass produced in the Solent region. On the instigation of Lord Beaverbrook, Minister of Aircraft Production, a representative of Supermarine accompanied by a constable toured the region commandeering bus depots, laundries and the like for makeshift factories. Overnight a cottage industry sprang up, prefabricating Spitfires which were taken by road to flight sheds at nearby airfields where they would be assembled, tested and then flown out to service units. Of the 22,000 odd Spitfires and naval Seafires built, about one fifth were constructed in the Solent region, with the design office being evacuated to Hursley Park House, near Winchester, where the prototypes of all new marks were built and test flown locally.

The growth of yachting in the Solent at the end of the nineteenth century had attracted Sam Saunders, a member of a long standing Thames boat building family, to Cowes. Sam began joining plywood panels together by stitching them with copper or brass wire. This was called Consuta which made them very strong but light and ideal for speedboat construction. Utilising Consuta, Saunders diversed into aviation and success came quickly due to a fortuitous encounter with the great pioneer, Tommy Sopwith, who constructed the wings for Saunders' canoe-like "Bat Boat" amphibian. In 1913 with Sopwith's pilot, Harry Hawker, at the controls the "Bat Boat" won the £500 Mortimer Singer (sewing machine) Prize for amphibians in the Solent and became Britain's first successful marine aeroplane. Saunders spent the First World War fulfilling Government

Saunders/Sopwith Bat boat at Cowes circa 1912   *Photo: Beken of Cowes*

contracts, building Avro 504 trainers and Felixstowe coastal flying boats. With the coming of peace Saunders drew upon his wartime experience and began designing flying boats. Unfortunately these never attained the same recognition as his marine craft and by 1928 the aviation division was in crisis.

Across the water at Portsmouth Airport the arrival of the Airspeed Aircraft Company in 1933 was the exception to the rule. With little interest in marine aviation their move south from York was purely economic. Small but innovative, Airspeed produced some excellent aeroplanes the best known being the "Oxford", the principle twin engine trainer for the RAF during World War Two and the "Horsa" assault glider, extensively used at Arnhem. In 1915 Sir Richard Fairey erected flight sheds on Hamble Spit to test fly the naval floatplanes that were built at his Hayes, Middlesex works. Here Fairey built the Seafox, one of which went on to gain fame for carrying out the gunnery spotting during the Battle of the River Plate. Another pioneer who set up a factory in the yachting village was Sir Alliott Verdon-Roe (hence Avro). Envisaging a demand for marine aircraft he erected a factory with a landing strip and slipway into Southampton Water. Verdon-Roe planned to erect a "garden city" of 350 artisans' houses in the village, but in the event only 24 houses were built. The projected flying boats did not flow from the hangars, but instead came hundreds of Avro 504 biplanes, the principle trainers for the services during the First World War. On this same field in 1926 the Spanish autogiro pioneer Don Juan de la Cierva established his development headquarters, using the fuselage of an Avro 504 for the first British built autogiro. In 1928 Verdon-Roe sold his interests to J.D. Siddeley, owner of Armstrong Whitworth Aircraft and the design office, headed by Roy Chadwick (of Lancaster fame), was moved to Manchester with the Hamble factory given over to the building of Armstrong Whitworth aircraft.

Still hankering to build marine aircraft, Verdon Roe and his remaining team relocated to East Cowes and amalgamated with Saunders to form Saunders-Roe (Saro), breathing new life into the ailing company. Saro launched a range of modern light amphibians, which received modest orders but their biggest success came with the elegant "London" coastal patrol aircraft, necessitating the building of the large "Columbine" hangar at East Cowes, which is still a very familiar landmark. Additional finance for Saro came from Whitehall Securities, who relocated another of their investments, Simmonds Aircraft, from Southampton to the old Wight Aircraft airfield at Somerton in West Cowes. Renaming Simmonds "Spartan Aviation" the new company complemented its partner, Saro, by specialising in light aircraft.

In 1942 the Brabazon Committee was formed to identify the needs of commercial aviation in post-war Britain. This included the need for a large flying boat, capable of crossing the Atlantic non-stop carrying a hundred passengers in luxury. When the leading flying boat designer, Sir Arthur Gouge, transferred from Short's to Saro, Cowes was elevated to Britain's best appointed marine aviation manufacturing base and was invited to design and build this "Queen Mary" of the skies. A seven year gestation period followed before the aircraft was to be rolled out of the Columbine hangar. Unquestionably a very beautiful aircraft and fitting for its name "Princess", it was to have ten gas turbine engines arranged in six nacelles. Unfortunately here lay one of the major headaches; with aviation gas turbine technology still in its infancy, delay followed delay. Eventually in 1952 a "Princess" lifted off from the Solent, years late, way over budget and looking for a role in life. BOAC had long since been wooed away from flying boats and were more than satisfied with the economics and practicalities of entirely operating land based airliners. With no clear future, work was stopped in mid development and the flying boats were cocooned to become the three "Sleeping Princesses".

The only Saunder-Roe "Princess" to fly is captured here flying over the Isle of Wight.

The island-hopping war in the Pacific had created a need for aircraft that could operate out of lagoons. In 1943 Saunders-Roe began studies for a revolutionary flying boat fighter to be powered by two jet engines. This was an extremely bold step because jet engines were very much in their infancy and it was not until July 1944 that the RAF even formed its first jet squadron. Undaunted, Saunders-Roe bravely commenced work on this machine designated the A/1, or colloquially the "Squirt" and it eventually made its first flight from Cowes in July 1947. By now the Pacific war had been won and the A/1 was just a good idea with nowhere to go with it making

Saunders-Roe SR A/1 Jet flying boat taking off in the Solent. This aircraft is displayed in the Southampton Hall of Aviation.

its inevitable final flight four years later. Despite its recent disappointments Saunders-Roe still accepted the challenge of being first in the field. They designed and flew a revolutionary mixed fuel fighter, using a Hydrogen Peroxide rocket for main thrust and a smaller jet engine for slow speed loitering. The result had the potential of being a world beater and would have been years ahead of its contemporaries. Flying for the first time in 1957 it was capable of speeds at over twice the speed of sound. Again Government policy blighted Saunders-Roe's genius and when the 1957 infamous Duncan Sandys "Defence White Paper" cancelled practically all manned fighter development, the SR 53 programme was terminated and this ended Saunders-Roe as an independent builder of aeroplanes.

The reason for the great success of the flying boat had been the lack of long runways throughout the world, but the development of land based aeroplanes during the war had led to the world being covered in hundreds of miles of concrete runways, negating the flying boat's only saving grace. On the water they were unweildy and difficult to manoeuvre and maintain, they had to share waterways with considerably more craft and in the air their boat-like shape was not conducive to efficient aerodynamics. Barely two years after returning to Southampton from Poole, BOAC's final flight departed from the port in November 1950. Even the promise of the charismatic "Princesses" could not reverse their decision and by 1958 all commercial flying had ceased in Southampton Water. In 1967 the "Princesses" were finally towed from the Solent up Southampton Water from Calshot Spit, now abandoned by the RAF and past Hamble Spit where the Fairey hangars had been turned over to boat building. The Avro sheds at Hamble were being used for light industry and the airstrip where Cierva first tested his British autogiro had reverted to being wasteland. Only the old British Marine Company Aircraft works still flourished in Hamble village. Here the Folland Gnat trainer, the original mount of the RAF "Red Arrows" were built. Journey's end for the "Princesses" was the river Itchen, birthplace of the immortal Spitfire. Close to the spot where fifty odd years previously Pemberton Billing had set up his workshop and started building aeroplanes, the last great British flying boats were beached and broken up. We have come the full circle.

Bibliography - *the Solent as a Naval and Military Waterway.*

ANON, 1973 *'Portsmouth in Defence of the Realm, an Imperial Legacy.'* Visit of the Hampshire Field Club and Archaeological Society to Portsmouth 12 May 1973.

ANON, undated. *'A History of Calshot Spit'.*

ANON, 1999. *'Victoria's Forts'.* Isle of Wight County Council.

Betts, R, 1992. *'Portsmouth Historic Dockyard'.* Portsmouth Naval Base Trust.

Cantwell, A & Sprach, P, 1981. *'The Needles Batteries'.* National Trust.

Cantwell, A & Sprach, P, 1986. *'The Needles defences', Solent Papers No 2.*

Coad, J. G. 1986 *'Calshot Castle'.* English Heritage.

Corney, A, 1965. *'Fortifications in Old Portsmouth'.* Portsmouth City Council.

Corney, A, 1984. *'Fort Widley and the Great Forts on Portsmouth'.* Portsmouth City Museum.

HMSO, 1976. *'Henry VIII and the development of coastal defence'.*

Magrath, P. 1992 *'Fort Cumberland 1747-1850 key to an Island's Defence'. Portsmouth Papers No 60.*

Mitchell, G & Cobb,P, 1987. *'Fort Nelson and the Portsdown Forts', Solent Papers No 3.*

Mitchell, G. 1988. *'Hilsea Lines and Portsbridge'. Solent Papers No 4.*

Mitchell, G & Cobb,P, 1984. *'Spit Bank Fort'.*

Mitchell, G & Sprach,P, 1987. *'Spit Bank and the Spithead Forts', Solent Papers No 1.*

Moore, D. 1988 *'Fort Gilkicker'. Solent Papers No 5.*

Moore, D. 1990 *'Fort Brockhurst and the Gomer Elson Forts'. Solent Papers No 6.*

Patterson, B.H. 1985. *'A Military Heritage - A history of Portsmouth and Portsea Town Fortifications'. Fort Cumberland and Portsmouth Militaria Society.*

Patterson, B.H. 1989. *'Giv'er a cheer Boys' - the Great Docks of Portsmouth Dockyard 1830 - 1914. Portsmouth Royal Dockyard Historical Society Publications No 5.*

Pope, F. 1977. *'The growth of the fortifications of Portsmouth Harbour'. Hampshire Architects Broadsheet No 8.*

Portsmouth Teachers Local Study Group, 1980. *'Local Studies Resources Guide to the defence of Portsmouth Harbour'.*

Rigold, S.E. 1978. *'Yarmouth Castle'.* English Heritage.

Riley, R.C. 1985 *'The evolution of the docks and the Industrial Revolution in Portsmouth dockyard 1698 - 1914'. Portsmouth Papers No 44*

Saunders, A.D. 1977 *'Hampshire Coastal Defence since the introduction of artillary'*. Royal Archaeological Institute.

Saunders, A. 1989 *'Fortress Britain'* Beaufont Publishing Ltd.

Temple Patterson, A. 1985. *'Palmerston's Folly'* - The Portsdown and Spithead Forts'. *Portsmouth Papers No 3.*

Temple Patterson, A. 1970. *'Portsmouth - A French Gibralter?'* - Portsmouth Papers No 10.

Williams, G.H. 1979. *'The Western Defences of Portsmouth Harbour 1400 - 1800'. Portsmouth Papers No 30.*

Bibliography - *the place of Cowes in the Military history of the Solent.*

Harding, D. *'Whites and the history of Cowes'*. Unpublished research.

Hyland, P. 1984 *'Wight: Biography of an Island'*. London, Victor Gollantz Limited.

Tagg, A.E & Wheeler R. L. 1989 *'From Sea to Air - The Heritage of Sam Saunders'*. Cross Publishing, Newport.

Williams, D.L. 1993 *'Whites of Cowes: Whites build, well built'*. Silver Link Publishing.

Southampton from Netley Beach

Netley Abbey

Chapter Five - Part One

THE ENCHANTED SHORE
Hampshire

'Calshot Castle'   John Frey, 1797

The Latin tag *Et in Arcadia Ego,* "I too lived in Arcady", decorates the tomb in the centre of Nicholas Poussin's (1594-1665) great work *'The Arcadian Shepherds'*, an allegorical idyll, painted in Rome in 1640 and now to be seen in the Louvre in Paris. The picture encapsulates the sublime and mystical wish to live in peace in natural and picturesque surroundings. Poussin's works were well known in England in the 18th century and are mentioned by William Gilpin, the Vicar of Boldre in the New Forest, in his *Remarks on Forest Scenery*, published in 1791. Gilpin was an advocate of the picturesque and relates beauty to nature. He disliked man's intervention.

"All forms, that are unnatural, displease. A tree lopped into a may-pole, as you generally see in the hedgerows of Surry (sic) and some other countries is disgusting. Clipped yews, lime hedges and pollards are, for the same reason disagreeable."[1]

The pursuit of the picturesque began with the Grand Tour of Italy, as Robin McInnes explains in the second part of this chapter, when he describes the discovery of the Isle of Wight. The label, "Grand Tour" came from *'A Voyage or a Complete Journey Through Italy,'* by Richard Lassels, published in 1670.[2]

The Grand Tour proper finished with the Napoleonic invasion of Italy in 1796. This turned the attention of would-be travellers and those bent on improving their minds to the works of earlier writers and explorers like Celia Fiennes, who remembered the Solent shore at Calshot. *"All round Calshot Castle, on the beach.....it is full of fine Cockle shells, so they heap them up round the Castle like a wall."[3]*

Drawings excited the would-be traveller, whether he or she would visit Italy or be inspired by nature's doings nearer to home. The artist, Thomas Rowlandson, 1757-1827, when in his mid-twenties, made a tour in a poste chaise, probably between September and October of 1784. He started in London and drew his way past Egham, Bagshot and Stockbridge to Salisbury. He then made for Southampton and Lymington, making an expedition on the Western Solent as far as the Needles and then up toward Spithead and Portsmouth on his return to the capital. He was accompanied by Henry Wickstead, a magistrate and fellow artist.

John Bullar wrote *'A Companion in a Tour Round Southampton'* in 1819. He travelled further afield to Lymington, Christchurch, Ringwood, Romsey, Winchester, Bishops Waltham, Titchfield, Gosport and Portsmouth. He noted villages, gentlemen's seats, curiosities and antiquities.[4]

Other artists followed Rowlandson in tempting the traveller. Anthony Devis (1729-1816) painted a view of the Needles from the Hampshire coast in 1792. Samuel Howett (1756-1822) also did a view of the Isle of Wight as well as vignettes of Lymington. Thomas Hurns (1744-1817) captured the Isle of Wight from Lymington. John Constable (1776-1837) did a charming little pencil drawing of Southampton and the Town Quay on the 12th October, 1816, ten days after his wedding to Maria Bicknel.[5] John Frey (fl. 1780-1800) captured Eagleshurst and J.M.W. Turner (1775-1851) did an atmospheric water-colour of Southampton Water.

The smoke, smell, bustle and clatter of the town as the industrial revolution began stimulated the wish to live simply with nature. Jane Austen in *Sense and Sensibility* (1811) wrote:

"I am excessively fond of a cottage; there is always so much comfort, so much elegance about them. And I protest, if I had any money to spare I should buy a little land and build one myself within a short distance of London where I might drive myself down at any time and collect a few friends about me and be happy."

Jane Austen moved to Chawton Cottage in 1809 and again in *'Sense and Sensibility'* she is perhaps comparing her own with the book's Barton Cottage. She goes on:

"As a house, Barton Cottage, though small, was comfortable and compact; but as a cottage it was defective, for the building was regular, the roof was tiled, the window shutters were not painted green, nor were the walls covered with honeysuckles."

The irony apparent in both these extracts - for the first is spoken by Robert Ferrars, an empty-headed fop - neatly underlines the somewhat absurd idealisation of the simple life by the wealthy classes.

According to Philippa Tristram in her chapter "Jane Austen's Aversion to Villas" in *'The Georgian Villa'*,[7] Jane Austen only uses the term villa twice in her published works. In Northanger Abbey she puts into the mouth of Isabella Thorpe, whom she has not much time for, *"There are some charming little villas about Richmond"*.

Romantic sketches, fiction and the desire for paradise gave way to near reality through a series of pattern books. The architect, Edward Gyfford, for example, in writing in his *'Designs for Small Picturesque Cottages and Hunting Boxes'* writes in the Preface:

Eaglehurst - Luttrell's Tower   *John Frey 1797*

"The plans in this volume are constructed on a small scale of accommodation, yet the elevations present an ornamented and picturesque appearance; they are calculated for the permanent residences of single gentlemen with a small establishment of servants; or for occasional occupation only, in the season of hunting and shooting, when, accompanied by a friend or two, the healthful sports of the field form the principal object for a temporary retreat from the more elegant amusements of the metropolis, or the more enlarged circle at the villa; and the accommodations are such as will, I flatter myself, be deemed sufficient for such occasional rustication; - some of the plans are sufficiently large for the permanent residence and required conveniences of a small family."

Southampton Water   JMW Turner

This concept continued the tradition of the Cottage Orné where the rustic dwelling on the outside was given convenience and comfort within. Gyfford's plan and drawing is:

"A design intended to accommodate only a Gentleman and his Friend in the season of shooting, and to be erected in a part of the country, probably remote from a principal town. The expense of this box will be about £160. It contains a kitchen, eating room and parlour, on the ground floor. The parlour occasionally to be converted into a bedroom, will, with those over the centre part make four bedrooms."[8]

This building owes much to the classical tradition, while the true Cottage Orné was in the vernacular style such as favoured by John Plaw in his *Rural Architecture or Designs From the Simple Cottage to the Decorated Villa* published in 1802[9]. John Plaw lived in Spring Place, near Southampton, and in 1795 brought out another book *The Ferme Ornée or Rural Improvements*.[10] In this he designed a fishing lodge that took up the rustic idea with tree trunks forming pillars, gothic windows and a thatched roof. Another plate showed a three bedroom cottage, with a ground floor plan like a shorn propeller hub, with thatched roof and a gigantic chimney at the apex. It was a real tour de force. He was very keen on mud walls and in the Preface he describes the technique as practised in France. The method was to *"construct the walls of dry earth, well rammed, or beaten together in a mould, like a case"*. He goes on to say that it is certainly cheap and the case easily shifted and used again. He also says *"the building is habitable as soon as it is formed, no danger being likely to arise to the inhabitants from damp walls."*

A cottage

Ackermann 1817

Ackerman's Repository of Arts, published in March, 1817, illustrates the difference between a cottage and a villa. The cottage is picturesque, yet full of *"modern"* comfort. The villa harks back to the younger Pliny, picked up by Robert Castell in his *Villas of the Ancients Illustrated*, of 1728.[11] The marine villa, Pliny's Villa Maritima, celebrated on the shores of the Bay of Naples,[12] was picked up by builders such as Sir Richard Worsley, with his Sea Cottage on the Undercliff of the Isle of Wight and others mentioned later by Robin McInnes in Part II of this chapter. Therefore, the cottage orné was not necessarily rustically ornamented, as the gothicised example from Ackerman's *"Repository of the Arts"* shows.

Much is made of the utility of such buildings for sporting purposes, particularly for fishing or shooting. However, the South Coast had its own call. This was the growing popularity of yachting encouraged first by George III at Weymouth and the Prince Regent at Brighton. Sea bathing, both in the Solent and in hot sea water baths on shore, became popular and drew people to the beach. Others became more interested in being on the water, rather than in it, and sailing as a sport gathered pace. Coach routes, particularly to Portsmouth and Southampton, and the coming of the railways made travel to the coast possible. The Isle of Wight was the main port of entry and departure for American visitors to Europe via Cowes, Portsmouth and Le Havre.

Thomas Jefferson in his Travels in Europe 1784-1789 records that:

"On July the 25th, 1784, Jefferson and Patsy landed at Cowes, on the Isle of Wight. After distributing tips to the ship stewards and leaving James Hemings and the phaeton at Cowes, the Jeffersons passed through Customs and breakfasted before crossing the Solent to Portsmouth where they lodged at Bradley's Crown Inn. Because Patsy had caught a cold and developed a fever, her father placed her under the care of a doctor Meak and a nurse. Until July the 31st, when they were to sail from Cowes to Le Havre in Captain Gray's ship, Jefferson made a brief circuit of nearby villages in a rented chaise."[13]

Therefore, rural retreats could be used as staging posts for journeys to the Continent and to America.

A Villa   Ackermann 1817

The mainland shore of the Solent is decorated with examples of picturesque cottages, marine and other villas. Many of these, perhaps the majority, have been demolished or obscured by later development. The backsides of other buildings now obliterate views of the water or the Isle of Wight. Of those that remain, some are no longer "picturesque", having been added to by owners in search of comfort inside, rather than retaining the romantic appearance without. Queen Victoria and Prince Albert stimulated the rush to the coast with the building of Osborne and by the time the Queen died this had accelerated, but at nothing like the pace that took place between the First and Second World Wars. The southern coast of England was built over from the Cliffs of Dover westward to the Southampton Water with hardly a break. Town and Country Planning Acts that came into place soon after the Second War slowed coastal building on green field sites, but intensification of development continued. Villas with large gardens were prime opportunities for bungalows and boxes many deep. Barge boards, mullion windows and honeysuckle were swept aside in favour of easily painted surfaces, plate glass windows and parks for car and boat. For all this, a journey along the Hampshire coast from Hayling Island to Hurst, occasionally venturing a little inland, can still be romantic and full of interest.

Hayling Island made a small attempt in the 1830's to emulate Brighton, but the effort died almost as it began. The detached Gothic villa of around 1850 in Sinah Lane reminds the passer-by that the island was at one time a lonely, romantic place of flat fields and little hamlets, shaded off into pitch mud flats thick with bird call. In the early 1820's the island was connected to the mainland by a bridge, linking it to Havant.

Further to the west, across the entrance to Langstone Harbour lies Portsea Island, now the home of Portsmouth that contains the four edge villages of Eastney, Southsea, Portsea and Hillsea on the northern edge. Southsea became fashionable during the first ten to fifteen years of the 19th century. The resort possessed a wild area that cut off Southsea Castle, one of Henry VIII's forts built between 1538 and 1540, along with Calshot, Hurst, Netley, Cowes and Yarmouth, from growing Southsea and Portsmouth. The land was reclaimed and became The Common. The land to the north was developed by Thomas Ellis Owen (1804-1862). Owen gave Southsea its character. He was an architect, a planner and a developer. Owen was twice Mayor of Portsmouth. Celia Clarke, who put together four guided walks to highlight the achievements of Owen, wrote in 1975 that he was influenced by Nash and his considerable achievement was *"in creating variety within a reasonable density. His ingenious plans and access arrangements were combined with a range of styles, from rustic to Regency, and winding, walled, tree lined lanes."*[15] One of Owen's earliest buildings in Southsea was Swiss Cottage, built in 1837, after Nash's Blaise Hamlet at Bristol. The Prospect Tower, added later, was much in vogue in early Victorian times in order to obtain a good view of the sea. Prince Albert and Thomas Cubitt incorporated such a tower in the Pavilion at Osborne.

Volage Villa[8] in Merton Road was built around 1860 and had a veranda with columns made of bark covered logs.

Across Portsmouth Harbour entrance and originally gathered around the top of Haslar Creek is Alverstoke. The Marquess of Anglesey, who kept his yacht Pearl at Cowes, was the patron of a new marine town, Angleseyville, that started with Crescent Road. The development would have been imposing in Brighton and is doubly so in Hampshire. Such terraces, villas and ornamental cottages are very much the sort of place where a retired naval officer could live with economy and pride not too far from the sea. Lord Ashburton certainly thought Alverstoke was just the place for his marine villa. He had Bay House, designed by Decimus Burton, built in the Tudor style in 1844. The Elizabethan chimney stacks now reach skyward over the old Gosport Grammar School. The building used to command wonderful views of Alverstoke Bay, eastward towards Spithead to the Isle of Wight. Another owner of the property was Colonel Ronald Sloane Stanley, the celebrated yachtsman. Decimus Burton was trained in the Royal Academy School. Burton and his father James played a large part in the development of Regents Park and Regent Street in London. They worked with the principal architect, John Nash.

To the west of the head of Fareham Creek, out of the town centre, lies Bishopswood, an overgrown cottage ornée that Pevsner reckons was built about 1800 and perhaps altered from an earlier farmhouse but greatly enlarged in the early 20th century. This cottage ornée still has its thatched roof. On the veranda, large tree trunks support the roof. Until recently the house did duty as the Bishop of Portsmouth's Palace.

Overlooking the Hamble River before the last reach that twists to the bridge is Brooklands, a Repton house with a gazebo by John Nash.[10]

At the entrance to the River Itchen lies what used to be the village of Weston. William Cobbett (1763-1835) remarked of the village *"To them that delight in water scenes, this is the prettiest place that I ever saw in my life"*. The village has changed dramatically, but the view from the shore still commands the

Volage Villa

Southampton Water and the comings and goings of ships. The village used to be part of the Weston Grove Estate owned by Thomas Chamberlayne.[11] Thomas owned the famous cutter *Arrow*, a competitor in the Round the Island Race of 1851 won by the schooner *America*. Unfortunately, she ran on the rocks east of Mill Bay on the Isle of Wight, managing to refloat and complete the race astern of most of the fleet. Weston Grove was demolished in 1940. Near by was Woolston House, again owned by the Chamberlaynes but now no more. The gardens of both remain. The Victoria History of Hampshire and the Isle of Wight records that there was, on the coast at Weston, "a curious old hut, entirely roofed with matted sea weed and said to be of considerable antiquity".

Leaving Southampton and hugging the western bank, is the ferry port of Hythe. The village's 1,100 foot long pier was built in 1880 and has a two foot gauge electric railway running along its length. Southwest of the pier is Forest Lodge, once the home of Captain George Robbins, the first Chief Constable of Hampshire when the police force was formed in 1839.[12] The house was built in 1730. Interest centres on the observatory or pagoda, that stood some 200 feet above sea level and looked out over Southampton Water. The house was also the home of Commander Edward Unwin, V.C., captain of the steamer River Clyde that acted as a landing ship on "V" Beach at Gallipoli. It is said more men were killed on and off her, than any other war time vessel.

Brooklands
Photo: Poppy Cooksey

The Pagoda at Forest Lodge, Hythe   *David Etheridge collection*

Forest Lodge, Hythe   *David Etheridge collection*

Further down Southampton Water, north of Fawley, within the Refinery on the site of the present round ball-like storage tanks stood Cadland House.[13] The mansion was demolished in 1948 to make way for the Fawley Oil Refinery. Henry Holland was responsible for the design of the original *marine villa*, fighting off competition from Robert Adam. Adam's design was similar to a small house in Scotland Adam designed for a Mr. Thompson, according to Alistair Rowan in his *Castles and Country Villas by Adam*.

The Hon. Robert Drummond, who built Cadland, was a son of the Fourth Viscount Strathallan killed at the Battle of Culloden in 1746, while commanding Bonnie Prince Charlie's cavalry. Robert's uncle, Andrew Drummond, started Drummond's Bank in 1715 and took young Robert and his brother Henry (whose son remodelled The Grange at Northington) into partnership. Robert Drummond employed Holland and Capability Brown to plan and create the Park. The team was also responsible for the thatched fishing cottage on the Solent's north shore in Stanswood Bay.

Cadland House   *Drawn by Henry Holland*

Rounding Calshot Castle, peeping out of the trees is Luttrells Tower. The Tower was built around 1740 to the designs of Thomas Sandby for Temple Simon Luttrell. Smugglers used to use the shore extensively and it is said Temple Simon Luttrell was much involved in their activities. The tower is now owned by the Landmark Trust and is available for holidays, being one of the Trust's most successful properties.

Across the lawn to the north of Luttrell's Tower lies Eaglehurst, which was designed by the Earl of Cavan, second in command to Sir Ralph Abercrombie in the Nile campaign, in a form that resembled his general's tent.[14] The wings with castellated towers were added later and the house was enlarged.

Further along the coast is Boarnhill, known as The Cottage, drawn by Rowlandson, and now Cadland House. As mentioned, the house was built by Robert Drummond as a fishing cottage, using the talents of Henry Holland and Capability Brown.[15] Gilly Drummond writes that *"Brown laid out the grounds to complement the enchanting folly of 1775. Holland designed a*

Eaglehurst   *David Etheridge collection*

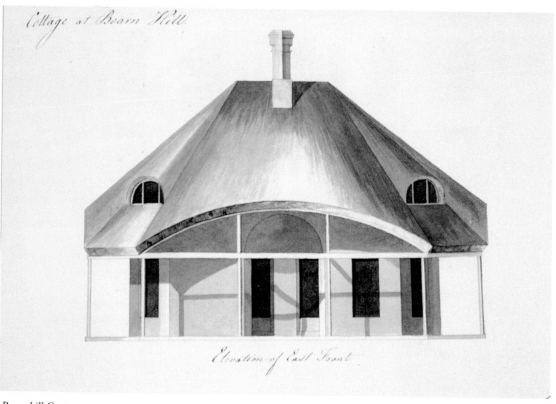

Boarnhill Cottage   *Design by Henry Holland*

Cowes

Chapter Five - Part Two
THE ENCHANTED SHORE
Isle of Wight

The discovery of the coastline of the Isle of Wight took place in the late 18th and 19th centuries at a time when exploration and travel to both historic and scenic sites throughout Europe was popular. It was part of the upbringing for young men from wealthy families to explore Europe on the Grand Tour and this interest in the culture and scenery of the European continent encouraged a desire to visit more remote and picturesque locations in Great Britain. As art and drawing was part of the education, and being before the days of photography, illustrated books provided a particularly important means of explaining the landscape and coastal scenery of areas such as Scottish Highlands, the coastline of Wales, Devon and Cornwall and other picturesque locations such as the Lake District and the Isle of Wight.

Some of these visitors to the Island shores came in the late 18th Century to visit a small number of wealthy gentry who had constructed seaside cottages (Cottages Ornés) along the remoter parts of the Isle of Wight coastline. It became fashionable for antiquarians and topographical artists to tour the Island, initially on horseback but later by carriage, to record the spectacular coastal scenery and antiquities.

One of the first of the new visitors to the Island was Charles Tomkins who in the 1770s undertook a riding tour which resulted in his *Tour of the Isle of Wight*, a lavish publication illustrated with 80 aquatints of Island coastal and inland scenes. His illustrations provide one of the first accurate records of life on the Island before the rapid period of expansion seen in the 19th Century. Tomkins returned in 1809 to undertake a commission for Charles Pelham, who later became Earl Yarborough the well-known yachtsman, and who played an important role in the development of the Royal Yacht Squadron at Cowes. A keen patron of the arts, Yarborough commissioned Tomkins to paint 58 watercolours of Island scenery in 1809, a unique record of life and landscape on the Isle of Wight at that time.

COWES CASTLE.

The flavour of the Isle of Wight in this period of discovery was captured by the author William Cooke who published a *New Picture of the Isle of Wight* in 1808. Cooke extolled the virtues of the Isle of Wight and the need for his publication as follows :-

"Its beauties are so celebrated as to attract the traveller from every quarter. At this period of increased taste for finer treasures of exploration, when the beauties of nature are more eagerly sought, and more highly relished; when a love of the arts so generally prevails, it is thought it may be acceptable to the public to have a picturesque portable companion directing the attention to each scene of beauty by means of original sketches."

The Isle of Wight was not of course undeveloped in the 18th Century. In fact parts of the Island were relatively prosperous with influential farming families occupying important country houses and Jacobean and earlier farms throughout the countryside. The change occurred towards the end of the 18th Century when the cottage orné became fashionable as a result of the influence of the important Regency architect, John Nash, who had built East Cowes Castle on the Island's Solent shore. Nash was a keen exponent of the cottage orné and this ornate form of seaside villa architecture flourished on the Isle of Wight as in some other favoured locations along the south coast of England.

These unusual properties with their architectural embellishments provided excellent subject matter for visiting artists particularly as many of the properties were set in remote and spectacular coastal locations. Early writers including Tomkins, Hassall, Wyndham, Sir Henry Englefield and others wrote about the residences of these gentlemen many of whom were very wealthy and could afford to buy original works of art or sponsor the publication of books which would usually include an illustration of their property.

The Bathing Place, Cowes   *John Hassell 1796*

East Cowes from West Cowes   *English School 19th c.*

Cowes

Brading   *William Daniell 1824*

Ryde Pier from Puckpool   *William Gray c.1855*

The eastern Solent from Southsea Common at sunset

128

English School c.1870

The creeks and estuaries bordering the Solent were relatively isolated spots with fishing being an important activity. Occasionally marine villas occupied wooded locations close to the shoreline although larger mansions such as Fernhill at Wootton provided a Gothic presence on the southern side of the high road leading to Ryde. Before entering the picturesque village of Binstead visitors passed Quarr Abbey, which had been founded in 1113 by Baldwin de Redvers, Earl of Devon. This was one of the first monasteries of the Cistercian Order and was an important monastery in its time until its dissolution by Henry VIII.

It is difficult to appreciate what some of the Island's smaller towns and villages would have been like in the early 1800s. Their character has been changed so much as a result of Victorian, Edwardian and later development. For example William Cooke, writing in 1808 said of Binstead:

"a short distance from Ryde, near the water's edge, is Binstead, charmingly situated and surrounded by woods. In the bosom of this sequestered village is the parsonage, which cannot fail to impress as one of the most beautiful on the Island. It is an elegant and captivating thatched cottage, charmingly placed on a verdant lawn embowered amongst the finest shrubs, adorned by trees of strikingly picturesque forms, amidst whose pendant foliage are glimpses of the water, the shipping and the opposite shore".

A short distance to the east was the town of Ryde, which at that time comprised two villages separated by several acres of meadows. During the early part of the 19th Century increasing development in this attractive location looking across towards Portsmouth led to their combination into a thriving, prosperous entry port to the Island. Although the prosperity of the town was further increased through the construction of the pier, in the early days much activity in terms of transit of goods to and from the Island took place on the sands. In the mid 19th century artists such as Copley Fielding and Edward Duncan captured these scenes in magnificent watercolours.

There is no doubt that the wooded Solent slopes in the vicinity of Ryde were popular locations for the construction of beautiful marine villas. Important residences such as Appley House, The Marina, St Johns and St Clare were all built close to the town. The wealthy landowners employed the leading landscape gardeners of the day such as Humphrey Repton to take the fullest opportunity of the topography and landscape to create a magnificent setting for elaborate garden parties, concerts and other events. The larger residences were often one of a number of properties owned by wealthy families who arrived with a large entourage of servants and other staff to stay for the summer season. Their houses were filled with the finest furniture, carpets and paintings, many of which had been acquired on their particular Grand Tour.

The coastline east of Ryde towards Bembridge was more sparsely developed although villas such as Fairy Hill and The Priory at Seaview, described by Charles Tomkins and illustrated by Thomas Walmesley under the title *Cottage near Ryde* were renowned for their beauty and setting in a luxuriant coastal landscape.

The busy harbour and waterway of Brading Haven separated St Helens from the Island of Bimbridge (sic) which could only be reached by an inland diversion around the head of the Haven. Subsequent reclamation and the construction of the railway and a carriage road encouraged the development of Bembridge, as it later became known. Flanked by the Island's central downs the low lying haven and Bembridge village were dominated by the downland behind, on which was situated a semaphore station that allowed information on shipping movements in the Channel to be passed to the Admiralty at Portsmouth. Later a handsome obelisk was constructed to commemorate Earl Yarborough, who had been able to pass instructions to the Captain of his yacht 'Falcon', which sailed frequently from Cowes and around the Isle of Wight to his marine villa at St Lawrence.

Priory Bay - Bembridge Point beyond William Gray c.1855

The original Needle Rock

Cowes, the Western Solent and the Isle of Wight Coastal Voyage

Travelling westwards from Cowes Parade the wooded slopes of the Solent were developed with marine villas, the hillside being dominated by Northwood House, and beyond, Westhill, a charming thatched cottage built by Admiral Sir Hugh Christian and which offered a magnificent view across the River Medina. The small hamlet of Gurnard, which derived its name from a species of fish caught in the Bay (earlier named Gurnet) was visited by the artist Tomkins on his 1809 tour. Taking a voyage along this part of the Solent in order to sketch the shoreline Tomkins describes his day out on the Solent as follows :

"The morning being fine, and the season the best for an aquatic excursion we weighed anchor and left Cowes Harbour with a gentle breeze from the west. In Gurnet Bay we caught a picturesque inland view of the country closed by the high downs of Alvington, Bowcombe, Mountjoy and the Castle of Carisbrooke. On reaching Gurnet Point we plainly saw, running to a considerable length, the gravelly ridge, supposed to be the isthmus which once joined the Isle of Wight to Hampshire."

Resulting from this voyage Tomkins produced charming watercolours of the Solent looking towards Calshot, Gurnard Bay and Cowes as well as a view from Rew Street in Gurnard looking across the Solent to Luttrell's Tower and Calshot Castle with a gypsy encampment in the foreground. Tomkins was the first of a succession of artists who came to Cowes and were impressed by the beauty of the Solent and its shoreline. Delicate views were portrayed in aquatint by Charles Raye in 1825 and later by Frederick Calvert in his colour plate publication *The Isle of Wight Illustrated* (1846).

Raye described the town of Cowes, which was just starting to develop as a resort and centre for yacht racing at that time in the 1820s, in the following way.

"The streets of Cowes are narrow and ill-built, but from the manner in which they rise one above another from the water's edge they do have a singular and not unpleasing appearance both from the sea and the opposite bank of the river. The convenience of this town for bathing has of late years occasioned it to become the resort of much fashionable company, also the general accommodations are very good."

The Needles

P J De Loutherbourg 1815

133

Yarmouth

The Parade was the centre of activity for yacht racing and promenading and Island artists including Charles Gregory and his son George illustrated scenes in meticulous watercolour. Later a succession of marine painters including Sir Oswald Brierly, George Chambers, John Wilson Carmichael and specialist marine painters such as William Lionel Wyllie, Edoardo De Martino and Arthur Wellington Fowles captured the atmosphere of the yacht racing and regattas. Westwards from Gurnard the coast was largely undeveloped although the once prosperous village of Newtown existed close to the coastline. The village had undergone a remarkable transformation from the important town of Franchville, the subject of repeated French attacks, to a huddle of small cottages with a ruined church. The silting up of the estuary and the decline of the salt industry were other factors which led to the demise of the town.

The most important town along the north-west coast of the Island was Yarmouth which was also a route for the transport of goods and passengers to the Isle of Wight. Repeated invasions by the French led to the construction of a castle by Henry VIII as part of his coastal defences scheme. Relatively isolated from the western end of the Island until a bridge was constructed across the Yar, the town was famous for its weekly market, its genteel residents and the George Hotel and other inns which were noted for their quality and hospitality. The narrow waters of the Solent between Yarmouth and the Needles were a focus for much interest by visitors on account of the amount of shipping activity and the presence of Hurst Castle and Hurst Spit. Coastal fortifications were added at Fort Victoria and Fort Albert and Victorian and Edwardian development of villages such as Totland made them holiday and residential locations regarded as of the highest quality. The peace and tranquillity of this part of the West Wight has remained largely to this day.

The coastal voyage

The northern ports of the Island, including Ryde, Cowes and Yarmouth, were convenient points for commencing a coastal voyage around the Island's 65 miles of coastline. The journey by paddle steamer or by smaller coastal craft or yacht was extremely popular, as indeed it is today, on account of the variety of coastal scenery. George Brannon, a local engraver and author, described the view of Yarmouth in the 1850s in the following way :

"The River Yar is best seen at the favourable moment of high water. It winds beautifully between gently rising banks imposed in which is here a mansion and there a cottage, whilst its course is marked by vessels, pleasure craft and a considerable number of swans. But at its junction with the Solent channel the river forms a busy picture of maritime life; the sea port town on one side and the sylvan village of Norton on the other. The prospect of this extensive landscape is deeply interesting ranging from Southampton Water to St Alban's Head. The harbour of Poole and the whole of the high lands westward has a charming effect when viewed against the glowing horizon of a declining sun on a clear evening".

Brannon also recommended visitors to take a voyage around the Isle of Wight. He published a guide in the 1840s entitled *A voyage around the Isle of Wight - being an indispensable handbook to every stranger who would fully enjoy the scenery of this delightful coast*. The guide describes the benefits of a coastal voyage in the following way:

"From the facilities afforded by the steam company, the trifling expense and above all, the variety and beauty of the scenery, a trip round the "Garden of England" is one of the most eligible, and certainly the most delightful the lover of aquatic pleasures and marine grandeur can possible enjoy. A highlight of the coastal voyage is the four mile section near Freshwater cliffs and Alum Bay. The magnificent and varied scenery here presented being produced by the ocean's destructive advances upon the western and southern sides of Freshwater Down, which formerly extended much further seawards than it does now, for the Needles and other detached rocks are known to have once formed part of the main range. Puffins, Gulls, Cormorants, Choughs, Eider Duck and other species assemble at these cliffs during the spring in prodigious numbers; crowning every pinnacle and crag and darkening the sky as they fly, whilst their various cries, however discordant in themselves, appear to harmonise delightfully with the wild sublimity of the scene".

Writing to Sir Henry Englefield in about 1811, the celebrated geologist and artist Thomas Webster said

"Alum Bay is so extraordinary I am unable to express in adequate terms the surprise I felt on first viewing it. From the shores of this bold sweeping bay the cliffs rise from 3-400 feet, destitute of vegetation but composed of vertical strata of the most brilliant coloured sands and clays, now in striking opposition and again blending in the most delicate tints; whilst the bold pinnacles and the indented surface break the outline and tend to harmonise the colouring to the hues of the rainbow. To the south, the vast chalk promontory, nearly 400 feet high, surmounted by the high steep down on which stands the lighthouse, stretches its perpendicular face for about half a mile of dazzling whiteness, except where sobered by the growth of Samphire and the tints of time, its extremity descending in bold irregularities to the celebrated Needles rocks."

Alum Bay
William Gray
c. 1860

Off Yarmouth   *William Gray c.1855*

Freshwater Bay   *William Daniell 1824*

Shipping off the Needles   *William Daniell 1824*

In the Western Solent   *T S Robins 1851*

137

William H Bartlett   *Scratchell's Bay*   *1830*

The Victorian period coincided with enormous interest in sciences such as geology and the Prince Consort was particularly interested in all matters of this kind. In 1846 he encouraged the British Institution to visit the Island and undertake a voyage which included excursions ashore at Alum Bay and Atherfield where the celebrated geologists of the time including Murchison and Fitton explained the unique geological situation and their understanding of its formation.

A visit to the Needles and round the headland towards Freshwater Bay was described by the antiquarian Sir Henry Englefield in 1816 :

"Nothing can be more interesting particularly with those who take pleasure in aquatic excursions, than to sail between and round the Needles. The wonderfully coloured cliffs of Alum Bay, the lofty and towering chalk precipices at Scratchell's Bay is of the most dazzling whiteness and elegant form - the magnitude and singularity of those spirey insulated masses, the Needles rocks, which seem at every instant to be shifting their position and give a mazy perplexity to the place. The screaming noise of aquatic birds, the agitation of the sea and the rapidity of the tide occasioning not unfrequently a degree of danger, all these circumstances combine to raise in the mind unusual emotions and to give the scenery a character highly singular and romantic. Scarcely a winter passes without one or more shipwrecks in this place; many vessels choosing to risk this shorter passage to and from Portsmouth instead of going round to St Helens. Two lighthouses are erected at Hurst Castle to direct the pilots to clear the Needles but in hazy weather fatal mistakes are all too frequent".

A favourite activity of wealthy gentry was shooting seabirds which nested in enormous numbers on the ledges on the chalk cliffs between the Needles and Freshwater Bay. Apart from the sport the birds and their eggs were eagerly sought by local residents as a source of food. Richard Worsley who wrote *A History of the Isle of Wight* in 1781 describes how these activities took place :

"The country people take these birds that harbour in the rocks, and their eggs by the perilous expedient of descending by ropes fixed to iron crows driven into the ground. Thus suspended they beat with sticks the birds as they fly out of their holes. A dozen birds generally yield one pound of soft feathers for which the merchants give eight pence. The carcasses are bought by the fishermen for sixpence per dozen for the purpose of baiting their crab pots."

Blackgang Chine

The eggs were also sold to visitors some of whom were prolific collectors whilst other species were stuffed and mounted in display cases. The risks of climbing the coastal cliffs around the Island were highlighted by William Cooke who in 1808 described how,

"an awful example of the danger attending this adventure has this year occurred. An artillery soldier from one of the neighbouring barracks, without experience, and it should seem without proper caution, attempted it alone, and is supposed to have neglected to fasten the rope around his body. However this might be, he was seen by the party at the signal house to fall headlong, dashing from crag to crag. His mutilated remains were found as a horrible spectacle among the rocks at the bottom of the cliff".

Puckaster Cove

Freshwater Bay or 'Gate' as it was known was so named because it was the only location along the south-west coast of the Isle of Wight where ships could pass through to find shelter and collect supplies of fresh water. The Cabin (now the Albion Hotel) was the haunt of George Morland, the celebrated artist, who fled there from London to escape his debtors towards the end of the 18th Century. Morland produced several superb paintings of the Isle of Wight coastline at that time.

The magnificent cliff line of the south-west coast of the Isle of Wight (or the 'back of the Wight' as it was known locally) was a predominantly rural area with a few farms, small manors and cottages occupied by fishermen or farm workers. The southern coastline continuing eastwards, known as the Undercliff, was also sparsely developed although it became increasingly fashionable from the 1840s. The sea cliffs at Blackgang range in height from 300 - 400 feet and in Victorian times it was possible to gain access from the cliff top to the shoreline.

A cascade of water ran over the rim on a hard band of sandstone and dropped vertically to the shore, this being captured by many artists and engravers and appearing as a popular view in early guidebooks. Following the wreck of 'The Clarendon' in 1836 a magnificent new lighthouse was built at St Catherine's Point and this was an important landmark and feature of interest on the coastal voyage. Prior to the extensive tree planting along the Undercliff, the rear scarp face of the Undercliff landslip presented a stark and rugged feature which extended for nearly 6 miles eastwards past the town of Ventnor to Bonchurch.

Undercliff Cave

A journey along the Undercliff coast from Ventnor to Blackgang was a highlight for early visitors to the Isle of Wight. Magnificent views could be obtained of the coast from the carriage route with elegant marine villas located in sheltered south facing positions in secluded locations. These included The Orchard, home of General Sir Willoughby Gordon, who was ADC to the Duke of Wellington in the Peninsula War, and his wife, an accomplished artist and potter, who prepared designs for Josiah Wedgewood, as well as major landowners such as Earl Yarborough at the Marine Villa at St Lawrence and John Hambrough who built Steephill Castle. The towers of Steephill Castle dominated the Undercliff skyline, the structure being constructed between 1833 and 1835. Reputed to have cost £250,000 to build the gardens were regarded as some of the most magnificent in the British Isles. Joseph Paxton the famous horticulturalist said:

"I have travelled from Stockholme to Constantinople but nowhere have I seen finer grounds than those at Steephill Castle."

Niton Undercliff
William Gray c.1855

St Lawrence - Steephill Castle beyond

George Childs c.1840

The southern coast of the Isle of Wight (St Lawrence to Ventnor)   George Brannon 1843

The town of Ventnor developed from a small fishing cove with an inn, a mill and a few cottages into a thriving seaside resort over a relatively short period between 1830 and 1870. Its fine situation on the southern slopes of St Boniface Down, the steepness of the development and roads led Victorians to compare it with some of the Italian resorts on the Amalfi coast. The town became increasingly popular as the benefits of climate for health were realised and the construction of a pier, as well as the completion of the railway line from Ryde to Ventnor secured its prosperity. To the east, the village of Bonchurch, set in a picturesque location amongst the trees, cliffs and rocks of the Undercliff became a centre for writers and artists in the mid to late 19th Century with Dickens, Macauley and many other famous authors and artists residing or spending the summer season there.

Ventnor from the East, Isle of Wight.

Ventnor from the west   *Henry B Wimbush c.1895*

Ventnor Cascade   *Henry B Wimbush c.1895*

Bonchurch from the sea   *Robert Carrick 1848*

The Vale, Bonchurch   *William Gray 1855*

143

The White Cliff, Ventnor (Wheeler's Bay).

This fine watercolour by William Gray called 'The White Cliff, Ventnor' shows a scene at Wheeler's Bay to the east of Ventnor in 1855. This Royal Academy exhibit provides a detailed view of fisherfolk at work in one of the many small fishing coves that existed around the Isle of Wight coastline in the nineteenth century. Noted for the richness of his palate, Gray, a professor of landscape painting, lived in Ventnor in the 1850s. His watercolours provide a vivid picture of life around the coastline at that time.

144

William Gray 1855

Unloading a coal boat at Horseshoe Bay, Bonchurch.

Thomas Miles Richardson was one of a number of important Victorian artists who regularly stayed at Seaside Cottage, Bonchurch to paint the coastal scenery. This magnificent watercolour shows a coal boat being unloaded on the foreshore whilst crew collect sand to re-ballast the vessel to allow departure on the next tide. Richardson painted extensively in the Alps and Mediterranean before visiting the Isle of Wight. It is believed the strong colours are a reflection of his watercolours from abroad. It is likely that William Gray, T C L Rowbotham and others were influenced by his work.

Thomas Miles Richardson Jnr 1861

The Undercliff coast

G Brannon

147

Rounding Dunnose Point the coastal voyage passed across Sandown Bay. The chines of Luccombe and Shanklin, which had been the haunts of fishermen and smugglers, were pointed out whilst the cliff-top development and establishment of esplanades on the foreshore at both Shanklin and Sandown took

place between 1850 and 1880. Between these two developing towns a small fishing community existed on the foreshore at Lake. The northern end of Sandown Bay and the eastern termination of the Isle of Wight is marked by Culver Cliff, a magnificent headland of chalk which contrasts with the ferruginous sands of Sandown Bay known as Red Cliff.

Luccombe   *Thomas Leeson Rowbotham c.1863*

Shanklin Head   *Frederick Calvert 1846*

Sandown Bay from Cowleaze Hill   *William Gray c.1855*

Near Luccombe   *William Gray c.1855*

Luccombe beach looking towards Culver.

This panoramic watercolour by Gray shows a scene on the beach at Luccombe where a small fishing community existed until the site was destroyed by a landslide in 1910.

William Gray c.1855

Culver Cliff

G Brannon

151

Queen Victoria's Experimental Squadron exercising in the Solent

mid 19th century lithograph

Rounding the often choppy waters off Culver Cliff the coastal voyage continued past Whitecliff Bay and Bembridge Point to re-enter the eastern Solent at St Helens. A distinctive landmark was the white tower, the only remains of the church of St Helens which had been lost through coastal erosion but with the tower remaining preserved as a landmark.

During the Victoria and Edwardian periods the development of the Solent shores continued and by the mid-20th century most of the urban frontages were fully developed. The popularity of an outlook across to the mainland remains as sought after today as it was when the Solent shoreline was discovered two centuries before.

Sunset Whitecliff Bay   *William Gray Jnr. 1875*

In the Solent - Sunrise   *English School*

Bibliography

Brannon, A. 1850, *'Voyage round the Isle of Wight,'* Wootton, IW.'

Calvert, F. 1846, *'The Isle of Wight illustrated,'* London.

Cooke, W. 1808, *'A new picture of the Isle of Wight,'* London.

Englefield, H. 1816, *'The Isle of Wight - a description of the history, geology and antiquities,'* London.

McInnes, RG & Butler, A. 1886, *'The Undercliff of the Isle of Wight in old picture postcards,'* European Library, Zaltbommel, Netherlands.

McInnes, RG. 1989, *'The Isle of Wight Illustrated,'* Cross Publishing, Ventnor.

McInnes, RG. 1990, *'The Garden Isle - Landscape paintings of the Isle of Wight,'* Cross Publishing, Ventnor.

McInnes, RG. 1993, *'A picturesque tour of the Isle of Wight,'* Cross Publishing, Ventnor.

Raye, C. 1825, *'A picturesque tour of the Isle of Wight,'* London.

Rowe, G. 1826, *'Views in the Isle of Wight,'* London.

Tomkins, C. 1796, *'A tour of the Isle of Wight,'* London.

Cowes Regatta.

Chapter Six
YACHTS & YACHTSMEN

The Adam or Eve of yachtsmen must have been the first person to lie on a log and push gingerly out from the shore for the sheer pleasure of being afloat. After a considerable leap in time, in 1588, the Armada year, it is often repeated that a small vessel was built for Queen Elizabeth I on the banks of the Medina for her personal use. The peculiarly named *Rat of Wight* was one of five ships supplied by the Isle of Wight to oppose the Spanish Armada.

The great Queen had sparked a Navy earlier. She had presented Ivan IV of Russia, Ivan the Terrible, with a small boat. A hundred years after the Armada, in 1688, Peter 1st, Peter the Great of Russia, found the boat mouldering in a lake north of Moscow, repaired and sailed her. In 1698, he came to London and studied naval architecture and ship building. On returning, Tsar Peter founded St. Petersburg in 1703 and the Russian Navy. He headed the world's first yacht club in 1718 and gave *Botik* (Little Boat) that he had rescued, the title "Grandfather of the Russian Navy". She is now in St. Petersburg, but her replica sailed in the Solent in 1998, the 300th anniversary of Peter the Great's visit to London and England's South Coast.

The name yacht, of course, was not recorded until the word appeared in *The Voyage of Stephan of Burrough* in Hakluyt's Voyages in 1598. The *White Ship* of Henry I, which is said to have left from Lepe, sinking on her return journey after hitting a rock in November 1120, would have been seen as a vessel dedicated for use by the King for national purpose and long before the word yacht came into general descriptive use. In the tragedy, the King lost his only legitimate son, William.

One of the first private vessels to record visiting the Solent was captained by Richard Ferris, who sailed from Tower Wharf in a sprit sail wherry painted green, the favoured Tudor colour.[1] Ferris records in his *The Most Dangerous and Memorable Adventure of Richard Harris* (published in 1590) that they "had a great storm" in the Solent. They later escaped from a pirate off the Runnel Stone and with the aid of "good sea stomachs" overcame the "high billows" and reached Bristol.

The word *yacht* came into the English language through the Dutch "jaght", via "jaghtschip", or literally a ship for chasing. The Dutch stole a march and discovered the pleasures of sailing through their splendid inland waters and the shoreline that was then protected by a maze of sandbanks that discouraged any interference from the outside. Their main advantage though, came from their exploitation of the herrings in the North Sea. The city of Amsterdam was said to be founded on herrings. In 1601, John Keymor wrote his pamphlet on the subject.[2] He held: *"There is more wealth raised out of herrings and other fish in Her Majesty's seas by the neighbouring nations in one year than the King of Spain hath from the Indies in four, and that there are 20,000 ships and other vessels, and about 400,000 people, set to work by both sea and land, and maintained only by fishing upon the coasts of England, Scotland and Ireland."* In this way, the Dutch built up a reservoir of mariners, born fishermen who were drawn on by their Navy and the Dutch East India Company, and as officers and hands for yachts.

The wealth of the city of Amsterdam produced a flowering of small, private vessels. The yacht *Mary* was presented to King Charles II by the city of Amsterdam in 1660. Pepys records in his diary for the 15th August, *"And after dinner by water to White-hall where I find the King gone this morning by five of the clock to see a Dutch pleasure-boat below the bridge".*[3]

Royal enthusiasm led to the building of royal yacht after royal yacht, developing the Dutch model by deepening the draught and altering the rig. Yachts were not only used for racing, pleasure and Royal purpose, but for carrying important people and despatches. Commissioners of the Navy and the dockyards, the Viceroy of Ireland and the Governors of the Isle of Wight were provided with their own "yachts".

Captain Grenville Collins, Hydrographer In Ordinary to Charles II, was despatched around the coast in the yachts *Merlin* and *Monmouth* between 1681-1688. He charted the sea coasts of England and Scotland and made good the deficiencies of the Dutch charts, all that were to be had before his *'Coasting Pilot'* was published.[4] Within this is one of the first accurate surveys of the Solent.

Mind you, not everyone saw the activity as a pleasure. Dr Samuel Johnson described "yachting", in 1759, as "being in jail with the chance of being drowned". As with the Dutch, sailing for pleasure began to flourish in sheltered waters. The Cumberland Sailing Society, the forerunner of the Royal Thames Yacht Club, was organised in 1775, prompted by the Duke of Cumberland. He turned to the water after gaining the nickname "Butcher" (following his pursuit and slaughter of the Jacobites after Culloden in 1746). In his quest for calm water, he had excavated the two mile long lake of Virginia Water, using military labour, and actively encouraged yacht racing.

Virginia Water became a sheltered marine playground for the Royal family, lasting from the time of George III through to the children of Queen Victoria. Among the ships was *Mandarin*, a small merchant vessel converted into a Chinese junk. The most powerful floating symbol though was the miniature frigate *Royal Adelaide*, armed with 22 one-pounder brass guns, ordered by William IV and launched on the lake in 1834. She was built to the lines of the frigate *HMS Pique*,[5] which left the ways at Plymouth Dockyard at almost the same time. *Royal Adelaide's* cannons were given to the Royal Yacht Squadron as a battery by Edward VII, then Prince of Wales, after the yacht was broken up in 1877.

Mock naval battles, or *naumachia*, had existed since the time of Julius Caesar and the idea flowered in the 18th and 19th centuries in England, not only privately on Virginia Water, but in such places as the 4th Duke of Newcastle's near 90 acre lake at Clumber Park. *Salamanca*, named in honour of Wellington's victory in 1812, was built in the same year by Linn Ratsey of Cowes. Another, the *Lincoln*, was on the lake until burnt at the beginning of World War II. A battery of guns poked out over the water from a miniature castle to complete the illusion of fresh water being salt.[6]

The 5th Duke of Newcastle, while Earl of Lincoln, became a member of the Royal Yacht Squadron. He had no doubt sailed in the pond yacht bearing his name. Lord Lincoln though called his sea-going schooner *Gitana*. The call of the sea, therefore, was heard from the lake.

East Cowes was busy building sizeable vessels from 1637 onward. Cowes was to provide the ideal place to start and finish small boat racing, with yachts competing in locally organised regattas. The word *regatta* came from the boat races held on the Grand Canal in Venice. The first English regatta was held on the Thames on the 23rd June, 1775. The Royal Yacht Squadron has a painting of an event off Cowes in 1776 between cutters of the Royal Navy. The war against France somewhat restricted any event that went out beyond the Wight. Indeed, when G.O. Fullerton went beyond the Needles in his yacht *Zephyr* in 1806, he was very nearly captured by a French privateer.[7]

Cowes gained the reputation of a bathing place. With the installation of sea water baths at the Vine Hotel around 1756 (on the site of the Fountain Arcade), Cowes became a fashionable resort in the late 18th and early 19th centuries when the French Wars prevented the aristocracy from visiting the continent or engaging in the "Grand Tour". It also became a favoured spot for those interested in a sea spectacle and, of course, for those who would venture out on the water. The gathering on the Solent and on the shore, led to the founding, in 1815, of the Yacht Club, later to become the Royal Yacht Squadron. This was, perhaps, the first use of the word "yacht" in the title of a British sailing club. In June of 1815, before the season really started, there was a meeting in the Thatched House Tavern at the bottom end of London's St. James's Street. The original centre for the Club on the Isle of Wight was the Hotel Medina or Aldred's Hotel in East Cowes. Later, the Vine Hotel in West Cowes was also employed for dinners. The original burgee of the club was plain white. The purpose of the club was broad - to bring together those interested in sailing and the sea. The 10th Rule of the first Regulations stated that on the 24th August a dinner would be held there at four o'clock, provided notice was given two days beforehand, together with an indication of the number of friends that a member proposed to introduce.

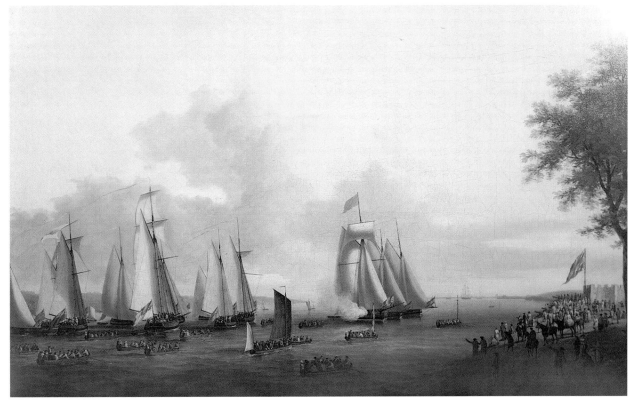

Cutters of the Royal Navy off Cowes   *Dominic Serres 1776*

One or two founder members of The Yacht Club were intrepid cruising yachtsmen before the club was formed. Sir William Curtis, who made his fortune by supplying hard-tack to the Navy [8], sailed to Spain in his cutter *Rebecca Maria*, a converted Arab dhow, to take a look at the Peninsular War. When the club was formed in 1815, he was not present, as by then he was bound for St. Petersburg. As an ex-Lord Mayor of London, he no doubt had gained inspiration from gazing at the Thames, then the water highway of the capital.

As far as the Yacht Club was concerned, yacht racing was a spectator sport. A prize fund was established to encourage competitiveness amongst local boatmen. There were exceptions. Joseph Weld and Thomas Asshton-Smith competed in a sailing match between the *Charlotte* and the *Elizabeth*. The match was strenuous and consisted of three races, the first from Cowes to Swanage and return. The second was to be from Cowes to the light vessel off Bembridge and return. However, Asshton-Smith's *Elizabeth* lost her mast off St. Albans Head in the Race and could not compete further. The first recorded Round the Island Race was in 1824, again between two keen racing members, James Weld in his *Julia* and C.R.M. Talbot in his *Giulia*. The Marquess of Anglesey, who had lost his leg at the Battle of Waterloo, raced against the Weld brothers in 1825 and swore that if his yacht *Pearl* was beaten he would burn her, but luckily he won.[8]

However, the majority of the membership of the now Royal Yacht Club liked the idea of floating about in comfortable boats, rather than racing. George IV became a member of the Club in 1817. He had owned a house on Cowes Parade in the early 1820's. The advantage of yachts were seen then as:

"They have all the accommodation of a house and are free from the inconvenience of a bad neighbourhood, for their site may be changed at pleasure. They have not only the richest, but also the most varied prospects. They are free from house duty and window tax, pay neither tithe nor poor rate, are exempt from Government and Parochial taxes, and have not only a command of wood and water, but may truly be said to possess the most exclusive fishery of any house in England."[9].

In this fashion, to quote the first history of the Royal Yacht Squadron, *"they avoided for as long as possible the fierce joys of the ownership of a racing vessel"*. The club used to parade, under the command of the Commodore, and sail gently round the Brambles and back to Cowes. The occasion was enjoyed by the public ashore. "Trunnion", though, writing in *Sporting Annals*, was critical.

"We have a right to presume that where so much wealth and splendour are wasted in the production of first rate specimens of naval architecture, the great object of so much competition must be to excel in the art of swift sailing, and yet we can gather no information upon the subject from the late evolution of the grand fleet at Spithead; on the contrary, this perfection would seem to be considered as an unnecessary appendage of those fanciful emblems of our wooden walls, and a squadron of English gabbards or Dutch dogers might as well have performed the manoeuvres so pompously described as the fleet in question." (9)

Well, perhaps this was the calm before the storm, for there were those who were competitive and unsatisfied by *"the mild gaiety of the annual meetings at Cowes"*.[9]

This rush for speed under sail led, in 1826, to a newspaper remarking that:

"These gentlemen, by building fast vessels and bestowing prizes upon the best sailors, create a spirit of emulation among the different branches of the artificers connected with nautical affairs and by introducing for trial new and extended machinery, perform services which no individual could or would undertake. So unrivalled are some of the yachts in the cut of sails and beauty of construction that they have received considerable attention from the Government."

Royal Yacht Club yachts started racing for cups in 1826.

The Navy was certainly impressed and the badge of their approval was a warrant empowering members of the Royal Yacht Squadron to wear a plain White Ensign with the Union flag in the corner. The White Ensign was not such a mark in the days before the 1860's. The red, white and blue squadrons were only abolished in favour of the universal white ensign of the Navy after that. Be that as it may, the Royal Navy bought *Pantaloon* from the Duke of Portland as a model for the ten gun brig and purchased Lord Belfast's East Cowes built *Waterwitch* which consistently out performed the Royal Navy by sailing circles around their ships. A correspondent wrote:

"The Navy will also be thankful to the Royal Yacht Squadron for bringing improvements to its notice which will give the seamen dry jackets and beds and such comforts never to be obtained at sea in other vessels previously constructed."

Such innovation did not apply to steam. In 1830, the Club banned steam engines unless they consumed their own smoke. This may be one of the first indications of a "green" movement in the middle of the Industrial Revolution. However, the rule was repealed in 1844.

Salt-water sailing and the gathering together of those interested in the sport began to spread around the Solent. The Royal Thames Yacht Club took over the hotel at East Cowes from the Royal Yacht Squadron. In 1840, the Royal Southern Yacht Club was founded with a clubhouse in Southampton's High Street. The Club later moved into Bugle Hall, a magnificent building that still stands by the old Wool House, the latter now the Southampton Maritime Museum. The Royal Southern was interested in the development of the Solent racing classes and this provided a stimulus for other clubs around the Solent.

The Royal London Yacht Club was instituted in 1838, originally as the Arundel Yacht Club, as members sailed from Arundel Stairs on the north bank of the Thames below the Strand. Like the Royal Thames before them, they made best use of London's river. They changed their name to the London Yacht Club, becoming "Royal" in 1849 at the behest of Queen Adelaide, "Royal Adelaide", the widow of William IV. In her well written and amusing history of the club, Bernice Slater quotes Field:

"There is no doubt that what may be termed a "middle class club" was required at Cowes........A great many yacht owners visit Cowes during the season, who no more hope or desire to be invited inside the R.Y.S. Castle than they do inside the Sultan of Morocco's harem."[10]

The "Red Squadron" was a nickname given to the Royal Victoria Yacht Club, founded in 1846. Ryde was the ideal place for yacht racing, being under the lee of the Island. George Ackers, Commodore of the Royal Victoria, was an ingenious man. He invented Ackers Timescales for Racing. These were generally in use until the Yacht Racing Association (now the Royal Yachting Association) came into being. He also designed a set of signal flags which, like the Royal Yacht Squadron's, were in general use until replaced by the International Code of Signals.

Solent yachtsmen must have looked on with interest on the 31st July, 1851 when the schooner *America* worked her way through the yachts, on her way to Cowes. "Like a rattle snake, she sneaked along", observed *Bell's Life*. *America* was there with a purpose, to display the superiority of her country in matters of naval architecture, construction and sail making, as part of Prince Albert's Great Exhibition that year. The Commodore of the New York Yacht Club, John Stevens, was blunt. He sent his challenge to the papers.

"The New York Yacht Club, in order to test the merits of the different models of the schooners of the Old and New World, propose through Commodore Stevens to the Royal Yacht Squadron to run the yacht America against any number of schooners belonging to any of the yacht squadrons of the Kingdom, to be selected by the Commodore of the Royal Yacht Squadron."[9]

The Earl of Wilton, the Commodore of the Royal Yacht Squadron, issued a slightly different challenge, for his Committee had decided to offer a cup of £100: "open to yachts of all nations, to

Lord Belfast's five yachts between 1825-1834: Therese (121 tons),
Harriet (96 tons), Louisa (139 tons), Emily (33 tons), and
Waterwitch (331 tons)

William. J. Huggins c.1834

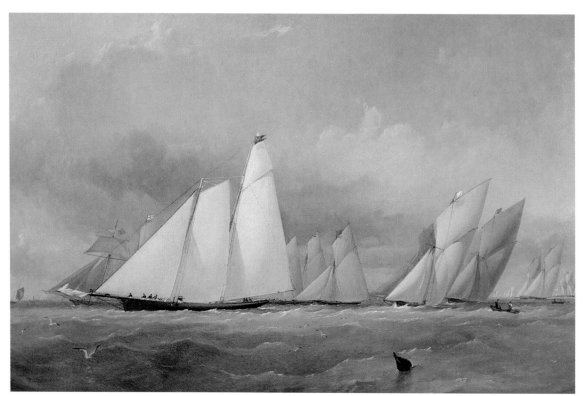

The schooner 'America' (170 tons) off Cowes, 1851

T.S. Robins

160

be sailed for under the sailing regulations of the Royal Yacht Squadron round the Isle of Wight."
[11] The race attracted fifteen starters along with three other yachts that entered but did not start. In those days, yachts were moored, in this case in two lines, north and south. On the starting gun at ten o'clock, most had weighed and were under way within half a minute. *America* was the last but she soon made up for this. A contemporary writer remembered:

"No foam, but rather a water jet rose from her bows and the greatest point of resistance, for resistance there must be somewhere, seemed to be about the beam, or just foreward of her mainmast, for the seas flashed off her sides at that point every time she met them; while the cutters were thrashing through the water and sending the spray over their bows, and the schooners were wet up to the foremast, the America was as dry as bone."[9]

Arrow went aground, the *Alarm* retired and *Aurora* was her only serious rival but she finished far astern. Lord Angelsey was so amazed by *America*'s performance that when invited to a party on board, could not resist leaning over the stern to see if she had a propeller. He was saved from falling overboard by Commodore Stevens who managed to seize his Lordship's wooden leg.

The impact on Cowes and the yachting world in general was volcanic for three reasons. Experts attributed her success to her beam being widest as far aft as her foremast, her hollow bow, and the fact that her sails were laced to her spars. *America*'s victory created publicity for Cowes. *The Times* and the *Illustrated London News* devoted many column inches to the event. The schooner's victory stimulated yacht racing and a call for shore side services. Shipwrights, riggers and sail makers were increasingly required.

We can now look back and see that *America*'s win and the advent of the America's Cup was the beginning of modern yachting. The great advances that we see today stem directly from her early example.

The beginning of the boom in yachting and yacht racing provided a demand for yacht skippers and yacht hands. The Itchen ferrymen provided a reservoir of experience. Fishermen from Itchen village found employment on yachts in the summer and went fishing in the winter. This pattern of employment for yacht hands went on until the early 1960's on the Hamble River. The Itchen Ferry cutter also took to fishing, after its original employment ceased. The owners of the cutters used to race the boats, encouraged by the prospect of winning silverware from the early Solent yacht clubs. Yachtsmen bought or copied these little cutters, usually between 22 and 28' overall, which were important in this competitive scene. Racing was encouraged by the Royal Southampton Yacht Club, founded in 1875, the Royal Portsmouth Corinthian Yacht Club, established in 1880, the Royal Albert Yacht Club that came into being in Southsea in 1864 and the Castle Yacht Club at Calshot, organised in 1887.

Calshot Castle, Headquarters of the Castle Yacht club from 1887

George Gregory 1890

Owners of larger yachts, who had previously relied on a skipper to helm and command, started taking the helm themselves. They were not averse to pulling on a rope either. Lord Dunraven remembered that he had to choose between the violin string and tarry hemp. He chose to go sailing. The "Corinthian Spirit", as owner participation came to be called, came from America in the middle of the 19th century and was incorporated in the title of yacht clubs such as the Royal Portsmouth Corinthian (1880) and the Royal Corinthian Yacht Club (1872). The Marquess of Ailsa was a notable exponent of the owner becoming a seaman. He raced in the Clyde and in the Solent. His real yachting fame came from helming to victory his two yachts *Bloodhound* and *Sleuthhound*. *Bloodhound's* mast now does duty on the Royal Yacht Squadron battery displaying a flurry of flags from the yard during racing from the Castle.

'Bloodhound' - owned by the Marquis of Ailsa. The yachts' mast is now within the Battery in front of the Royal Yacht Squadron and flies the Squadron flags and signals.

Photo: Beken of Cowes

Originally, small racing boats were divided into classes by overall length - under 21′, under 25′ and under 30′. This was replaced in 1887 by the Linear Rating Rule. Initially there were two and half, five and ten raters, but the rule and length changed in 1896, when two more rates were added - the half and the one rater. The advent of the "rater" brought fame to yacht designers. Nathaniel Herreshoff, the American yacht designer, introduced the fin keel and Charles E. Nicholson of Gosport responded with faster and faster boats. William Fife, who had built *Bloodhound* and *Sleuthhound* for Lord Ailsa at Fairlie on the Clyde, turned his hands to the "rater" and like a lot of his successful designs, these came south. They were all good looking, for Fife's motto was that a yacht had to be "eye sweet". Good looks and the idea that "what looks right is right" was to be the hallmark of both the Herreshoff and the Fife designs.

Strange sails began to appear. In the race between *Niobe*, designed by Hatcher in Southampton, owned by Mr. Gordon, and *Sphinx*, belonging to Herbert Maudesley, *Niobe* set a billowing sail that was labelled a "Ni-ob", taking the name of his boat. Maudesley followed suit with another version of this triangular running sail. The Itchen Ferry crews called the sail a "Sphinxer". Dixon Kemp, the great Victorian small boat designer and author, labelled it a spinniker, which soon changed to the modern name. Sails in those days and, indeed, up until the late 1960's, were principally made of cotton canvas and could not be put away wet or they would have gone mildewy and lost their strength. Drying sails is now a forgotten chore, in the age of artificial fibres.

In 1906, the first International Rule came in for smaller classes, and through this the six metre and all the other metre boats arrived. The six metre, which had the characteristics of a larger yacht, became the classic racing boat.

Such was the enthusiasm for "racing round the buoys" that during the summer and well into the autumn there was hardly an occasion when a white sail could not be seen off Cowes and other mainland and Island towns. Each year there was a Ryde Week, a Yarmouth Week, and a Lymington Week, hosted by local yacht clubs. Some of the clubs were founded late in the 19th and early 20th centuries, but have grown in importance, such as the Royal Lymington, founded in 1920. One of the most remarkable clubs, providing summer and winter racing for the many, is the Island Sailing Club, based in Cowes. Formed in 1889, the club specialises in small boat sailing and organises the "Round the Island Race". The Island, as it is known, was the idea of General Charles Baring, a keen sailor in spite of losing his arm in the Crimean War; he lived at Nubia House, Cowes, overlooking The Green. The famous photographer Kirk had his shop and studio at 67 High Street, until it was burnt down, and the General purchased the site, together with the land running down to the river, where the club is now based.[13]

Cowes Roads became celebrated for the racing, which could be viewed with great excitement from The Parade, the Royal Yacht Squadron Battery and The Green. The sight of large yachts thundering towards you as they tacked down to Egypt Point, flying before the wind under spinnaker before crossing the Cowes Yacht Club lines, was a sight to be remembered. The cries of "starboard" or "water", sometimes decorated with one or two other words, could be heard through the thunder of flapping sails. The smell of salt-water, seaweed and, during Cowes Week, a whiff of coal smoke and hot oil from steam launches, was all part of the scene.

The large steam yachts provided the back drop. In "The Week", they were anchored right down to Egypt in the west and toward Osborne Bay in the east. Their launches dropped guests on The Parade, at the various steps, including those of the Royal Yacht Squadron. Launches hung on to Victoria Pier on the Parade (now demolished), when the ferries allowed, waiting for their charges. The mix of sail and steam provided some of the finest scenes of yachting activity to encourage the artist's brush or the photographer's talents.

Queen Victoria's purchase of old Osborne House from Lady Isabella Blachford in 1845, gave great encouragement to the yachting scene. The Royal Yacht, *Royal Charlotte*, had been built at Woolwich in 1824 and "taken to pieces" in 1832. She was succeeded by the first *Victoria & Albert*, a paddle wheel steam yacht with sails, one funnel and two masts. She was not commissioned until 1843. The Queen and Prince Albert required a taxi to take stores, carry Royal despatches, courtiers, "cabbages and Kings". *Fairy*, launched in 1845, made a speed of over 13 knots and discharged her passengers and cargo occasionally at the jetty in Osborne Bay, but

Entrance to Southampton Water

William Frederick Mitchell 1867

Cowes Road with the Earl of Crawford's Valhalla, (1490 tons)   *Charles Dixon 1899*

more usually Trinity Pier, East Cowes. She was described as the tender to the *Victoria & Albert*, but really spent most of her time serving Osborne House. *Fairy* was succeeded in this task of tender by the royal yachts *Elfin* and *Alberta*. The three yachts had clipper bows and counter sterns inspired by the clipper ship. The Queen's yachts set the scene, therefore, and inspired some of the most beautiful powered vessels to come alive from a naval architect's board. *HMY Alberta* was, perhaps, the most eye catching of all.[7]

A long line of steam yachts came from the offices of G L Watson of Glasgow. His vessels did much to improve the view from the shore. The habit spread to America and to the *Corsairs* of J Pierpoint Morgan. His third *Corsair*, built in 1899, was one of the most beautiful power yachts ever built. She graced Cowes on a number of occasions. If she had a rival, as far as looks were concerned, it would have been *Nahlin*, one of the last of G L Watson's great steam yachts and his most graceful. *Nahlin* was built for Lady Yule in 1930 and, although she cruised extensively, was seen off Cowes. *Nahlin* was chartered by King Edward VIII to cruise the Mediterranean with

Mrs. Simpson, later the Duchess of Windsor.[8] *Nahlin* may come back to Cowes, for she is in the process of being restored, having slipped from being the Romanian Royal Yacht to a power school ship and then a restaurant on the Danube. The three masted topsail schooner *Sunbeam*, built and owned by Thomas, later Earl Brassey, from 1874 to 1919 had the same clipper form, with a 350 IHP steam auxiliary engine. She was the first yacht to circumnavigate the world. One of *Sunbeam's* cruises which started in 1876, was described by Mrs Brassey in her published log, *Sunshine & Storm in the Far East*, which ran to several editions.

HMY Alberta   *Photo: Beken of Cowes*

166

Nahlin

Photo: Beken of Cowes

Lady Brassey died on *Sunbeam* while on a cruise around Australia in 1887. Lord Brassey became the Governor of Victoria some eight years later. *Sunbeam* was often seen in Cowes Roads.[9] Both Earl Brassey and her subsequent owner, Lord Runciman, were members of the Royal Yacht Squadron.

Lady Brassey did a lot with her books to encourage long distance sailing and exploring distant lands in a yacht. Another amateur sailor and member of the Cruising Club (Royal Cruising Club) who was to have a remarkable affect on small boat cruising was Erskine Childers. Childers was a friend of Walter Runciman, though his boat was a good deal smaller, and he could well be described as a *Corinthian* sailor. In 1896, he sailed his *Marguerite*, or "Mad Agnes", a half deck, 18′, sailing boat from Greenhithe to Cowes and then later on to Poole, returning via the Needles to the Solent.

Sunbeam

Photo: Beken of Cowes

Erskine Childers yacht 'Vixen', owner at the helm - sailing in the Solent   *Le Fann*

In Childers' log he recorded that he *"ran straight on past Cowes, under the lee of the Kaiser's yacht Hohenzollern and German fleet."* He remarked that Cowes was a *"bewildering spectacle.....every sort of anchorage occupied with every size and sort of steam and sailing yacht. The whole edged with English and German battleships, the Hohenzollern conspicuous, the latter a marvellous compound of destructive force and graceful luxury."*[16] Childers cruised to the Baltic in 1897. In 1903, on his return from the Boer War, he published the first spy novel, *The Riddle of the Sands*, the best sailing story in the English language. The saga was based on Erskine Childers' experiences when cruising the North German coast in 1897, in his yacht Vixen.

The Solent, though a starting point for many an epic voyage, has waters of considerable challenge to the competitive sailor. This so called sheltered stretch of water may be whipped into an angry scene by strong winds and fierce tides, especially when opposed to one another. Local knowledge is vital to success and those who possessed the necessary expertise were and are in great demand. Few large yachts were built in the 1880's and in 1892, there were only two boats in the "Big Class", *Iverna*, built for John Jameson, and the first *Meteor*, owned by the German Emperor. The Secretary of the Yacht Racing Association and Yachting Editor of *The Field*, Dixon Kemp, thought *"that no more large racing yachts will be built"*.[17]

Kemp's gloom was soon relieved by the announcement that Lord Dunraven was to build a new *Valkyrie*, continuing his challenges for the America's Cup. The Prince of Wales commissioned G L Watson to design perhaps the most famous of all first class racing yachts, the Royal Cutter *Britannia*. Soon after came the announcement that the American yachtsman, Phelps R Carroll, had asked Herreshoff to design the cutter *Navahoe*. *Navahoe* crossed the Atlantic to challenge the British yachts in 1893, the year *Britannia* was launched. The British fleet was joined by Soper's cutter *Satanita*. The revival of big class racing was dramatic and set the scene that lasted through to 1939, with time off for the Great War.

Britannia's lines were perfection and she continued to turn heads and win cups until George V died in 1935 and she was scuttled. From 1893, out of 635 starts, *Britannia* won 360 prizes, including 231 firsts. Her best year was 1895, when out of 50 starts she gained 40 prizes, 38 being firsts..[18] G L Watson gave her a "spoon bow" that departed from the classic clipper bow or the straight stem of yachts like Dixon Kemp's *Zoraida*, built at Blackwall on the Thames in 1888 and still afloat, as a houseboat, in Wootton Creek. As the clipper bow faded for racing yachts, so did the ginger bread work on the trail boards, leaving only the cavita line scored into the hull below the bulwarks to emphasise the sheer and draw the eye fore and aft. Some makers left their mark at each end. William Fife rejoiced in a carving of a dragon, tongue out. The first dragon may

Royal cutter 'Britannia'   *Photo: Beken of Cowes*

have decorated the yacht of the same name, and as she was successful, the idea was repeated and became Fife's celebrated mark.[15]

Racing flags were a part of the heraldry of yacht racing. The Prince of Wales' was blue on the hoist, red on the fly - half and half - with his feathers centred, half on the blue, half on the red. Before the First War, flags of the larger classes appeared on the racing programme so that people armed with binoculars on the shore could discover the yachts names and owners. Burgees, ensigns and racing flags also decorated the pages of *Lloyd's Register of Yachts*, first published in 1878 and so continued annually, with breaks for the two wars, until 1980. The racing flag came down, so to speak, in the early 1970's, along with the burgee, the latter sadly demoted to the starboard crosstree. The cause was the "broccoli", or electronic gadgetry sprouting from the top of the mast. A few clubs, such as the Royal Yacht Squadron and the Royal Cruising Club, required their members to continue to fly their burgees properly and owners overcame the problem with a longer burgee stick. The racing flag slowly disappeared in favour of battle flags hoisted on the forestay when the day was done. After the 1960's, when the Solent became more and more crowded, an International Code Flag fluttered from the backstay to advertise the racing class. Flag etiquette began to suffer too about this time, with sailors less proud of their bunting, wearing privileged ensigns without the necessary burgee and leaving the ensign to flutter until the fly was frayed and colours faded. The smart Sunday ensign, often made of silk in the old days, all but disappeared. Another casualty that followed the loss of the racing flag was the end of season photograph of the yacht under sail, decorated with a string of racing flags indicating the number of prizes won during the season. The only colour left today is the spinnaker and pop art on the hull.

The First World War broke with the invasion of Belgium on the Monday of Cowes Week in 1914. The Kaiser's brother had already arrived in Cowes. The Kaiser's yacht, *Meteor*, enroute to Cowes, slipped away in tow of a German destroyer. However, Frau von Krupp's schooner *Germania* was captured and secured in Southampton (now a protected wreck off the Florida coast).The ferries for the Island ceased, resuming under a war schedule. An enterprising

West Solent restricted class sloop 'Jade' owned by Air Commodore J C Quinnell.   Photo: Beken of Cowes
Her string of racing flags indicate that in the 1946 season she won 23 firsts,
25 seconds and 5 thirds.

gentleman, who had been denied the use of the ferry, made his way to Lepe, only to be turned back by an armed soldier.

Large yachts, many from Cowes, joined the Yacht Patrol. Some owners were lucky enough to be given command of their own vessel. One of those in charge of seeing whether a yacht was suitable for war service, Captain H S Lecky, observed, *"There is very little that is delicate about the best yachts except their appearance."*[19] Everything began to go grey, and for those on the Solent shore who were used to seeing the sails of the huge "J" Class racing yachts, the shining white hulls and buff funnels of powered craft, the colours of the "proper" yacht, it looked as if the "closing down sale" had begun.

In Cowes and the little ports around the Solent, the boat building yards were converted to do war work, causing a break in fitting out the larger classes of yachts until after the war. However, the pause gave pride of place to the six metre class, which was boosted by the British American Cup, started in 1921. This competition was quickly followed by the Seawanhaka Cup for individual sixes.

The twelve metres revived and the class forwarded the yachting career of the celebrated aircraft designer and builder T.O.M. Sopwith. His skill and enthusiasm led to greater things with his two challenges for the America's Cup in *Endeavour* in 1934 and in *Endeavour II* in 1937. His first challenge came as near as any British competitor to success in recapturing the America's Cup.

Meteor III & Germania' racing   Photo: *Beken of Cowes*

'Endeavour' owned by T.O.M Sopwith, designed by Chaules Nicholson   Photo: *Beken of Cowes*
and a challenger for the America's Cup in 1934

The event of most moment in yachting between the two wars was the formation of the then Ocean Racing Club. The Club was determined to have an event that would rival the Bermuda Race. As a result of this, the 600 mile Fastnet Race was born. The first race was on a course from Ryde, around the Fastnet Rock, to finish at Plymouth. The memorable first race, in 1926, was won by Commander E G Martin in the converted Le Havre pilot cutter *Jolie Brise*. The following year, the start of the Fastnet was moved to Cowes. The event was the fore runner of what became known as "ocean racing". The sport took thousands of people to sea under the blue burgee with a white seahorse of the Royal Ocean Racing Club.

The big class did revive after World War I, and the most celebrated races were between the King's cutter *Britannia* and the great Herreshoff schooner *Westward*, owned by T B F Davies and skippered by Alf Diaper, one of the most famous Solent yacht skippers. Davies was a rough diamond and a very able sailor. He had a full command of the English language, and some words not usually included in the dictionary! One day King George V carried *Westward* beyond the mark by having an overlap and preventing the great schooner from going about, until the King chose his moment. *Britannia* could achieve the manoeuvre in short order, but for *Westward* it was a different matter. She soon fell far behind. At dinner that evening aboard the Royal Yacht, the King asked Mrs Davies what her husband had said during the incident. Mrs Davies replied diplomatically, "Nothing unusual Your Majesty". Those who saw *Westward* running before the wind under full sail never forgot the sight. Sadly, following the example of the King's cutter, *Westward* was scuppered on the death of T B F Davies. So ended the rivalry between two of the finest yachts ever built. The fierce competition is best illustrated by the story told by John Nicholson, the son of the great designer Charles E. Nicholson. The King summoned the latter to Buckingham Palace to ask his advice and remarked, "Whatever we do to improve Britannia, we must beat that damned schooner."[20]

"Yachting" was giving way to "sailing" for the small one design classes which gained strength after the First World War. The "X" Class, designed by A. Westmacott and just over 20' overall, was launched in 1908. The Royal Lymington Yacht Club took a great interest in promoting this class, which has continued to the present day, for they now number 194. Another

Schooner 'Westward' owned by T B F Davies   *Photo: Beken of Cowes*

Royal Lymington and Berthon Boat Company one design was the West Solent Restricted Class. These had the air of a miniature eight metre and it was also possible to cruise in them. West Solent's were just over 34' in length and were one of the first of the cruiser/racers. However, the class did not survive as a Solent class beyond the early 1960's. The Berthon Boat Company, formerly Inman & Co and before that G Inman & Son, is one of the oldest boat yards in the Solent. The combination of yard and club made Lymington the western centre of Solent yachting.

Colonel John Moore-Brabazon, later Lord Brabazon of Tara, used his Redwing *Tara* to experiment with a novel form of propulsion. Fascinated by the auto gyro, he fitted a similar rotor on his yacht, a leap of faith in a class that was first established in 1896. He found the yacht performed well to windward, better than that achieved using the original rig. Unfortunately, the concept had a spectacular end which discouraged Brabazon and others. The yacht was moored in Cowes Roads when one of the crew let go the controls for the rotor, which spun wildly, in Force 5 driving the little boat into others, the rotor doing spectacular damage.[21]

Experimentation continued with other craft and the Solent Waters were churned up by racing power boats. The Hon Ernest Guinness bought a First World War high speed motor boat, *Oma*. Although she already had three engines, he was determined she should go faster and installed a 450 hp Napier-Lion engine that drove an aircraft propeller on the stern, adding satisfaction, but only three knots in speed.

In August 1939, the clouds of war were gathering when the public assembled on The Green, which had been given to Cowes by G.R. Stephenson in 1863, to watch the start of the Fastnet Race. The race was won by the then Ikey Bell's yawl *Bloodhound*, built to the 12 metre rule by Camper & Nicholson. After the war, *Bloodhound*, then owned by Sir Miles Wyatt, became one of the most famous ocean racers. Her fame continued, for the dark blue yawl was used for cruising when the property of the Duke of Edinburgh.

A number of Cowes yachts played a strong part in the war. For example, the Duke of Westminster's *Cutty Sark*, an ex First World War "S" Class destroyer was bound for St Nazaire with a party of Royal Engineers aboard to blow up the harbour, but was damaged in Raz de Seine. *Narcissus*, along with other yachts, took part in the Dunkirk evacuation and rescued hundreds of troops before hitting a mine. *Philante*, owned by Tom Sopwith, which played a strong part in the America's Cup challenges by towing the two *Endeavour*'s across the Atlantic, escorted convoys in the build up to the invasion of North Africa.[8]

Photo:
Beken of Cowes

Philante was owned by T.O.M., later Sir Thomas Sopwith. She towed the two Endeavours across the Atlantic for the 1934 and 1937 America's Cup Challenges and in World War II escorted convoys in the build up to the invasion of North Africa. Philante is now the Norwegian Royal Yacht 'Norge'.

In May of 1942, Cowes suffered the worst air raid of the War. On the 12th August of that year, the Royal Yacht Squadron Castle, together with other Cowes buildings, were commissioned as HMS Vectis. Later in 1942, the Castle became the headquarters of "J" Force, under the command of Captain John Hughes Hallett, who was awarded the DSO in the Dieppe Raid. Also taking part in the Dieppe Raid were three of the fleet of Free French sumarine chasers which were stationed from 1941 at what is now the UKSA at Cowes and which did so much to contribute to the protection of our coasts and convoys. Serious damage was again done to Cowes on the night of the 15th/16th May, 1944. A string of bombs exploded just west of the Castle, one on the lawn, and others on the Promenade, with a few in the sea.

In the Solent Waters, the gallant little *Campeador*, as her crew were labelled by *The Times* (23rd July 1940), was blown up by a German magnetic mine on the 22nd of June 1940. On board was her owner, Temporary Lt V W McAndrew, RNVR who was killed. There were only two survivors. The wreck lies half way between Ryde Pier and Old Castle Point, a silent reminder of the part Solent yachts played during the Second World War.[22]

Photo:
V W McAndrew

The 'Gallant little Campeador', sunk 22nd June 1940 between Ryde Pier and Old Castle Point

The spectacle of the invasion fleet gathering in the Solent will never be forgotten by those watching from the shore. King George VI took the salute from the Royal Yacht Squadron Battery at Cowes on the 24th of May 1944, the brass cannons glinting in the sun.[23] Within a fortnight, on the 6th June, the invasion fleet was off the coast of Normandy and the crowded Solent anchorage empty. Old stagers later remembered that "you could have walked over to the Island on their decks, they were packed so closely together". Incidentally, Prime Minister Winston Churchill wore his yachting cap with the Royal Yacht Squadron badge, on many war time naval occasions. He had become an Honorary Member of the Club when he was the First Lord of the Admiralty in 1911, retaining his membership until his death. Churchill's image is embroidered on the Overlord Tapestry displayed in the D-Day Museum, Portsmouth.

Soon after peace returned, the sport of sailing was given great encouragement by the presentation of a Dragon Class yacht, *Bluebottle*[19] to the Duke and Duchess of Edinburgh by the Island Sailing Club in April 1948 . The Dragon Class led the re-birth of "round the buoys" sailing in the Solent. The Duke of Edinburgh encouraged the renewal of interest in international yacht racing after the War by his presentation of a challenge cup to be competed for by Dragons belonging to any nation. His friendship with another great competitive yachtsman, Uffa Fox, who was accepted by many as the uncrowned "king" of the Isle of Wight, was a further catalyst to

'Bluebottle' - presented to the Duke and Duchess of Edinburgh by the Island Sailing club in 1948

Photo: Beken of Cowes

Solent sailing. Uffa Fox had started building dinghies, including the famed 14′ international, on an old chain ferry up the Medina River before the Second World War. From Uffa's drawing board came the "Flying 15", so bringing the keel class to the dinghy sailor. The most famous of that class was *Coweslip,* built in 1949 and presented by the people of Cowes and East Cowes to the Duke of Edinburgh. The class flourished, but her sister classes, the Flying 10, the Flying 25 and the Flying 50 did not succeed in the same way.

The West Solent Restricted Class was revived in 1946, followed quickly by the Six Metres. Colonel R G J Perry won a Silver Medal in this class at the Helsinki Olympics in 1952. This renewed interest in yacht racing culminated in the 1958 challenge for the America's Cup by Hugh Goodson and a Royal Yacht Squadron syndicate in *Sceptre*. It was a brave effort, but she was soundly beaten by the American Defender *Columbia*.

Captain John Illingworth, Royal Navy, yacht designer, with his ultra light, reverse sheer, *Myth of Malham,* won the Royal Ocean Racing Club's Fastnet Race in 1947 and 1949. Illingworth brought new ideas and new blood to ocean racing. He was a minimalist when it came to gear brought aboard. More than two pairs of socks were frowned upon, because they were unnecessary weight.

In contrast, weight, along with power and seaworthiness were the essential requirements for off-shore power boat racing. The event that did most to improve the performance of small, fast boats on salt-water was the *Daily Express* Power Boat Race, the brain child of Max, later Sir Max Aitken. This race began in 1961. The exposure of small boats at high speed to rough water led, in fits and starts, to the creation of an all weather, high speed hull form. This concept came to a very successful conclusion, for example in the Royal National Lifeboat Institution's 52′, 18 knot Arun Class lifeboat.

The feats of Sir Francis Chichester were responsible for many new challenges. The Single Handed Trans-Atlantic Race in 1960 led to the OSTAR event. Renewed interest in long distance sailing and racing came in the wake of Sir Francis' solo round the world event in 1966/67, which, in turn, led to the Whitbread Round the World series that began in 1973.

Start of the Whitbread Race   Photo: Beken of Cowes

Sir Owen Aisher with his series of yachts named *Yeoman* and Sir Ted Heath with his *Morning Cloud*s provided a major boost to the sport of ocean racing that went far beyond the Solent, culminating in Ted Heath winning the Sydney-Hobart in 1969. This growing interest led to the Admiral's Cup International Team event, organised as part of Cowes Week every two years and including the Fastnet. These are held in Cowes Week in "on" years when many more yachts attend.

Changes in the pattern of yacht racing were in the offing and responded to a new work and social imperative. The "big bang" in the City and its effect on business throughout the Kingdom meant the office desk became an anchor and long weekends necessary for off-shore racing were no longer available, except for owners prepared to pay their crews. The professional skipper and crew again became part of the scene. As yachts became lighter, faster and with taller rigs, crews were required to balance the boat by sitting with their legs outside the hull on the weather side. This may have been acceptable for "round the buoys", but it was not a side of the sport of ocean racing that generally appealed. Another problem was family responsibilities. It was no longer acceptable to push off on Friday and return on Tuesday. "Round the buoy" racing, to a degree, avoided these conflicts.

As a result of the great expansion in yacht racing, the clubs in Cowes came together to improve their organisation. Since 1964, Cowes Week has been run by Cowes Combined Clubs. Further changes in the organisation and profile of the sport of yachting have come with the increasing importance of sponsorship, initially for Round the World events, but now spreading throughout the racing calendar. Sponsors became more and more important and yachtsmen began to understand that this was not philanthropy, or entirely driven by an interest in their activities on the water. It was good business, giving high profile to the sponsors. Advertisements began to appear on the hulls of yachts and even below the Battery of the Royal Yacht Squadron. Cowes Week became a major sponsorship opportunity.

Although foreign yachts had visited these shores before, international yacht racing really began in Cowes with the victory of the "low, black schooner" *America* over all comers in the race round the Island in August, 1851. In the 150 years since 1851, the intense competition for such prestigious international trophies such as the America's Cup, the Whitbread Round the World Race and the Daily Express Offshore Power Boat event has contributed many advances in design, materials and gear. Off-shore racing yachts like *Mari-Cha* recorded speeds up to 26 knots when surfing, while reaching or before the wind. New materials meant sails no longer had to be dried after racing and running rigging no longer required storing with care to ensure strength and life. Navigation was aided by electronic gadgetry and positions at sea could be fixed exactly. Way Points entered the language. There was competition for the waters of the Solent with large, commercial vessels and cruise ships.[21] Many of the problems were eased by good co-operation between the Royal Navy, Associated British Ports and the Solent Cruising & Racing Association. The latter was founded in 1895. The Solent Forum also brought all Solent users together, in order to understand and discuss current and future problems and opportunities.

The Royal Yacht Britannia & commercial shipping and sailing in the Solent   *Photo: Beken of Cowes*

In August 2001, there will be the largest ever gathering of yachts in the Solent on the 150th anniversary of the race for what was to become the most famous trophy in the history of yachting - the America's Cup. This Jubilee event will pay tribute to the start of international competitive yacht racing. The event will celebrate the past glories of yachting, with participants which include those large yet elegant yachts of the Edwardian and between the Wars eras, the "J" class and the 12 metres. It will showcase the latest in yachting technology here in these Solent waters which have seen such striving for improvement since the Yacht Club was first established in 1815. We shall recognise, too, the part these enclosed and challenging waters have played in producing our young sailors for other great events, including our successes on the water at the Olympics. The Solent has truly been the cradle of yachting.

Bibliography

1. Anon. 1907, *'British Yachts & Yachtsmen,'* The Yachtsmens Publishing Company, London.
2. John Keymer. 1664, Pamplet, printed in London.
3. R.C. Latham & W. Matthew (Ed). 1995, *'The Diary of Samuel Pepys,'* Vol. 1 (1660) Harper Collins, London.
4. Captain Greenville Collins. 1693, *'Great Britain's Coasting Pilot,'* W&J Mount and T. Page, London.
5. David Lyon. 1993, *'The Sailing Navy List,'* Conway, London.
6. Michael Cousins & Patrick Eyres. 1995, *'Naumachia, the Parkland Phenomenon of Mock Naval Battle,'* New Arcadian Journal, No. 39/40.
7. Charles Percy Jones. 1930, *'History of Lymington,'* Chas. T. King, Lymington.
8. Ian Dear. 1985, *'The Royal Yacht Squadron 1815-1985,'* Stanley Paul, London.
9. Montague Guest & William Boulton. 1903, *'The Royal Yacht Squadron,'* John Murray.
10. Spencer Herapath. *'The Royal Yacht Squadron,'* The Field, 20th November, 1976.
11. Bernice Slater. 1988, *'The Royal London Yacht Club 1838-1988,'* The Royal London Yacht Club, Cowes.
12. Douglas Philips Birt. 1974, *'The History of Yachting,'* Elm Tree Books, Hamish Hamilton, London.
13. J.C. Damant. 1989, *'The Island Centenary Edition 1889-99,'* Island Sailing Club, Cowes.
14. Erik Hofman. 1970, *'The Steam Yachts,'* Nautical Publishing Company, Lymington.
15. May Fife McCallum. 1988, *'Fast and Bonnie,'* John Donald Publishers Ltd., Edinburgh.
16. Maldwin Drummond. 1985, *'The Riddle,* Nautical Books' (Conway Maritime Press Ltd), London.
17. Ian Dear. *'Dixon Kemp, Yachting's Greatest Authority,'* Classic Boat, March, 2000.
18. John Irving. c.1938, *'The King's Britannia,'* Seeley Service, London.
19. J.B. Atkins. 1939, *'Further Memorials of the Royal Yacht Squadron,'* Geoffrey Bles, London.
20. John Nicholson. 1970, *'Great Years in Yachting,'* Nautical Publishing Company, Lymington.
21. Lord Brabazon of Tara. 1956, *'The Brabazon Story,'* Wm Heinemann Ltd, London.
22. Cecil Hunt. 1941, *'The Gallant Little Campeador,'* Methuen & Co. Ltd., London.
23. Martin Doughty. 1994, *'Hampshire & D Day,'* Hampshire Books, Hampshire County Council.

Chapter Seven
YACHT PHOTOGRAPHY

Mariette (This was taken in 1997 when the lovely craft came over from the U S A)　　　　　　*Photo: Beken of Cowes*

"The way for a yacht to enter your heart, is to sit alone at the helm, through a quiet star covered night and let her do the sailing, with just a whisper of wind to fill the sails and give her a gentle ripple at the bow. The hours merge into time, and the dawn is an intrusion on something so rare."

I would like to meet the person who wrote that; to me, it says everything there is to know about sailing, and it is my work (and joy) to try and record these moments in time and freeze them forever on film.

The first thing, in our work, is to know your subject. A yacht is a living thing, it has voluptuous curves, it has power and yet delicacy - it has majesty. In the lightest of airs, it moves swanlike, without effort or noise, as if plucked by magnetism. Everyone is different, just as every hour of the day, with changing sunlight, changing winds and variable seas. On deck the crew very often are poised to resemble a ballet and at other times project a scene of passionate men in battle with the sea.

My father, Frank Beken, had the good fortune to have lived in the period of the early 1900's with all those beautiful gaff rigged yachts like the *Royal Britannia*, the *Valkyries*, the great schooners *Westward, Cecily, Meteor*'s of the Kaiser, and all the *Shamrocks* of Sir Thomas Lipton. What wonderful yachts, and what a challenge. To meet this challenge, as a marine photographer, one must know one's subject material. Frank Beken, myself and now Ken Beken, know all about the art of sailing, it having been their main sport. One automatically sees things that would spoil pictures - ropes hanging over the hulls, fenders, sails not hoisted taut, crew in bad positions. One should photograph a yacht as one would photograph one's own debutante daughter, to show her at her best.

Frank Beken, 1880 - 1970   *Photo: Beken of Cowes*

Meteor IV, 1909

The Solent is and always will be a wonderful area for sailing, for racing can be held under any weather conditions and any time of the year, in rough conditions, and courses can either be held in the lee of the mainland, or the island. The ebb and flow of the tide trains helmsmen to pick and choose their course for the next mark, with a close inshore course to stem against that flood tide. It is my contention that the ebb and flow of the tides, the wind variations that can occur, and the fact that one can race or cruise in the Solent area safely, in any weather, will breed a better helmsman and crew, for seamanship is what it is all about.

I recall as a young man in the early thirties racing my 14 ft dinghy close hauled down the Solent, and meeting the Royal Racing Yacht Britannia on the port tack. She graciously came about, giving me right of way.

Ladies Day Race, 1895   *Photo: Beken of Cowes*

Britannia & Westward   *Photo: Beken of Cowes*

Noryema 4   *Photo: Beken of Cowes*

I also remember her later in the year with her deck awash, preparing to gybe all standing, the water cascading off her deck port and starboard like waterfalls as she pulled her spinnaker out on her boom (which was a whole tree in itself). Some sixty years ago I remember Ben Chaplin, a mast headman on one of these great yachts; these men remained about 60 feet up the mast for the whole race in very strong winds force 5-6... they bred tough seamen in those days.

Cowes Weeks with those great yachts were classics. I recall being on the starting line of the Royal Yacht Squadron, with a strong westerly blowing, 10 seconds to go for the start with the schooner *Westward* of 300 Tons, *Britannia*, *Velsheda* and *Endeavour* of the 'J' Class, and *Astra* and *Candida*, all of 120 feet in length with just a few feet between stem and stern close hauled on the Starboard tack. We were in our 25 ft launch (at 6 knots) in amongst them, at the crack of the gun they all came about, the noise was deafening of the jib sheets, the wooden blocks and tackle, as they shot into the eye of the wind and then off on the other tack, with the crews sweating their guts out heaving the sheets in. For us to manoeuvre, photograph at the right angle, and prejudge their movements to take as many photographs as possible was hectic, for in a few minutes they were out of range.

Cameras to be used at sea were limited, and Frank Beken had to invent his big wooden box camera holding a glass plate of 8 x 6 inches in size, and firing off the shutter by biting a rubber bulb. This absolutely revolutionised photographing at sea, every negative becoming very sharp and all horizons level. In earlier days a firm "West of Southsea" took photographs at sea. The negatives were 15 x 12 inches, on similar glass plates, and West used his camera on a tripod, so he must have been on a very stable big boat from which he took his photographs. His collection was finally bought by Frank Beken, for history. There was also another photographer based in Cowes by the name of Kirk, who ceased photographing in 1939. His collection was sold to the general public.

HMS Drake leading the 1st Cruiser Squadron, 1903   *Photo: Beken of Cowes*

HMS Implacable 1903

Photo: Beken of Cowes

America (This was taken in 1997 when the lovely craft came over from the U S A)

Photo: Beken of Cowes

Velsheda (Taken in the Solent in 1997 and reconstructed - new colour etc.)

Photo: Beken of Cowes

As with great artists, composition, light and shade are all important. We depend on the elements critically for results, and yet they are our worst enemy. Rough seas give fine pictures but they cause bad movement of our boat, while rain and of course sea water have also to be dealt with.

At the start of the war yachting of course ceased, and the only vessels to be seen afloat were torpedo boats, destroyers, gun ships of all calibre. Frank Beken had a contract with the Admiralty to photograph all these new vessels built locally in the Solent. This was a great challenge, with some of them travelling at you at 45 knots in all weathers. The old camera withstood the challenge, and all the glass negatives show to this day, 55 years after, a brilliant wartime collection.

Whilst my father was photographing the Naval Vessels, I was operating a 73 ft Vosper launch in the R.A.F. Air Sea Rescue, on one occasion operating from Lerwick in the Shetland Isles. One crash call I shall never forget, being called out to rescue a dinghy from a British crashed aircraft 40 miles off Bergen, Norway. We found them and returned to Lerwick which took us 6 hours, with a Force 7 gale lashing our stern. The Vosper breached continuously, despite all efforts by towing buckets etc to stop it - Man's control of the sea stops at the shoreline.

Back to civilian life in 1945 and returning to Cowes, the old launch was recovered (I was told it was hidden in a haystack during the war,) and once more I went to sea. Yachts were in short supply for a year or two, but as more people came out of the Forces, yachting began to increase. Inevitably as the years went by, designs of yachts changed dramatically, and fibre glass hulls started to increase and take their toll of the classic wooden hulls; the building of marinas in various ports was probably due to fibre glass hull not absorbing water, so that it could stay afloat most of the year instead of the yacht being hauled up and put in storage under cover from September to April.

The speed of colour film started to increase, and I had to design a camera similar to the big box one, but, to take 5 x 4 inch negative, still to be fired by biting a rubber ball. Fortunately the speed of the shutter had been increased to I/400 sec. which cut our boats movement drastically.

As the years went by, we had changes in launches, firstly a Bruce Campbell design and then a Boston Whaler, remarkable for its stability on the water, its speed and also its all round visibility. This enabled us to accept contracts to photograph all the liners from around the world which arrived through the Solent, both in colour and black and white, amongst these was the first nuclear powered ship the *Savannah*.

Glasgow (when the Captain saw the Beken launch he accelerated to get some action!)

Photo: Beken of Cowes

Rendez-Vous - in a sudden gale   Photo: Beken of Cowes

In the mid 1950's the America Cup challenge raised its head. The 12 metre class were the suggested yacht. *Sceptre*, a potential challenger designed by David Boyd, and built in Scotland raced against *Flica, Kaylena Evaine* etc in trials in the Solent. She finally challenged in 1958, but lost the first four races. I photographed the races off Rhode Island, after having my 5 x 4 box camera stripped to pieces by the Customs officer on arrival, for he could not believe it was a camera!

The designs of the yachts racing in the Solent were rapidly modernising, masts becoming taller, booms shorter, and we also had to modernise our cameras. The big black box was put out to grass and the Hasselblad took its place with a shutter speed of I/500th of a second. This together with the speed of the Boston Whaler opened up the potential to obtain more positions to show the yacht in various different angles, both to our benefit, but also to that of the owners, who could study their yacht, and also those of other owners, to see any flaws in hull or sail design. The Admirals Cup races sparked a new breed of designers from around the world, with the racing being so cut-throat that the preceding year's design almost came out of date in the following year.

The great Fastnet races are to us most challenging, with many yachts of lovely design - here is an interesting remark made by a Scandinavian skipper to me -

"We love the Solent area for sailing, for with the great variation in weather patterns in the South of England, it ensures we design a yacht for all weathers, and not one for light or heavy weathers which occur in other parts of the world".

Original first hovercraft

Photo: Beken of Cowes

Carabistouilles (an action shot by Ken in 1999)

Photo: Beken of Cowes

Mercury *Photo: Beken of Cowes*

Kenneth J and Keith A *Photo: Beken of Cowes*

"That is where all the English Lords and Ladies live" -

That was a comment made by a Captain of a Russian Tall Ship to his crew pointing to Cowes. Many years later a Russian Hydrofoil, straight from the Volga paid a visit to Cowes during Cowes Week. It held a cocktail party aboard and half way through, ran out of soft drinks and even water. The inevitable result did more for the Russian/British relationship than the rest of Cowes Week.

Cowes has changed in the last 50 years - and yet it has not, for it has an atmosphere of sailing and welcome that is known and appreciated the world over. The difference between the Solent and other yacht racing venues of the Mediterranean and North European areas is perhaps most marked after the day's racing has finished. Abroad, the crews tend to distribute themselves far afield in various clubs and restaurants. In Cowes Week etc, clubs and restaurants are within a stones throw of each other, parties and dances last well into the early hours of the morning - I remember photographing a certain Class 1 ocean racer the next day with all the crew still in Black tie...

Now in this year of 2000, Maxis will be thrashing their way through hundreds of yachts; the Round the Island Race hopes to have 2000 entries to mark the Millennium. In 2001, the 150th Anniversary of the America's Cup will be celebrated at Cowes. The Solent will be packed with yachts and boats of all types from all over the world for this event, and the Bekens as ever, with their Royal Warrants to Queen Victoria, King George V and H.R.H. The Duke of Edinburgh, will be out there, putting on record for ever these wonderful events.

To all seagoing people, may I quote -

"Adventure on, and if you suffer, swear
That the next adventurer shall have less to bear;
Your way will be retrodden, make it fair."

Chapter Eight
THE SOLENT TODAY

The Solent today is, perhaps, one of the most intensively used coastal areas in the UK. Extending from Hurst Spit to Selsey Bill and including the north coast of the Isle of Wight, it is home to over one million people. Man has long exploited the shores of the Solent for its favourable natural environment; in the past and today its harbours have been important strategic defence locations and this is reflected in the area's rich natural defence heritage. It is also an area of significant economic activity with two major ports and a wide range of other maritime industries. Additionally, it is used extensively by the local population and visitors for recreational pursuits. The Solent is north west Europe's premier yachting location and contains the fourth biggest concentration of watersport activities. Against this background of human use, the natural environment of the Solent retains its importance in a national, European and international context. Over eighty per cent of the Solent's coastline has been designated for its conservation interest; this includes its waders and wildfowl and the habitats and species of its shores, such as saltmarshes and intertidal mudflats. The Solent is unique in that it is an estuarine complex, consisting of twelve estuaries and harbours. The characteristics of these estuaries and harbours vary across the site, but all are interdependent component parts of the overall estuarine complex. With a coastline of approximately 370 kilometres and covering an area of 36,000 hectares (138 miles^2) the Solent is one of the largest estuaries in the UK. The total UK estuarine resource is 530,000 hectares (Solent is fifteen percent).

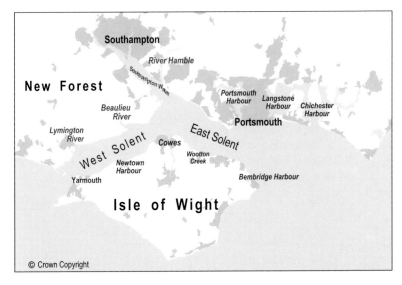

The Solent is an estuarine complex of twelve harbours and estuaries

The River Medina, Cowes and East Cowes and Cowes Roads

The Solent's Economy

The Solent's sheltered natural harbours and inshore waters made it an ideal location for ports to develop. On the mainland, activity centres on the privately owned Port of Southampton and Portsmouth Commercial Port, which is owned by Portsmouth City Council. On the Island, Cowes is the main focus for port activity, being the only location on the Island with deep-water channels capable of handling bulk cargo carrying ships.

The recreational boating industry also has a strong base in the Solent area. Numerous companies provide the services and goods required by the people who participate in recreational boating activities. Every September, Southampton plays host to an international boatshow, and hosts a series of other maritime events such as the BT Global Challenge 'Round the World Yacht Race'. Additionally, the Solent supports other major industrial concerns such as Fawley power station, the adjacent Esso oil refinery and the naval shipbuilding company, Vosper Thornycroft, which is located on the banks of the River Itchen. The area is also a leading centre of excellence in maritime research, providing a home to three academic institutions, all of which have specialist coastal courses and maritime research programmes.

Recreation and the Solent

The Solent has a long association with sailing and yachting and is acknowledged as a site of international importance for boating activity. Yachting events take place throughout the year, with major events such as Cowes Week and the 'Round the Island Race' featuring predominantly in yachtsmen's diaries. It is estimated that around nine hundred yachts participate in the various Cowes Week events. In addition to sailing, numerous other watersports activities have come to the Solent in more recent times. On a fine summer's day, one can see motor and sail boats of all different shapes and sizes, windsurfers, personal watercraft users, swimmers, water-skiiers, divers, surfers, anglers and canoeists all using the waters of the Solent. In addition to the more active recreational pursuits, as in other coastal areas, many people just enjoy coming to the water's edge to admire the scenery, go for a stroll and watch the ships and boats sail past. On a fine Sunday afternoon people of all ages, both locals and visitors, fill the Solent's beaches and country parks as they take in the sea air and appreciate this coastal resource. The value of the Solent to the people that come to visit its shores should not be underestimated.

The Natural Environment

There are twenty-seven Sites of Special Scientific Interest, three Special Protection Areas, three National Nature Reserves and one Special Area of Conservation covering different parts of the Solent and its shores. Its sheltered location along with its complex of estuaries, open inshore waters and coastal and marine habitats provides a haven for many different coastal and maritime plants and animals. It lies at the transition between the warm 'Lusitanian' waters of the western English channel and the colder 'Boreal' waters of the North Sea, which means that many of the species that it supports are at the limits of their natural ranges. This rich wildlife heritage has developed in parallel to the ever increasing human use of the coastal zone over hundreds of years. Although still ecologically important, a combination of increasing human pressures on the coast and sea level rise could mean that the flora and fauna of the Solent find they have no place to go in the future.

Maritime businesses exhibiting their products at the Southampton International Boatshow

The Solent is intensively used for recreational pursuits

Management of the Solent

Fragmentation of responsibility

The responsibility for the planning and management of the Solent lies with numerous authorities. In total there are twenty-six relevant authorities who have statutory duties to manage the various parts of the Solent system. Key authorities include the local and strategic planning authorities, who guide and regulate land use and development down to the mean low water mark. The harbour authorities in the Solent have powers and responsibilities relating to navigation, access, moorings, conservation, pollution control and waste management. Vessels in the Eastern Solent are regulated by the Queen's Harbour Master based at Portsmouth, the Western Solent is currently unregulated and Southampton Water is regulated by Associated British Ports. In addition to the planning and harbour authorities, various competent authorities issue licences and consents to control and regulate the numerous human activities that take place across the site. For example, the Environment Agency is responsible for pollution prevention and control, water resources, flood defence, fisheries, conservation, navigation and recreation and the Sea Fisheries Committees manage and regulate the inshore fishing industry.

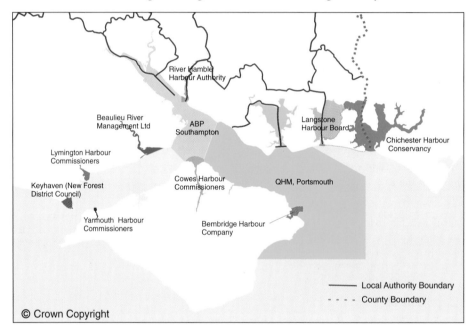

Numerous organisations have statutory responsibilities in the Solent

The need for a co-ordinated approach

With so many different authorities and agencies having management responsibilities across the Solent system, there is a danger that this estuarine complex will be managed in a piecemeal fashion with a lack of co-ordination across the area. Such fragmentation can lead to situations where one activity or interest thrives at the expense of another. The plethora of legislation, which includes European Directives, national laws and local bye-laws compounds the problem. We must remember that the Solent is a natural system, which does not recognise the administrative boundaries drawn up by humans. A management decision taken in one location, for example the construction of a new coastal defence, could impact in a negative way in another location, for example, through exacerbated coastal erosion. The key to successful management is for all the agencies and authorities to take a co-ordinated approach and work together for the benefit of the whole system. The benefits of taking such an approach have become increasingly widely recognised throughout the 1990's. The term 'Integrated Coastal Zone Management (ICZM)' has come to encompass this concept of working together.

The multiplicity of plans in the '90's

A second strand of coastal management throughout the 1990's has been the development of management plans for a wide variety of purposes. There are now over forty management plans covering the Solent and the vast majority of these have been developed over the last ten years (see table 1). This has led to calls of 'plan overload' from some sections of the coastal community and there is now growing support for the rationalisation and integration of some of these plans. The themes of rationalisation, integration and consolidation are likely to dominate coastal management over the next ten years. The plans are driven from a variety of sources. Shoreline Management Plans, Estuary Management Plans and Biodiversity Action Plans are driven by the national agenda. The influence of Europe can be seen in the development of management schemes for European Marine Sites and river basin management plans are looming on the horizon as a result of the proposed EU Water Framework Directive.

Type of Plan	Number in the Solent
Structure Plan/Unitary Development Plan	3
Local Plans	8
Coastal/Estuary Management Plans	11
Shoreline Management Plans and Strategy Plans	6
Biodiversity Action Plans	3
European Marine Sites Management Plans	1
Coastal Habitat Management Plans	1
Coastal Strategies	2
Local Environment Agency Plans	5

Table 1. Examples of management plans covering the Solent

Some of the plans have statutory backing, such as the management schemes for European Marine Sites, others are centrally funded but non-statutory such as Shoreline Management Plans, whereas Estuary Management Plans are both voluntary and locally funded by the coastal community. One of the greatest benefits of the development of management plans has been the bringing together of all those organisations with an interest in the coastal zone. The regular meetings that these plans entail raise awareness and understanding of issues and allow people to meet each other face to face and discuss working in partnership together. This saves on resources, maximises output, facilitates conflict resolution and ensures that the system is managed in a more integrated manner.

Development of a Management Scheme for the Solent European Marine Sites

The development of a management scheme for the Solent European Marine Sites provides a good example of how all the relevant authorities in the Solent need to work together. The scheme will provide protection for the Solent's habitats and species that have been designated under either the EC Birds or Habitats Directives. It will illustrate how the numerous activities that take place in the Solent should be managed to prevent detrimental impacts on the environment. The UK Regulations that transpose these Directives into national law state that there can be only one management scheme for the site and the Solent's relevant authorities have formed a group to work together to develop this scheme. The development of a single scheme of management across the whole Solent reflects the interdependent nature of the habitats and species within the site. Birds do not stop at local or harbour authority boundaries, they may use several sites for feeding and roosting and sediment patterns and movements across the Solent determine the state and location of saltmarshes and mudflats.

The Development of the Standing Conference on Problems Associated with the Coastline (SCOPAC) and the Solent Forum

The need for closer working partnerships within the Solent's coastal community led to the establishment of two coastal fora, the Standing Conference on Problems Associated with the Coastline (SCOPAC) in 1985 and the Solent Forum in 1992. These two groups provide structures for the exchange of ideas and information on the Solent. Both organisations meet regularly to discuss and inform the Solent's coastal community on topical issues affecting the planning and management of the Solent.

SCOPAC

The seeds of SCOPAC were sown at a two day conference entitled 'Problems Associated with the Coastline', organised by the Isle of Wight County Council in April 1985. The Conference addressed a wide range of issues relating to coastal defence and protection and concluded that closer working arrangements were needed amongst the 'Operating Authorities' who have responsibilities for coastal defence along the coast of central southern England. Hence SCOPAC was born and held its inaugural meeting in 1986. After fifteen years, support for SCOPAC and its work is still strong. It organises regular meetings, conferences and seminars, has a website and produces a newsletter. It also commissions extensive research on the natural processes and coastal defence issues in its study area. The success of SCOPAC stimulated the development of similar coastal groups throughout the country and most areas in the UK now have a SCOPAC equivalent.

Hurst Spit - guardian of the Western Solent

SCOPAC is unique among all the current Coastal Groups in that it provides a formal structure, for a body lacking formal powers, through the delegation of action to the elected members from each of its constituent local authorities. This improves public accountability and ensures that statutory support is given to SCOPAC's work. An example of this work is the research study that it is commissioning on climate change. This will review the potential impacts of climate change on the central south coast and the implications, particularly for coastal defence. This provides an excellent example of how working in partnership can deliver real benefits to the organisations who need to manage the coast. Climate change is, perhaps, the biggest issue that the coast faces today, particularly the low lying heavily populated coasts of the South, and the findings of this study will be extremely valuable in helping SCOPAC members to respond to the likely impacts of predicted changes.

Solent Forum

The Solent Forum is a grouping of organisations, which have an interest in the Solent and its management. Formed by a handful of organisations in 1992, it has now grown to eighty members from fifty different organisations. The work of the Forum covers the full spectrum of coastal issues, including the social, economic and environmental pressures on the coast. The Forum meets on a bi-annual basis to discuss topical Solent issues, the meetings cover a wide range of subjects and all organisations are given the opportunity to discuss any concerns that they may have. The Forum is funded by thirteen of the key players on the coast, has one full time Forum officer and an independent Chairman. Although the Solent was one of the first coastal fora to be established, it is not unique in having such a Forum. Many of the estuaries in the UK have similar structures- to the west of the Solent is the Dorset Coast Forum and to the east the West Sussex Coastal Liaison Panel. On a more local level, there are liaison committees, which represent the users of the Solent's component harbours and estuaries.

One of the main achievements of the Forum to date has been the publication of a strategy for the Solent, in December 1997. Entitled 'Strategic Guidance for the Solent' this publication looks at all the issues that affect the Solent today, what the position is, what action needs to be taken and which is the appropriate authority to take that action (see table 2). It provides a holistic overview of the Solent's natural and human systems and attempts to integrate and reconcile conflicts and disseminate and encourage existing best practice. To assist in the implementation of this strategy, it developed five flagship projects that the Forum Officer has been working on for the last three years. Outputs from these projects include: a major science conference held in 1998; a website that gives information on the work of the Forum and its members; regular newsletters and a fact-file on the Solent; training seminars and the collation and distribution of information on all aspects of the Solent. Most important, perhaps, is the vehicle that the Forum provides for the face to face contact of coastal practitioners. Developing personal contacts is key to the success of any form of integrated management.

Table 2. Issues covered in the Strategic Guidance for the Solent

Conservation of the Solent's Heritage
> Landscape and Seascape
> Historic Heritage and Maritime Archaeology
> Nature Conservation

Support for Sustainable Development
> Marine Aggregates
> Oil and gas
> Recreation
> Naval Base and Defence Interests
> Fisheries
> Marine Industry
> Transportation
> Ports and Shipping

Protection of Human Life and the Environment
> Environmental Quality
> Safety
> Emergency Planning
> Coast Protection and Sea Defence

Issues affecting the Solent at the beginning of the new Millennium

Development Pressures

The Solent, like many other coastal areas around the UK, has many human demands placed upon it. For centuries people have lived by the Solent, used it for recreational pursuits and located their businesses adjacent to its shores. Access to the waterside is, therefore, in heavy demand. History shows us that many settlements grew up around the shores of our coast or by the banks of rivers. Humans have also claimed land back from the sea for their use, such as the land reclamation that has taken place for commercial and recreational developments in Portsmouth Harbour and Southampton Water. In the past much of the shores around Portsmouth Harbour were used by the Royal Navy for military purposes. Since the rationalisation of the armed forces, large tracts of prime coastal land have been released and are now

Re-development in Portsmouth Harbour showing the construction of Gunwharf Quays

subject to urban regeneration for housing and recreational purposes. The levels of re-development in Portsmouth Harbour are some of the most significant seen in any of the UK's estuaries. 'The renaissance of Portsmouth Harbour' is the name of the multi-million pound millennium project that has been transforming the harbour's shores in recent years.

There is also pressure for development on the western shores of Southampton Water, by the Port of Southampton, owned by Associated British Ports, which has plans to construct a new container terminal on a site known as Dibden Bay. The existing site of the Port of Southampton all lies to the east of the River Test and these proposals would mean port development on the New Forest coast of Southampton Water for the first time. There are strong arguments both for and against the proposals. Opposition centres on the local impacts that the terminal will have on the New Forest coastline, in particular on the local residents and the site's wildlife interests. Dibden Bay was designated as a Special Protection Area for its European bird interest in 1998. The arguments for development include the provision of jobs for local people and the strategic

Container ship travelling up Southampton Water to the Port of Southampton

importance of the Port of Southampton as a European hub port. As a nation, we all demand the goods that are brought to us by international shipping with little thought as to how they arrived or what the impact of importing them is on the local community. How do we choose whether the needs of the local people and wildlife should override those of the nation as a whole? Inevitably this major proposal will be dealt with at a Planning Inquiry, where each side is given the opportunity to present its case, the final decision being taken by the Secretary of State.

During the late 1980's and early 1990's the Solent's natural attributes made it a focus for the rapidly expanding maritime leisure industry. Demand for marina developments was high and new marinas were constructed, often with associated housing and leisure facilities, such as Ocean Village in Southampton and Port Solent at Portsmouth. However, there was growing concern that the number of developments was having a serious adverse impact on the intertidal areas and the habitats and species that such areas support. In the 1990's, the balance swung in the favour of the protection of the environment. While this is to be welcomed, there are some that will argue that

the balance moved too far in favour of the environment. Local marinas and boatyards can now face significant difficulties in trying to carry out essential work, such as maintenance dredging, that is fundamental to their survival. The bureaucracy and environmental legislation can be bewildering and the cost of employing consultants to undertake environmental assessment prohibitive. Where should the balance be between the needs of the environment and local business? Both are fundamental components of the coastal system and need to learn to co-exist. In this new millennium we need to work towards achieving this balance. This is what sustainable development is all about, the process of getting the environmental, social and economic aspects of the system to dwell side by side; flexibility and give and take is required by each of these aspects successfully to achieve this goal .

Luxury waterside housing at Hythe Marina Village

Coastal defence and flooding

The coastline of the Solent is defended along most of its length, reflecting the substantial urban population and the number of commercial, domestic and industrial properties. A combination of climate change, leading to higher sea levels and more severe weather events (and intensive use of the coastal zone) can result in flooding in vulnerable areas. Low lying estuaries such as the Lymington River are increasingly subject to flooding from both the sea and rivers. The cost of defending people and their property can run into millions of pounds for a single coastal defence scheme, the cost being met predominantly by the taxpayer at present. In the near future we face a situation where the effects of climate change will cause these costs to escalate. There is concern that natural coastal barriers such as Hurst Spit could breach in the future, leading to widespread flooding along parts of the New Forest coast. In the late 1990's, shoreline management plans were developed for the Solent to take a strategic look at how specific coastal units could be defended. Whilst being a welcome start to addressing some of the problems that will arise from coastal flooding, much more work needs to be done. In the long run we may seriously have to accept retreat of parts of the shoreline in the face of natural change. The escalating insurance costs from living or operating a business on the coast may facilitate this inland migration.

Cumulative impact

One concern that has come increasingly to the fore in recent years is the potential cumulative impact of the various proposed developments and activities in the Solent. This is particularly true since the introduction of the Conservation and Natural Habitats Regulations in 1994, which give the relevant authorities in the Solent a statutory duty to assess proposals in the light of existing and future planned developments. In isolation, a particular plan or project may not have a significant impact on the site but in combination a series of developments could cause a substantial loss of coastal habitat. There has been concern on the Isle of Wight over the cumulative effects of offshore marine aggregate extraction. The fears are that, over time, extraction could cause changes in coastal processes, which could exacerbate the coastal erosion problems faced by south Wight. Similarly, on the mainland, English Nature has expressed concern about the cumulative effects of small-scale developments in intertidal areas, such as the construction of new slipways.

In practice local planning authorities face a difficult task in trying to assess what the cumulative effects of new developments will be, particularly when they need to take into account all the planned and existing developments across the whole Solent. There is no comprehensive collection of information on what is happening around the Solent, as data is fragmented between the local planning authorities. To try to resolve this issue the authorities in Portsmouth Harbour are working together to try and obtain a comprehensive picture of the development pressures in the Harbour. The work that is being undertaken will provide a pilot approach that will be rolled out across the Solent and transferred to other parts of the UK.

Challenges for the Next Millennium

This chapter concludes by reviewing what the challenges in the Solent will be over the next millennium. The ongoing focus, as has been the case over the latter half of the last century, is on the balancing of environmental, commercial and recreational interests. Over one million people now live within easy reach of the Solent and recreational pressures can place significant strains at certain 'honeypot' sites. Urban regeneration is a topical issue with the release of Ministry of Defence land in Portsmouth Harbour and surrounding areas. Waterside locations will continue to be sought after by marine businesses and people wanting a 'sea view'. Traffic congestion, although not unique to the coast, is one of the main limiting factors in people being able to obtain access to the Solent's many attractions. The increasing number of different types of watersports and greater participation levels could lead to a greater potential for conflict between recreational users. Perhaps the most significant challenge is how climate change will impact on the Solent, bringing its own set of issues to address and exacerbating current problems.

It is estimated that sea level in the Solent will rise fifty centimetres by 2050. This is a result of a combination of the effects of global warming and the isostatic sinking of Southern England after the last ice age. Much of the Solent's coastal plain is less than 10 metres above sea level and parts of the West Sussex coast are already below sea level. Historically, humans have not only utilised the coastal zone but reclaimed land back from the sea. In the future, it is likely that the sea will try to take back this land along with other areas that are low lying such as river and coastal flood plains. As land is lost and the coastal zone 'squeezed' competition between the various uses will intensify. It is not only rising sea levels that the people, plants and animals of the Solent will need to deal with, but also more extreme events such as winter gales cause flooding and damage habitats, buildings and infrastructure. Living or working on the shores of the Solent in a hundred years time may prove a hazardous and expensive occupation.

The Solent's contours and bathymetry

Those who manage and own land on the Solent's shores will have some difficult decisions to make in future years about how to cope with the impacts of climate change. How do you decide where to defend and who will meet the costs? The current presumption is to protect people and property and the taxpayer currently meets most of this cost, but as costs escalate should those who live or operate businesses by the coast make a contribution to defending their location? There is also the question of recreational and wildlife sites and whether there will be a place for such sites in the future. The coast has great recreational value, but how do you value, hence justify, the spending of large sums of money to protect a coastal footpath instead of building a new hospital? As mentioned earlier in this chapter, over eighty percent of the Solent's coastline is covered by a conservation designation and those who manage the coast have an obligation to conserve these habitats and species. In an ideal world, coastal habitats would migrate inland as sea levels rise, but on much of the Solent's shores this land is not available. Inevitably priorities and choices must be made; it is the coastal planners and managers of today and the future who must make these choices and shape the Solent for future generations.

Over the last ten years, the Solent's planners and managers have begun to put in place the frameworks needed to manage the Solent into the future. Although there is much still to do, we must recognise and appreciate the progress that has been made in coastal management throughout the 1990's. The work of SCOPAC, Solent Forum and numerous other organisations has contributed to the understanding and need to manage the Solent as an integrated unit, if problems such as climate change are to be successfully addressed. The development of Shoreline Management Plans (SMP's) has started to tackle some of the issues about which sections of the Solent should be defended in the future and which should be left to return to the sea. These plans were prepared by a consortium of organisations working together to deliver the best possible options for both the natural and human aspects of the coast.

Delegates on a SCOPAC field study visit, reviewing coastal defence issues in the Solent

We must learn to build on and expand upon the work that has been undertaken in the Solent over the last ten years. Co-ordination and co-operation between all those with responsibilities and an interest in the Solent should, hopefully, help to make the Solent a better place despite the challenges, both natural and human, that lay ahead. By working in partnership let us hope that the state of the Solent at the turn of the next millennium will be one for which the people of that day will be proud of the achievements of their ancestors.

What kind of Solent will we leave for the next generation?

References

Badman, T. and Sisman, K., 1997, *Strategic guidance for the Solent*. Southampton: Solent Forum

McInnes, R.G., 2000, *SCOPAC-Revised Terms of Reference. Newport, Isle of Wight:* SCOPAC

McInnes, R.G., 1994, *A management strategy for the coastal zone.* Ventnor, Isle of Wight: South Wight Borough Council

McInnes, R.G, Jewell, S and Roberts, H., 2000 *European Union LIFE Project on Integrated management of coastal zones.* IW Centre for the Coastal Environment: Newport, Isle of Wight

McInnes, R.G, Jewell, S and Roberts, H., 1998. *Coastal Management on the Isle of Wight, UK.* IW Centre for the Coastal Environment, Newport

McInnes, R.G, Jakeways, J and Tomalin, D., 2000. *European Union LIFE Project-Coastal change, climate and Instability.* IW Centre for the Coastal Environment. Newport, Isle of Wight

Bray, M.J, Carter, D.J, Hooke, J.M and Taussik, J., 1997 *SCOPAC -A Critique of the past- a strategy for the future.* Portsmouth: SCOPAC

New Forest District Council, 1997. *Coastal Management Plan.* Lyndhurst. New Forest District Council.

Inder, A *et al.,* 1991. *A Strategy for Hampshire's coast.* Hampshire County Council: Winchester

Yarmouth and the western Solent

INDEX

Illustrations in bold type

THE UNOFFICIAL COMPLETE ENCYCLOPEDIA OF
Formula One

Dear James,
Happy Birthday!
With lots of love
from Mum & Dad
2018

THE UNOFFICIAL COMPLETE ENCYCLOPEDIA OF

Formula One

MARK HUGHES

FOREWORD BY JENSON BUTTON

LORENZ BOOKS

This edition is published by Lorenz Books

Lorenz Books is an imprint of
Anness Publishing Ltd, Hermes House,
88–89 Blackfriars Road, London SE1 8HA
tel. 020 7401 2077; fax 020 7633 9499
www.lorenzbooks.com; info@anness.com

© Anness Publishing Ltd 2004

UK agent: The Manning Partnership Ltd,
6 The Old Dairy Melcombe Road, Bath BA2 3LR;
tel. 01225 478 444 fax 01225 478 440;
sales@manning-partnership.co.uk

UK distributor: Grantham Book Services Ltd,
Isaac Newton Way, Alma Park Industrial Estate,
Grantham, Lincs NG31 9SD
tel. 01476 541080; fax 01476 541061;
orders@gbs.tbs-ltd.co.uk

North American agent/distributor: National
Book Network 4501 Forbes Boulevard,
Suite 200, Lanham, MD 20706
tel. 301 459 3366; fax 301 429 5746;
www.nbnbooks.com

Australian agent/distributor: Pan Macmillan
Australia, Level 18 St Martins Tower,
31 Market St, Sydney, NSW 2000;
tel. 1300 135 113; fax 1300 135 103;
customer.service@macmillan.com.au

Publisher: Joanna Lorenz
Editorial Director: Helen Sudell
Senior Editor: Sarah Ainley
Text Editor: David Malsher
Editorial Reader: Jay Thundercliffe
Design: Michael Morey
Photography: Sutton Motorsport Images
Indexer: Helen Snaith
Production Controllers: Pedro Nelson
and Ben Worley

1 3 5 7 9 10 8 6 4 2

Contents

Foreword

"I've known Mark since I first came to Formula One in 2000. He's charted the various highs and lows of my career in the pages of *Autosport* with a lot of insight. Here he gives the full story of Grand Prix racing right from the very start up to the present day. There's technical stuff as well as sporting. It's a good read, and hopefully in some future edition it will tell the story of my first Grand Prix victory."

Jenson Button

▼ Jenson Button completed his first season with the BAR-Honda team in 2003 in superb form and led both the final races, in America and Japan.

▲ Jenson Button
at the 2003 German
Grand Prix.

▶ Jenson Button's
BAR-Honda at
Monaco in 2003.

Introduction

It was man's very nature that made motor racing so inevitable. Clever enough to have devised the car, he is intrinsically competitive enough to have then made racing cars a mere formality. The ultimate form of the discipline came to be called Grand Prix racing in 1906, just 11 years into the sport's history, and Formula One Grands Prix are still the pinnacle of the sport today. What also remains, unaltered through over a century, is the essence of the sport. The qualities it demands of drivers, who face the ultimate stakes, and technicians, who experience the most intense of challenges, make it arguably the most majestic of all sporting endeavours.

▼ David Coulthard winning in Australia in 2003.

▼ Kimi Raikkonen celebrates his first Grand Prix win in Malaysia in 2003.

Though latterly it has become more overtly commercial than in the past, that is simply a reflection of the world in which the sport exists, just as the cars have mirrored the level of technological sophistication of the modern industrial world. It shouldn't be forgotten that motorsport was conceived as much with business in mind – by a group of pioneer car manufacturers – as it was for sport. Formula One owes its existence to business, and always has, but the superficial trappings melt away to nothing in the intensity of battle, once the start flag has dropped or the lights have gone out. Between that moment and the chequered flag, the sport exists in its purest form.

▼ The youngest winner: Fernando Alonso at the Hungarian Grand Prix in 2003.

▼ Michael Schumacher takes championship number six.

The History of Formula One

The thread of the sport's lineage is long and sometimes complex. But it is very clearly a thread, a brilliantly vivid one in which heroes have been made, celebrated and – over the decades – largely forgotten. The nature of the sport gives it a here and now intensity, and leaves the past in black and white dusty memory. But revisiting the deeds of the drivers, the manufacturers, engineers and designers can bring their achievements back to life, and lend them their true perspective. Here, we look at the men, the cars and the races that made their mark on history, stretching from the first true motor race in 1895 right up to the present day.

◄ Ayrton Senna's last race. Senna's Williams FW16 follows the safety car at Imola, 1 May 1994.

The Seeds are Sown

Motor racing is very nearly as old as the motor car itself. Karl Benz and Gottlieb Daimler are widely credited with the invention of the car – each had their first petrol-fired prototypes running in 1885 – and within a decade the first significant motor race took place.

In the early years cars did not race round and round, but from place to place. The organizers did not charge an admission fee to watch, and the cars were not recognizably different from those driven as a means of transport. But the sport's essence, to get from the start to the finish against both the clock and each other, was exactly as it has been ever since.

The First Race

Although the car was born in Germany, France can be said to have invented motorsport. The first true race was a contest from Paris to Bordeaux and back, a distance of just over 1190 kilometres (740 miles) on public highways. Twenty-seven vehicles congregated at Porte Maillot in the early hours of 11 June 1895 and, one by one, were sent on their way. Only those in the car – of whom there had to be at least two – were allowed to work on the car during the race, using only those tools carried with them.

The event was devised by a group of pioneer manufacturers with the

▲ Emile Levassor's Panhard-Levassor car in the 1894 Paris–Rouen reliability trial that led to the 1895 race.

idea of publicizing the practicality and speed of the motor car. The winner, Emile Levassor, was a partner in the firm of Panhard et Levassor, an old French engineering company that had recently embraced car manufacture. Levassor's drive was heroic. He had

planned to change over with his relief driver some time before Bordeaux but, finding him asleep at around 3am, decided to continue. In fact, he drove the entire event, and the relief driver became simply a passenger. As he passed each time control still in command of the race, news of Levassor's epic solo performance spread like wildfire and when he arrived back in Paris in the afternoon of 13 June,

▲ Chevalier René de Knyff seated on the Panhard-Levassor car that won the first Paris–Bordeaux race in 1898.

◄ Degrais competing in the Paris–Madrid race of 1903.

▼ Callan is pictured here in his Wolseley motor during the Circuit des Ardennes race, Belgium, 1903.

thousands were there to greet him. With an average speed of just under 24km/h (15mph), he was five hours ahead of the next man. The new sport had its first hero.

The heat of competition fed a technology drive that advanced the car at breakneck speed – to the great benefit of the customers. Pneumatic tyres and the steering wheel were just two of the more obvious advances the sport generated in its early years. By 1901, racing machines were capable of up to 120km/h (80mph). Meanwhile, sales of the motor car soared: France produced 13,000 of them in 1903.

The First Tragedy

The sport's honeymoon period came to an abrupt end later that same year. Millions of spectators lined the route of the Paris–Madrid race in May 1903 to watch in awe the cars that were, by now, powered by monstrous engines of up to 14 litres. It was a tragedy waiting to unfold. Competitors Marcel Renault, Lorraine Barrow, Philip Stead

and two riding mechanics were all killed in various brutal accidents along the route. But the biggest, most unacceptable tragedy occurred in the town of Chatellerault, when a child walked into the road and a soldier ran to pull him clear. Tourand's car hit them, killing both, before veering into the crowd, killing one spectator and injuring many more.

As cars and distraught competitors rested overnight in Bordeaux, the French government stepped in and stopped the race. The silent cars were pulled to a train by horse and transported back to Paris. City-to-city racing was over.

▼ Fernand Gabriel wins the 1903 Paris–Bordeaux race in a Mors that produced 70hp. It marked the end of city-to-city racing.

From Cities to Circuits

T he tragedy of the 1903 Paris–
Madrid race came close to killing
the sport for ever. It was only granted a
reprieve by a saner approach. No longer
would races run through major towns
with big population centres; they would
instead utilize the roads of sparsely
populated rural areas. More critically,
no longer would the races run from
place to place, but instead around
roads comprising circuits, thus making
the routes easier to police.

The New Era of Circuit Racing

The first major event of the new format
had been the 1902 Circuit des Ardennes
in Belgium, ironically the race that
immediately preceded the 1903 Paris–
Madrid. The race comprised six laps
of an 80-kilometre (50-mile) circuit of
public roads through the countryside,
and was won by Englishman Charles
Jarrott in his French Panhard.

The success of the event and the
end of city-to-city racing meant that
the Circuit des Ardennes became the
blueprint for the new era of the sport.
One of the first post-tragedy races run
to this new format was the Gordon

Bennett Cup, held in pre-republic
Ireland in 1903.

Gordon Bennett was a millionaire
newspaper magnate and a vital early
supporter of motor racing. As well as
helping to fund the first races and

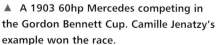

▲ A 1903 60hp Mercedes competing in
the Gordon Bennett Cup. Camille Jenatzy's
example won the race.

giving them the lifeblood of publicity
through one of his publications, the
Paris Herald, he also devised the
competition that made the sport
truly international, and that bore
his name.

The Gordon Bennett series was first
held in 1900. Countries could enter
up to three cars each in the race. From
1903 each country was identified by
the colours of its cars. The winning
nation would host the following year's
event. France dominated initially but,
in winning the 1902 event for Britain
(by virtue of being the only finisher),
Selwyn Francis Edge ensured that the
Royal Automobile Club had to have an
Act of Parliament passed to host the
1903 race in Ireland; racing on the
public highway had always been
forbidden by British law.

Camille Jenatzy won the race for
Mercedes, and thereby took the event to
Germany for 1904. The French industry
didn't take kindly to being beaten in

◀ Christian Lautenschlager was first to
the finish in a Mercedes in the 1908 French
Grand Prix at Dieppe.

what it saw as its own specialist field, and after winning the event in 1904 and being the winning host in 1905, the French declined to stage the event the following year. The Automobile Club de France had instead devised another competition in which no restrictions would be put on the number of entrants a country could provide. The name of this competition was the "Grand Prix". Its lineage continues to this day.

The First Grand Prix

Held at Le Mans in 1906, the inaugural Grand Prix was won by the Renault of Ferenc Szisz, a Hungarian who had previously been Louis Renault's riding mechanic in the city-to-city races. The event was a great success and other countries copied its format, though it would be many years before the term "Grand Prix" was applied to races outside of France. For now, the USA came the closest, with its American "Grand Prize".

For the 1908 event, the Paris-based international governing body of the sport formulated regulations to ensure uniformity from country to country. Motor racing flourished, even surviving a mass pull-out by manufacturers concerned at spiralling costs and the first downturn of sales. As early pioneers such as Panhard and Mors faded, Mercedes remained very much

a central force and was joined by Fiat and Peugeot.

By 1914, on the eve of World War I, the French Grand Prix attracted 13 manufacturers and 33 cars. The race saw an epic fight between the twin-cam 16-valve Peugeot of Georges Boillot and the might of the Mercedes team. Christian Lautenschlager's Mercedes won after Boillot retired on the last lap. The engine of Lautenschlager's car was based on that which would soon be put to use in fighter planes.

▲ Vincenzo Lancia in his Fiat at the very first Grand Prix, held near Le Mans, France, in 1906.

▼ *(left)* The front cover of the French periodical *La Vie au Grand Air* shows Hungarian driver Ferenc Szisz at the wheel. He was the winner of the first recognized Grand Prix held near Le Mans in 1906.

▼ *(right)* Ferenc Szisz in his Renault at Le Mans, 1906. Szisz and the French manufacturer won the race that year.

Boom Between Wars

The armistice period that followed World War I accelerated the pace of technology, and lessons learned there were soon applied in motorsport. Advances made in metallurgy and in understanding the combustion process more fully meant that engine efficiency rocketed. The 1921 Fiat's 8-cylinder motor became the blueprint for racing engines for decades to come.

Grand Prix Racing Spreads

In 1922, the new Monza track near Milan hosted the Italian Grand Prix. This was a purpose-built race circuit – it was the first time a major European race hadn't been held on public roads – and it enabled Grand Prix race promoters to charge spectators an entrance fee for the first time. Soon afterwards, other tracks were built in a similar vein, such as Montlhéry on the outskirts of Paris, and Sitges just south of Barcelona.

Most of the races continued to be run on public roads however, and in order to stop speeds escalating out of control, a 2-litre formula was imposed for 1922. This signalled a parting of the ways between European and American

▲ Rudolf Caracciola in his Mercedes-Benz on his way to winning the 1937 Swiss Grand Prix. German cars now dominated racing.

▼ Luigi Fagioli (Mercedes) passing Soffietti (Maserati) at the 1935 Monaco Grand Prix.

▼ Independent team owners came to the fore from the mid-1920s to early 1930s.

racing which, until this time, had overlapped. The American Duesenberg team had won the 1921 French Grand Prix, while European cars had dominated for a time at the Indianapolis 500. American racing was chiefly conducted on closed tracks, not public roads, and with its wide open spaces, the American car industry was producing passenger cars with ever-bigger engines: the new European 2-litre formula was an irrelevance there.

The Pioneering Teams

Such was Fiat's dominance during the early 1920s that rival manufacturers had to resort to poaching technical staff from Fiat in order to compete. It was in this way that Alfa Romeo and Sunbeam became serious Grand Prix forces, with the former team being advised by one of its drivers, Enzo Ferrari. Sunbeam became the first British constructor to win a Grand Prix, when Henry Segrave triumphed in France in 1923.

The economic downturn of the late 1920s saw manufacturers pull out of the sport and, for a time, wealthy independent team owners formed its backbone, with specialist car companies such as Bugatti and Maserati providing the hardware. It was during this time that Tazio Nuvolari graduated to the sport from motorcycle racing, and created such a sensation that he is still often cited as the greatest driver who ever lived.

Hitler came to power in Germany early in 1933, and he immediately identified Grand Prix racing as a powerful tool in propagating the image of Aryan superiority. Backed by Nazi subsidies, Mercedes-Benz and Auto Union entered the competition with revolutionary new models in 1934 that rendered the various Italian and French machinery completely obsolete. Their independent suspensions allowed huge horsepower gains to be utilized and, before long, speeds of up to 320km/h (200mph) were being reached. The German domination continued until the cessation of Grand Prix racing on 1 September 1939, the day that Britain declared war on Nazi Germany.

◄ *(left to right)* **Manfred von Brauchitsch, Christian Kautz, Tazio Nuvolari and Hermann Muller at the Donington Grand Prix, Donington Park, England, in 1938.**

▼ **Tazio Nuvolari, Auto Union, during the 1938 Italian Grand Prix.**

Post-war Recovery

During the period of German domination before the outbreak of World War II, several constructors had turned instead to voiturette (small car) racing. With Germany in no position to partake in international motorsport in the early post-war years, pre-war voiturette Alfa Romeos, Maseratis and ERAs formed the basis of an early revival of the sport.

The Birth of Formula One

The reconstituted governing body arranged a loose calendar of "premier" Grands Prix for 1947, and for the following year it announced a new Grand Prix formula: Formula One. Sensibly, it catered for existing machinery and was therefore largely based on the pre-war voiturette formula, which allowed for supercharged engines of 1.5 litres. As a means of bolstering the grids, Formula One also catered for unsupercharged engines of up to 4.5 litres, in order to encourage the entry of the sportscar-derived racers that had performed a similar makeweight class in the immediate pre-war period.

With their Italian factories in ruins, wheeling out their pre-war cars and winning some Grands Prix was a vital tonic for Alfa Romeo, which was the dominant racing force in these early post-war years. Ironically the car – dubbed the "Alfetta" – had been created under the guidance of Enzo Ferrari, who had now ceased to be Alfa's racing manager and had instead

▲ Froilán González wins his own and Ferrari's first Championship-status Grand Prix at Silverstone in 1951, defeating the previously all-conquering Alfa Romeos.

become a constructor in his own right. Alfa's financial plight precluded it from taking part during 1949 and, in their absence, the Ferrari marque racked up its first Grand Prix victories.

▲ The Argentinian Juan Manuel Fangio, five times World Champion.

◀ Juan Manuel Fangio in his Alfa Romeo 158 during the 1950 International Trophy at Silverstone.

▼ Juan Manuel Fangio in his Alfa Romeo 158 Alfetta during the Belgian Grand Prix, at Spa-Francorchamps in 1950.

▲ Giuseppe Farina pictured at home, shortly after winning the first Drivers' World Championship in 1950. He won the British, Swiss and Italian Grands Prix.

The World Championships

Alfa was tempted into a return in 1950 by the inauguration of a World Championship. In a move designed to regain the sport its pre-war following by popularizing its appeal, the contest would find a "World Champion" driver. Points were awarded based on the results of six nominated Grands Prix. The first race of the World Championship was held round the perimeter track of a disused British wartime airfield called Silverstone. Actually, all of the Grands Prix were held on European soil, but the "world" title was justified by the inclusion of results from the American Indianapolis 500 race. This anomaly continued for much of the decade until genuine Grands Prix outside Europe began to appear on the calendar.

Alfa Romeo won every Grand Prix in 1950, and the title contest was fought out between their drivers Giuseppe Farina and Juan Manuel Fangio. The former just got the verdict on account of a better reliability record, though it was the Argentinian Fangio who set the pace. Fangio went on to his first world title in 1951, but from mid-season of that year, his supercharged Alfa Romeo was pushed hard by a new challenger – the unsupercharged V12 Ferrari.

Technology 1951

Ferrari 375

After trying – but failing – to beat Alfa Romeo with a similar 1.5-litre supercharged car in 1950, Enzo Ferrari and his designer Aurelio Lampredi re-assessed. They had noted that the pre-war 4.5-litre unsupercharged Talbots could occasionally push the much more powerful Alfas uncomfortably close over a race distance by virtue of using less fuel and therefore making fewer refuelling stops. The rationale behind the 375 of 1951 was of a 4.5-litre car more modern than the Talbots that would retain an economy advantage over the Alfas but close the power deficit. Its V12 engine produced around 330bhp at a time when the Alfas were giving over 400bhp, but critically it consumed fuel at around 7.2km/g (4.5mpg) rather than the 2.9km/g (1.8mpg) of its rival, which had such high supercharger boost pressure that fuel was needed for cooling as well as combustion. The turning point came at Silverstone in 1951, when José Froilán González was able to run his 375 wheel-to-wheel with Fangio's Alfa, and then pull clear when the supercharged car had to make its inevitable early pit stop. Enzo Ferrari was famously quoted as saying he felt as if he had killed his mother, given his former close links with Alfa.

▼ José Froilán González on his way to the first Championship-status Grand Prix win for Ferrari at Silverstone in 1951.

Ferrari Maintain Italy's Lead

Ferrari's speed in the second half of 1951 put Alfa Romeo on the defensive. As the newer design was honed into an ever-faster machine, the development potential of the Alfetta – which had debuted in 1937 – hit a brick wall. Having retained the championship by the skin of their teeth, and without the finances to design and build a new model, Alfa made an honourable withdrawal at the end of the year.

Switch to Formula Two

The departure of Alfa Romeo left Formula One with a problem: Ferrari now had no worthwhile competition. Maserati was operating on a hand-to-mouth basis, building and selling outclassed cars while making plans for the future. There was the almost mythical BRM, an exciting idea borne of British post-war optimism and

▲ Ascari in the Ferrari 375 at the 1951 German Grand Prix. This marked his first Championship-status victory.

▼ Belgian Grand Prix 1952: Alberto Ascari in his Ferrari. The Italian won every Grand Prix he contested for a dominant season.

Shapers

Enzo Ferrari

The founder of the most revered of all racing teams described the essence of his ability as "a flair for the agitation of men". Ruthless and autocratic, he was also shrewd and single-minded, traits that were evident from his days as racing manager for Alfa Romeo in the 1920s, right up to his death in 1988. He was a moderately successful driver in the early 1920s, but his real value to Alfa came as an organizer; it was he who succeeded in poaching key technical staff from Fiat, for instance. His links with Alfa were finally severed in the late 1930s, and in 1948 the first Grand Prix car bearing the name of "Ferrari" appeared on the track.

His relationships with his drivers and other key personnel were often stormy as the success of his race team overrode any human considerations, though for certain rare men – Peter Collins in the 1950s and Gilles Villeneuve in the 1980s being the most notable – he made exceptions.

financed by that country's industry. The power potential of its supercharged V16 engine was said to be fantastic, but no-one knew for sure because it never hung together long enough to find out. It was a frail hope on which to rest a World Championship contest.

Race promoters, fearing no-one would come to watch a Ferrari demonstration, switched their main races to Formula Two, a junior category for 2-litre unsupercharged cars. The governing body followed suit and announced that the 1952 and 1953 World Championships would be for Formula Two cars. Ironically, Ferrari dominated anyway, with its lead driver Alberto Ascari achieving a sequence of successes that has yet to be equalled. He won six of the seven Grands Prix comprising the 1952 season, followed by a further five in 1953, and in the course of his run he established a record of nine consecutive victories that still stands today.

Ascari's luck ran out in the final race of 1953, at Monza, where he lost a thrilling battle to chief rival Fangio, who was driving the ever-improving Formula Two Maserati. Ascari and Fangio, the two fastest drivers in the world at the time, shared the front row of the grid, but the latter made a poor start as Ascari surged into the lead ahead of his Ferrari team-mate, Farina. Fangio's friend and Maserati team-mate Onofré Marimon then slipstreamed past both Ferraris to lead as Fangio made up the lost ground and made it a four-car slipstreaming battle. Time after time, the positions changed between the four until, at half-distance, Marimon was forced to pit with a radiator leak. He rejoined a lap down but, crucially, still with the leaders on the road.

Into the last corner of the last lap, Farina made a desperate bid for victory, and leader Ascari spun trying to avoid contact as Farina ran wide. The spinning Ascari was hit by Marimon, allowing Fangio to nip through for his first victory since breaking his neck at this same track the year before.

▶ **Alberto Ascari and Ferrari took their second World Championship title in 1953.**

▲ Ascari leads Fangio, Farina and Marimon in the battle of the 1953 Italian Grand Prix.

◀ Ascari takes the plaudits again in 1953. His sequence of nine consecutive wins is a record that has not yet been broken.

The Brief Return of the Factories

Motor racing had been invented by the big European customer-car producers, and largely dominated by them until the advent of World War II. Thereafter, with their factories in ruins, they had little choice but to stay out of it, Alfa Romeo's flurry with their pre-war cars notwithstanding.

The Specialists

In their place, the sport came to be dominated by specialist race car constructors, such as Ferrari, Maserati and Gordini, who built cars for sale to race entrants and ran their own teams of "works" machines. The specialist constructors existed on revenue from the sale of their machines, from start and finish money from race organizers, and from trade deals with suppliers who could then advertise their part in the ensuing success.

But in 1954, with the post-war recovery process now well established, the factories began to return. First Mercedes-Benz, then Lancia announced Grand Prix programmes and the fact that they had respectively signed Fangio and Ascari, the top two Grand Prix drivers, signalled the seriousness of their intent.

▲ **Lancia's D50 was an even more advanced design than the rival Mercedes.**

The Return to Formula One

With such an undertaking of support, the governing body felt confident in the reintroduction of Formula One as the basis for the World Championship. This time the formula stipulated engines of no more than 2.5 litres unsupercharged. Ferrari and Maserati came up with new

▼ **Mercedes-Benz W196** *Stromlinienwagen* **exiting Champel Curve at Silverstone in 1954. The streamlined body of the car did not suit the airfield circuit.**

machines, but when Mercedes unveiled the W196 racer, the different scale of their resources became very clear.

Fangio gave the car a win first time out, in the 1954 French Grand Prix, with his team-mate Karl Kling close behind, and the rest nowhere. For the remainder of the season, the Mercedes would be beaten only twice, and Fangio duly delivered the Championship – something he repeated for the company after an even more dominant performance in 1955, this time backed up by the highly promising young British driver, Stirling Moss, who took his first victory that year at Aintree.

▼ Stirling Moss in his Maserati 250F at the 1954 British Grand Prix. He retired from second place with only ten laps to go.

The Factories Withdraw Again

The introduction of the Lancia D50 had been delayed until the end of 1954, but it set pole position by a full second in its debut race, and looked set to give Ascari victory before breaking down. In concept it was arguably even more advanced than the Mercedes, but the financial problems of the parent company meant its potential was ultimately untapped. Ascari's death while testing a Ferrari sports racer in May gave Lancia the justification it needed to withdraw from the sport at the end of 1955.

Mercedes withdrew too, for reasons even more catastrophic. In by far the biggest tragedy the sport has ever suffered, over 80 spectators were killed in the 1955 Le Mans 24 Hours sportscar race, when a Mercedes was launched into the crowd after hitting another car. The fall-out affected all of motor racing and several Grands Prix were immediately cancelled. Mercedes suddenly found its participation in the sport changed from a public relations benefit to a liability, and it pulled out at the end of that year, not to return for a very, very long time. All of which, of course, left Formula One back in the hands of the specialists, with significant long-term consequences.

Technology 1955

Mercedes W196

Innovation and attention to detail was everywhere on this landmark racer. Its eight cylinders were fed by inlet and outlet valves that were not closed by conventional springs but by "desmodronic" actuation, whereby they were directly mechanically controlled for more accuracy and reliability. Its chassis was not the conventional metal ladder frame with bolstering tubing. Instead, the tubing was arranged in such a way that its geometry formed a load-bearing structure and the heavy ladder frame was dispensed with; this was termed "spaceframe" construction. Its brake drums were initially mounted inboard

▲ The two Mercedes-Benz W196, driven by Juan Mauel Fangio and Karl Kling, receive attention behind the pits. Fangio has his back to the camera, on the left.

rather than within the wheels, thus reducing the unsprung mass of the car, to the benefit of road-holding. But the most visually dramatic feature was its all-enveloping bodywork that made traditional open-wheelers look previous-generation. Ironically, this induced a handling imbalance and the car more usually ran in more conventional open-wheel form.

▼ The enclosed-wheel "streamliner" bodywork was only used occasionally.

The Unstoppable Fangio

▼ Five times Formula One World title holder Juan Manuel Fangio driving through Becketts in the Ferrari D50.

T he specialist constructors were quick to take advantage of the factory withdrawals. Enzo Ferrari's shrewdness was never more apparent than when he contrived to get paid for taking over the assets of the Lancia Grand Prix project – including the D50 cars, which were a big advance over the existing Ferraris. Fangio was signed up to drive them and he duly delivered the 1956 Championship, his fourth and Ferrari's third.

Fangio and Ferrari

But it was a far from smooth road to glory for both parties. Enzo Ferrari and Fangio failed to hit it off, and there was a lot of tension and mutual distrust in the team. As they arrived at Monza for the final round of the title contest, Fangio's biggest threat was his own team-mate, Peter Collins, the young British driver, who was a particular favourite of the boss.

Fangio was in the leading group, a couple of places ahead of Collins, when he suffered a steering-arm breakage on lap 18 and pulled into the pits to retire the car. At that time, teams were allowed to use more than one driver in a single car and have them share the

points. When the third Ferrari driver, Luigi Musso, pitted to refuel, he was asked if he would hand his car over to Fangio. He refused.

This meant that Collins, now in third place, stood poised to win the title. But when he came in for a tyre stop on the 35th lap and saw Fangio standing

watching, he immediately jumped out and offered his car to him. Fangio took it and with it finished second – enough to clinch him the title. It was a supreme act of sportsmanship from Collins. Asked why he had done it, he simply replied, "Because Fangio deserved it." Fangio was indebted.

▲ Fangio (2) behind the lead car, in action for Maserati.

◀ Juan Manuel Fangio takes the winner's garland after winning the 1956 German Grand Prix.

Maserati and "That" Race

Fangio was approaching 47 years old as the 1957 season began. He had originally planned to retire at the end of 1955, but an economic crisis in his home country of Argentina had persuaded him to continue. But any thoughts that his competitive spirit was waning were utterly demolished in 1957. Neither he nor Ferrari had any interest in continuing their partnership, and he switched instead to Maserati, who had continually refined and developed their 250F model over the last three years until it was a beautifully responsive and balanced machine, just the sort of car in which Fangio could display his genius.

At the German Grand Prix, Fangio clinched that year's Championship – his fifth – with his final Grand Prix victory. It was also his greatest. Around the mountainous 14-mile Nürburgring

◄ Juan Manuel Fangio in his Maserati at Monza in 1957.

▼ Mike Hawthorn and Peter Collins lead Fangio's Maserati at the German Grand Prix of 1957.

circuit, he overcame a mid-race delay in the pits to claw back a 51-second deficit, a task that had looked impossible. He broke and re-broke the lap record on each subsequent lap, leaving it at 9 minutes 17.4 seconds, over 8 seconds faster than his own pole position time. The Ferrari drivers were unable to respond, and he passed them both on the last lap. Fangio later recalled that on that day he had driven at a level he had never reached before, and did not wish to reach again. Many regard it as the greatest race ever driven.

The British Challenge

Britain had enjoyed its moments of Grand Prix glory, but never for any great duration. Sunbeam had won races in the 1920s in partnership with Henry Segrave before becoming financially strapped. In the late 1930s, rising British star Richard Seaman displayed such immense promise that he was employed by the Nazi-backed Mercedes team and actually won the 1938 German Grand Prix. He suffered a fatal accident while leading the 1939 Belgian Grand Prix.

The New British Breed
What occurred in the 1950s was quite different; it was a movement, and for the first time it became conceivable that the centre of motor racing might move away from France and Italy, its twin homes for half a century.

British law had never allowed the road racing seen in those countries, and consequently British motorsport initially took a different direction, being centred around the specially-built enclosed circuit of Brooklands. This was in essence an oval shape: no corners, just flat-out running around a dramatic, banked track. The demands of this sort of racing were rather different to those of traditional road circuit-based Grands Prix. But World War II rendered Brooklands unusable as a race track as

▲ Tony Brooks *(left)* and Stirling Moss after winning the 1957 British Grand Prix. Moss took over Brooks' car after his own suffered problems.

▼ Harry Schell drives his Vanwall at Castle Combe in 1955.

▼ Brooklands hosted the British Grand Prix in 1926 and 1927 but more usually held domestic events around its speed bowl.

much of it was demolished to make room for expanded aircraft-manufacturing facilities.

What the war gave British motor racing in place of Brooklands were dozens of redundant wartime airfields. These made ideal race venues, and the tracks more nearly reproduced the demands of continental road racing. Concurrent with this, the country's governing body, the RAC, approved a new low-cost, entry-level class of racing, Formula 500 (later renamed Formula Three). This catered for motorcycle-engined cars of 500cc and attracted an entirely new breed of driver to British sport. No longer was it exclusively an idle pastime of wealthy men; it attracted ambitious young

talent who wished to become professionals. Stirling Moss and Peter Collins were the outstanding graduate drivers of this formula. Among their rivals were three men later to have a huge influence on Grand Prix racing outside of the cars: John Cooper, Ken Tyrrell and Bernie Ecclestone. The 750 Motor Club, another post-war British attempt at low-cost motorsport, was meanwhile proving incredibly fertile ground for engineering talent, with Colin Chapman as its vanguard.

Vandervell and British Success

Concurrent with these movements was another British initiative, but a private one: that of the industrialist Tony Vandervell. He had become a very wealthy man as the boss of Vandervell Bearings, whose patented "thinwall bearing" was behind major efficiency gains in aircraft and car engines. With the aim of one day having his own

Grand Prix team, he initially bought customer Formula One race cars from Enzo Ferrari. Called the "Thinwall Specials", these modified Ferraris were the precursors to the Vanwall, which first appeared in 1955. Using his industry contacts to the full, Vandervell

commissioned de Havilland aircraft aerodynamicist Frank Costin to design a highly advanced body, while the engine was a scaled-up version of that used in Norton motorcycle racers. By 1957, it was the fastest car in Formula One, and Stirling Moss and Tony Brooks took it to a shared victory in the British Grand Prix of that year. It was the first wave of British success, and was soon to be followed up in devastating fashion as the young racing community that had built up around Formula 500 transformed itself from a movement to a revolution. In the space of a couple of seasons, the whole fabric of Formula One had changed fundamentally.

▲ (left) British driver Stirling Moss in his Vanwall at Aintree for the 1957 British and European Grand Prix, where he lapped at 144.5km/h (89.85mph).

◄ The young Stirling Moss with his 500cc Formula Three car.

Walls Come Tumbling Down

"Suddenly, there were green cars all around me. I wasn't part of that world. I drove red cars. It was time to leave." The words are those of Juan Manuel Fangio, who retired part-way through the 1958 season after a record five world titles, four of them in the Italian colours of red. British racing green had reached a landmark in the 1957 Italian Grand Prix, where the race organizers had to change the grid formation to 4-3-4 from the usual 3-2-3, in order to get an Italian car onto the front row. The fastest three qualifiers were Vanwalls.

British Racing Green

For 1958, a new world title was initiated – for constructors. This ran alongside the Drivers' Championship. Vanwall won it, but their success was spread between Moss and Brooks, who were therefore pipped to the Drivers' Championship by Ferrari's Mike Hawthorn (and even he was British). Ferrari effectively had only one driver in the championship fight after the

▲ A relaxed Mike Hawthorn in the pits during practice for the British Grand Prix at Silverstone in 1956. Driving the BRM P25, Hawthorn was an early leader in the race, but he soon retired.

death in the German Grand Prix of Peter Collins.

But for all the glory days enjoyed by the streamlined, thoroughbred Vanwalls, the year's most significant victory went to a tiny, runtish-looking jumped-up Formula Two car, also British. Called a Cooper, it won the opening race of the season in Argentina. Driven in this race by Moss, it signalled the arrival into the rarefied Grand Prix ranks of the Formula 500 movement.

Because the cars of Formula 500 had used motorcycle engines with chain-drives, the logical place to put the engine had been between the driver and the driven rear wheels. This brought further, unforeseen, advantages. The pre-war Auto Unions had been "mid-engined" too, but they were monster cars whose size disguised the superiority of the layout, and thus left it unexploited until the Coopers – father and son, Charles and John – came along.

The Coopers Pave the Way

Because Formula One had been the preserve of small specialist teams since the pull-out of Mercedes and Lancia, the engineering was not progressive. As specialists rooted in the fabric of Grand Prix racing, Ferrari and Maserati had neither the resources nor the breadth of vision to fundamentally re-evaluate; they simply honed and refined. Vanwall, another specialist, had been created in the image of Ferrari. But Cooper came from leftfield, from different roots entirely, and they were not constrained by any convention other than those established in a very young junior formula.

It soon became clear that the funny little car with its engine in the "wrong" place – which had precipitated jeers of derision when it first turned up at practice in Argentina 1958 – had made instant dinosaurs of thoroughbreds. The DNA of the Grand Prix car had just been altered.

◀ Mike Hawthorn laps Giulio Cabianca on the start/finish straight of Monza in 1958. Hawthorn finished second.

▲ The supremely gifted Stirling Moss, who, along with Tony Brooks, helped British Formula One racing take on the Italians.

▲ Moss winning the 1957 Pescara Grand Prix in his Vanwall, one of the three victories they took that year.

▼ Tony Brooks, for Vanwall, wins the Belgian Grand Prix at the Spa-Francorchamps circuit in 1958.

Front Engine's Last Goodbyes

There was to be no stopping Cooper in 1959. The car with which Moss had won the Argentinian Grand Prix in 1958 had not been a proper Grand Prix machine, merely a Formula Two car with a slightly enlarged engine.

The "Garagistes"

Encouraged by this success, the Coopers set about building a proper Formula One car. But though its lines were sleeker, and its engine more powerful, it was built very much to the formula of their breakthrough Argentina car. Not only did it retain the mid-engined layout, but it utilized parts from wherever they could be found, and adapted them as required: a gearbox based on that of a road-going Citroën, key suspension parts borrowed from the Volkswagen Beetle, and steering components from a Triumph. The engine was bought in from Coventry Climax, who had developed it out of what was originally a fire-pump motor.

If Ferrari and Maserati, who always made their own engines and components, had been previously considered racing "specialists" to distinguish them from the big

▲ **Tony Brooks won the 1959 French Grand Prix in his Ferrari Dino 246 V6, but by then he was fighting against the tide of Coopers.**

car-producing factories, this took the concept several stages further. Cooper simply designed and assembled their cars and used a network of specialized sub-contractors to provide necessary hardware. Enzo Ferrari contemptuously

described them as "garagistes". He also famously said his cars would never have mid-mounted engines as "the horse should pull the cart, not push it".

Here to Stay

The network of racing specialists that had formed in Britain around Cooper and the Formula 500 movement was soon servicing other constructors.

▼ **Jack Brabham's Cooper on the Oporto circuit of the Portuguese Grand Prix in 1960.**

Technology 1959

Cooper T51

A centralization of the car's masses was the critical advantage endowed by the mid-engined layout. In much the same way that a door with heavy weights bolted to the middle would be easier to move than one with the weights bolted to the outer edge, the mid-engined car was able to change direction quicker and with less momentum. In scientific terms, it had a lower "polar moment of inertia" than a traditional front-engined car.

The benefits of the layout multiplied. Because the front of the car didn't have to accommodate the engine, it could have a lower frontal area, making it quicker down the straight and more economical. Because no propshaft was needed to carry drive from a front engine to rear wheels, the car could be lower, giving benefits on the straights and in the corners. No propshaft and a lower

body meant it could be smaller and lighter, and therefore quicker to accelerate, brake and manoeuvre. The 1959 Cooper weighed in at 460kg, a massive 20 per cent lighter than the rival Ferrari 246. Even with 60 brake horsepower less, the Cooper had it covered. The weight and aerodynamic benefits meant less fuel was needed,

▲ Masten Gregory driving a Formula One Cooper T51 at Aintree in 1959.

furthering its weight advantage at the start. The lower weight also made it gentler on its tyres, which would thereby retain their grip for longer. The advantages for car and driver just kept snowballing.

A whole community of geographically close teams formed in the south of England, knowledge between them spread fast, and soon these "garagistes" were dominating the Grand Prix grids.

That community has formed the mainstay of Formula One ever since.

Ferrari's beautiful front-engined dinosaurs fought valiantly against an irresistible tide in 1959, and their driver

Tony Brooks was unlucky to miss out on the championship to Cooper's Jack Brabham. But there was no going back. Formula One had changed for ever and mid-engined cars were here to stay.

▲ Jack Brabham, driving for Cooper, was the 1959 World Champion.

▶ Tony Brooks' front-engined Ferrari (24) fights it out with Jack Brabham's rear-engined Cooper (8) in the 1959 French Grand Prix.

Rear-engine Revolution Completed

With a further development of their mid-engined wondercar, Cooper steamrollered their way to the 1960 World Championship – again with Jack Brabham as their driver – in a yet more convincing demonstration of the layout's superiority.

Ferrari Converts

As Ferrari continued to campaign hopelessly outdated front-engined machines, they were left outclassed, and even Enzo Ferrari was forced to eat his words about the horse pushing the cart. At the Monaco Grand Prix, his team debuted a prototype that had been crudely converted to the mid-engined layout. The lessons learned from this were applied as the team effectively wrote off the 1960 season to prepare for 1961, when a new 1.5-litre (unsupercharged) formula was due to replace the 2.5-litre one that had run since 1954.

Cooper and Lotus

The closest rival to Cooper in 1960 was another British constructor, Lotus. Using the same bought-in Coventry Climax engines as Cooper, and relying on the same network of specialist

sub-contractors, Lotus built their first mid-engined car for the 1960 season. Team boss Colin Chapman had a reputation as a brilliantly original thinker from his days in the 750 Motor Club in Britain. It was partly his pride in this reputation that had prevented him

▼ Jack Brabham, winner of the Portuguese Grand Prix, 1960, in the Cooper T53. Brabham benefited from the absence for much of that season of Stirling Moss.

▲ Jack Brabham, winner of the British Grand Prix, 1960, in the Cooper T53, on his way to a second successive world title. This confirmed front-engined cars were dead.

from copying the Cooper mid-engined formula earlier; Lotus had struggled with front-engined Formula One cars in 1958 and 1959.

With his Lotus 18, Chapman combined the Cooper's layout with a much more scientific approach.

▲ After giving Cooper its first Grand Prix victory in Argentina in 1958, Moss continued to rack up wins for the marque in 1959.

The spaceframe chassis had a more sophisticated geometry, and the suspension was designed to give the tyres an easier time. His obsession with weight reduction was reflected in a kerb weight of just 390kg, still the lightest winning Grand Prix car of all time. As part of the 1961 regulations, the sport's governing body stipulated a minimum weight of 450kg, fearing that cars such as the Lotus were frail. Regulation minimum weights have been a feature of Formula One ever since.

Maybe the fear was justified. Stirling Moss gave the Lotus its first victory at Monaco in 1960, but two races later broke his back when practising for the Belgian Grand Prix. He was thrown out of the car after crashing because a rear wheel had fallen off due to hub failure. It put Moss out for most of the year, and gave Brabham and Cooper their relatively easy runs to the Drivers' and Constructors' Championships.

▼ **Winner Jack Brabham in the Cooper T53 at the British Grand Prix, Silverstone, 1960.**

Shapers

John Cooper

John Cooper and his father Charles founded Cooper Cars in the late 1940s to produce machines for the new British Formula 500 series. Charles had been an amateur racer at Brooklands pre-war, and John was a fairly successful competitor in the new formula, though he soon hung up his helmet to concentrate on the business, which was run from a garage in Surbiton, near London. Coopers became the dominant machines in the low-cost junior series and drivers such as Stirling Moss, Peter Collins, Ken Tyrrell and Bernie Ecclestone all cut their teeth in them.

Easy-going and friendly, John formed a stark contrast to the short-tempered Charles, and the two rowed frequently. Nonetheless, it was John who had the vision and who took the technical concept of the Formula 500 cars and applied it to bigger, faster

▼ John Cooper in 1968.

machinery, until even Formula One surrendered to his funny little cars. His trademark victory somersault at the trackside became very familiar in 1959 and 1960. He later lent his name to the Mini Cooper and stayed in Formula One until 1968, thereafter concentrating on his garage business. He died in 2001.

Ferrari Bite Two Bullets

Ferrari came back with a vengeance in 1961. Preparation was the key to their success. The British constructors had opposed the formula change to 1.5 litres. The governing body had made the change to combat escalating speeds, but the British teams believed it would leave them without suitable engines, thereby effectively handing the competitive advantage to Ferrari, who made their own engines. This became a self-fulfilling prophecy as the British teams failed to make adequate provisions for the formula change, while Ferrari concentrated on readying their new engine and cars.

Ferrari Returns

The subsequent Ferrari 156 was the team's first effort at a proper mid-engined car, and even though its chassis was not as advanced as those already produced by Lotus or even Cooper, its engine was considerably more powerful than the 1.5-litre version

▲ Phil Hill's Ferrari finished third in the Monaco Grand Prix, Monte Carlo, 1961. It was the start of his title campaign.

of the Coventry Climax the British teams relied upon. It recalled another of Enzo Ferrari's famous maxims: that he built engines with wheels on.

Only one thing kept the Ferraris from completely annihilating the opposition: the genius of Stirling Moss. In the privately-owned Lotus of his entrant Rob Walker, Moss twice beat the Ferraris – at Monaco and Germany. But in championship terms, the contest was between Ferrari drivers Phil Hill and Wolfgang von Trips. Hill won, becoming America's first World Champion after von Trips crashed to his death at Monza in the penultimate round of the championship. Fourteen spectators died with him.

By the end of the year, Coventry Climax had produced a new V8 1.5-litre engine that for 1962 gave Lotus power

▼ Winner Phil Hill in the Ferrari 156 leads team-mate Wolfgang von Trips at the 1961 Belgian Grand Prix. They led a Ferrari 1-2-3-4.

parity with Ferrari, enabling their superior chassis technology to give them the winning edge once more.

BRM Triumphant

Stirling Moss had received career-ending injuries at the beginning of the season, and it was Lotus' works driver Jim Clark who assumed his mantle as the accepted number one. Yet it was Graham Hill and BRM who won the 1962 world crown on account of a better reliability record than the Lotus.

It was the culmination of over a decade's effort from BRM, a team

originally set up as a trust funded by contributions from British industry. By this time, however, it was privately owned and rather better organized. The P57 with which Hill won the title was powered by BRM's very own V8 engine. It was this that transformed the fortunes of the team, turning it from a laughing stock to a world beater. Hill's determination played a key part in driving the team forward.

◄ Graham Hill, here wearing a cap featuring the same London Rowing Club colours as his helmet, won the 1962 title.

Technology 1962

Lotus 25

Lotus redefined Formula One technology with the monocoque construction of their 25 model. Instead of a spaceframe of metal tubing clothed with panels, the aluminium shell was load-bearing and tubing was discarded. The monocoque was stiffer and lighter than the spaceframe, and enabled the suspension to work more effectively. It was also far safer in the event of a serious impact. The technique had long been used in aircraft, but this was its first Formula One application. The entire design of the car was

tailored to the compact dimensions of lead driver Jim Clark, with a cockpit just wide enough to accommodate him and no wider. He was also reclined to an almost horizontal driving position of 35 degrees. It all resulted in an impressive cross-sectional frontal area of just 0.37sq m (3.98sq ft), which compared to 0.54sq m (5.81sq ft) for the rival Ferrari car of 1962.

◄ The gearbox and exhaust end of the revolutionary Lotus 25, the pacesetter of Formula One from 1962–65.

◄ The 25 unclothed, showing just how tightly it was tailored around Jim Clark's dimensions. Chapman confers.

▲ Jim Clark giving the thumbs-up after taking his Lotus 25 to victory in the 1963 Dutch Grand Prix, on his way to the title.

Clark Becomes the Master

The combination of the Lotus 25 and Jim Clark could not be denied indefinitely, and in 1963 they stormed to victory in seven of the World Drivers' Championship's ten rounds. Frequently their level of performance reduced the rest to bit-players: in the Dutch Grand Prix, Clark lapped the field; in France he led from start to finish, despite a couple of broken valve springs. If he failed to win, it was usually because something in the car broke.

Clark and Chapman
Scotsman Clark had formed a symbiotic relationship with Lotus boss, Colin Chapman. Here was the greatest driver of his era working in harmony with the greatest designer. Few doubted that all records would succumb to the pairing.

It did not always go to plan, however. In 1964, some of the unreliability bugs returned and John Surtees was waiting to pounce. The

▲ Jim Clark (*left*) and Colin Chapman, arguably the greatest pairing of driver and designer ever seen in Formula One.

▼ Jim Clark takes victory in the 1965 French Grand Prix at Clermont Ferrand in his Lotus 33, an update of the 25 model.

Shapers

Colin Chapman

Widely cited as the greatest Formula One designer of all time, Colin Chapman's Lotus cars repeatedly took Formula One technology down new roads, leaving the rest to follow in the dust trails of his fertile mind.

He set himself up as a secondhand car trader while studying engineering at London University, and later designed, and competed in, a trials car based on a pre-war Austin 7, dubbed a "Lotus". While training as a pilot in the Royal Airforce, Chapman built a circuit racer for 750 Motor Club events. So successful was he with it that he took orders for replicas; Lotus, the cutting edge of Britain's Formula One invasion, was born.

The success of the business meant that Chapman had to withdraw from racing cars himself, though his driving

talents were considerable. He was even given a drive in the 1956 French Grand Prix by Vanwall, and was quick in practice but a non-starter in the race after damaging his car.

Colin Chapman died from a heart attack in 1982, aged 54. Everyone who worked with him attests to his enormous charm, yet for each of these stories there's another telling of a hard, and ruthless edge. In business, as in car design, he would always search for the loophole, and this trait left his memory tarnished by his involvement in the DeLorean Motor Company scandal of the early 1980s.

◀ **Chapman, here sitting in the Lotus 25, frequently took technology from elsewhere and applied it to Formula One.**

former motorcycle champion had begun his Formula One career at Lotus but was now at Ferrari, where he helped hone a new V8 machine, and clinched the title in the final round after Clark's oil pipe came adrift. Surtees remains the only man to have won world titles on two wheels and four.

Clark and Lotus re-established themselves in 1965, the final year of the 1.5-litre formula. They won six of the nine races they contested on their way to both the Drivers' and the Constructors' titles, missing one round in order to compete in the Indianapolis 500 in America. They won that too!

▼ **(left) John Surtees, 1964 World Champion for Ferrari. Surtees was already a multiple world title winner on motorbikes when he began his Formula One career.**

▼ **(right) Surtees' 1964 season came alive with victory in that year's German Grand Prix around the 14 mile Nürburgring.**

Return to Power

ormula One cars were given their power back in 1966, with the inauguration of a new 3-litre formula. The 1.5-litre regulations had run their allotted time, and there was a hope from the governing body of tempting the American car manufacturers into the sport, to make it appeal more genuinely to a global audience.

Factories Stay Away

Already a Japanese company, Honda, had entered Formula One and had won the final race of the old formula, at Mexico in 1965. Those who controlled the sport hoped this might herald the return of full factory participation in Grand Prix racing. But it was not to be. Whilst Honda produced some

▲ Jack Brabham's 3-litre Brabham BT19 leads Jim Clark's 2-litre Lotus 33 in the 1966 Dutch Grand Prix at Zandvoort.

▲ Denny Hulme, 1967 World Champion, driving for Brabham. A solitary figure, he retired from Formula One in 1974.

◄ Race winner Jack Brabham leads the Coopers of John Surtees and Jochen Rindt in the 1966 German Grand Prix.

▼ Hulme leads Clark and Brabham on the first lap of the 1966 Dutch Grand Prix. Clark led, but later suffered a car problem.

▼ Jim Clark, Lotus 49, won first time out with the brand new Ford DFV engine, at the Dutch Grand Prix, Zandvoort, 1967.

exceptionally powerful engines, their chassis technology was a long way behind the established top teams, and their success was very sporadic.

The "garagiste" era initiated by Cooper in the late 1950s had made Formula One such a specialized exercise, far removed from road-car production, that a factory could no longer expect to come in and immediately dominate. Although Cooper themselves were, by now, a spent force, their influence was everywhere – in the format of the teams doing the winning and in the offshoots created directly from Cooper.

The Cooper Legacy

Jack Brabham, Cooper's former lead driver, won the world title for a third time in 1966, this time driving a Brabham car. He was not the only ex-Cooper driver to incorporate the lessons learned there and set up on his own either: Bruce McLaren had done the same thing and would win McLaren its first Grand Prix in 1968.

But a major manufacturer, Ford, did become involved. The European off-shoot of the American car giant funded the development of a new Formula One engine from Cosworth of Britain, the DFV. Labelled as a Ford, this motor would fill the role of providing off-the-shelf Formula One horsepower previously taken by Coventry Climax. It debuted in the Lotus 49 of 1967, and instantly proved the class of its field, but early unreliability let the title slip to the Brabham of Denny Hulme.

Technology 1967

Cosworth DFV

Keith Duckworth, in partnership with Mike Costin, formed Cosworth Engineering in 1958. The company made its name with some devastatingly successful racing engines in the junior formulae, often based on Ford production units.

Helped by a £100,000 investment from Ford, Duckworth designed the V8-cylinder DFV (double-four-valve). It was probably the first Formula One engine designed with the dimensions of the car specifically in mind, and not only was it decently powerful, with an initial 405bhp, but it was also small, relatively light and could be packaged very efficiently. It was also made sufficiently stiff that it could be mounted in such a way that it formed

part of the car's rigidity. This helped the suspension to do its job.

It won first time out, with Jim Clark in the 1967 Dutch Grand Prix, and won for the final time in 1983, in narrow valve-angle DFY form, in the back of Michele Alboreto's Tyrrell at Detroit. It took over the role of the standard Formula One engine and totalled 155 Grand Prix wins to become the most successful of all time. It was one of the most important parts of the matrix of specialist suppliers that allowed the British race car community to thrive and dominate Grand Prix racing.

◄ Keith Duckworth, designer of the revolutionary Cosworth DFV engine, looking at his handiwork, 1967.

Making a Lethal Game Safer

The long-overdue safety movement in Formula One truly began one wet afternoon in June 1966, when Jackie Stewart suffered a terrifying accident in the first lap of the Belgian Grand Prix, from which he was fortunate to emerge with his life.

Stewart's Great Escape

The Spa-Francorchamps circuit, nestled in a forested Ardennes valley, always featured changeable weather and though the track was dry as the race began, when the leaders first arrived at Malmédy some miles down the road, they were confronted with a sudden downpour. Eight drivers spun, some of them many times. Among them was Stewart, whose BRM overturned in a ditch after striking a stone wall. Trapped inside and with petrol from the tanks leaking down onto him, Stewart was convinced the car's hot exhausts were about to trigger a fire.

With no marshals at the scene, he was rescued by fellow drivers Graham Hill and Bob Bondurant, who had to borrow a spanner from a spectator in order to remove the steering wheel to facilitate Stewart's exit from the car. It then took 20 minutes for an ambulance

to arrive. As an illustration of how little forethought was being given to driver safety, it was horrific.

Stewart's Crusade

From that moment and for the rest of his career, Stewart fought tirelessly for improved safety standards, and was highly unpopular with race organizers, circuit owners – and even some fellow drivers – for doing so.

▲ A cigarette-wielding fire marshal douses the Cooper T86B of Brian Redman, following a high speed accident at Spa in 1968.

▼ *(left)* The Spa track of the mid-1960s shows the lethal proximity of houses and solid objects.

▼ *(right)* Richie Ginther's 1961 Ferrari 156 with roll-over bar; but Ginther still wears just a T-shirt instead of fireproof overalls.

The wearing of helmets had only been compulsory since the beginning of 1952, and since then there had been very little safety progress. Seatbelts had not had universal take-up as many drivers feared being trapped by them in a burning car. The wearing of fireproof overalls only came into vogue in the late 1960s, around the time that the first full-face helmets began to appear – though many drivers still opted for open-facers in the following years, showing how difficult change was.

Standards began to improve in car construction. The 1969 regulations stipulated compulsory on-board fire extinguisher systems and sealed rubber bag fuel cells within the tanks. These were the first safety regulations since the introduction of cockpit roll-over bars in 1961.

But the biggest struggle was with circuit owners. It came down to a Stewart-led drivers union – the Grand Prix Drivers' Association (GPDA) – to act militantly and demand changes. Trees were felled from trackside locations, Armco barriers were erected, barbed-wire fencing cleared, marshal training improved, and circuit medical facilities upgraded. Eventually, medical helicopters would be present every time the cars ran, ready to ferry injured drivers to hospital. In time, some venues – notably the public road circuit of Spa-Francorchamps where Stewart had crashed in 1966 – were deemed too dangerous and fell from the calendar.

◄ Monaco had one of the worst safety records in Formula One during the 1960s. Lorenzo Bandini died here in 1967, the flames from his car fanned by a helicopter taking film footage.

▼ *(left)* There was scant protection for the spectators, let alone the drivers. Sixteen spectators were killed during Formula One races of the 1960s.

▼ *(right)* Lotus mechanics look on at the remains of the Lotus 49B of Jackie Oliver, after he crashed in practice in France in 1968 as a result of aerodynamic turbulence.

The changes helped, but the sport remained lethally dangerous. In the 1960s, 12 drivers and 16 spectators were killed in Formula One events. Several more Grand Prix drivers died competing outside of Formula One, notably the great Jim Clark, who was killed in a Formula Two race at Hockenheim shortly after breaking Fangio's all-time record of Grand Prix victories. He had racked up win number 25 in South Africa on New Year's Day 1968. Even the world's greatest driver could become a victim.

Money Talks

Commercial sponsorship hit Formula One in 1968, when Imperial Tobacco plastered their Gold Leaf brand livery over the Team Lotus cars. Until this time, such a practice had been restricted to American national racing, while Formula One teams had plugged only trade backers, with small stickers for tyre, fuel, oil or brake brands in exchange for a free supply of their wares. The Lotus deal took things onto a different scale entirely.

Advertising Enters Formula One

The competitive push of the teams, notably Lotus' Colin Chapman, had led them to pressure the governing body to relax restrictions on commercial advertising on the cars in order to give them bigger budgets for development and design. This duly happened at the end of 1967, and Lotus were the first to take advantage. National racing colours – something first established in the 1900 Gordon Bennett competitions – soon became a thing of the past. Ferrari were an exception, though team boss Enzo Ferrari was able to show disdain for the new trend only because his team had been acquired by motor giant Fiat in 1969, giving financial security but retaining Enzo's autonomy. He was now able to get back to full strength.

► **Winner Graham Hill clutching his Monaco trophy, 1968. The victory put him into a firm lead of the championship.**

▲ **Race winner Graham Hill in the Lotus 49B made it four wins around the Principality. Monaco Grand Prix, 1968.**

Life After Clark

Lotus bounced back from the death of Clark, largely thanks to the grit and determination of Graham Hill. With team boss Colin Chapman devastated, Hill took the initiative and in winning the very next Grand Prix following Clark's death, helped the team recompose itself. That was in Spain and in winning the following event in Monaco too, Hill put himself and Lotus in command. Nonetheless, to win the fight they had to fend off two very serious challenges: Jackie Stewart in

▼ **By winning the 1968 Spanish Grand Prix immediately after the death of team-mate Jim Clark, Graham Hill helped Lotus recover.**

the new Matra and reigning champ Denny Hulme in the McLaren. All three contenders were powered by the Ford Cosworth DFV engine.

Stewart's French-built and designed Matra was run by his former Formula Three entrant, Ken Tyrrell, as the pair re-established their partnership to form what would become one of the sport's golden liaisons. Their first victory came in Holland that year but their greatest was at the Nürburgring in a wet and foggy German Grand Prix. Stewart won by over four minutes in one of the greatest performances ever seen around the formidable 14-mile circuit. Hulme won the next two events, with Stewart again on top in the penultimate race. Going into the final round, in Mexico, it was a three-way title shoot-out between Hill, Stewart and Hulme.

Hulme was an early retirement as the race developed into a thrilling dice at the front between Hill and Stewart, with the pair passing and re-passing. Eventually, falling fuel pressure began to lose Stewart power, enabling Hill, Lotus and Gold Leaf to win the race and the Championship. Hill's grit had got the job done once again.

▲ Bruce McLaren (McLaren M7A) leads Jackie Oliver (Lotus 49B) at the Mexican Grand Prix, Mexico City in 1968. McLaren finished second and Oliver third.

▲ Bruce McLaren (McLaren-Cosworth M7A) finished in sixth place at the USA Grand Prix, Watkins Glen, in 1968.

▼ Johnny Servoz-Gavin (Matra MS10) crashed out on lap 71 of the Canadian Grand Prix, Mont-Tremblant, in 1968.

Downforce: The Genie Escapes

At the 1968 Monaco Grand Prix, the Lotus 49 appeared in revised "B" trim. On either side of the nose were two small wings, while the rear bodywork featured an upsweep designed to provide similar download at the rear. The concept of downforce had arrived in Formula One, heralding a completely different scale of performance. It has been with the sport ever since. By the next race, at Spa, Ferrari and Brabham appeared with devices that took the principle a step further, featuring full-width rear wings, separate from the body, mounted direct to the gearbox. Chris Amon took pole position in the Ferrari by the huge margin of 3.7 seconds.

Aerodynamic Technology

The principle essentially involved taking an aerofoil shape, as used for aircraft wings, and turning it upside down so that it provided downforce instead of lift. If air is forced to travel a longer distance over a lower surface than an upper one, it creates a pressure that will force the car to the ground, through the medium of the tyres. In this way, braking and cornering capacity is increased hugely.

Mounting the wings higher up on the car got them out of the disturbed

▲ Jochen Rindt's Brabham BT26 in the 1968 Canadian Grand Prix shows the ugly and dangerous heights wings had reached.

▼ Chris Amon drives the Ferrari 312 to second place in the British Grand Prix at Brands Hatch in 1968.

airflow created by the car itself, and within just a few races, almost all the cars were running front and rear wings mounted on hugely high stalks, feeding the loads directly into the suspension. Teams also began to experiment with wings that could be retracted on the straights to overcome the straightline speed penalty of their drag. It all made for a bizarre spectacle – and a highly dangerous one.

Wings of Unreason

At the Spanish Grand Prix of 1969, Graham Hill crested a rise in his Lotus, and his rear wing snapped off its mounts. Suddenly shorn of its downforce, the car became airborne and crashed heavily. As Hill was making his way back to the pits to get the team to warn his team-mate Jochen Rindt, the sister car suffered exactly the same failure over the same crest, and cannoned off Hill's abandoned wreck. Rindt was trapped in the car but fortunately had suffered only a broken nose. It was a miraculous escape for both drivers, not to mention the spectators. The governing body decided

it had to act, and at the next Grand Prix it banned wings outright. After a subsequent meeting with constructors, a compromise was reached; wings were allowed once more, but no longer could they be either movable or mounted to the suspension. Less effective fixed wings mounted only to the bodywork were allowed, with dimensions and height drastically reduced.

Amid all the controversy, Jackie Stewart and his Ken Tyrrell-run Matra-Ford glided from one immaculate victory to another on the way to their first World Championship. Jochen Rindt was the only one to consistently challenge them, but his Lotus lacked reliability. The Ford Cosworth DFV engine took victory in every single race with Matra, Lotus, Brabham and McLaren cars.

▲ Remarkably Jochen Rindt escaped from this wing failure-induced accident with just a broken nose. It led to wing restrictions.

▲ The remains of Hill's Lotus 49B after his 1969 Spanish Grand Prix accident. He broke a leg in the US Grand Prix later that year.

▲ Jackie Stewart, in car, and Ken Tyrrell pose for some publicity shots for a brand of whiskey at the Canadian Grand Prix, 1969.

The Stewart Years

ochen Rindt and Jackie Stewart were widely acknowledged as the world's two best drivers as the new decade began. But their competitive circumstances were about to change. Matra, now backed by Chrysler France, could not be seen running Ford engines and so the arrangement with Stewart and Tyrrell came to an end. While making plans to have his own machine built for the following year, Tyrrell purchased a car from a manufacturer new to Formula One, March, for the 1970 season. Unfortunately it wasn't up to the task of sustaining a championship challenge.

◄ Jackie Stewart (left) with Jochen Rindt at the British Grand Prix, Brands Hatch in 1970. Rindt was later made Posthumous World Champion of 1970.

▼ Rindt, in the Lotus 72C, wins his fourth Grand Prix in a row at Hockenheim, Germany, in 1970.

A Brutal Season

Jochen Rindt, by contrast, found himself behind the wheel of a new Lotus, the 72, that moved the technical goalposts of Formula One and gave him a real advantage. After a stunning win at Monaco in the old 49 model – where he pressured race leader Jack Brabham into running wide and hitting the barriers on the last lap – Rindt took up residence in the 72 and reeled off four successive victories. Although he was not to know it, these effectively secured

him the World Championship crown. Rindt was killed practising for the Italian Grand Prix, through a suspected wheel hub failure. In the remaining four races, no-one overhauled his points score and he became the sport's only posthumous World Champion.

It had been a particularly brutal season, with Piers Courage and Bruce McLaren also killed. With his friends being slain around him, Stewart worked harder than ever on his safety campaign. But he still found time to dominate the

1971 season in his new Tyrrell-Ford, with which he won six races.

The five he didn't win were split between his own team-mate François Cevert, the Ferraris of Mario Andretti and Jacky Ickx, and the Yardley Cosmetics-sponsored BRMs of Jo Siffert and Peter Gethin. The latter triumphed in Italy, where his race average of 241km/h (151mph) is still the fastest recorded in a Grand Prix. Thereafter chicanes were installed in the super-fast Monza track for reasons of safety.

▼ Winner Peter Gethin (BRM, *right*), Ronnie Peterson (March) and François Cevert(Tyrrell) at the Italian Grand Prix, 1971.

Technology 1970

Lotus 72

While the advent of wings in 1968 made Formula One cars substantially faster round a circuit on account of their vastly improved braking and cornering capabilities, the aerodynamic drag they created actually made the cars slower on the straights than before. The 1970 Lotus 72 – conceived by Colin Chapman, translated into reality by Maurice Phillippe – brilliantly resolved the conflicting requirements of downforce and straightline speed.

Its wedge shape made the cigar-like structures of before obsolete. This, combined with the re-siting of the radiators from the front to the side of the car, lowered the frontal area while the wedge bodywork itself helped create downforce. This enabled smaller wings to be fitted for equivalent downforce; powered by the same Ford Cosworth DFV engine, the 72's terminal speed was 14km/h (9mph) higher than the 49's, its predecessor. Other novelties included inboard brakes front and rear to lower the car's unsprung mass, and

rising-rate suspension to resolve the requirements that the very different aerodynamic loadings of high- and low-speed corners placed upon it.

▲ The launch of the Lotus 72 in 1970. The radical car took a few races to be fully sorted but it was devastating thereafter. It was still winning in 1974.

New Eras Beckon

(T) he seeds that eventually flowered to make Grand Prix racing one of the biggest sports in the world were planted some time in 1971. Jack Brabham had retired from racing at the end of 1970 and, at the age of 44, he sold up and went back home to Australia. Initially his designer Ron Tauranac took over the reins of the Brabham team, but later in 1971 Bernie Ecclestone – the late Jochen Rindt's manager – also bought into it.

Big Business
It gave the Brabham team a new lease of life, but very few at the time realized the enormous implications for the future of Formula One. Ecclestone's ownership of a team made him party to business dealings with the race organizers, whom he felt were exploiting the teams. As an incredibly astute businessman, he banded the teams together and negotiated on their behalf. The much-improved deal he secured them was just the start. He also had the vision to see the true business

▲ Bernie Ecclestone (*left*, with Brabham designer Gordon Murray) brought a new era to Brabham – and to all of Formula One.

▼ Emerson Fittipaldi winning the 1972 British Grand Prix at Brands Hatch, on his way to becoming the youngest champ.

potential of Formula One to international sponsors, and so set about securing worldwide television coverage.

Fittipaldi and Lotus
On the track, Emerson Fittipaldi became the youngest-ever World Champion when he clinched the 1972 title at the age of 25 years, eight months and 29 days. The livery of his Lotus 72 had been changed from Gold Leaf to the black and gold colours of John Player Special cigarettes in one of the sport's most distinctive branding exercises. Treadless, "slick" tyres, introduced to Formula One in 1971 but originating from drag-racing, were the norm now, giving a greater surface area of rubber, and therefore more dry-track grip. The combination of downforce and slicks saw cornering forces rise to 2g.

Fittipaldi's Championship campaign had been eased somewhat by Jackie Stewart suffering a stomach ulcer, but for 1973 the Scot came bouncing back to take his third title. At Monaco he scored his 26th Grand Prix win,

breaking the record held by his friend, the late Jim Clark, and at the German Grand Prix he took his 27th and final race victory. At the end of the season, 34-year-old Stewart retired. But at Watkins Glen in the United States, the death of his team-mate François Cevert in practice for what was going to be Stewart's final race, had illustrated that the Stewart-initiated safety campaign had to continue.

▲ *(left)* François Cevert in 1973. The Frenchman perished at the end of the season, on the verge of great success.

▲ *(right)* Emerson Fittipaldi (Lotus) leads winner Jean-Pierre Beltoise (BRM) at Monaco in 1972. It was to be BRM's last victory.

Shapers

Bernie Ecclestone

The Mr Big of modern Formula One started out as just another Formula 500 racer in the early 1950s, combining this with his business of selling second-hand cars and motorcycles in south London. Ecclestone wasn't a bad driver, but his real talent lay in the world of business. He cut his links with the sport after the fatal accident of his close friend Stuart Lewis-Evans in the 1958 Moroccan Grand Prix, and made his fortune in property dealing.

He returned as the business manager of Austrian driver Jochen Rindt in the late 1960s. Rindt was killed at Monza in 1970, but Ecclestone this time stayed around and bought into the Brabham team, following the retirement of its founder Jack Brabham. From that time

onward, Ecclestone almost single-handedly transformed Formula One into a big business and, eventually, one of the biggest sporting series in the world. In the process, he made most of the team owners extremely wealthy, and himself even more so.

Along the way, Ecclestone's Brabham team gave Nelson Piquet world titles in 1981 and 1983, though Ecclestone sold the team in 1987. As head of the Formula One Constructors' Association (FOCA), he continues to wield enormous – some would say ultimate – power in the sport.

◄ Bernie Ecclestone, Brabham owner, at the South African Grand Prix in 1972. Big changes were coming.

The Ferrari Renaissance

Ferrari were badly in the doldrums by the end of 1973. They had just suffered an appalling season in which they never came close to winning a race, and they hadn't been World Champions since John Surtees' triumph of 1964. The top British teams with their "garagiste" kit-cars, using bought-in components, had basically run rings around the Italian thoroughbreds, with their exclusive self-made engines, for the best part of a decade. It was time for a reorganization.

Ferrari Revamps

Enzo Ferrari took the bull by the horns. He made wholesale changes to his technical team, and recruited a new driver line up. A brilliant young lawyer with close family ties to Fiat's Agnelli family, Luca di Montezemolo, was put in charge of the day-to-day running of the team, while Mauro Forghieri was made head of Formula One development. He toiled away to produce the 1974 312B3 model. Distribution of masses

▲ *(left)* Ferrari designer Mauro Forghieri and Niki Lauda in 1974, the two driving forces behind Ferrari's success.

▼ The new Ferrari 312T of Clay Regazzoni *(left)* alongside the previous 312B3 model in the pits at the South African Grand Prix, Kyalami, in 1975.

was his theme. The powerful flat-12 engine – used since 1970 – already brought the centre of gravity down low. Forghieri now set about centring the masses of the car as much as possible too, to make it more manoeuvrable. To this end the cockpit and fuel cells were moved forward within the wheelbase.

Concurrently, Ferrari signed a promising young Austrian driver, Niki Lauda. His technical feedback and appetite for endless hours of pounding round Ferrari's new Fiorano test track pleased Forghieri immensely. Together, they made the 312B3 1974's fastest car – as Lauda's nine pole positions testified. Some impetuosity on Lauda's part, and the occasional glitch from the car, handed the title to Emerson Fittipaldi and McLaren. But for 1975 there would be no such weaknesses as Lauda and Ferrari annihilated the opposition with the new 312T model. After a gap of 11 years, Ferrari were once again on top of the world.

▶ Winner Emerson Fittipaldi, in the McLaren M23, at the Canadian Grand Prix, Mosport Park, in 1974.

▼ (right) Winner Emerson Fittipaldi, in the McLaren M23, leads second-placed Niki Lauda at the Belgian Grand Prix at Nivelles, in 1974.

▼ (left) Emerson Fittipaldi, the 1974 World Champion, driving for McLaren.

Technology 1975

Ferrari 312T

The 312T was the car that broke a seven-year Championship-winning streak for Ford Cosworth DFV-powered machines. It was the masterpiece of Ferrari's chief designer Mauro Forghieri.

At the car's heart was Forghieri's flat-12 cylinder engine, which had first appeared in 1970. With the cylinders arranged in two horizontally-opposed lines of six, it had a lower centre of gravity than the vee-cylinder formation of the DFV, which benefited handling. With 12 smaller cylinders, it also had a greater combustion chamber area, lower inertia and fewer heat losses, allowing it to rev higher and produce more power. But 12 cylinders also meant it was heavier and thirstier. With 495bhp, it had around 35bhp more power than a DFV of the time, but was 25kg heavier and had to carry an extra 20kg of fuel at the start of a race.

The innovation of the Ferrari 312T was Forghieri's transverse gearbox. This further centralized the masses of the car, and enabled its handling to be more responsive. Forghieri also opted for the maximum width allowed by the regulations which meant more frontal area but brought a twofold advantage: firstly,

centre of gravity was lowered further; secondly, it facilitated wide but short fuel tanks, which allowed a short wheelbase despite a long engine, thereby getting around a key drawback of a 12-cylinder engine, to the benefit of the car's direction-changing ability.

▼ Clay Regazzoni won twice in the 312T in 1975 and 1976, as support to team leader Niki Lauda.

The Greatest Story Ever Told

After a fiery mid-season accident, Niki Lauda came back from the dead to fight for the 1976 World Championship, a contest that went down to a dramatic final round in the rain and mist of Japan, overlooked by the menacing Mount Fuji. Lauda's rival was an English former public schoolboy, James Hunt, who could have arrived straight out of a comic-strip. Dashing, blond and caring little for convention, his beautiful model wife had left him for film star Richard Burton earlier that season. It all made for the most fantastic story, one that transcended the sport and brought Formula One unprecedented public attention throughout the world.

Lauda vs Hunt
Lauda began the season as he had ended 1975, by winning in dominant fashion. By the time of the German Grand Prix in August he looked comfortably on his way to a second successive title, despite the often brilliant showings of Hunt in the Marlboro-McLaren. But then Lauda crashed, his Ferrari caught fire and he

◄ James Hunt at the South African Grand Prix in 1976, where he took his second successive pole position for McLaren.

▼ James Hunt in the McLaren M23, finished in third place in the 1976 Japanese Grand Prix, securing him the title by one point.

Technology 1977

Renault RS01

When the 3-litre formula was announced for 1966, there was a clause in the technical regulations stipulating that forced-induction engines could be no bigger than 1.5 litres. It was assumed that such a penalty would prevent anyone building a supercharged or turbocharged engine, the costs of which were expected to be exorbitant. Supercharged engines – whereby a mechanically-driven compressor compresses the fuel/air mix into the cylinders, massively increasing the power – had last been seen in Formula One in 1951. But at that time, exotic alcohol-based fuels that kept the extreme internal temperatures in check were permitted. Since 1958, only

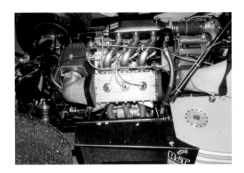

▲ The 1.5-litre V6 was very compact, albeit heavy, thanks to ancilliaries needed for the turbo and its cooling.

▼ Jean-Pierre Jabouille gave the RS01 its first race at Silverstone in 1977, qualifying 21st and retiring in the race.

conventional pump-fuel had been allowed. Despite this, Renault reckoned they could make a success of the turbo engine – whereby exhaust gases rather than a mechanical device drive the compressor. In its initial form, the 1.5-litre V6 produced 500bhp – slightly more than most conventional 3-litre engines were giving. As if the engine were not innovation enough, the Renault was also the first Formula One car to feature radial tyres rather than crossplies, courtesy of Michelin.

It would take many years before Renault could make a turbo engine reliable, but when they did, it released previously undreamed-of horsepower and changed the face of Formula One.

was trapped inside. Some fellow drivers pulled him out but he had suffered critical lung damage through inhalation of the flames. For days his life hung in the balance, and he was even granted the last rites. But, remarkably, he made a rapid recovery. Facially scarred, he returned three races later and finished fourth at Monza in one of the most astonishing performances ever seen in any sport.

He pulled out of the final race in Japan after one lap, unwilling to risk his life in conditions of virtually zero visibility. Hunt finished the race third, taking the Drivers' title by one point.

The story was made even better when in 1977 Lauda succeeded in regaining his crown. Better still, one

of his key victories came in Germany, albeit at a different track; his 1976 accident had ensured that the famous Nürburgring – recognized as the most demanding Grand Prix track of all since being built in 1926 – would never again host a Formula One race.

The 1977 British Grand Prix marked a key moment in Formula One history in the form of an unconventional yellow car that qualified only 21st fastest. It was the first Grand Prix start in 69 years for Renault. More significantly, it signified the arrival in Formula One of turbo-powered engines.

◀ The battle-scarred Niki Lauda returned to retake his World Championship title in 1977, and then he promptly left Ferrari.

The Magic of Ground Effect

The Lotus 78 of 1977 had a magic trick within it, one that took Formula One technology down a new road and would soon increase grip exponentially. In the process, it enabled the band of British constructors that had dominated Formula One for two decades to have a fighting chance against the return of the factories that Renault's entry to the sport now represented.

Lotus Innovations

With the 78 model, Lotus brought the concept of "ground effect" to Formula One. When air is funnelled through a small aperture that then opens out into a wide expanse, it creates a negative pressure. Give this area a seal with the ground and it will suck down. This in essence is how the Lotus worked, giving it a big grip advantage over its closest rivals.

Only car unreliability kept Mario Andretti from comfortably winning the 1977 World Championship with the Lotus 78. For 1978, the Lotus 79 represented an evolution of the concept, and this time the performance advantage it brought was massive. Andretti's only rival for the world crown was his team-mate Ronnie Peterson, but Peterson was contracted to be in a support role to Andretti,

► American racing legend, Mario Andretti, won the 1978 World Championship using the ground-effect Lotus 78 and 79 models.

▲ Swede Gunnar Nilsson won the 1977 Belgian Grand Prix in the ground-effect Lotus 78. He died from cancer in 1978.

and on a couple of occasions finished a dutiful second to him when he could conceivably have passed.

Andretti clinched the title at the Italian Grand Prix, but it was in tragic circumstances. Peterson died as a result of injuries sustained in a startline collision. His car slid beneath a barrier in the force of impact, breaking one of his legs. He was hospitalized but died later that evening from a brain embolism triggered by the broken bone. It was a tragic end to Lotus' glorious season.

▼ Andretti winning the 1977 Italian Grand Prix in the Lotus 78. Its slow straightline speed was corrected in the 79 model.

▲ The aftermath of the first lap crash which claimed the life of Ronnie Peterson at Monza on 10 September, 1978.

▶ Ronnie Peterson tragically succumbed to his Monza injuries after a fine season. He was lying second in the Championship.

Technology 1978

Lotus 79

The previous year's Lotus 78 had been the first Formula One car to utilize ground effect. Contained within its side pods were venturi channels, small apertures opening out into a bigger area. When air flowed through these, channels it created a negative pressure, which was sealed off via skirts running along the bottom of the pods, thereby sucking the car to the ground.

The problem with the 78 model was that the centre of pressure was too biased towards the front of the car, necessitating a bigger rear wing to balance the handling, at the cost of straightline speed. In its layout, the 79 addressed this problem, and more fully exploited the potential of the concept. Quite by chance, ground effect also

brought the decade-old Cosworth DFV engine back into play as the most suitable engine for the job. Since the mid-1970s, Ferrari had taken full advantage of the lower centre of gravity endowed by their flat-12 motor to produce the fastest cars in the competition. But efficient ground effect demanded side pods with plenty of open space behind them, in order to

▲ Ronnie Peterson followed Mario Andretti home in the Spanish Grand Prix of 1978, both Lotus 79-propelled.

speed up the airflow and increase the suction. This meant that the cylinder banks of the Ferrari were now in the worst possible place, while those of the DFV, angled upwards in a vee-shape, were perfectly situated.

Safety: Still a Way to Go

R onnie Peterson's fatal accident
at the 1978 Italian Grand Prix
illustrated just how far there was still to
go, over a decade after Jackie Stewart
initiated the safety campaign. Peterson
was the only Formula One driver to be
killed on-track that year, suggesting
some improvement since 1970 when
three drivers succumbed. But the
average for the decade was still slightly
more than one driver death per season.
The figures also showed that there
would be a death or serious injury for
every 40 accidents – a big improvement
over the 1960s, but still far too high.

Taking Safety Seriously

Professor Sid Watkins, a British
neurologist and motor racing fan,
had been asked by Bernie Ecclestone
to attend some races with a view to
making suggestions about how to
improve medical facilities. He was
present that day at Monza but had no
position of authority. His observations
of events there indicated many areas
where big improvements could be
made relatively easily. Soon after,

▲ *(above and inset right)* John Watson in
the carbon-fibre McLaren MP4/1, in which
he survived unscathed from a huge accident
at Monza.

▼ Catch fencing halts the errant cars of
Jochen Mass and Nelson Piquet in the 1980
Belgian Grand Prix.

▲ Sid Watkins, FISA Doctor, is swarmed by
the Coca-Cola girls at the Brazilian Grand
Prix, Rio de Janeiro, in 1981.

▼ Denny Hulme leads Jackie Stewart through a newly-installed chicane at Monza in 1972, designed to keep speeds in check.

Watkins was made chief medical officer for all Grands Prix, which gave him absolute authority. He can bring a meeting grinding to a halt if he is not satisfied with any aspect of safety. The medical facilities of the circuits have since improved immeasurably.

Safety vs Advantage

In terms of car design, new regulations for 1973 stipulated that the space between the monocoque skins had to be filled with hardened foam to provide a deformable structure, and the fuel tanks had to be better insulated. But thereafter, the advent of ground effect cars made it more desirable from an aerodynamic performance point of view to have the cockpits far forward within the wheelbase, even to the extent that drivers' feet were sometimes ahead of the axle line of the front wheels, making them especially vulnerable. A regulation banning this practice didn't come into effect until 1988.

Circuit safety improved throughout the decade. Greater run-off areas were beginning to be provided on the fast corners, tyre barriers were erected, as was catch fencing, which would wrap itself around an errant car and thereby slow its progress. This, however, created a secondary hazard in that the poles to which the fencing was attached could strike a driver's head. The 1980s would see the catch fencing replaced by gravel traps. As a downside to the safety movement, several demanding corners – highlights of the track – were lost from the circuits as chicanes were installed before them to slow cars down to a safer cornering speed.

▲ Safety crusader Jackie Stewart in his post-retirement role of TV commentator talks viewers through a Lotus 79.

▲ Alan Jones and Gilles Villeneuve make use of the catch fencing at the British Grand Prix at Silverstone in 1981.

TV: Spreading the Word

The fairytale story of the 1976 Lauda vs Hunt epic was probably the spark that got television companies interested in Formula One. The British Broadcasting Corporation televised the championship finale – something of a departure from its previous policy of screening the Monaco and British Grands Prix only. In 1978, the BBC began televising every race.

Formula One Goes Global
If Hunt's performances can be said to have been responsible for bringing the BBC in, it was a pattern repeated as drivers of other nations were successful. Australia's Alan Jones began winning races on a regular basis in 1979, triggering Channel Nine's season-long coverage for the following year.

Emerson Fittipaldi's success in the early to mid-1970s saw interest in Formula One soar in Brazil, and the television companies responded appropriately. In each case, the broadcasts were such a success that they remained regular fixtures even after those drivers had left the sport or ceased to be successful. France was an early television convert, thanks to the success of the Elf programme in backing the nation's promising junior drivers until they reached Formula One; by 1978, there were seven French drivers there.

The rights to broadcast Formula One were – and are – negotiated by Bernie Ecclestone. Initially the terms were not too fierce, as he sought to lead them into the sport gently and thereby make it a more attractive place for sponsors

▲ *(left)* James Hunt's 1976 epic title race with Niki Lauda, and his glamorous profile, generated lots of interest from racing fans.

◄ Arguably the dice of the decade unfolded as Gilles Villeneuve and René Arnoux fought over second, France 1979.

▼ Jody Scheckter won the 1979 World Championship after taking his Ferrari to victory three times.

▼ Clay Regazzoni takes the flag at Silverstone 1979 to give the Williams team its first Grand Prix victory.

to be. But steadily, the process snowballed and, as the money rolled in, so the sport became bigger news, and so the fee increased. The television companies happily paid up, as the sport was attracting ever-more television advertising revenue.

Television and Live Drama

By the end of the 1970s, it was all just beginning to take off. There was some particularly good footage to show in 1979, most memorably in the French Grand Prix where Gilles Villeneuve's Ferrari and René Arnoux's Renault fought one of the most desperate and thrilling wheel-to-wheel battles ever seen, frequently trading rubber or running wide onto the grass in the closing laps of the race. In all the excitement, it was easy to overlook the fact that this was a fight for second place; some way ahead of them, Jean-Pierre Jabouille was himself making a bit of history. In winning the race for Renault, he gave the turbocharged engine its first ever Formula One victory.

At Silverstone for the next race, Clay Regazzoni gave the British Williams team its first win, initiating a lineage of success for them that continues to this day. His team-mate Alan Jones dominated the second half of the season in the ground-effect FW07 model. But it was Ferrari's Jody Scheckter who took the title thanks to three victories and superbly consistent finishing in between.

▼ Clay Regazzoni's Williams in action.

Entente Incordiale: The Battle for Control

Bernie Ecclestone's increasing power and influence through the 1970s had made the sport's nominal governing body, the FIA (Fédération Internationale de l'Automobile), very nervous. When the body elected a new president, Jean-Marie Balestre, in 1978 he vowed that he was going to wrest control of the sport back where it belonged. He included in that mission statement financial control as well as sporting and technical.

David vs Goliath
The body headed by Ecclestone, the FOCA, represented the interests of the independent teams, most of whom were British. It didn't include Ferrari, nor the car-producing factories of Renault and Alfa Romeo, both of whom had recently joined Formula One. Balestre, an outrageously manipulative politician, succeeded in exposing a fault line of conflicting interests between the FOCA and non-FOCA teams.

For 1980, Balestre attempted to ban the sliding skirts used on the sidepods of the cars that were a critical part of their ground effect performance. His stated objection was that they made the cars so much faster that circuits were having to be constantly changed, with ever-greater run-off areas, just to keep pace.

The British constructors, all of them relying on the venerable bought-in Cosworth DFV engine, felt that it was only their superior chassis technology

▲ *(top)* Jean-Marie Balestre, FISA President, talks with Bernie Ecclestone, Brabham team owner and FOCA member.

▼ Jody Scheckter finished second at the United States Grand Prix (West), Long Beach, Florida, in 1979.

▲ *(above)* Pole sitter Nelson Piquet, in the Brabham BT49, took his first Grand Prix win at the USA (West) Grand Prix in 1980.

▼ Max Mosley, March team owner, at the Canadian Grand Prix, Mosport Park, October 1977.

that was preventing Formula One being dominated by a small number of money-no-object factory teams, with their own more powerful engines. The sliding skirts were an essential element to this chassis superiority.

On the Brink of Divide

The argument bubbled on throughout 1980 before the sport split into two camps during the off-season of 1980–81. FOCA announced its own Championship and published a series of dates. Six teams, including Ferrari, Renault and Alfa Romeo, stayed loyal with the governing body, and it looked for a time as if there would be two conflicting World Championships. A South African Grand Prix took place in January with just the FOCA teams. It was a sure recipe for a complete commercial disaster.

Shapers

Jean-Marie Balestre

Noted as bombastic and highly controversial during his time as president of FISA, the sporting arm of the FIA, Balestre did many positive things for the sport during his time at the helm.

After serving in the war as an undercover agent for the French Resistance – posing as a member of the French SS – he established a successful French racing motor magazine, *Autojournal*. He is also given credit for popularizing kart racing, and founded the world karting commission. He rose to a position of authority within French national motorsport and this led to his presidency of the Paris-based world governing body. It was Balestre who established specific crash test requirements for Formula One cars and in so doing raised safety standards enormously. He was re-elected in 1987 and stayed in charge until the 1991 elections when he lost to Max Mosley, who for years had been Ecclestone's key partner in FOCA.

▼ Carlos Reutemann in the Williams FW07B finished third at the Belgian Grand Prix at Zolder in 1980.

It was a farcical situation and a compromise was finally brokered by Enzo Ferrari. In a meeting at the Ferrari base of Maranello, Balestre and Ecclestone both signed an agreement – called the Concorde Agreement – that is, essentially, the basis on which the sport of Formula One runs today. FOCA was granted the commercial negotiating rights on the FIA's behalf, while the FIA retained control of all sporting and technical regulations.

Many years later Ecclestone revealed that he had been about to telephone Balestre to surrender when Balestre called him to suggest a compromise! At last, the racing could get underway again, though feelings of distrust between the two sides continued to flare up from time to time.

▼ Jean-Pierre Jabouille, Renault RE20, retired on the first lap with clutch failure. Belgian Grand Prix, Zolder, 1980.

Specialists vs The Factories

G round effect had arrived just in time to give the British specialist teams a weapon against the exotic turbo engines of the returning factory outfits. It did not take long for Renault to devise their own ground-effect chassis though, and so while the British teams were fighting to have turbos banned, they were also researching avenues through which they could get their own.

On Even Ground

There was a brief window – before Renault had made their engines fully reliable and before the specialist teams had sourced turbos – where a competitive equilibrium between the two was established. That window comprised the 1980 and 1981 seasons.

Alan Jones gave Williams its first World Championship in 1980, pushed hard by the Brabham of Nelson Piquet. The Renaults by now were running close to 600bhp – an advantage of around 100bhp over the DFV cars – and won three races in the hands of René Arnoux and Jean-Pierre Jabouille, but their chassis, despite featuring ground effect, lagged behind those of the best specialist teams and their engines repeatedly blew up.

▲ Alain Prost in the Renault RE30, en route to his first victory and on home soil at the French Grand Prix, Dijon-Prenois, in 1981. It was the first of 51 wins for the Frenchman.

◄ 1980 World Champion Alan Jones retired at the end of 1981 after another great season with Williams. He later returned, but without the same level of success.

▼ Prost's Renault dices hard with Jones' Williams in the 1981 German Grand Prix. It was a classic factory vs specialist team fight: the Renault had superior horsepower, but the Williams had a better chassis.

▼ Portuguese Grand Prix winner Alain Prost (*centre*) with second-placed Niki Lauda (*left*) and third-placed Ayrton Senna (*right*) in 1984.

final race of 1983, armed with the turbo, he had driven an extremely strong race, closing down on the leader before his engine expired.

Lauda Holds Off

As the 1984 season progressed, it soon became clear that Prost, as the younger, hungrier man, had a clear edge in speed. But Lauda had the guile and cunning of experience and he put it to superb use. They arrived at Estoril, Portugal, for the final round with nine points up for grabs and Lauda just 3.5 points ahead.

Prost qualified on the front row and quickly established a big lead in the race. Lauda had qualified a disastrous eleventh, and for much of the race was stuck in tenth, making no progress. As cars dropped out ahead, Lauda moved up to seventh. Assuming Prost was going to win this race, Lauda needed to finish second in order to clinch the title. He then began to get a move on, quickly disposing of Johansson, Alboreto and a young driver in his first season, Ayrton Senna. Now Lauda was third, with just Nigel Mansell's Lotus between him and a third world title. Lauda could make no gains on the Lotus, but at around three-quarter distance, Mansell was

suddenly lapping much slower – his brakes were failing. Lauda duly picked him off and cruised to his third title – five years after retiring!

The McLarens retained their dominant form into 1985, but Lauda suffered an appalling reliability record. By contrast, Prost glided from win to win, and took his first title by a comfortable margin. Only in Zandvoort, for the Dutch Grand Prix, was there an echo of 1984, when Lauda resolutely

held off a charging Prost in the closing stages to take his 25th – and final – Grand Prix victory. At the end of the season, Lauda retired once again, and this time he stayed out for good. It was a remarkable end to a remarkable two-part career.

▼ Niki Lauda's McLaren MP4/2B leads second-placed team-mate Alain Prost to take his twenty-fifth and final Grand Prix victory at Zandvoort, Holland, in 1985.

Prost vs Williams

By the tail-end of 1985, with Alain Prost well on his way to winning the title, the pace of the McLaren-Porsches was finally overcome by that of the Williams-Hondas, which won the final three races. For 1986 Williams enlisted double World Champion Nelson Piquet to partner Nigel Mansell, and thus made themselves favourites for the title. But that was to reckon without an intense personal battle between the two Williams drivers – and also the supreme skills of Prost.

The Race for Pace

The McLaren-Porsche successes had been built on a compact, fuel-efficient engine, the specification of which was largely laid down by McLaren designer John Barnard. As a paying customer that had exclusively commissioned the

▲ The Williams-Honda mechanics work on Nelson Piquet's car at the 1986 British Grand Prix at Brands Hatch.

engine from Porsche, McLaren were able to dictate what they needed rather more effectively than Williams, whose engines were supplied free of charge by Honda.

The Porsche's compact dimensions had allowed Barnard to design an aerodynamically efficient car. Since 1983, ground effect side venturis and skirts had been banned and so the emphasis came back to upper bodywork and maintaining a good balance between low drag and high downforce. Barnard's McLarens were tightly waisted around the engine, giving a healthy airflow to the rear wing of the car.

Fuel stops had been banned since 1984 and a fuel limit of 220 litres imposed. The trick for engine designers was to reach an efficiency level that still allowed a reasonable amount of turbo boost to be used. In this, the Bosch electronic control of the Porsche was supreme, and very much key to McLaren's world titles of 1984 and 1985. By 1986, however, Honda had caught up – and even surpassed – Porsche in this respect. Their engines were giving over 900bhp for the races and an astounding 1200bhp in high-boost qualifying trim. Williams had also begun to use the underfloor of the car,

◀ The dominance of the Williams-Hondas in 1987 was emphasized at the British Grand Prix. They were over a lap clear at the end.

▼ Nelson Piquet's Williams FW11B leads at the start of the 1987 Austrian Grand Prix at the Osterreichring. He finished second.

aft of the regulated flat-bottom area that extended to the rear axle line, to create more downforce. A sharp upwards sweep of the underbody formed a "diffuser" that created ground effect.

The Guile of Prost

Williams' year got off to a terrible start even before the season began as team boss Frank Williams was crippled in a road accident. He missed most of the year as designer Patrick Head stepped up to run the show. Mansell and Piquet fought like demons, fuelled by an intense dislike of each other. Prost's car wasn't usually as fast, but he won whenever the Williams faltered and sometimes – such as at Imola and Monaco – he simply out-drove and out-thought the Williams drivers. Going into the final round at Adelaide, Mansell had a six point lead. By lap 63, the three title contenders were in the

first three positions in the order of Piquet, Mansell, Prost. If it stayed like this Mansell would be Champion. But with 19 laps to go, Mansell's rear tyre exploded at around 300km/h (190mph). He wrestled the car to a stop, but his title was gone. Piquet was called in for a precautionary tyre change, leaving Prost to win the race and an unexpected second Championship.

The End of Turbo

In 1987, Williams extended their speed advantage over McLaren, and this time the title fight was between Piquet and Mansell, even though in winning the Portuguese Grand Prix, Prost broke Jackie Stewart's record of 27 wins. Piquet won the title after Mansell injured his back in a crash during practice for the penultimate round in Japan.

► Nigel Mansell wrestles his Williams FW11 back under control after his rear tyre blew on the Brabham Straight costing him the 1986 World Championship crown.

Changing of the Guard II

In a surprising development, Honda switched its supply of engines for 1988 from Williams to McLaren. As part of the deal, McLaren acquired the services of Ayrton Senna, who had driven a Honda-powered Lotus in 1987. In Senna and Prost, McLaren had possibly the most explosive driver line-up of all time. In Gordon Murray's MP4/4, it also had one of the greatest car designs. The combination produced the most dominant season enjoyed by any team in the modern era of Grand Prix racing. McLaren won 15 of the 16 races comprising the Championship.

It was the final year in which turbocharged engines would be allowed. The governing body had introduced a 3.5-litre non-turbo class in 1987 and then limited the turbos

yet further for 1988. They were not allowed to run any more than 2.5-bar boost (it had been limited to 4-bar in 1987) and they had to do a race distance on no more than 150 litres of fuel. For the non-turbo engines there was no fuel limitation. By 1989 the turbos would be outlawed. Controlling costs was put forward as the rationale behind this, but more likely it suited both the manufacturers and appeased the smaller teams, who had been calling for a turbo ban for years.

◀ Ayrton Senna in 1988.

▼ Senna's McLaren MP4/5 prepares to head out on to the track as team-mate Alain Prost waits in the pits.

▼ Gerhard Berger's Ferrari F187/88C leads team-mate Michele Alboreto to an emotional 1-2 home finish at the Italian Grand Prix, Monza, in 1988.

Although it had been the turbocharged format that had attracted Renault to Formula One in 1977, and their subsequent success that had enticed other big manufacturers into the sport, those manufacturers had no intention of leaving Formula One just because of a return to normally-aspirated motors. Indeed, turbocharging was beginning to fall out of fashion for road-going engines as a new emissions law loomed, so the change of formula suited them fine. The turbo era had introduced them to Formula One and changed the scale of money in the sport, but its increasing global reach and image had more than justified the investment.

The massive financial investment by manufacturers had allowed the top teams to grow quickly in size and resources. Teams invested in wind tunnels and research and development programmes, and as quickly as new regulations were issued to control performance so new research-led solutions appeared. McLaren and Honda demonstrated as much in 1988 when even with the severe turbo engine restrictions, they dominated and easily eclipsed the non-turbo runners. Resources were now everything.

▲ Enzo Ferrari, racing driver from a different era and founder of the Ferrari marque, photographed c.1983.

Senna vs Prost

Senna clinched the Championship from Prost at the last round. In a parallel to the Lauda-Prost McLaren line-up of 1984, the younger, hungrier Senna was the quicker driver, but Prost had guile. It was an uneasy relationship from the start and would develop into a hostile one the following season.

The only 1988 race not won by McLaren was the Italian Grand Prix, where Senna, leading, was tripped up lapping a backmarker. With Prost already out, it gifted Ferrari a 1-2 result on home soil. Just a few weeks earlier, the team's founder, Enzo Ferrari, had died at the age of 90. He had been the last link to a very different age.

Prost Makes a Stand

T he new non-turbo 3.5-litre era made little difference to McLaren and Honda's form. Like the returning Renault, who supplied the Williams team, Honda opted for a V10 engine, judging it the ideal compromise between the all-out power of a V12 and the compact packaging and economy of a V8.

Bitter Inter-team Rivalry

With up to 685bhp, the Honda was the most powerful engine in the field in 1989, leaving Senna and Prost to once again fight for the title. At Imola, the second round of the Championship, the pair fell out over a pre-race agreement not to fight into the first corner. Senna led clearly at the start and Prost didn't force the issue, but then the race was restarted after an enormous fiery accident for Gerhard Berger's Ferrari brought out the red flags. On the restart Prost led cleanly away, but this time Senna forced his way down the inside on his way to winning the race. Prost was furious, and from that moment on the pair were sworn enemies. The advantage see-sawed between them as the season played

out and, into the penultimate round in Japan, Prost was ahead on points. Senna needed to win here to keep the title fight open until the final round. The Frenchman dominated the first half of the race, but gradually Senna began to reel him in. On lap 47, just six from

▲ The moment when Alain Prost and team-mate Senna tangle to a standstill at the Japanese Grand Prix, Suzuka, 1989.

▼ After their collision, Alain Prost walks away mistakenly believing his car had been damaged in the accident.

▼ Senna pits for a new nosecone after his collision with Prost at Japan in 1989. Prost had already retired from the race.

the end, Senna made a move under braking into the chicane from a long way back. Essentially, it gave Prost the choice: either he gave way or had a collision. In no mood for compromises, Prost deliberately turned in on Senna and they tangled. They sat gesturing to each other in their stationary cars before Prost jumped out, falsely believing his machine had suffered suspension damage.

Senna restarted, returning to the track via the escape road, then pitted for a new nosecone, and came back to win the race. But he was subsequently disqualified for his use of the escape road, and the title went to Prost. Senna was furious, as was McLaren team boss Ron Dennis because Prost had already announced he was leaving McLaren for Ferrari in 1990. This result meant he would be taking the number one (reserved for the World Champion), with him. But the war between Prost and Senna was not over yet.

Technology 1989

Ferrari 640

Ferrari came back strongly in 1989, with a radical new John Barnard-designed car that Nigel Mansell and Gerhard Berger took to three victories. Powered by a V12 engine, its biggest innovation was a semi-automatic clutchless gearbox worked by electro-hydraulics.

Gear paddles on the back of the steering wheel – one for up, the other for down the box – replaced the conventional gear lever. It meant the cockpit could be narrower, to the benefit of the aerodynamics, and the mechanism could change the gears

faster than any driver. It also meant the driver could have two hands on the wheel at all times, which on certain types of corner with heavy braking into a tight apex, found him a lot of time.

It was an innovation that was widely copied, and it is now a standard feature of all Formula One cars.

◄ Gerhard Berger was thankful for the Ferrari 640's strength after surviving a huge impact at Imola in 1989.

▼ Berger didn't enjoy quite the same success with the 640 as Nigel Mansell. The car proved quick but unreliable initially.

Prost and Senna: War

he separation of Prost and Senna into separate teams did nothing to dilute the intensity of their battles in 1990. On the contrary, it now gained an even sharper edge. It was a finely-matched season between the two of them. Senna was the world's fastest driver aided by the Honda V10, still the most powerful engine. His nemesis Prost enjoyed the benefits of a Ferrari that was a little down on power but which had a clear handling advantage.

Neck and Neck
Senna began the season strongly, but Prost hit back with three consecutive mid-season victories. One of these, in Britain, was at the expense of his team-mate Nigel Mansell who was commanding the race until his gearbox played up. In an emotional outpouring afterwards, Mansell announced that he was going to retire at the end of the

▲ Ayrton Senna (*left*) and Alain Prost end up in the gravel after their run-in at the Japanese Grand Prix, Suzuka, in 1990.

▼ Senna (*left*) goes down the inside of Prost at Suzuka in 1990 with no intention of lifting off for the looming corner.

▼ Senna (*right*) and Prost walk back to the pits after retiring from the 1990 Japanese Grand Prix.

▼ Ayrton Senna at Monaco in 1991. Victory here was part of a campaign that took him to his third – and final – world title.

year. He was unhappy at the way Alain Prost had walked into what had been Mansell's team and been able to centre it around him.

A win for Prost in Spain made it five victories to the six of Senna, and then came Japan, the scene of their famous altercation the year before. Senna set pole, slightly quicker than Prost. The Brazilian then complained that the grid layout left him on the dirty side of the track, which would make him potentially slower off the line than Prost. He asked that the sides be changed, so he could benefit from his pole position. He was livid when the request was refused.

With this and their accident the year before as a backdrop, Senna had a ruthless plan if, as he feared, Prost was able to out-accelerate him away from the lights. Prost duly got ahead at the start, and the pair of them headed down to the first corner, braking from around 225km/h (140mph). Or at least Prost braked. Senna did not even lift the accelerator, and in a cynical move hit the back of the Ferrari, taking them both off into the gravel trap and retirement from the race. Now, with just one race to go, Prost could no longer catch his rival's points score.

► Winner Nigel Mansell at Silverstone in 1991. He pushed Senna close for the Championship as preparation for 1992.

Senna was World Champion for the second time.

Mansell had since "unretired", having been talked into returning to the Williams team which had enjoyed a promising 1990, with Riccardo Patrese and Thierry Boutsen scoring a win apiece in the improving Renault-engined car. It was a good move: the Ferrari effort imploded in 1991, while

the Williams-Renault gradually emerged as the fastest car of all. Mansell was able to push Senna's now V12 Honda-powered McLaren hard, but Ayrton was able to hang on for title number three. After falling into complete disarray, the Ferrari team sacked Prost two races before the season finished for being publicly critical about his car. He took a sabbatical the following year.

Gizmos to the Fore

Williams had followed Ferrari's early lead in developing a semi-automatic electro-hydraulic gearbox in 1991. Their chief aerodynamicist Adrian Newey had also come up with a highly efficient chassis. What Newey wanted to do now was make the next step – active ride. After much haranguing of technical director Patrick Head, Newey was finally given the go-ahead to develop what would turn out to be the dominant machine of 1992.

Active Ride

As long ago as 1983 active ride had been tried by Lotus, but the technology of the control systems of that time were insufficiently sophisticated. In 1987, both Lotus and Williams had won races with active ride cars, but at the time there didn't seem to be enough benefit over conventionally-sprung cars, and the developments were shelved.

By the early 1990s, the control systems were much improved and the cars were more pitch-sensitive than ever before – their aerodynamic effectiveness varied a lot according to the pitch of the car. There was an

▲ Adrian Newey, Williams chief designer, who was responsible for the all-conquering Williams FW14B.

▼ Nigel Mansell, winner of the Brazilian Grand Prix, 1992. Mansell took the FW14B to victory in the first five races that season.

enormous increase in aerodynamic performance to be had by keeping the ride height of the cars constant at all times. Active ride was perfect for this. Instead of springs and dampers, the suspension featured computer-controlled hydraulic actuators that would react in a split-second to the loads put on the car, and keep the ride height constant at all times, eliminating pitch, dive and roll.

The resultant Williams FW14B was a devastating tool. Mansell won the first five Grands Prix of 1992 and took nine victories during the season, both record-breaking statistics. He clinched the world title at the Hungarian Grand Prix, with five races still to go.

Early in 1992 Williams had taken the precaution of signing Alain Prost for 1993, and Prost took over leadership of the team as Mansell failed to agree financial terms and left to go Indycar racing. Mansell was replaced by test driver Damon Hill.

Traction Control

Not only did every serious team have active ride by 1993, but traction control

was an almost universal feature too, whereby computers would cut power to the wheels when excessive wheelspin was detected. In some cars, notably the Benetton B193, this system was combined with an automatic "launch control" system; the driver just pressed buttons to "arm" the system, then another as the lights changed and the car would automatically make the optimum getaway. The Benetton also featured four-wheel-steer. Williams introduced anti-lock ABS braking to their cars part-way through the season, while McLaren was working on a programme that, when perfected, would give different chassis settings from corner to corner.

While the other teams may have caught up with Williams in 1993 in the number of electronic gizmos used, the aerodynamic efficiency of the FW15 and the power of its Renault V10 made it by far the fastest car, which enabled Alain Prost to clinch his fourth title fairly comfortably. He took his 51st and final Grand Prix victory at the German Grand Prix at Hockenheim to set a record that would stand for some years. At the end of that season Prost retired.

▲ Damon Hill in the Williams FW15C takes the chequered flag for his first Grand Prix victory at the Hungarian Grand Prix, Hungaroring, in 1993.

◄ Race winner Nigel Mansell at the Mexican Grand Prix, Meixco City, 1992. Mansell set a new world record that year of nine wins in one season.

▼ Race winner Alain Prost in the Williams FW15C at the San Marino Grand Prix, Imola, Italy, in 1993.

The Senna Tragedy

Ayrton Senna, the world's greatest driver, was killed live on television on 1 May 1994. Just the previous day, Roland Ratzenberger had perished at the same Imola track. These were the first driver fatalities at a Grand Prix for 12 years. While this emphasized the great safety strides that had been made, the shocking events of Imola shook Formula One into a new safety initiative as the sport's right to exist came under scrutiny in a way unseen since the Le Mans tragedy of 1955.

De-humanizing the Sport
The 1994 season had started on a controversial note with the banning of "driver aids". Traction control, launch control, ABS braking, active suspension, and pits-to-car telemetry that enabled settings to be changed from the pits while the car was on the track, were all deemed illegal. The governing body, headed by Max Mosley, felt that the gizmos were de-humanizing the sport, damaging its public appeal. Concurrently, refuelling pit stops were reintroduced.

Senna, newly signed for Williams-Renault, had struggled in the opening two races against the Benetton-Ford of Michael Schumacher. Ever since making a startling Formula One debut at Spa in 1991, the German had been considered the man most likely to inherit Senna's

▲ **Ayrton Senna in the Williams FW16 follows the painfully slow safety car after the startline crash at the San Marino Grand Prix.**

▼ **Senna embarks on his final lap before tragically losing his life in an accident on lap six at Imola, 1 May 1994.**

▼ Roland Ratzenberger lost his life the day before Senna, at Imola. The Austrian was in his first season of Formula One.

throne as the world's number one. The early races of 1994 confirmed as much as Senna struggled with a car suffering an aerodynamic flaw and lacking the traction and stability of Schumacher's car. The change in regulations appeared to have slowed Senna's car more than Schumacher's.

Death at Imola

Senna was leading Schumacher at Imola when the race came under the jurisdiction of the safety car, soon after the start, in order that debris from a startline accident could be cleared up. Upon the resumption of racing, Senna was pushing extremely hard to keep Schumacher at bay when he lost control through the flat-out kink of Tamburello. He hit the retaining wall

Shapers:

Max Mosley

As President of the sport's governing body, the FIA, since 1991 Mosley has been extremely pro-active on the safety issues of the sport, and has successfully fended off an EEC initiative that threatened to wrest exclusive control of the sport away from the FIA. Through the FIA, Mosely has also initiated a vigorous safety testing procedure for road car manufacturers in an effort to transfer safety lessons learnt in racing to the road.

An urbane lawyer, he is the son of former English Fascist leader, Sir Oswald Mosley. He took up racing in the 1960s, competing as high as Formula Two, and in 1969 he co-founded March Engineering, which entered Formula One the following year. The team won three Grands Prix in the 1970s, and the company became a highly successful customer race car producer.

▲ Max Mosley, President of the FIA. He pushed through extensive safety measures after Imola in 1994.

Mosley was a key member of FOCA, and in the early 1980s fought hard alongside Bernie Ecclestone, wrestling the FIA for control of the sport. The poacher became gamekeeper when he was elected as former foe Jean-Marie Balestre's replacement in 1991.

at around 210km/h (130mph), and a suspension part flew off and pierced his helmet, inflicting fatal injuries.

At the Monaco Grand Prix, where Karl Wendlinger went into a coma following impact with a protective barrier, Max Mosley announced a series of regulation changes to address the safety issue. Stepped-bottom regulations limiting ground effect were imposed from the very next race, together with a pit lane speed limit.

From 1995, engine capacity would be reduced to 3 litres and cockpits had to feature protective raised sides. The FIA's safety programme has been ongoing since the deaths at Imola in 1994, with a series of ever-tougher crash tests and compulsory safety features introduced on a regular basis.

▼ A scorching start helped Michael Schumacher's Benetton to victory in the 1994 French Grand Prix.

Damon's Debacles

Following the death of Ayrton Senna, the 1994 season distilled into a controversial duel between Benetton's Michael Schumacher and Williams' Damon Hill. The German was widely acknowledged now as Formula One's greatest exponent, while the early aerodynamic problems of the Williams were quickly sorted to make it Formula One's fastest car.

Life After Senna
Schumacher had taken victory in the first four rounds before Hill made his seasonal breakthrough, with victory in Spain. Spookily, it echoed his late father Graham's achievement of 1968, when victory at the same race had acted as a much-needed tonic for a team devastated by the loss of its number one driver. Here, Damon did much the same thing for Williams. For all that, Schumacher astonished by finishing second in a car that for much of the race was stuck in fifth gear.

At the British Grand Prix that year, Schumacher was given a draconian race ban for the relatively minor infringement of overtaking on the warm-up lap. This was later changed to a two race ban! Combined with his disqualification from victory in the Belgian Grand Prix – because the underfloor wooden plank, which ensured the regulation stepped-bottom rules were met, had been ground away

▲ Damon Hill (*left*) and Michael Schumacher in the midst of a robust battle for the lead, Belgium, 1995.

◄ Schumacher's professional foul on Hill, Adelaide 1994, ensured the German took his first world title.

▼ Michael Schumacher tries a daring move inside Damon Hill at the 1995 Portuguese Grand Prix at Estoril.

▼ Race winner Michael Schumacher in the Benetton B195 at the 1995 Monaco Grand Prix, Monte Carlo.

▲ Michael Schumacher shows his anger after colliding with Hill during the race. Italian Grand Prix, Monza, 1995.

when he spun on a kerb – it somewhat artificially made the final round in Australia a title-decider.

Schumacher and Hill quickly pulled away from the rest of the field, both stretching themselves to their very limits. It was Schumacher who cracked first, glancing the wall before rejoining the track. This had happened out of Hill's sight, and as he then made a dive for the inside at the next corner, Schumacher turned in on him and terminally damaged the Williams' suspension. Schumacher was champion

▲ Schumacher discusses tactics with technical director Ross Brawn (*centre*) and Pat Symonds (*left*) at Silverstone in 1994.

▼ Schumacher and Benetton completely dominated the 1995 championship, frequently humiliating Hill and Williams.

under the most controversial circumstances in what had been an intensely controversial season.

There was to be no doubting the outcome in 1995 though. Benetton was newly equipped with a Renault engine like that in the Williams, which nonetheless retained its status as Formula One's fastest car. Despite this, Schumacher and the Benetton team consistently out-performed Hill and Williams, taking nine victories on the way to a comfortable title. Schumacher and Benetton technical director, Ross Brawn, repeatedly won races through superior pit stop strategies, as they formed an incredibly close working relationship.

Schuey Joins Ferrari

After winning two consecutive World Championships with a relatively unfancied team, what next was there for Michael Schumacher? It would have been quite straightforward to have negotiated a place at Williams, who had the fastest car and biggest depth of technical talent. It would probably have been the work of a moment to make himself part of Mercedes-Benz's ambitious Formula One plans in partnership with the mighty McLaren team. What he did instead was accept motorsport's biggest challenge: he transferred to Ferrari, the biggest name in Formula One, but a team in disarray that hadn't been a championship contender for years.

▲ Ferrari President Luca di Montezemolo (*left*) and team manager Jean Todt (*right*): architects of the Ferrari revival.

Ferrari Steadies Ship

Scuderia Ferrari had been through some turbulent times since the death of its founder Enzo Ferrari in 1988, but a measure of management stability seemed to arrive following Luca di Montezemolo's appointment as president of the company in late 1991. A man close to the Agnelli family of parent company Fiat, Montezemolo had been Ferrari's Formula One team manager in the 1970s, but since then had risen through the corporate ranks. No longer could he devote his time

▼ Despite an uncompetitive car, Michael Schumacher won three times in the 1996 Ferrari, aided here by the rain at Barcelona.

▼ Michael Schumacher with Ferrari technical director Ross Brawn (*left*) at the 1997 French Grand Prix at Magny-Cours.

▲ Michael Schumacher in the Ferrari F310B took second at the 1997 German Grand Prix.

to the running of the Formula One operation, and for this role he recruited Jean Todt, a man with a brilliant reputation as a team organizer honed first in rallying, then with the Peugeot sportscar squad.

The Long Road to Success

With money no object, Todt wanted the best available and so he recruited Schumacher. What the German found when he arrived was a team still rebuilding. By the standards of a top Formula One team, the on-site technical facilities were lacking. Technical director John Barnard had set up a satellite operation in Britain where he designed and built the cars. When Schumacher tested the new V10-engined F310 model he realized immediately he was in for a difficult season. Its handling was woeful, and its reliability worse. Somehow he managed to win three races with it in 1996, but at no stage that season was he or the Ferrari team in Championship contention. For 1997, Barnard had produced a much better

car but his Ferrari contract was coming to an end. Schumacher pushed to have the team recruit the man with whom he had shared success at Benetton, Ross Brawn. With him came Benetton chief designer Rory Byrne. The triangle was reunited. From that moment, Ferrari just got better.

▼ Ferrari's line-up (*left to right*): Paulo Martinelli (engine chief), Michael Schumacher, Ross Brawn (technical director), Jean Todt (sporting director), Rubens Barrichello, and Rory Byrne (chief designer).

▼ Michael Schumacher's Ferrari F310B finished second at the San Marino Grand Prix at Imola in 1997.

Second Generation Champions

With Michael Schumacher struggling in his first year at Ferrari, 1996 represented Damon Hill's best chance yet for a world title, equipped as he was with the latest Williams-Renault model, the FW18.

Damon Comes Good
He made full use of the opportunity with a series of very polished performances, but often he was made to work very hard by his new team-mate, a Formula One rookie by the name of Jacques Villeneuve. It made for a fascinating inter-team battle, two second-generation Formula One drivers fighting not only each other but the memory of their late and legendary fathers, Graham Hill and Gilles Villeneuve.

Villeneuve Jr had already created a sensation in the United States, where he had won the Indycar championship and the Indy 500. He made a startling Formula One debut in the Australian Grand Prix, bagging pole position and looking set to win until a late slide across the grass damaged a radiator and handed victory to Hill. Damon's greater experience showed over the season with a more consistent level of competitiveness, and he clinched the Championship in Japan with a mature drive to victory. Villeneuve, though, created some moments of spine-

▲ Jacques Villeneuve and Damon Hill at the British Grand Prix, Silverstone, in 1996.

tingling drama, never more so than at Estoril's final corner, when he did the unthinkable by overtaking Michael Schumacher round the outside.

Villeneuve vs Schumacher
Controversially, Williams didn't renew Damon Hill's contract for 1997, and he was replaced by Heinz-Harald Frentzen. This left Villeneuve to battle

with Schumacher's Ferrari for the world title. Their fortunes see-sawed through the season, and the showdown came in the final at Jerez, Spain. There, Schumacher was leading but Villeneuve, on new tyres, was catching fast after his pit stop. Electing to surprise the Ferrari driver, he made a move down the inside from a long way back. By the time Schumacher realized what was happening, it was too late. He turned in on the Williams, but succeeded only in bouncing off it and landing beached in the gravel trap. It left Villeneuve free to cruise to the title, though there was controversy in that he allowed the McLarens of Mika Häkkinen and David Coulthard to pass him in the late stages in exchange for their help earlier in the race, when they did not attack him in the midst of his battle with the Ferrari.

Ironically, one of the chief architects of this Williams World Championship, chief aerodynamicist Adrian Newey, had already left the team and headed for McLaren. This coincided with Renault withdrawing from official participation in the sport, leaving the Williams team's strength much reduced for the future. It would be some time before it recovered from such a double blow.

◀ "I've made it at last!", Damon Hill in the Williams FW18 becomes the 1996 World Champion at the Japanese Grand Prix.

▲ Hill with the 1996 World Championship trophy after winning the Japanese Grand Prix at Suzuka, 1996.

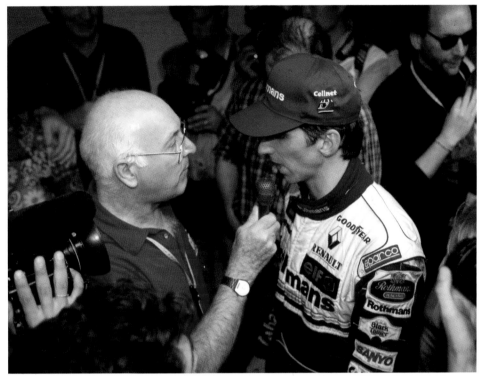

▲ Murray Walker (*left*), in his final Formula One race commentary for the BBC, interviews Hill, the new 1996 World Champion.

▼ Michael Schumacher turns his Ferrari into the passing Williams of Jacques Villeneuve, in a vain attempt to take his rival out of the race.

The McLaren Wonder Years

Everything conspired in McLaren's favour for the 1998 season. Formula One's technical regulations were radically altered just as brilliant aerodynamicist Adrian Newey arrived at the team. The Mercedes engines powering the cars were at the peak of their development, and the Bridgestone tyres gave them a performance advantage over the Goodyears on Michael Schumacher's Ferrari.

McLaren Overcome Restrictions

The FIA had been concerned about rising lap speeds, and their solution for 1998 was two-fold. Firstly, the maximum width of the cars was reduced from 2 metres to 1.8, so reducing the available ground effect-generating under-floor area, as well as limiting the mechanical grip. Secondly, slick tyres were outlawed and replaced by grooved tyres, giving a smaller surface area of rubber on the track. The effect was to make the cars more

▲ McLaren designer Adrian Newey.

▼ The McLarens of Häkkinen and Coulthard lead at the first corner of the Australian Grand Prix, Melbourne, in 1999.

skittery, and initially they were as much as 2 seconds per lap slower than they had been in 1997, though further technical development soon began to reduce this deficit.

The Cool Finn

McLaren's MP4-13 model brilliantly resolved the issues arising from the new regulations, and gave Mika Häkkinen and David Coulthard a flurry of victories. Ferrari fought back though, and came on very strong in the second half of the season. Michael Schumacher went to the final round in Japan with a chance of the title, but a dominant drive from Häkkinen sealed it for the Finn and his team.

Mika had a rather easier time of it in 1999 when Schumacher broke a leg in a crash at Silverstone. However, the strength of Ferrari showed when their number two driver, Eddie Irvine, took the title battle all the way to the final round. But again Häkkinen sealed it.

▼ David Coulthard in the McLaren MP4–14 at the Monaco Grand Prix in 1999.

▲ Mika Häkkinen and the McLaren MP4-13 took third place at the French Grand Prix at Magny-Cours in 1998.

▼ Häkkinen took third at the Malaysian Grand Prix at Sepang in 1999, this time driving the McLaren MP4-14.

Technology 1998

McLaren MP4-13

The new narrow-track/grooved tyre regulations of 1998 gave designers the chance to fundamentally re-evaluate the requirements rather than fine-honing existing themes. The McLaren design team, led by Adrian Newey, did this better than anyone else.

The tyre grooves substantially reduced the amount of rubber in contact with the track surface, placing mechanical grip at much more of a premium than before. Previously, aerodynamic performance had over-ruled all else, but McLaren actually surrendered some of that in order to claw back mechanical grip lost to the new regulations. In partnership with tyre suppliers Bridgestone, they opted for bigger front tyres, which more than made up in terms of grip what had been lost through increased drag. They gave the car a lower nose section too, reasoning that the limitation of under-body airflow would be more than compensated by the lowering of the centre of gravity.

Powered by a Mercedes-Benz V10 engine that produced 800bhp, it was the fastest car, and gave the McLaren team its first world title for seven years.

▼ Häkkinen's McLaren MP4-13 at the Hungarian Grand Prix in 1998.

The 21-year Itch

Michael Schumacher's dream of bringing world championship glory back to Ferrari finally came true in 2000, five years after joining. In each of those years the team were successively more competitive, as designer Rory Byrne and technical director Ross Brawn fine-honed their use of the huge resources at their disposal. The Ferrari F1-2000 was the first car to be created from the on-site wind tunnel. A 90-degree vee angle in its V10 lowered the centre of gravity from the previous motor's 80-degree angle. New materials enabled the cylinder heads to be smaller and lighter.

For each of the previous three years, Ferrari had to develop their way to mid-season competitiveness after beginning the season trailing either Williams or McLaren on speed. This car was fast right from the off – and that made the critical difference. Schumacher won the first three Grands Prix of the year and over the course of the season took a

▲ Ferrari's Michael Schumacher is elated after winning at Japan in 2000, while Mika Häkkinen (*far left*) and David Coulthard (*right*), for McLaren, look somewhat less so.

▼ The start of the Japanese Grand Prix, 2000. Häkkinen gets the jump on Schumacher.

further six. He clinched the title by winning an incredibly tense duel in Japan against his only rival, McLaren's Mika Häkkinen.

This was the first time since Jody Scheckter's 1979 success that a Ferrari driver had won the world title. The

▼ Luca di Montezemolo (*right*), president of Ferrari, talks with Hiroshi of Bridgestone tyres at the San Marino Grand Prix, 2002.

team president Luca di Montezemolo was present in Japan to witness the culmination of the work he had begun when he took up the post nine years earlier, when the team had been in

complete disarray. His dream had converged with that of Schumacher, Brawn and Byrne, the three men who had already won world titles together at Benetton.

▲ Michael Schumacher, in the Ferrari F1-2000, leads team-mate Rubens Barrichello at the British Grand Prix, Silverstone, in 2000. Schumacher took third place in the race.

Shapers

Ross Brawn

Brawn became best-known as the man whose brilliant pit strategies at both Benetton and Ferrari won countless races for Michael Schumacher. But as technical director of Ferrari, he was also an organizational genius with the necessary technical background to structure the Italian team in a way that brought the longest period of sustained success in its long history.

Brawn had been a highly successful designer before his partnership with Rory Byrne enabled him to step back. He began his motor racing career in 1976 as a research and development engineer at Williams. There, he learned an enormous amount from resident design chief Patrick Head in all aspects of Formula One car design. After spells as chief designer at Beatrice and

Arrows, he was recruited by Tom Walkinshaw's TWR team and designed the fabulously successful Jaguar XJR-14 sports racer. When Walkinshaw bought into the Benetton Formula One team, Brawn went with him, and worked alongside Rory Byrne for the first time. Here, the golden partnership took form. When Michael Schumacher joined the team, the triangle was complete.

For only one year – 1996, when Schumacher joined Ferrari but Brawn and Byrne stayed at Benetton – was the partnership broken up. Never have three such brilliant individuals worked together for so long in Formula One. That in itself goes a long way to explaining their success.

◄ Ferrari technical director Ross Brawn.

Ferrari Break All Records

Ferrari and Michael Schumacher actually strengthened their hold on Formula One during 2001 and 2002. The German superstar gave the Italian marque the greatest run of sustained success in its long and glorious history, and in the process he made himself the most statistically successful Formula One driver of all time.

In the 2001 Hungarian Grand Prix he clinched his fourth world title and equalled the record of 51 Grand Prix victories secured by Alain Prost eight years earlier. At the very next race, at Spa in Belgium, Schumacher surpassed that record. By the end of 2002 he had secured his fifth World Drivers' Championship, equalling the all-time record of Juan Manuel Fangio, and his career race win tally stood at an astonishing 64. Ferrari also took its fourth consecutive World Constructors' Championship in this year, a feat it had never before achieved. In winning 11 Grands Prix in 2002 alone, Schumacher also set the benchmark for the number of victories during a season, beating a record he had previously shared with Nigel Mansell.

◀ Ferrari's Michael Schumacher makes his trademark victory leap on the podium after winning the Spanish Grand Prix in 2002. McLaren's David Coulthard (*right*) finished in third place.

▼ (*left*) Rubens Barrichello's Ferrari F2002 (*below*) inches past team-mate Michael Schumacher to take an unexpected victory at the United States Grand Prix, Indianapolis, 2002.

Behind the awesome numbers lay Ferrari's ever-greater technical resource, and the brilliant use made of it by Rory Byrne and his design team. But in 2001 the Ferrari, while the fastest all-round car, was frequently out-powered by the BMW motor in the Williams chassis. When Formula One rookie Juan Pablo Montoya aggressively took his Williams past Schumacher's Ferrari to lead the Brazilian Grand Prix, many heralded the arrival of a new challenge to Schumacher's dominance. But despite several more exciting dices with the champion, Montoya's competitive circumstances actually declined in 2002 as the Williams FW24 proved no match for the F2002 Ferrari.

At the 2002 Italian Grand Prix, BMW proudly announced that its engine was the first in Formula One to break the 19,000rpm barrier. At this astronomical speed, the 3-litre V10 motor was achieving around 880 horsepower, making it the most powerful engine in Formula One.

BMW had re-entered Formula One with Williams in 2000. Also returning at that time was French tyre company Michelin, absent since 1984 and looking to break Bridgestone's dominance. With Williams in 2001 and 2002, and McLaren in 2002, Michelin returned to the race winner's circle, but the dominance of the Bridgestone-shod Ferrari meant such victories were perhaps fewer than their product warranted, a situation Michelin shared with BMW.

It was an illustration of how the various facets of the sport were being dwarfed by the scale of Ferrari's dominance – to the extent that calls were being made to liven up what was becoming an overly predictable show. Ferrari had courted controversy in Austria in 2002 when it instructed its second driver, Rubens Barrichello, who had led all the way, to move over in the last few hundred yards and hand victory to Schumacher. After the championship was sewn up several other races were stage-managed between the Ferrari drivers, such was their dominance. It was a development that did not go down well with fans of the sport.

Among moves being considered by the governing body were weight penalties for success and a new system of driver contracts that could see them change team for each race. That such radical departures were being contemplated illustrated the staggering extent of Ferrari's superiority.

▲ Juan Pablo Montoya in the Williams-BMW FW24 *(left)* and team-mate Ralf Schumacher, *(right)* squeeze out Schumacher's Ferrari F2002.

▼ Michael Schumacher *(left)* collects his Drivers' Championship Trophy at the FIA Prize Gala, while Jean Todt *(centre)* collects the Constructors' Trophy for Ferrari.

Schumacher Knocks 'em for Six

Ferrari's Michael Schumacher broke the all-time World Championship record in 2003 by scoring his sixth title. The previous record – Juan Manuel Fangio's five – had stood for 46 years. However, in contrast to the one-way dominance of Ferrari in 2002, the 2003 season was a classic, with a superbly tight battle for the World Championship between four drivers from three different teams.

Schumacher's 2002 dominance had led to falling television viewing figures. The governing body's response was a new set of sporting regulations for 2003. The points scoring system was revised, with a smaller gap between first and second and points down to eighth place instead of sixth – all designed to keep the title fight running longer. One-lap qualifying, whereby each driver took to the track on his own and had only one chance in which to set a time that would determine his grid position, was introduced. Furthermore, fuel could not be added to the car between qualifying and the race – meaning that there was a trade-off to be made between qualifying speed and pit stop strategies. These latter two changes had the effect of mixing the grids up slightly. But the

biggest contribution to the closely-matched 2003 competition was the improvement in the speed of the Williams-BMW and McLaren-Mercedes teams, aided considerably in both cases by the big advances made by their tyre supplier, Michelin. The rival Bridgestone

▲ Juan Pablo Montoya's win at Monaco kick-started the Williams team's 2003 season.

◀ McLaren's Kimi Raikkonen took his first Formula One victory in the 2003 Malaysian Grand Prix, and pushed Michael Schumacher for the world title throughout the season.

tyres, so dominant the year before, were left trailing, and this left Ferrari facing up to a very tough job.

Ferrari used its 2002 title-winning car for the first four races of the new season, while its new F2003-GA model underwent further development. Michael Schumacher won only one of those four races, and it became clear that he had a bigger fight on his hands than in the previous year. He gave the old car a glorious send-off by winning the San Marino Grand Prix. Two weeks later the new model, with a longer wheelbase, enhanced aerodynamics and more powerful engine, was given a victorious debut by Schumacher in the Spanish Grand Prix. Further wins in Austria and Canada meant that at the season's halfway point he appeared to be on-course to correct his shaky start to the year.

As it transpired, that Canadian win would be his last for quite some time. The Williams team had raced its new FW25 model from the beginning of the year. Radically different to its 2002 predecessor, with a much shorter wheelbase and Ferrari-like compact gearbox, it took the team some time to fully understand how to extract its full potential in terms of mechanical and aerodynamic set-up. The breakthrough came at the Monaco Grand Prix where Juan Pablo Montoya took an impressive victory. From this point onwards, the Williams was usually the fastest car around. In fact, the biggest problem for the team was that its two drivers, Montoya and Ralf Schumacher, were so closely matched that they were taking points off each other, as well as rival drivers from other teams.

Meanwhile, McLaren's Kimi Raikkonen kept scoring high places, adding to his victory in Malaysia, the second round of the series. McLaren had modified their 2002 car, with which to start the season, and the initial plan had been to then replace it with the radical new MP4-18. Development hitches with that car, and the continuing success of the MP4-17D, meant that the new car never did appear. Raikkonen's strong finishing record kept him in contention for the title right until the final round.

Raikkonen's team-mate David Coulthard won the opening round, in Australia, but otherwise had a rather low-key season. Michael Schumacher's team-mate at Ferrari, Rubens Barrichello, won the British Grand Prix in a superlative display and sealed Schumacher's title by winning in the final round, in Japan. In the two races prior to this, Schumacher had returned to winning form.

Giancarlo Fisichella gave the Jordan team a freak victory in an accident-shortened and very wet Brazilian Grand Prix. The season's other winner was Spanish newcomer, Fernando Alonso, driving for the Renault team. Aged just 22 years and 26 days, Alonso became the youngest ever Grand Prix winner, and the first from Spain, when he took victory in the Hungarian Grand Prix. Having withdrawn as an engine supplier after winning the 1997 World Championship with Williams, Renault had returned as a fully-fledged team in 2000 when it bought out Benetton. Under the control of former Benetton boss Flavio Briatore, Renault became increasingly competitive, and Alonso's result in Hungary marked its first victory as a team, rather than an engine supplier, for 20 years.

▲ Michael Schumacher was made to work hard for his win in the 2003 Spanish Grand Prix by Fernando Alonso's Renault.

▶ Schumacher celebrates his record-breaking sixth world title.

A – Z
Constructors

In 1895, Panhard-Levassor took one of the pioneering, new-fangled motor cars it was trying to sell to the public, and modified it with an override switch on its engine-speed governer. Thus was created the first winning racing car.

Although a divergence quickly formed between road cars and racing machines, for many decades racing car constructors tended to be the same teams as those who built customer cars for the public. In the late 1920s, specialist teams began to form, relying on racing for their existence. Some, like *Scuderia Ferrari*, relied on the hardware of manufacturers. Others, like Maserati, began building their own machines. But still the factories were the dominant constructors.

But by the end of the 1950s, Formula One was being dominated by a new breed that were constructors in a more literal sense. Pioneered by Cooper, these teams assembled their cars using bought-in components. This formed the blueprint for Formula One constructors for the next 20 years. But with the commercial success of Formula One came the return of the big car-producing factories – but this time with a difference; they usually entered the sport in partnership with an existing specialist team.

This mix of specialist understanding with factory financial clout characterizes the Formula One constructor of today.

◀ The drama of the pit stop.
Mika Salo's Toyota lays rubber.

Alfa Romeo

Within months of producing its first road-going cars in 1910, this Turin-based company was involved in racing to publicize its products. It reached the front rank of the sport in the 1920s when, aided by one of its drivers, Enzo Ferrari, it poached key racing technical staff from the bigger Fiat concern.

Chief among these staff was the brilliant designer, Vittorio Jano, who created the company's first successful Grand Prix car, the P2. Introduced in 1924, it won the inaugural World Manufacturers' Championship the following year. Jano's P3 of 1930 was the first genuine single-seater Grand Prix car and remained successful for many years, sealing its immortality

◄ The Alfa 158 "Alfetta" was conceived pre-war as a voiturette racer but had a successful post-war career as a Championship Grand Prix winning car.

▼ Bruno Giocomelli's Alfa leads the 1980 USA Grand Prix. He was dominating the race until the coil failed at three-quarter distance.

Alfa Romeo	
Country of origin	Italy
Date of foundation	1910
Active years in Grands Prix	1924–39, 1946–51, 1979–85
Grand Prix victories	10 (+ 42 pre-championship)

when Tazio Nuvolari took it to victory against the far more advanced German cars in the 1935 German Grand Prix.

The German domination eventually led to Alfa concentrating on voiturette ("small car") racing in the late 1930s, with an elegant 1.5-litre machine dubbed the "Alfetta". Designed by Giocchino Colombo under the direction of Alfa's now racing manager, Enzo Ferrari, it got a new lease of life post World War II when Formula One was created along the lines of the old voiturette formula. It won Giuseppe Farina the inaugural World Drivers' Championship in 1950, with team-mate Juan Manuel Fangio following up with the 1951 title.

Thereafter the company withdrew from Formula One. It returned as an engine supplier to Brabham in 1976 before committing itself to an unsuccessful constructors role from 1979 to 1985.

Auto Union

▼ The Auto Union V16 at the French Grand Prix in 1934.

his company was created in 1932 with the merger of four German car manufacturers. Its boss, Baron Klaus van Oertzen, was a racing fan and took the company into Grand Prix racing after the Nazi party offered subsidies for any company representing the Fatherland in the sport.

Van Oertzen commissioned former Mercedes engineer Ferdinand Porsche to design a car for the new 750kg formula of 1934, and he came up with a stunning mid-engined V16 design. Like the rival Mercedes, its independent suspension was a novelty and proved to be the trigger that allowed previously unheard of horsepower to be utilized. Hans Stuck won races in the car's first season and a development of it dominated 1936 with Bernd Rosemeyer. When the latter driver was

Auto Union	
Country of origin	Germany
Date of foundation	1932
Active years in Grands Prix	1934–39
Grand Prix victories	15 pre-championship

killed attempting a world speed record for the company, he was replaced by the legendary Tazio Nuvolari, who enjoyed much success in 1938 and 1939 in new V12 supercharged versions.

However, World War II left the constituent parts of the company in different countries, under different regimes, splitting it up. Today's Audi is one of the descendants.

▲ H. P. Muller in an Auto Union V16 during the European Mountain Championship round at Grossglockner in 1939.

► Tazio Nuvolari in action at Donington Park, England, in 1938, winning the 250-mile International Grand Prix at an average speed of 129.53km/h (80.49mph).

Ballot

The French Ballot company made its mark in the sport first in the American Indianapolis 500 race, and subsequently in Grand Prix racing, in the early 1920s.

Founded by Ernest Ballot, a French maritime engineer who had been producing road-going engines, the company switched to production of Hispano-Suiza V8 aero engines during World War I. This accelerated the company's understanding of engine technology and, encouraged by racing driver René Thomas, Ballot branched out into the manufacture of racing cars in 1919. For this, the company employed designer Ernest Henry, who had been responsible for the first twin-cam Grand Prix car, the 1912 Peugeot.

Henry's new design proved to be the pacesetter at Indianapolis for several years in succession, beginning in 1919, though appalling luck meant it never did win the event. An adaptation of this car won the 1921 Brescia Grand Prix with former Peugeot driver Jules Goux, but this was the company's final moment of glory within the sport. Henry was recruited by the rival Sunbeam concern and Ballot withdrew.

It thereafter concentrated on production cars until being bought out in the early 1930s by the same Hispano-Suiza company for which it had built aero engines during the war. Shortly afterwards, founder Ernest Ballot was dismissed.

▼ Ernest Ballot oversees preparation of his team cars in the pits, 1921.

▲ Ballot adapted its Indianapolis car for Grand Prix racing in 1921.

◄ Ballots were the fastest cars at the Indianapolis 500 from 1919 to 1922 but failed to win the event.

Ballot	
Country of origin	France
Date of foundation	1906
Active years in Grands Prix	1919–22
Grand Prix victories	1 pre-championship

Benetton

The famous Italian fashion clothes manufacturer first appeared in Formula One as a sponsor of the British Tyrrell team in 1983; founder Luciano Benetton was attracted by the image-boosting profile of the sport.

After a further spell sponsoring the Alfa Romeo team, Benetton decided to become a Formula One constructor in its own right when the opportunity of purchasing the British former Toleman team presented itself in time for the 1986 season. This, it was felt, represented better value than simply being a sponsor, and the team itself was already up and running. The resident designer Rory Byrne proved himself a highly gifted man and his BMW turbo-powered B186 was competitive enough to give the team – and its driver Gerhard Berger – their first Grand Prix success at Mexico 1986.

Sporadic success followed until the team was put on a more solid footing with the recruitment in 1989 of Flavio Briatore, a friend and business associate of Luciano Benetton. In partnership with Ford, competitiveness grew. For 1990, racing entrepreneur Tom Walkinshaw bought a share in the team, bringing with him designer Ross Brawn. Although Walkinshaw subsequently left, the technical partnership of Brawn and Byrne proved exceptionally fertile, especially so when blended with the driving gifts of the startling newcomer Michael Schumacher. The German won his first Grand Prix for the team in 1992, and two years later

Benetton	
Country of origin	United Kingdom
Date of foundation	1986
Active years in Grands Prix	1986–2001
Grand Prix victories	27 (+ 1 Constructors' Cup)

the team secured the World Drivers' Championship. This feat was repeated in 1995, this time with Renault power in place of Ford.

For the 1996 season, Schumacher left Benetton for Ferrari, and within a year Brawn and Byrne had followed him there. This rather decimated the team, despite the return of Gerhard Berger. The Austrian took Benetton's final Grand Prix victory at Hockenheim in 1997. The team continued for another four years, but in 2000 it was bought by Renault. In 2002, the Benetton tag was dropped in favour of the name of the parent company. The Renault Formula One cars are still built in the former Benetton premises in England.

◀ Michael Schumacher celebrates victory in the 1995 Pacific Grand Prix.

▼ Schumacher's 1995 win at Aida clinches Benetton's second successive championship.

Brabham

▼ Jack Brabham at the 1966 French Grand Prix, becoming the first man to win in a car bearing his own name.

After winning two World Championships with Cooper in 1959 and 1960, Jack Brabham found the team's impetus running out in the seasons that followed. For 1962, he decided to branch out on his own, and his Brabham team became one of the core British teams – using bought-in components in the way Cooper had pioneered – that came to dominate the sport in that era.

Brabham initially built customer racing cars for the lower formulae, partly to fund the Formula One team. The cars were all designed by Ron Tauranac, a friend of Jack Brabham's from their days in Australian dirt-track racing. They soon proved highly effective. Dan Gurney gave the team its first Grand Prix victory in France in 1964. In the same country two years later, Jack became the first man to win a Grand Prix in a car bearing his own name. This was the foundation for winning the World Drivers' and Constructors' Championships of that year. In 1967, Brabham's second driver Denny Hulme gave the team its second successive championship double.

◄ The Brabham BT3 made its Grand Prix debut in the hands of the team owner, Jack Brabham. He retired on lap nine of the 1962 German Grand Prix with a broken throttle linkage.

Brabham retired at the end of 1970, and returned home to Australia. The team was initially bought by Tauranac, but soon after it was sold again, this time to Bernie Ecclestone, who had managed the late Jochen Rindt, a former Brabham driver. Ecclestone gave the team a new lease of life, aided by the brilliant young South African designer, Gordon Murray.

In winning the 1981 world title, Nelson Piquet gave the Ecclestone-era Brabham its first title success. It was a feat the team repeated in 1983, this time in partnership with BMW. This association saw Brabham pioneer the use of electronic engine management and pits-to-car telemetry. Furthermore, in 1982, Murray re-introduced the tactical pit stop to Formula One racing, after a gap of three decades.

Ecclestone sold the team in 1987. It stuttered on, ever less successful, until going out of business in 1992.

Brabham	
Country of origin	United Kingdom
Date of foundation	1962
Active years in Grands Prix	1962–92
Grand Prix victories	35 (+ 1 Constructors' Cup)

◄ Brabham reintroduced tactical pit stops to Formula One, as here, with Nelson Piquet making a stop at Silverstone in 1983.

BRM

British Racing Motors was the brainchild of Raymond Mays, a successful racing driver of the 1930s, who had also initiated the ERA company of that time. With the post-war BRM project, Mays devised the idea of a motor racing trust, with financial and resource contributions from British industry. The resulting car would advertise British engineering excellence to the rest of the world through the medium of Formula One racing. To this end, designer Peter Berthon came up with a hugely complex machine, with an engine of 16 tiny cylinders, which complied with the 1.5-litre supercharged regulations for Formula One.

The engine was said to have a power potential of up to 600bhp, which, if true, would have made it a match for the all-conquering Alfettas of the time. Unfortunately, the car proved horrifically unreliable and, after interminable delays, it fell into obsolescence when the technical regulations were changed. What had been billed as a world-beater became a laughing stock.

In the mid-1950s, industrialist Alfred Owen bought out the company, retaining Mays as a consultant. For the 2.5-litre formula a much simpler car, the P25, was built, and Jo Bonnier won the team's first Grand Prix in Holland 1959. The 1.5-litre formula of 1961–65 marked the team's glory years. With the

▲ Graham Hill, here in the 1962 French Grand Prix, gave BRM its one and only world title in 27 years of trying.

BRM

Country of origin	United Kingdom
Date of foundation	1948
Active years in Grands Prix	1950–77
Grand Prix victories	17 (+ 1 Constructors' Cup)

▼ Jo Siffert dominated the 1971 Austrian Grand Prix for BRM. It was the team's last fully competitive season.

mid-engined V8 P57 of 1962, Graham Hill won the World Championship. In 1965 Jackie Stewart took his first Grand Prix victory with the team after a dramatic dice with team-mate Hill.

Early mistakes were repeated when the 3-litre formula was introduced in 1966, as the team produced a heavy and inefficient H16. A V12 engine originally designed for sports car racing brought a measure of respectability back to the team in the early 1970s, but by the middle part of that decade, the team – under the direction of Owen's brother-in-law Louis Stanley – was under-funded and lacking direction. Its last Grand Prix appearance came in 1977.

Bugatti

E ttore Bugatti was an eccentric self-trained Italian artist-cum-engineer who gave the world the fabulous and beautiful Bugatti line of cars, built in Molsheim in the Alsace region of France in the 1920s and 1930s. These were exquisite and exotic machines to which the rich and famous aspired. Ettore also designed and built devastatingly successful racing cars, notably the Type 35, introduced in 1924 and still winning Grands Prix in the early 1930s.

Before setting up Bugatti cars in 1910, Ettore had received commissions from manufacturers such as Peugeot and de Dietrich, and during World War I he designed a 16-cylinder aero engine, the internal design of which influenced racing car builders in the early 1920s. The Type 35 was the first truly successful Bugatti Grand Prix car, taken to major victories by a whole host of drivers. Its twin-cam derivative, the Type 51, continued the winning lineage. But the German domination of the mid-1930s left Bugatti unable to respond, at a time when it was going through internal difficulties.

▲ The type 59 model took over from the 35/51 late in 1933 but was soon overwhelmed by the new German cars.

◀ Driver Maurice Trintignant (in white hat and raincoat) at the new Bugatti T251 Formula One car tests in 1956.

Ettore's son Jean, a talented stylist for the company, was seen as Ettore's natural heir but was killed testing a sports car in 1939. Ettore himself died in 1947. The company continued from one financial crisis to another but managed to create a radical mid-engined Formula One car, the 251, in 1956. However, the car was under-developed and, ultimately, unsuccessful and the company died soon after.

Bugatti	
Country of origin	France
Date of foundation	1909
Active years in Grands Prix	1921–39 and 1956
Grand Prix victories	35 pre-championship

◀ Bugatti's type 35/51 ran at the frontline of Grands Prix from 1924 until 1933. For a time the car formed the backbone of Grand Prix racing.

Connaught

A Connaught became the first British car ever to win a Formula One race when Tony Brooks took victory in the 1955 Syracuse Grand Prix, a non-championship event. It was also the first Formula One victory for a car equipped with disc brakes.

Rodney Clarke, a brilliant engineer, was the brains behind the Connaught team. Kenneth McAlpine, construction company heir and amateur racer, was the money. After beginning in British club racing in the early 1950s, Connaught graduated to Grand Prix when the World Championship was switched to Formula Two cars for 1952.

Lack of a suitable engine always

▲ The A-type Connaught was a popular Formula Two car in the early 1950s. Here, Margulies in an example from 1951.

Connaught	
Country of origin	United Kingdom
Date of foundation	1949
Active years in Grands Prix	1952–58
Grand Prix victories	0 (1 non-championship)

▼ Archie Scott-Brown showed the potential of the B-type Connaught in several British non-championship races.

hindered the company upon the reintroduction of Formula One, but the quality of the chassis and the new-found advantages of disc brakes worked in the car's favour. The team didn't participate in a full season, but Brooks' Syracuse victory – which came against a highly competitive field of Maseratis – showed what Connaught might have achieved had it been sufficiently funded.

Clarke had some brilliant innovations under development – such as a mid-engined, monocoque construction car that was years ahead of its time. Partly due to Clarke's fastidious

nature, such developments never saw the light of day, and the potential of this constructor was not widely seen. Its advanced philosophy was evident when it became the first Formula One team to have its own wind tunnel. But progress was slow, and, at the end of 1957, the company ceased to be as McAlpine tired of investing in it. Bernie Ecclestone bought some of the assets and made an ill-starred attempt to qualify for a couple of Grands Prix the following year, but the company itself was dead, a tale of unfulfilled potential.

Cooper

The Cooper team forever changed the convention of where a Formula One car's engine was situated – and a lot more besides. After a breakthrough victory with a tiny mid-engined car at the Argentina Grand Prix in 1958, the days of front-engined cars were numbered. It also heralded the domination of Formula One by specialist British assemblers, using bought-in components, making the sport less reliant on road car-producing factories.

Father and son Charles and John Cooper ran the team from a garage in Surbiton, near London. They initially set up in the early post-war years as manufacturers of cars for the then new Formula 500 series, a low-cost formula for cars powered by 500cc motorcycle engines. With engines designed for chain-drive, the logical place to put the engine was in between the driver and the rear wheels. The Coopers took this F500 convention all the way to Formula One, the breakthrough for them being when engine suppliers Coventry Climax came up with a twin-cam engine, giving the Cooper reasonable power for the first time.

Jack Brabham took works Cooper-Climaxes to victory in both the 1959 and 1960 World Championships, and Formula One changed forever. No

▲ In winning the 1960 British Grand Prix, Jack Brabham put Cooper well on the way to its successive World Championship.

Cooper	
Country of origin	United Kingdom
Date of foundation	1948
Active years in Grands Prix	1952–68
Grand Prix victories	16 (+ 2 Constructors' Cups)

▼ Cooper's final race victory came with Pedro Rodriguez in 1967 in South Africa.

longer would the sport's health be at the whim of road car manufacturers, as Cooper's method divorced the technicalities of the cars from road car convention, and at the same time opened up Formula One to specialists lacking the financial resource to fund engine design and build programmes.

Ironically, other British specialist constructors created in a similar vein, such as Lotus, Brabham and McLaren – the latter two companies created by former works Cooper drivers – leapfrogged Cooper. Using Maserati engines, the team took its final race victory with Pedro Rodriguez in South Africa in 1967, and withdrew at the end of the following year.

Delage

This French constructor sealed its place of immortality within the sport when, in 1927, it won all four major Grands Prix comprising the season, with its lead driver Robert Benoist.

Founded in 1905 by Louis Delage, the former chief of development at Peugeot, the company began by producing road-going cars. It then entered voiturette ("small car") racing for publicity. The company's first Grand Prix car came in 1912, and was highly sophisticated for the time, with desmodronic valve actuation and a five-speed gearbox. Two years later, René Thomas took a Delage to victory in the Indianapolis 500.

Delage	
Country of origin	France
Date of foundation	1905
Active years in Grands Prix	1912–27
Grand Prix victories	7 pre-championship

Grand Prix success came in the 1920s, first with a V12-engined car and later with the straight-8 that came to dominate in 1927. However, the development costs of these cars came close to bankrupting the company and it withdrew from the sport. It was later bought-out by Delahaye, and Louis Delage was pensioned off. He died in relative poverty in 1947.

▲ Robert Benoist in the 1924 French Grand Prix held in Lyons. He drove the 2-litre V-12 Delage 2LCV to third place. Note the driver's protective face mask.

▼ The Delage 1.5 litre model in action at the 1927 British Grand Prix at Brooklands.

Duesenberg

By winning the French Grand Prix in 1921, Jimmy Murphy made Duesenberg the first American manufacturer to triumph in a major European race. But the company's racing credentials had already been established by success in America, notably the Indianapolis 500. The cars were the beautifully-engineered creations of the brothers Fred and August Duesenberg. Unusually, they began in racing before diversifying into road car production, with some of the most luxurious and sought-after machines of the 1920s and 1930s.

Divergence in technical regulation between American and European racing after 1921 meant that Duesenberg did not stay around to build on its successful European foray, and instead went on to dominate the Indy 500.

Duesenberg	
Country of origin	USA
Date of foundation	1914
Active years in Grands Prix	1921
Grand Prix victories	1 pre-championship

▲ *(top)* The Deusenbergs shocked France by winning the French Grand Prix at Le Mans in 1921.

▲ *(above)* Jimmy Murphy in a Deusenberg at the French Grand Prix, Le Mans, 1921.

◄ Tommy Milton in a Duesenberg at Indianapolis in 1920.

Ferrari

Enzo Ferrari had been a works driver with Alfa Romeo in the early 1920s, and subsequently became its general "fixer", recruiting key technical staff from Fiat, for example. He took an Alfa Romeo dealership and formed a race team, Scuderia Ferrari, which for a time became the official race entrant of Alfa Romeo. He finally split from Alfa in 1939, with the intention of building his own cars.

In 1948, the first Grand Prix Ferrari appeared. It enjoyed some success in 1949, but this was largely due to the absence of the previously dominant Alfa Romeo. When the latter team returned in 1950, Ferrari was again reduced to also-ran status. The breakthrough came the following year, when Ferrari's designer Aurelio Lampredi came up with a 4.5-litre normally-aspirated car that, through its fuel-thriftiness, was able to defeat the supercharged Alfas at the British Grand Prix, driven by José Froilán González.

The first World Championships came in 1952 and 1953 with Alberto Ascari, and there followed further titles for Juan Manuel Fangio in 1956 and Mike Hawthorn in 1958. A new 1.5-litre formula for 1961 saw Ferrari more prepared than anyone else and the red cars dominated the championship, driven by Phil Hill and Wolfgang von Trips. John Surtees took another title for the team in 1964. There was then a barren period until the mid-1970s, when the combined forces of designer Mauro Forghieri and driver Niki Lauda brought a four-year sequence of victories

◄ The Monaco Grand Prix was one of five victories that Niki Lauda took in 1975 on his way to the first Ferrari World Championship for 11 years.

Ferrari

Country of origin	Italy
Date of foundation	1946
Active years in Grands Prix	1948–present
Grand Prix victories	166 (+ 13 Constructors' Cups)

that yielded two Drivers' and three Constructors' World Championships.

Jody Scheckter and Gilles Villeneuve brought the team another Constructors' title in 1979, with Scheckter also taking the Drivers' honours. Ferrari then took the 1982 and 1983 Constructors' Championships before another barren period, as the British teams overtook them in the depth of their technology.

Enzo died in 1988, after which the team came under the full control of Fiat, which had bought into it in 1969. A period of success came in 1989–90, with innovative John Barnard-designed cars, whose chassis were conceived and built in Britain, but it was the arrival of former manager Luca di Montezemolo in 1991 that led to more sustained success – and with cars that were once more of Italian manufacture.

Michael Schumacher joined in 1996, and with the arrival of his Benetton technical partners, Ross Brawn and Rory Byrne, a new era of success dawned. They took a close championship win in 2000, and dominated in 2001 and 2002. A record-breaking fifth consecutive world constructors' title came in 2003.

▼ Michael Schumacher's victory in the 2002 British Grand Prix helped Ferrari to its fourth consecutive constructors' title.

Fiat

▼ Felice Nazzaro driving for Fiat at Targa Florio in 1907.

R ight from its birth at the turn of the 20th century, the Milan-based Fiat concern saw racing as essential to its image and its technical education. It graduated to international motor racing in 1904 and its ambitious philosophy was demonstrated when it pioneered the progression from side-valve to overhead-valve engines. It was later an early convert to the overhead-camshaft motor.

In 1907, Fiat won all three major races of the season with their lead driver Felice Nazzaro, backed up by Vincenzo Lancia, both of whom had been inherited when Fiat bought the Ceirano company in 1900. Fiat remained a major force in Grand Prix racing up until the outbreak of World War I.

Newly informed by the technology drive of war, Fiat again set the technological pace in the early 1920s, thanks to a brilliant group of engineers, directed by Guido Fornaca but also including Vittorio Jano. The philosophy

Fiat	
Country of origin	Italy
Date of foundation	1900
Active years in Grands Prix	1904–24 and 1927
Grand Prix victories	12 pre-championship

behind their straight-eight engine of 1921 proved highly influential for decades to come. Fiat was the dominant Grand Prix force in 1922 and 1923 (when it was the first to win a Grand Prix with a supercharged engine), but by 1924 rival teams had begun to poach its technical staff. This triggered the company's withdrawal at the end of the year. It made a brief –

and victorious – comeback in 1927, but generally concentrated on its production range thereafter. In 1969, the company acquired Ferrari as one of its specialist satellites.

▼ David Bruce-Brown in his Fiat 14.1-litre model at the 1912 French Grand Prix at Dieppe.

Hesketh

▼ James Hunt ended his and Hesketh's first year of Formula One with second place and a lap record in the USA Grand Prix.

T he British Lord, Alexander Hesketh, brightened up the Formula One scene in the mid-1970s with his eccentric but successful team that was built around the talents of designer Dr Harvey Postlethwaite and leading driver James Hunt.

Hesketh himself projected the image an of an aristocratic dilettante – and his team remains the only one to have included a grand piano as part of its race weekend cargo – but Postlethwaite and Hunt were gifted and committed. The three parties found themselves thrown together by circumstance. Separately, neither Hesketh nor Hunt had enjoyed great success in the junior categories of the sport but decided to graduate to Formula One together in 1973. To this end, a car was purchased from the March team, and with it came promising March boffin, Postlethwaite.

With Postlethwaite's modifications, the March performed far better than the similar cars of the works team, culminating in second place and a lap record for Hunt in the 1973 American

Grand Prix. For the following year Postlethwaite designed a new "Hesketh" car. At the 1975 Dutch Grand Prix Hunt took the Hesketh to a fairy tale victory over the mighty Ferrari of that year's World Champion, Niki Lauda.

But it was close to the final hurrah. Even a Lord didn't have money to burn indefinitely and, with no significant commercial backers, the team released Hunt and Postlethwaite and resorted to running pay-drivers for a further couple of seasons before pulling out completely.

Hesketh	
Country of origin	United Kingdom
Date of foundation	1972
Active years in Grands Prix	1973–78
Grand Prix victories	1

▼ Hunt withstood pressure from Lauda's Ferrari to win the 1975 Dutch Grand Prix.

Jordan

▼ Damon Hill gave Jordan its first Grand Prix victory at a wet 1998 Belgian Grand Prix.

Guided by the entrepreneurial Irishman Eddie Jordan, this team made what seemed at the time to be a financially suicidal bid to graduate to Formula One in 1991, and, remarkably, they made it work.

With lots of wheeling and dealing and a very respectable car from designer Gary Anderson, Jordan made its mark during its first Formula One season of 1991 after a successful decade in the junior ranks of Formula Three and Formula 3000. In between scoring points that took them to fifth place in the Constructors' Championship, Jordan took a lap record in Hungary, had one of its drivers, Bertrand Gachot, jailed for assault, introduced Formula One to the talents of Michael Schumacher – and then immediately lost him to a bigger team.

Hovering for the first few years on the brink of financial disaster, Jordan steadily built itself up, helped by partnerships first with Yamaha then Peugeot. Rubens Barrichello gave the team its first pole position at Spa in 1994. Four years later this was the

◄ Giancarlo Fisichella won the team's fourth victory in the rain of Brazil in 2003.

venue of Jordan's first Grand Prix victory, as Damon Hill and Ralf Schumacher drove their Mugen-Honda-powered cars to a Jordan 1-2.

Heinz-Harald Frentzen scored two further victories for the team in 1999 and was an outside championship contender until the penultimate race of the season. The team has never been quite able to repeat such form but it remains one of the sport's most high-profile and imaginative participants.

Jordan	
Country of origin	United Kingdom
Date of foundation	1991
Active years in Grands Prix	1991–present
Grand Prix victories	4

◄ Bertrand Gachot giving the Jordan team its Formula One baptism at the 1991 USA Grand Prix in Phoenix, Arizona.

Matra

This French missile manufacturer entered the sport in 1964 when it took over the ailing Bonett sports car constructor, the founder of which was a friend of Matra chief, Marcel Chassagny.

Matra put engineer Jean-Luc Lagardère in charge of the new subsidiary and he enthusiastically committed to a long-term programme of competition, comprising Formula Three, Formula Two, and eventual graduation to Formula One. Backed by Elf, this came in 1968. The company had designed a new V12 engine for the project but hedged its bets by supplying a car to Ken Tyrrell, who fitted it with the dominant Ford Cosworth DFV V8 and had it driven by Jackie Stewart. The Cosworth-engined car proved more competitive than the Matra-powered one and Stewart only narrowly missed out on the World Championship that year.

For 1969 Matra withdrew its own team to further develop the V12, but Stewart and Tyrrell enjoyed a dominant season in the Matra-Ford, making Matra World Constructors' Champion in only its second year of Formula One. Ironically, it proved to be the team's final flourish of Formual One success.

A marketing tie-up with Chrysler France for a road car made the Matra-Ford politically unacceptable, and the Tyrrell arrangement came to an end.

▲ Jackie Stewart scored his fourth victory in five races in a Matra 1–2 finish at the French Grand Prix, Clermont Ferrand, 1969.

▼ Jean-Pierre Beltoise sits on the grid and finished in ninth place at the French Grand Prix, Rouen-les-Essarts, 1968.

Matra	
Country of origin	France
Date of foundation	1964
Active years in Grands Prix	1968–72
Grand Prix victories	9 (+ 1 Constructors' Cup)

Matra reintroduced its V12 engine but despite several competitive showings from 1970–72, it failed to win a Grand Prix. The company withdrew from the category at the end of 1972 to focus on sports car racing. Some years later, the V12 Matra engine got a taste of Formula One success, powering Jacques Laffite's Ligier to victories on three occasions between 1977 and 1981.

Mercedes

▼ German constructors Mercedes and Auto Union together dominated Grand Prix racing from 1934–39.

Gottlieb Daimler is co-credited with the invention of the motor car. He did not live to see the completion of the "Mercedes" model he was working on at the turn of the century. Mercedes was the name of the daughter of Emile Julinek, the Austrian importer for the company. The car's name change from Daimler came in recognition of how big a progression this 1901 model was over anything previously seen. When Mercedes officially entered competition in 1903, it quickly ended the domination of the French Panhard and Mors marques.

The company regularly came in and out of the sport as it developed new technologies that fed its production car and aero-engine programmes. It was the first team to race an overhead-cam engined car, in 1906, and it won the French Grand Prix of 1908 and 1914.

In 1923, Mercedes introduced the supercharger to racing but its next period of sustained success didn't come until the inauguration of the 750kg

Mercedes

Country of origin	Germany
Date of foundation	1901
Active years in Grands Prix	1903–08, 1914, 1926–39, 1954–55
Grand Prix victories	9 (+ 29 pre-championship)

formula of 1934 when, with Nazi party backing, Mercedes rewrote the rules of Grand Prix technology. With ever-more powerful cars that were soon reaching over 322km/h (200mph), the "silver arrows" – so named because of their bare aluminium bodies – dominated until the outbreak of World War Two.

It was 1954 before the company re-entered Grand Prix racing. It did so with the highly progressive W196, with Juan Manuel Fangio taking the car to victory on its debut in France. Fangio and Mercedes took the World title that year, and in 1955. Indeed, during two seasons of racing, the W196 was beaten on only three occasions. But at the end of the 1955 season, the company was forced to withdraw from the sport after one of its cars was launched into the crowd at the Le Mans 24 Hours sports car race, killing more than 80 of the spectators.

Following that catastrophe, it was to be a very long time before the company felt comfortable re-entering the sport. It did so first in sports car racing in the late 1980s, before entering Formula One with Sauber from 1993. After two years it switched its engine supply to the long-established McLaren team, and eventually this became one of the sport's greatest liaisons. McLaren-Mercedes dominated Formula One in 1998 and 1999, and continues to be a major force.

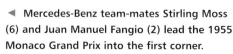

◀ Mercedes-Benz team-mates Stirling Moss (6) and Juan Manuel Fangio (2) lead the 1955 Monaco Grand Prix into the first corner.

Mors

Mors was one of the most successful pioneer racing manufacturers at the dawn of the sport in the late 19th and early 20th centuries.

Emile Mors, chief of one of France's leading telegraph equipment companies, founded the company in the 1890s and competed himself in some of the early city-to-city races. An injury in one of these events caused him to retire from competitive driving, but he employed others to do so for him. Using ever-more monstrous engines, Mors came to vie with Panhard as the fastest racing car of them all.

The Mors of Fernand Gabriel was victorious in the tragic Paris–Madrid

Mors	
Country of origin	France
Date of foundation	1897
Active years in Grands Prix	1897–1908
Grand Prix victories	11 pre-championship

race, in 1903, that caused city-to-city racing to be banned for all time. It was never to win a major event again. Mors built its last Grand Prix racing car in 1908 after failing to keep pace with technology advances introduced by more progressively engineered cars from the likes of Mercedes, Renault and Fiat. The company was later bought out by Citroën.

▲ *(right)* The 1902 Paris–Vienna type Mors, drivern by Augières at Archères, near Paris. He set a new land speed record of 123.4km/h (77.13mph).

▶ The 1903 Mors "Dauphin" shows an early attempt at steamlining.

McLaren

Kiwi Bruce McLaren left Cooper to form his own team in 1966. Within two years he had joined his former Cooper team-mate Jack Brabham in the exclusive club of men who have won Grands Prix in cars bearing their own name.

Tragically, Bruce never lived to see the colossus that his team came to be. He was killed testing a Can-Am sports car at Goodwood in 1970. His partner Teddy Mayer took over the running of the team – which was highly successful in Indycar and Can-Am racing, as well as Formula One – and steered it to its first World Championship, in 1974, with Emerson Fittipaldi and the Gordon Coppuck-designed M23 model. Two years later, James Hunt used an M23 in his dramatic title victory over Niki Lauda.

By the late 1970s, the team had lost its technical impetus, and its sponsor

◀ Bruce McLaren – here in third place – eventually won this race at Spa in 1968 for the team's first Formula One victory.

Marlboro arranged for a merger between McLaren and Marlboro's Formula Two team, Project 4, run by Ron Dennis. Dennis brought with him designer John Barnard who then produced the first carbon-fibre Formula One car, the McLaren MP4/1. This won a race in its first season and established the new era McLaren as a serious competitive force. World Championships

followed with TAG-Porsche power in 1984, 1985 and 1986, and with Honda in 1988, 1989, 1990 and 1991. During the 1980s and 1990s McLaren, together with Williams, dominated the sport, with Niki Lauda, Alain Prost and Ayrton Senna bringing championship glory to the team. A new partnership with Mercedes yielded titles in 1998 and 1999 with Mika Häkkinen. Since Häkkinen's retirement at the end of 2001, another Finn, Kimi Raikkonen, has led the team.

◀ Mika Häkkinen won the 1998 Monaco Grand Prix on his way to his first, and the team's tenth, drivers' title.

▼ Ayrton Senna leads eventual winner Alain Prost in the 1988 French Grand Prix. Their MP4/4s won 15 out of 16 races that year.

McLaren	
Country of origin	United Kingdom
Date of foundation	1966
Active years in Grands Prix	1966–present
Grand Prix victories	137 (+ 8 Constructors' Cups)

Panhard

A Panhard-Levassor was the very first winning race car, taking the finish of the 1895 Paris–Bordeaux–Paris more than five hours ahead of its nearest competitor. It was driven by one of the partners in the business, Emile Levassor. The other partner was Louis-René Panhard.

A friend of Levassor's had gained the French commercial rights to the German Daimler engine, leading to Panhard and Levassor diversifying from their core engineering business to car manufacture. Racing was recognized as essential in both improving technology and advertising the capability of the automobile in general. Indeed, Emile Lavassor was one of the driving forces in the early days of the sport.

Using ever bigger, more powerful engines, Panhard dominated the early city-to-city events, though eventually it

Panhard	
Country of origin	France
Date of foundation	1895
Active years in Grands Prix	1895–1908
Grand Prix victories	22 pre-championship

began to be challenged hard by rival, Mors. Like that company, Panhard failed to keep up with advances introduced by more progressive companies and, again like Mors, it built its last Grand Prix racer in 1908, the year that Louis-René Panhard died. Thereafter, guided by Panhard's sons, it concentrated on production cars until the 1960s, when Citroën bought it out.

▲ The very first winning racing car won the 1895 Paris–Bordeaux–Paris race but wasn't eligible for the prize money on account of it having only two seats!

▼ Lebron's Panhard in the Circuit des Ardennes race in 1905.

▲ Henry Farman in a Panhard-Levassor passing through Criel-sur-Mer, Dieppe, in the 1908 French Grand Prix.

Peugeot

Peugeot was already a very old company when the motor car was first invented, having begun as a steel works, producing everything from steel rods for insertion into fancy dresses to bicycles. It produced a steam car in 1889, but was soon converted to the benefits of the petrol engine by Gottlieb Daimler. Using Daimler-engined cars, Peugeot took part in the very first city-to-city races and later produced its own power units, designed by Louis Rigolout, who was also the company's nominated race driver.

Peugeot then lost interest in racing as it built up its production facilities. In 1906, a splinter group was formed, Lion-Peugeot, to produce bicycles and light cars. This company entered the new voiturette ("small car") class of racing, and became the dominant force there, with drivers Jules Goux, Georges Boillot and Paulo Zuccarelli. A 1911 reorganization brought the two companies back together and the racing core of the former offshoot planned its first full-size Grand Prix car. Designed by Ernest Henry, the 1912 Peugeot L76 model broke new technical ground in having twin overhead camshafts driving four valves for each engine cylinder.

It was a revolutionary concept, making up in technology what it conceded to its rivals in engine size – at 7.6 litres it was just over half the size of the 14.1-litre Fiat. After a closely matched race against the Fiat, Boillot took the car to victory in the 1912 French Grand Prix, and so brought the era of the racing monster to an end. Peugeot won again in 1913 and also took the American Indy 500 that year – something it repeated in 1916 and 1919. Henry left the company during

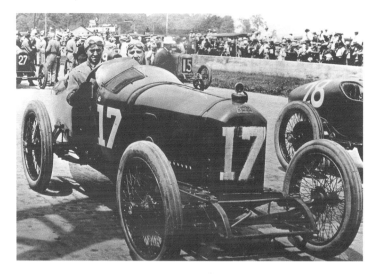

◄ Dario Resta won at Indianapolis for Peugeot in 1916. The progressive design of the car influenced a whole generation of imitators.

▼ *(left)* Goux took fourth at Indianapolis in 1914 but had won the event at his and Peugeot's first attempt in 1913.

▼ René Thomas in the Peugeot L3 won the Coupe de la Meuse at the Circuit des Ardennes, Belgium, in 1912. This car was a voiturette version of the Grand Prix car.

the war, Boillot was killed and then Goux departed too, leaving Peugeot bereft of racing experience. There was an attempt on the Indy 500 in 1921 with a radical but hopelessly unreliable machine. This triggered a retirement from frontline racing.

It returned to sports car racing in 1990 and made a Formula One engine for McLaren in 1994. This partnership lasted just one year and in six subsequent seasons with the Jordan and Prost teams, it failed to win a race. Peugeot withdrew from the sport at the end of the 2000 season.

Peugeot	
Country of origin	France
Date of foundation	1889
Active years in Grands Prix	1895–1902 1906–14
Grand Prix victories	13

Renault

The son of a button manufacturer, Louis Renault first got into car manufacture after devising a successful improvement to the gearbox of his own de Dion car in the 1890s. Backed by his brothers Fernand and Marcel, he set up a factory to produce Renault cars. Louis and Marcel raced these machines in the early city-to-city events.

The brothers and the little Renaults were brilliant performers, often beating cars massively more powerful. But in the catastrophic 1903 Paris–Madrid race, Marcel was one of the fatalities. Louis finished second in that event, but retired from competitive driving thereafter. The newly inaugurated Grand Prix competition of 1906 led Renault back to the sport, producing a new car for Ferenc Szisz – formerly Louis's riding mechanic – to drive. He took it to victory. The company continued racing until 1908.

It returned, 69 years later, with a car that was to change the face of Formula One racing: the turbo-charged RS01. Jean-Pierre Jabouille's Renault took victory in the 1979 French Grand Prix, the first for the turbocharged engine, and before long the rest of the grid was forced to follow suit. After missing out on the 1983 World Championship,

▲ The winning car of the first ever Grand Prix was this Renault, driven by Ferenc Szisz.

Renault withdrew as a works team at the end of 1985, though it continued to supply engines to other teams.

This continued after the turbo era. In 1989, it debuted its V10 engine with the Williams team. This configuration was as widely copied as the earlier turbo. Renault V10s powered Williams and Benetton to five World Drivers' titles between 1992 and 1997, after which it withdrew once more. It returned as a works team in 2002, having bought out the Benetton team. Fernando Alonso's victory in the 2003 Hungarian Grand Prix marked a return to winning ways.

Renault	
Country of origin	France
Date of foundation	1898
Active years in Grands Prix	1901–08, 1977–85 2002–present
Grand Prix victories	16 (+ 2 pre-championship)

▼ Jarno Trulli in the Renault R202 retired from the 2002 Malaysian Grand Prix. The team had re-entered Formula One that season.

Sunbeam

▼ Jean Porporato in a Sunbeam at Indianapolis in 1915. He qualified in sixth position but retired with piston failure.

Victory in France in 1923 made Sunbeam the first British constructor to win a Grand Prix.

First and foremost a production car company, its technical director Louis Coatalen was a big believer in racing and took the company into voiturette ("small car") competition in 1910. With third, fourth and fifth places overall, Sunbeams took the first three places in the voiturette class of the 1912 French Grand Prix. The class victory was repeated a year later.

Coatalen recruited former Peugeot designer Ernest Henry to produce a Grand Prix car for the new 2-litre formula of 1922. It proved ineffective against the new Fiats, leading to

Sunbeam	
Country of origin	United Kingdom
Date of foundation	1904
Active years in Grands Prix	1911–26
Grand Prix victories	3 pre-championship

Henry's replacement by one of the Fiat's designers Vincent Bertarione. For 1923, the Italian produced a car so similar to the 1922 Fiat that it was instantly dubbed "the green Fiat". It proved very effective and enabled Henry Segrave to come through for victory in France – ironically after the faster, newly-supercharged Fiats had retired when dominating.

For 1924, Sunbeam development engineer Captain Jack Irving devised Sunbeam's own supercharger, and in compressing the fuel/air mixture rather than merely the air, it allowed for lower internal temperatures and therefore more power. So equipped, the 1924 Sunbeam dominated the French Grand Prix from the start but retired with electrical trouble.

Soon afterwards, poor financial performance forced the termination of the company's racing programme, though it was later successful in securing world speed records.

▼ Henry Segrave in the Sunbeam 2-litre at the French Grand Prix in 1925.

Tyrrell

▼ Jackie Stewart gives the Tyrrell its first Grand Prix outing in 1970 at Canada. He would win the 1971 title with the car.

Ken Tyrrell was a timber merchant who had been moderately successful as a driver in the British Formula 500/Formula Three series in the 1950s. But he found his true vocation as a team entrant. In 1964, he teamed up with a promising young Scottish driver, Jackie Stewart, and together they stormed to victory in the British Formula Three Championship.

Stewart immediately graduated to Formula One, leaving Tyrrell to find further success as an entrant in Touring Car and Formula Two racing. Stewart continued to drive for Tyrrell in between his Formula One commitments, and for 1968 the pair were reunited properly in Formula One. Tyrrell had arranged that he be provided with a Matra chassis in which he would install the Ford Cosworth DFV engine. With Stewart driving, the team were close runners-up in the World Championship that year. Still with a Matra-Ford they went one better in 1969, dominating the season.

The Matra association then ended, and after purchasing a March for 1970 as a stop-gap, the first "Tyrrell" car appeared at the end of that season. Designed by Derek Gardner, the chassis had clear Matra influences. Powered by the ubiquitous Ford Cosworth DFV, it dominated the 1971 season as Stewart took his second world title. Tyrrell took the corresponding constructors' title in its first full season of racing.

The team remained a major force for the remaining two years of Stewart's career, but Jackie retired from the sport after securing title number three in 1973. Stewart's intended replacement, François Cevert, was killed practising for what was due to be Stewart's final race, a body blow to the team. Tyrrell instead recruited Formula One new boys Jody Scheckter and Patrick Depailler and enjoyed some success, but the glory days of Stewart were over.

A six-wheeler in 1976 gave the team lots of publicity as well as a 1-2 at the Swedish Grand Prix, but it was never repeated. The four-wheel replacement, the 008, won the 1978 Monaco Grand Prix with Depailler, but the team was struggling to generate commercial backing as Formula One entered a

▲ Jody Scheckter leads second-placed team-mate Patrick Depailler to take the first and only victory for a six-wheeled car.

▼ Jean Alesi – here in the 1990 Mexican Grand Prix – gave the team its last strong year. He scored second at Phoenix.

Tyrrell	
Country of origin	United Kingdom
Date of foundation	1970
Active years in Grands Prix	1970–98
Grand Prix victories	23 (+ 1 Constructors' Cup)

slicker, more expensive age. There were some bright spots – Michele Alboreto won a couple of races in the early 1980s, and Jean Alesi showed that the 1990 Tyrrell 019 was perhaps the best chassis on the grid – but overall the trend was downward.

The team was bought out at the end of 1997 by British American Tobacco. Ken Tyrrell died in 2001, aged 77, and the Formula One world mourned one of the last direct links to an earlier era.

Vanwall

▼ 1958 Vanwall Formula One car. Its sleek aeronautic-inspired lines helped make it the quickest car in a straight line.

Vanwall won the inaugural Formula One World Constructors' Championship in 1958, and so achieved the ambition of its founder Tony Vandervell, the British industrialist who had vowed to one day beat Ferrari.

Vandervell was the proprietor of Vandervell Bearings, whose patented "thinwall" bearing had been a major breakthrough for several manufacturers – including Ferrari – in making their engines more efficient. Vandervell had originally been part of the BRM trust, but left in frustration at the "management by committee" of that team in its early days. Instead, he persuaded Enzo Ferrari to sell him a series of Formula One cars that were then modified and raced as "Thinwall Specials".

The natural progression from this was a fully Vandervell car. This first appeared in 1955 and was labelled the "Vanwall". In place of the Ferrari engine was a four-cylinder unit derived from the single-cylinder Norton motorcycle race engines. Vandervell later commissioned de Havilland aerodynamicist Frank Costin to design a highly advanced low-drag body for it. Costin, in turn, suggested that Vandervell commission Lotus' Colin Chapman to make modifications to

Vanwall	
Country of origin	United Kingdom
Date of foundation	1955
Active years in Grands Prix	1955–58
Grand Prix victories	9 (+ 1 Constructors' Cup)

▼ Tony Vandervell (*left*) with mechanics at Pescara, Italy, in 1957.

the chassis and suspension. The combined result of all this development was that the Vanwall was the fastest car of 1957, and Tony Brooks and Stirling Moss gave it its first victory in the British Grand Prix of that year.

Brooks and Moss won six Grands Prix for the team in 1958, ensuring the Constructors' title. But in the final race of the season, at Morocco, third team driver Stuart Lewis-Evans crashed and received fatal burns. Vandervell, in failing health anyway, was devastated by the loss of his driver and he announced his retirement from the sport. The team did struggle on for another couple of seasons, appearing sporadically, but the serious challenge was over. Vandervell died in 1967.

▲ Stirling Moss and Tony Brooks in 1957. These two gifted drivers ensured Vanwall's first Grand Prix win at Aintree that year.

Williams

▼ Alan Jones in the Williams FW06 ran a sensational race at Long Beach in 1978, to firmly establish the team for the first time.

F rank Williams founded the team that came to dominate Formula One for much of the 1980s and 1990s in 1977. A keystone to its success was his chief designer Patrick Head.

Prior to this, Williams had eked out an existence on the fringes of Formula One, grabbing the occasional result but being perpetually underfunded. With the Head-designed Williams FW06 of 1978, the team's form enabled it to attract decent backing. The follow-up FW07 of 1979 gave the team its first victory, at the British Grand Prix, with Clay Regazzoni. Team-mate Alan Jones went on to dominate the second half of the season before giving the team its first World Championship in 1980.

Williams driver Keke Rosberg took the last ever DFV-powered World Championship in 1982. From the end of 1983, Williams went into partnership with Honda, a combination that yielded World Constructors' Championships in 1986 and 1987; Williams driver Nelson Piquet took the World Champion title in the latter year. After being surprisingly

Williams	
Country of origin	United Kingdom
Date of foundation	1977
Active years in Grands Prix	1977–present
Grand Prix victories	112 (+9 Constructors' Cups)

dropped by Honda, Williams took up with Renault, and this led to an even more dominant spell. A Williams-Renault driver was Champion in 1992, 1993, 1996 and 1997.

Since 2000, BMW has been the team's engine partner, and together they have been winning races on a regular basis since 2001.

◄ Nelson Piquet leads Nigel Mansell as the two Williams fight over victory in the 1987 British Grand Prix. Mansell won.

▼ Juan Pablo Montoya tests the BMW Williams FW24 on an artificially wet track at Valencia, Spain, in 2002.

Constructors: The Current Challengers

Today's Formula One grid comprises ten teams. Five of these – Ferrari, Jordan, McLaren, Renault and Williams – have winning pedigrees. The remaining five aspire to join their ranks. These are the challengers.

◄ Minardi at the German Grand Prix, 2003.

▼ Sauber at the Hungarian Grand Prix, 2003.

Ready for Battle

In recent years, major road car producing manufacturers have entered Formula One, sometimes as engine suppliers, as in the case of Mercedes, BMW and Honda, and sometimes as fully formed teams, as with Jaguar, Renault and Toyota. Formula One has provided the manufacturers with a superbly effective global marketing platform.

At the same time, the level of financial investment they have brought to their Formula One programmes has increased the cost of competing for everyone. For those few teams not in partnership with one of the major manufacturers, these are very tough times indeed.

This was emphasized at the beginning of both 2001 and 2002, when the Prost and Arrows teams respectively went out of business. The three remaining teams not aligned to manufacturers – Jordan, Minardi and Sauber – are striving to be the Davids to the manufacturers' Goliaths.

The team names at the forefront of Formula One – Ferrari, McLaren and Williams – have been the same for some time, and joining their winning circle is not easy. But, in 2003, Renault showed that it could be done, breaking back into that elite group by taking its first victory in 20 years. Toyota is fancied as the next manufacturer to make that breakthrough.

▲ The challenger teams in action in 2003: *(from top)* Jaguar, BAR-Honda, Minardi, *(left)* Sauber, *(right)* Toyota.

BAR

Guided by Craig Pollock, the manager of 1997 World Champion Jacques Villeneuve, the tobacco giant British American Tobacco decided to create its own Formula One team. To this end it bought out the Tyrrell team and renamed it British American Racing, shortened to BAR.

The team was formed around Villeneuve, who drove the first BAR car in the 1999 Australian Grand Prix. It proved a difficult debut season as the team failed to score a single point.

With newly-acquired Honda works engines it improved during 2000, and Villeneuve scored a series of points finishes. Pollock resigned at the end of 2001 and was replaced by David Richards, whose Prodrive company has taken rallying World Championships with Subaru. Completing the new-broom era, original driver Villeneuve was replaced for 2004 by the Honda-favoured Takuma Sato.

BAR	
Country of origin	United Kingdom
Date of foundation	1999
Active years in Grands Prix	1999–present
Grand Prix victories	0

▼ Olivier Panis driving the BAR-Honda 004 at the Canadian Grand Prix, Montreal, Canada, in 2002.

▲ *(top)* Jacques Villeneuve at the Spanish Grand Prix, Barcelona, in 1999. The team suffered a dismal first year.

▲ *(above)* Jacques Villeneuve drove the BAR Honda 003 to third place in Barcelona in 2001. It was the team's first podium.

Jaguar

▼ Eddie Irvine drove superbly to finish third in the 2001 Monaco Grand Prix, securing the first podium for the team.

Jaguar is the Formula One challenge of the Ford Motor Company. Still a young team, it has suffered a difficult gestation since its arrival in 2000.

Initially, Ford went into partnership with former World Champion Jackie Stewart, whose team Stewart Grand Prix won the 1999 European Grand Prix with Johnny Herbert. But Ford bought Stewart out in that year, wishing to own the team outright and re-brand it after its luxury car brand.

Several changes of management have characterized its efforts so far but results have been slow to come. Niki Lauda was replaced as boss pre-season 2003, but Mark Webber has since shown that progress has been made.

Jaguar	
Country of origin	United Kingdom
Date of foundation	2000
Active years in Grands Prix	2000–present
Grand Prix victories	0

◀ Eddie Irvine acknowledges the plaudits for his third place at Monaco 2001. He equalled this result at Monza in 2002, but these were the highlights of three years' effort for the team.

▼ Spaniard Pedro de la Rosa pushes hard in the Jaguar R3 during the Austrian Grand Prix in 2002.

Minardi

Italy's "other" Formula One team after Ferrari, Minardi, has been part of the sport since 1985, when Formula Two constructor Giancarlo Minardi graduated to the upper echelon.

It has been a struggle for the tiny, underfunded team, but in the USA in 1990, Pierluigi Martini did give Minardi a front row qualifying position. He also scored the team's best-ever result with fourth place in the Portuguese Grand Prix in 1991.

Team founder Minardi sold his majority shareholding in the 1990s to Gabriele Rumi, who in turn sold out to airline boss Paul Stoddard in 2001. The team's plucky fight against the odds has won it many fans.

Minardi	
Country of origin	Italy
Date of foundation	1985
Active years in Grands Prix	1985–present
Grand Prix victories	0

▲ Pierluigi Martini – Minardi's most successful driver – leads Stefan Bellof's Tyrrell in the 1985 Dutch Grand Prix.

▼ Mark Webber in the Minardi Asiatech PS02 during practice for the Austrian Grand Prix at the A1-Ring in 2002.

Sauber

After a successful campaign in sports cars that included World Championships and victory in the Le Mans 24 Hours, the Swiss-based Sauber team graduated to Formula One in partnership with Mercedes in 1993.

The Mercedes link came to an end in 1995. After a similarly short partnership with Ford, Sauber has found a level of stability using customer Ferrari engines since 1998.

Since that time the team has steadily improved its competitiveness to the point that it finished fourth in the World Constructors' Championship of 2001, ahead of many teams with factory engine partnerships.

With Kimi Raikkonen in 2001 and Felipe Massa in 2002, team boss Peter Sauber has earned a reputation as a talent scout. Both drivers had highly impressive Grand Prix seasons with Sauber as Formula One rookies. When McLaren bought out Raikkonen's Sauber contract for 2002, it gave the team a significant boost in budget.

▲ *(top)* Sauber versus Sauber. Jean Alesi and Johnny Herbert tangle at the Argentine Grand Prix, Buenos Aires, in 1998.

▲ *(above)* J.J. Lehto in the Sauber-Mercedes C12 at the Italian Grand Prix, Monza, in 1993. The team was in partnership with Mercedes during its first season of Formula One.

◄ Nick Heidfeld qualified only 17th in the 2002 Monaco Grand Prix, but he had helped to take the Sauber team to fourth place in the previous year's title chase.

Sauber	
Country of origin	Switzerland
Date of foundation	1970
Active years in Grands Prix	1993–present
Grand Prix victories	0

Toyota

▼ Allan McNish in the Toyota TF102 at the 2002 Monaco Grand Prix in Monte Carlo.

The world's third biggest motor manufacturer entered Formula One for the first time in 2002. Bravely, it decided to do so on its own rather than in partnership with an existing specialist team. Having enjoyed great success in the sport of rallying, it used the same Cologne base to establish its Formula One operation, although the impetus comes very much from the parent company in Japan.

Chief designer Gustav Brunner – a veteran of several Formula One teams, including Ferrari – designed the TF102 chassis into which the all-new Toyota V10 engine was installed. The car created a good impression immediately, with straightline speed as good as that of the top teams. It was also uncannily reliable for a brand new design, with Mika Salo scoring World Championship points in two of its first three races.

The facilities and investment underlying Toyota's first Formula One season left few onlookers with any doubts that this would, in time, come to be a serious force in Formula One. A more competitive season followed in 2003 as the team built up its experience of this very exacting sport. The team poached Renault's technical director Mike Gascoyne at the end of the year.

▲ Mika Salo's Toyota TF102 finished sixth in the debut race for Toyota at the Australian Grand Prix, Melbourne, in 2002.

Toyota	
Country of origin	Japan
Date of foundation	2001
Active years in Grands Prix	2002–present
Grand Prix victories	0

▼ Both Toyota drivers Mika Salo and Allan McNish get involved in a first corner accident at Melbourne in 2002.

A – Z
Drivers

The same competitive urge to drive a machine faster than the next man has produced over a century of heroes. Through the ages of wildly differing machinery and circumstance, that basic urge has remained the same, as has the basic technique of balancing grip against power through steering and throttle control.

It was always a dangerous sport and despite the elimination of many unnecessary perils, it remains inherently so. Many of these heroes didn't get to live out the natural span of their lives. Here then are the men who excelled in a sport with the highest of stakes.

◄ The start of the Monaco
Grand Prix, Monte Carlo, 2002.

Jean Alesi

A spectacular Formula One career that lasted for over 12 years yielded only one victory but produced countless moments of high drama and astonishing car control.

Alesi graduated to Formula 3000 in 1988 as the French Formula Three Champion, and the following year he clinched the Formula 3000 crown with Eddie Jordan Racing. That season he made his Formula One debut with Tyrrell, making a big impression by coming home fourth in his first event. He created an even bigger impact in the first race of 1990, at Phoenix, when after leading in the Tyrrell and being passed by Ayrton Senna, he cheekily re-passed the great Brazilian before surrendering to the inevitable and finishing second.

Such performances led to a string of offers from top teams for 1991, among them Williams and Ferrari. In a decision of dubious wisdom, he chose the latter, then spent five years in a sequence of Ferraris that were rarely as quick as the top cars. His sole victory came in Canada in 1995, his final year with the Italian team.

Alesi spent the next six seasons in a succession of ever-less competitive cars from Benetton, Sauber and Prost. A mid-2001 switch to Jordan was a last gasp opportunity to regain form and rescue his career, but he was dropped at the end of the year.

Jean Alesi	
Nationality	French
Seasons	1989–2001
Teams driven for	Tyrrell, Ferrari, Benetton, Sauber, Prost, Jordan
Number of major victories	1

◀ Jean Alesi celebrates his first Grand Prix victory at Montreal, Canada, in 1995.

▼ (*below*) Alesi came second for Ferrari at the San Marino Grand Prix at Imola in 1995.

▼ (*bottom*) Jean Alesi, in the Ferrari 412T2, took second place at the German Grand Prix, Nürburgring, in 1995.

Fernando Alonso

By winning the 2003 Hungarian Grand Prix for Renault, Fernando Alonso became the youngest ever driver to win a Formula One race. It also marked the first time that a Spaniard had won a Grand Prix.

The 2003 season was Alonso's first with a competitive team, though he had made his debut with Minardi in 2001 as a 19-year-old. As a six-year-old he had been encouraged by his father – himself a keen amateur kart racer – to take up karting in Spain. Over the following years he became one of the country's top exponents of the sport, and this led to his graduation to car racing in 1999, when he won the Spain-based Formula Nissan Championship.

This gave him a test drive with Minardi and it led to a seat within the F3000 category, the stepping stone to Formula One. During this time Alonso's obvious talent was noticed by Renault Sport boss, Flavio Briatore, who put him on a long-term contract.

After his debut Formula One season with Minardi, he took up the position of test driver for the Renault team, and from there he graduated to a seat with the race team in 2003. His sensational form has led many to mark him out as the future successor to Michael Schumacher as the sport's number one driver, and has created an explosion of Formula One interest in Spain.

Fernando Alonso	
Nationality	Spanish
Seasons	2001–present
Teams driven for	Minardi, Renault
Number of major victories	1

◀ Alonso has ignited Formula One interest in his native Spain.

▼ Alonso became the youngest-ever Grand Prix winner, at 22 years 26 days, when he triumphed in Hungary in 2003.

▲ Fernando Alonso's Renault has a comfortable lead at the 2003 Hungarian Grand Prix.

Chris Amon

The brilliant New Zealander has the unfortunate reputation as the greatest driver never to win a Grand Prix. He began his Formula One career as a 19-year-old in 1963 – for many years he held the record as the youngest driver to start a Grand Prix – and ended it as a disillusioned 32-year-old in 1976. In between, he gave some virtuoso performances that stood comparison with any of the greats of the sport, but he added to his natural bad luck by a sequence of poor career moves.

Indulged by his farming father, Amon began racing in New Zealand, where he was spotted by Formula One team owner Reg Parnell, who took him into Formula One with his privateer team. Amon won the Le Mans 24 Hour sportscar race of 1966 in partnership with Bruce McLaren, but not until he signed with Ferrari for 1967 did his potential become clear. He took fourth in that year's championship, but in 1968, with a more competitive car, he was often the fastest man around. He retired from a 40-second lead in Spain and an even more dominant position in the closing stages in Canada. It seemed only a matter of time before such form gave him the world title.

▲ Chris Amon in 1968.

▼ Chris Amon's Ferrari 312 took second place at the British Grand Prix, Brands Hatch, in 1968.

Chris Amon	
Nationality	New Zealand
Seasons	1963–76
Teams driven for	Parnell, Cooper, Ferrari, March, Matra, Tecno, Tyrrell, Amon, BRM, Ensign, Wolf
Number of major victories	0

In the non-championship Tasman series of 1967–68, he raced wheel-to-wheel with the great Jim Clark. In the same competition the following year, he triumphed over future champion, Jochen Rindt. He left Ferrari at the end of 1969, just as the team came good, and left March at the end of 1970, as it was on the verge of producing the car that would take Ronnie Peterson to second in the 1971 World Championship. In France in 1972, he drove one of the greatest races of all time when, after leading comfortably in his Matra, he suffered a puncture then came back to take third. After retiring in 1977 he returned home to New Zealand.

Mario Andretti

Often cited as the most versatile racing driver of all time, Andretti was a champion in Formula One and Indycar racing, and he has won in everything from dirt-track racing to NASCAR stock cars.

Of Italian descent, Andretti moved to America as a child. Together with his twin brother Aldo, he began racing dirt-track midget cars, leading eventually to a full-time drive in the USAC Championship that included the famous Indianapolis 500 race. As a rookie, he won the USAC Championship in 1965. At Indianapolis that year he came to the attention of Lotus boss Colin Chapman, who promised him a Formula One drive whenever he felt he was ready.

Mario Andretti	
Nationality	American
Seasons	1968–82
Teams driven for	Lotus, Ferrari, Parnelli, Alfa Romeo
Number of major victories	12

◀ **Mario Andretti won the 1978 World Championship driving for Lotus – taking six victories along the way.**

▼ **Mario Andretti took pole position and finished in third place as a Ferrari stand-in at the Italian Grand Prix, Monza, in 1982.**

He felt ready by the end of 1968 – and promptly put his Lotus on pole position on his Formula One debut at the American Grand Prix. He didn't race in Formula One full-time until 1976, but in between he won the 1971 South African Grand Prix for Ferrari. In 1976, he returned to Lotus, and together they won the final race of the year. This was a prelude to a brilliant two-season run with the ground-effect Lotus 78 and 79 models, culminating in the 1978 World Championship. Lotus' competitiveness went downhill subsequently, and Andretti spent his final Formula One season in 1981 with Alfa Romeo. Ferrari called him up as a stand-in at the 1982 Italian Grand Prix – and he responded with pole position, showing that at the age of 42, he still had it.

Thereafter, he finished off his career in American Indycar racing, winning for many years before finally retiring from motorsport at the end of 1994.

◀ **Winner Mario Andretti leads Jo Siffert at the South African Grand Prix, 1971.**

René Arnoux

Arnoux was one of the generation of French drivers of the 1970s who began their careers at the Winfield Racing Drivers' School and succeeded in each category as they moved up the ladder. Arnoux's progress wasn't as smooth as those of some of his peers, but when he got his big Formula One break in 1979, with Renault, he made maximum use of it. In a Formula One career lasting 11 years, he took 18 pole positions and seven race wins with Renault and Ferrari.

After winning the 1977 Formula Two Championship with the Martini team, they graduated to Formula One together in 1978. It was an underfunded effort and they struggled, but for 1979 Renault wanted to expand to running two of its radical turbocharged cars, and Arnoux's promise and nationality made him a shoe-in for the drive. He won his first Grand Prix in Brazil in 1980, and driving alongside Alain Prost in the

▼ (below) Winner René Arnoux in the Renault RE20 at the South African Grand Prix in 1980. It was his second victory.

following two years he proved every bit as fast, if not as calculating. After famously disobeying team orders to win the 1982 French Grand Prix, his days at Renault were numbered. For 1983 he was recruited by Ferrari.

He took three victories in his first season with the Italian team, entering the final round with an outside chance of taking the world title but ultimately finishing third. After performing erratically, he was sacked by Ferrari early in 1985 and this signalled the end of his frontline career. He returned with Ligier in 1986 and served out four more Formula One years before quietly retiring at the end of 1989.

◄ René Arnoux was one of the fastest drivers of the early 1980s.

▼ (bottom) Arnoux, here in his final full season with Ferrari, at Austria in 1984. He won three times for the Italian team.

René Arnoux

Nationality	French
Seasons	1978–89
Teams driven for	Martini, Renault, Ferrari, Ligier
Number of major victories	7

Alberto Ascari

The man who would be 1952 and 1953 World Champion was just seven years old when his father, Antonio, was killed while leading the 1925 French Grand Prix. Alberto subsequently began racing motorcycles and, just prior to the outbreak of World War II, he made his car racing debut.

Post-war, he was signed by Maserati and enjoyed considerable success there in 1948 and 1949. His senior team-mate Luigi Villoresi adopted him as his protégé and guided his subsequent career. In 1950, the pair were recruited by Ferrari, where they stayed for the next four years.

Ascari quickly demonstrated that he was the only driver on the same level as the legendary Juan Manuel Fangio, and the two had some epic dices. For 1952, the World Championship was changed from Formula One to Formula Two regulations, and Ferrari produced the fastest machine. It was under these circumstances that Ascari reeled off the most dominant championship display ever seen. He missed the first race to compete in the Indianapolis 500, but won every single subsequent round of the contest. Despite increased pressure from Fangio's Maserati in 1953, he took his second title quite comfortably. For 1954, he was recruited by Lancia but

Alberto Ascari	
Nationality	Italian
Seasons	1947–55
Teams driven for	Maserati, Ferrari, Alfa Romeo, Lancia
Number of major victories	15

◀ Alberto Ascari, driving a 2-litre Ferrari 500, celebrates his win at Silverstone, 1953.

▼ (left) Alberto Ascari and and Luigi Villoresi.

▼ Alberto Ascari led the 1951 French Grand Prix in the Ferrari 375.

delays in readying the new D50 model meant he did very little racing. Highly superstitious, it has been claimed he was obsessed with the idea that destiny would not allow him to live longer than the 36 years his father had enjoyed.

At 36 years old, he was lying in second place in the 1955 Monaco Grand Prix when he crashed into the harbour. He was only slightly injured. A few days later, he visited Monza to watch his friend Eugenio Castellotti test a Ferrari sports car, before asking if he himself might try the car. In an accident that has never been fully explained, Ascari left the road and was killed.

Antonio Ascari

Ascari worked his way into the racing seat through a succession of jobs as a mechanic and tester before World War I. Post-war, he established himself as an Alfa Romeo dealer in Milan, and through that connection began racing works Alfas.

This was at a time when the Milan-based company was just emerging as a serious Grand Prix force, and Ascari's arrival upon the international scene was sensational. In his first big-time event, Cremona 1924, he gave the brand new Alfa Romeo P2 a debut victory. He then came to within three laps of winning the French Grand Prix before going on to a dominant victory in Italy.

Within the space of a few months, Ascari had made serious claim to be the world's fastest Grand Prix driver. He opened his 1925 account with a start-to-finish victory in the Belgian Grand Prix. He was leading by a long way in the French Grand Prix of that year when rain began to fall, and everyone but Ascari reduced their pace considerably. But he pressed on, and eventually he slid wide. A rear wheel became entangled in some fencing, and the car flipped upside down. It was before the days of crash helmets or roll-over bars, and Ascari's injuries were fatal.

Antonio Ascari

Nationality	Italian
Seasons	1924–25
Teams driven for	Alfa Romeo
Number of major victories	2

▲ *(left)* Antonio Ascari for Alfa Romeo at Monza in 1924, his first year in Grand Prix.

▲ *(right)* Antonio Ascari (*left*) with young Alberto, seated in the car, and Enzo Ferrari (*second from left*).

▼ Antonio Ascari driving for Alfa Romeo at the French Grand Prix, Montlhéry, 1925.

Rubens Barrichello

The other half to Michael Schumacher of the dominant Ferrari team, the Brazilian Rubens Barrichello has performed with distinction for four years alongside the champion. During that time he has won seven Grands Prix and he finished runner-up to Schumacher in the 2002 World Championship.

Prior to his stint at Ferrari, Barrichello had served a seven-year apprenticeship in Formula One with the Jordan and Stewart teams, showing regular flair and promise but never quite managing to win a race. After a successful karting career in Brazil, Barrichello came to Europe in 1990 and established a big reputation in the junior categories, winning the European GM Euroseries that year and following it up with victory in the 1991 British Formula Three Championship.

His Formula One debut came in 1993, with Jordan. In that year's European Grand Prix at Donington, he drove brilliantly to run in second position to his countryman and idol

Rubens Barrichello	
Nationality	Brazilian
Seasons	1993–present
Teams driven for	Jordan, Stewart, Ferrari
Number of major victories	7

◀ Barichello has been a critical part of Ferrari's success into the new millennium.

▼ Barrichello takes victory in the 2003 Japanese Grand Prix.

Ayrton Senna before retirement. It took a long time to convert such potential into Formula One success, but he finally achieved his first win at Hockenheim in the 2000 German Grand Prix.

He was at the centre of the Ferrari controversy in 2002 when the team instructed him to give way to his team-mate Schumacher in the Austrian Grand Prix, despite having led the race from the start. He complied in the last few hundred yards of the race, triggering an outcry from those who felt the team were doing the sport a disservice. In 2003, Barrichello won both the British and Japanese Grands Prix and was a critical element in securing Schumacher's record sixth title.

Robert Benoist

▼ Robert Benoist in 1922.

Benoist's Grand Prix immortality is assured by his feat of winning all four Grands Prix of 1927 for Delage.

The son of a Rothschild gamekeeper, he began racing bicycles and worked for the Grégoire car company shortly before World War I. He volunteered as a pilot for the war and survived being shot down; he was also credited with shooting down one enemy plane. After the war, he began cyclecar racing and was a dominant champion in 1923. This brought him to the attention of Delage, with whom he made his Grand Prix debut in 1924. He finished third in that year's European Grand Prix at Lyons. He then shared victory with team-mate Albert Divo in the 1925 French Grand Prix, after the Alfa team withdrew following the death of Antonio Ascari.

As the Delage became ever-more competitive, so Benoist's career flowered, culminating in his victorious 1927 season. Delage then withdrew from racing, leaving Benoist to serve the rest of his career with Bugatti, for whom he won the Le Mans 24 Hours sports car race in 1937.

Robert Benoist	
Nationality	French
Seasons	1924–36
Teams driven for	Delage, Bugatti
Number of major victories	5

During World War II Benoist was a leading member of the French resistance against German occupation, and he received training in Britain. Working in collaboration with fellow Grand Prix drivers William Grover-Williams and Jean-Pierre Wimille, he was highly successful in the field before being captured and executed by the Gestapo.

▲ Louis Chiron *(left)* and Benoist in 1928.

◄ Benoist in action at the European Grand Prix, San Sebastian, Spain, in 1926.

Gerhard Berger

In a Formula One career stretching from 1984 to 1997, Berger took victories with Benetton, Ferrari and McLaren, though he never managed a sustained challenge for the world title.

The Austrian's rise through the sport's junior ranks was rapid, and partly funded by his father's transport company. He made a big step from Renault Five racing to Formula Three in 1983, and was immediately competitive. By the end of 1984, he was making his Formula One debut in an ATS-BMW with over 800 horsepower. His abundant natural ability meant he adapted comfortably.

After a season driving for Arrows in 1985, he was recruited by the new Benetton team for 1986. At the end of that season he gave himself and the team their first victory, with a winning drive in Mexico. His performances had attracted the attention of Ferrari, with whom he scored two consecutive victories at the end of 1987.

In the early laps of the 1989 San Marino Grand Prix, a wing failure sent him into the wall at Imola's flat-out Tamburello corner. The impact was massive and the Ferrari erupted in flames. Remarkably, he was pulled out of the car with just slight burns to his hands, a broken rib and fractured shoulder blade. Two races later he was back behind the wheel.

▲ Gerhard Berger in 1987, during the first of two stints driving for the Ferrari team. He won the final two races of that year.

Gerhard Berger	
Nationality	Austrian
Seasons	1984–97
Teams driven for	ATS, Arrows, Benetton, Ferrari, McLaren
Number of major victories	10

In 1990, he was recruited by McLaren to partner Ayrton Senna, but he wasn't the same standard as the Brazilian. He served three years alongside Senna before returning to Ferrari for a big money offer. He helped improve the team's performances and won the 1994 German Grand Prix. He left in 1996, when Ferrari recruited Michael Schumacher, and returned to Benetton, where he served out his career, winning the 1997 German Grand Prix before retiring. He later took up the post of motorsport director with BMW.

▲ Berger's Benetton locks a wheel on the way to third place in the 1997 Brazilian Grand Prix in Sao Paulo.

▶ Berger's Ferrari (left) attempts to fend off Damon Hill's Williams in the 1994 Canadian Grand Prix. Berger finished fourth, two places behind Hill.

Georges Boillot

Boillot appeared like a meteor in Grand Prix racing, winning on his debut in France in 1912, and establishing himself as the fastest and most daring driver up to the outbreak of World War I. Serving as a pilot in the French Air Force, he was killed in action in 1916.

His car racing career began in the voiturette ("small car") class, with Lion-Peugeot, in 1908. He soon came to be the dominant driver of this category, and when Lion-Peugeot and the parent Peugeot company were reunited in 1911, he was central to the plan of building and racing a full-size Grand Prix car.

This car was the ground-breaking twin-cam, four-valve-per-cylinder L76. Boillot took it to victory on its debut at Dieppe. He repeated this result in the French Grand Prix of 1913, before setting pole position and a lap record

▲ Georges Boillot finished first in the 1910 Mont Ventoux hill climb in the Lion-Peugeot.

▼ *(left)* Boillot won the Mont Ventoux hill climb in 1913 in the Peugeot 5.7 litre.

▼ *(right)* Georges Boillot.

on his debut at the Indianapolis 500 in 1914. Later that year, in the French Grand Prix, he drove a heroic race in a Peugeot that was, by now, outclassed by the latest model from Mercedes. He kept the faster German cars at bay for almost all of the race's seven-hour duration, but retired on the final lap with engine failure.

He was shot down after attempting to take on seven German scout planes single-handed. He was awarded a posthumous *Legion d'Honneur*.

Georges Boillot	
Nationality	French
Seasons	1912–14
Teams driven for	Peugeot
Number of major victories	2

Pietro Bordino

▼ Pietro Bordino driving for Fiat in the 2-litre Grand Prix of 1924.

As the lead driver with the crack Fiat squad, Bordino was the man to beat in the early 1920s.

He had begun as a Fiat riding mechanic pre-war, alongside aces Felice Nazzaro and Vincenzo Lancia. His driving debut for Fiat was at the 1921 Brescia Grand Prix where his speed was sensational, leading comfortably until sidelined by mechanical problems.

Through 1922 and 1923, he won a whole flurry of major Grands Prix, and had there been a World Championship then he would have won titles in both

years. Fiat withdrew from Grand Prix racing at the end of 1924, and Bordino wasn't seen for a while. The company made a one-off comeback at the 1927 Milan Grand Prix, which Bordino completely dominated.

He was practising for the 1928 Targa Florio race in a Bugatti when he hit a dog, jamming his steering and causing him to crash into a river with fatal results.

◄ Bordino's new Fiat at the Monza Grand Prix of 1927.

Pietro Bordino	
Nationality	Italian
Seasons	1921–28
Teams driven for	Fiat, Bugatti
Number of major victories	3

▼ Bordino – in the Fiat 802 – retired from the 1921 Italian Grand Prix at Brescia but set a lap record of 150.35km/h (93.43mph).

Jack Brabham

This tough Australian who began his career midget-racing on the cinder tracks of his home country won three World Championships, the last of them in a car bearing his own name. This stands as a unique achievement in the history of the sport.

After a highly successful career in Australia, Brabham arrived in Britain in 1955 and hooked up with the Cooper team. A highly technical driver, Brabham was able to help Cooper develop its mid-engined cars, first of all in sports cars and subsequently in Formula One.

In 1959, Brabham in the mid-engined Cooper emerged victorious from a final-round championship showdown against Tony Brooks in the front-engined Ferrari. It was the final nail in the coffin for the traditional Grand Prix car. Brabham repeated his success in 1960 but the Cooper was about to be leapfrogged by Lotus.

Sensing that Cooper was a spent force, Brabham set up on his own, recruiting his friend from midget-racing, Ron Tauranac, to design the

▲ Jack Brabham, in the Brabham BT33, taking his 14th and final Grand Prix victory at Kyalami, South Africa, in 1970.

Jack Brabham

Nationality	Australian
Seasons	1955–70
Teams driven for	Cooper, Brabham
Number of major victories	14

Brabham BT3, which made its debut in 1962. Brabham seemed content to let his employed driver Dan Gurney lead the team and was planning to retire from the wheel at the end of 1965. But then Gurney left to set up *his* own team, leaving Brabham as the lead driver once again. This coincided with the new 3-litre formula, and Brabham's shrewdness of engine choice and cockpit skills gave him his third title.

He remained a front rank driver until his retirement at the end of 1970, when, at the age of 44, he sold up and returned home to Australia.

▲ Brabham at the Mexico Grand Prix in 1969, where he finished the race in third place after starting from pole position.

◀ Brabham retired from the 1966 Italian Grand Prix at Monza, but he won that year's championship regardless.

Tony Brooks

Brooks vies with Stirling Moss as the greatest driver never to have won the World Championship, though his quiet, less thrusting manner meant he has never achieved the same fame as his contemporary.

Brooks came to prominence in 1955 when, in only his second race outside the British club scene, he won the Syracuse Grand Prix for Connaught. Although it was a non-championship event, this was the first Grand Prix victory for a British car and driver for over 30 years. On his aeroplane flights there and back, he was studying for his final exams in dentistry.

Although Brooks received the qualification, he never did take up dentistry, as his huge talent made him much in demand within the sport. After a season with BRM in 1956,

▲ Tony Brooks, driver for Vanwall, Aston Martin and Cooper cars, in 1958.

▲ Brooks winning the German Grand Prix at the Nürburgring for Vanwall in 1958.

Tony Brooks	
Nationality	British
Seasons	1955–61
Teams driven for	Connaught, BRM, Vanwall, Ferrari
Number of major victories	6

he was recruited by Vanwall to drive alongside Moss in 1957. The pair proved extremely evenly-matched and took a shared victory in the British Grand Prix. Brooks won three times in 1958, helping Vanwall to the World Constructors' title.

For 1959, he moved to Ferrari and was unlucky to lose out in the title showdown with Jack Brabham. He

was hit from behind off the line by his team-mate and insisted on pitting for a damage inspection, unwilling to risk his life. He finished the race third, but otherwise would probably have won both the race and the championship.

It was his last competitive season. Wanting to return to Britain, he was obliged to take drives in inferior cars, and he retired at the end of 1961.

► Tony Brooks in his Ferrari during practice for the 1959 Italian Grand Prix. Clutch failure at the start of the race lost him a likely victory in the World Championship that year. He never came so close again.

David Bruce-Brown

As one of the stars of American racing, Bruce-Brown was recruited by the visiting European teams in the 1910 and 1911 American Grand Prize races. Against the cream of American and European racing combined, he won both times for Benz and Fiat respectively.

Highly impressed by his speed and intelligence, Fiat brought him over to Europe to compete in the 1912 French Grand Prix. He was leading the race against the Peugeot of Georges Boillot when he retired.

Commonly hailed as the best driver in the world at this time, he was killed during practice for the 1912 Vanderbilt Cup in Milwaukee.

David Bruce-Brown	
Nationality	American
Seasons	1910–12
Teams driven for	Benz, Fiat
Number of major victories	2

▲ David Bruce-Brown at the wheel of his Benz, at the Savannah Grand Prix, 1910.

▼ Bruce-Brown in the 1911 Vanderbilt Cup. He was killed in this event the following year.

Jenson Button

▼ Jenson Button in the Williams-BMW FW22 at the Japanese Grand Prix, Suzuka, in 2000.

Button burst onto the Formula One scene in sensational fashion in 2000 when, as a 20-year old, he was plucked from the junior ranks of racing to drive in Formula One for the mighty Williams-BMW team. By finishing sixth in Brazil 2000, his second race for the team, he became the youngest British Formula One driver ever to score a world championship point. He went on to several more stunning performances during his debut year, including out-qualifying Michael Schumacher on his first visit to the Belgian Grand Prix.

Despite generally out-performing his Williams team-mate, Ralf Schumacher, in the latter stages of the 2000 season, Button was moved aside at Williams to make way for Juan Pablo Montoya in 2001. The Colombian was already on a long term contract with Williams and Button had been used as a stand-in.

Nonetheless, it had enabled him to show his talent at the highest level, and he transferred across to the Renault team for the next two seasons. In 2003, he drove alongside Jacques Villeneuve at BAR-Honda and proceeded to out-perform the former world champion. He led both the American and Japanese Grands Prix. Button remains Britain's brightest Formula One prospect.

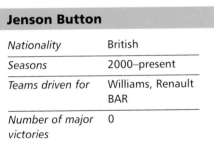

Jenson Button	
Nationality	British
Seasons	2000–present
Teams driven for	Williams, Renault BAR
Number of major victories	0

▲ Jenson Button in 2003.

▼ Jenson Button in the Renault F1 R202 at the Monaco Grand Prix, 2002.

Rudolf Caracciola

One of the all-time great Grand Prix drivers, Caracciola's career was intertwined with Mercedes in the 1920s and 1930s. He first made his reputation with some astonishing Grand Prix drives in the hopelessly heavy and unsuitable SSK sports car. With this he fought for victory in the first Monaco Grand Prix of 1929; twice he took the car to victory in the German Prix around the tortuous Nürburgring.

When Mercedes could offer him no racing programme for 1932, Caracciola switched to Alfa Romeo, where he instantly matched the speed of the legendary Tazio Nuvolari. He badly injured a leg in a practice accident at Monaco in 1933, and this came close to ending his career.

◄ Rudolf Caracciola in his Mercedes W163 during the 1939 French Grand Prix. He retired after hitting a wall.

He was tempted back by Mercedes as it re-entered Grand Prix racing under the Nazi regime in 1934. His silky touch had not deserted him and he was European Champion in 1935, '37 and '38. Rudi's greatest performances invariably came in the rain, where his uncanny feel led to the tag of "reinmeister".

After spending the duration of World War II in exile in Switzerland, Caracciola did not return to Grand Prix racing post-war. He died in 1959.

▲ Rudolf Caracciola, the European Champion of 1935, 1937 and 1938.

► Manfred von Brauchitsch and Caracciola, both driving for Mercedes, fight for the lead in the 1937 Monaco Grand Prix.

Rudolf Caracciola

Nationality	German
Seasons	1926–39
Teams driven for	Mercedes, Alfa Romeo
Number of major victories	17

François Cevert

C evert was being groomed by Ken Tyrrell as Jackie Stewart's heir, ready to take over as Tyrrell's lead driver after Stewart retired. With his talent, film star looks, intelligence and charm, he looked set to be a major star. He had spent three seasons under the combined tutelage of the two masters and looked set to be one of the elite of Formula One drivers. But in qualifying for the 1973 American Grand Prix – ironically due to be Stewart's final race – Cevert was killed attempting to secure pole position. Jackie withdrew, and the rest of the Formula One world mourned with him.

Cevert benefited from Elf's drive to promote young French talent. After winning a scholarship with the Winfield Racing School in 1968, he had proved very quick in Formula Three and

Formula Two, and he made his Formula One debut with the Elf-sponsored Tyrrell team in 1970. At the end of 1971, he won the American Grand Prix. In 1973, he dutifully followed Stewart home on three occasions, though the Scot later confided he believed Cevert could have passed him had he chosen to.

▲ François Cevert celebrates his first and only Grand Prix victory at Watkins Glen, USA, in 1971. It was the scene of his death two years later.

▼ Cevert at Montjuich Park, Spain, in 1973, where he finished second to his mentor, Jackie Stewart.

▲ Cevert in 1972: his film star looks belied talent and determination. A very bright future looked assured.

François Cevert	
Nationality	French
Seasons	1970–73
Teams driven for	Tyrrell
Number of major victories	1

Fernand Charron

This French former cycle racer was the most successful of the first ever generation of racing drivers. Employed by Panhard, he made his reputation by winning the two biggest events of 1898, the Marseilles–Nice and the Paris–Amsterdam–Paris races.

Fast and daring, his British rival Charles Jarrott said of him: "Dare-devil, dashing and full of the winning spirit, his wins were hard-fought and hard-won. Without being what is ordinarily called nervous, he was nevertheless a mass of nerves, and he received little assistance from his physique to carry him through the strain and stress of driving a racing car at full speed throughout the long day. He is slightly built, small, dapper and quick as lightning when the occasion calls for quickness... As a really brilliant driver, Charron at his best had no equal."

▼ Charron in the Marseilles–Nice race of 1898. Winning this race helped to establish his reputation as a driver.

▲ Fernand Charron driving the Panhard in which he won the 565km (351-mile) Paris–Bordeaux race of 1899.

▼ Fernand Charron (right) driving a Panhard-Levassor in the Tour de France race of 1899.

Fernand Charron	
Nationality	French
Seasons	1897–1901
Teams driven for	Panhard
Number of major victories	4

Louis Chiron

▼ Chiron established himself as a frontline Grand Prix driver in Bugatti's type 35 model.

One of the major stars of Grand Prix racing in the late 1920s and 1930s, Chiron continued driving in Formula One until the mid-1950s.

A native of Monte Carlo, his early career was synonymous with Bugatti. He first began winning major races for this constructor in 1928, though not until 1931 did he finally manage to win his home Grand Prix.

He later transferred across to Alfa Romeo and produced what was arguably his finest drive when he took his Alfa P3 to victory in the 1934 French Grand Prix against the faster cars of Mercedes and Auto Union.

He continued his career post-war, but not with the same degree of success. After retiring, he was asked by Monaco's Prince Rainier to run the Monaco Grand Prix. He did so until his death in 1979, aged 78.

Louis Chiron	
Nationality	French
Seasons	1928–58
Teams driven for	Bugatti, Alfa Romeo, Mercedes, Talbot, Lancia
Number of major victories	14

◄ Chiron, here in his role of running the Monaco Grand Prix, talks to Juan Manuel Fangio.

▼ Chiron in a Scuderia-Ferrari Alfa Romeo P3 in 1934.

Jim Clark

The greatest driver of his era, Clark was World Champion in 1963 and 1965 and, at the time of his death in 1968, he had won more Grands Prix than anyone in the sport's history. He drove for Lotus throughout his Formula One career.

A Scottish farmer, he was adopted as a protégé by amateur racing driver Ian Scott-Watson. His early successes came in a variety of saloons and sports cars in local club racing. The break into the big time came after testing a Lotus Formula Two car at Brands Hatch, where he was trading times with the team's Formula One star Graham Hill. Lotus boss Colin Chapman was stunned when he subsequently learned that this was Clark's first ever drive in a single-seater.

Clark subsequently became a works Lotus Formula Two driver, and within a few months was making his Formula One debut in Holland in 1960. Chapman and Clark came to form a very close relationship, and as each man was a genius in their respective fields of design and driving, phenomenal success followed. As well as winning in Formula One, they also took the American racing world by storm with victory in the 1965 Indy 500.

Clark was 32 and at the height of his powers when he was killed in a Formula Two race at Hockenheim on 7 April 1968.

Jim Clark	
Nationality	British
Seasons	1960–68
Teams driven for	Lotus
Number of major victories	25

▲ Jim Clark dominating his final Grand Prix at South Africa in 1968.

▶ Jim Clark, World Drivers' Champion of 1963 and 1965.

▼ Clark gives the Lotus 25 its debut at the 1962 Dutch Grand Prix. He would win two world titles with this car and its derivative.

Peter Collins

Collins' place in motorsport folklore was guaranteed when he gave up his chance of winning the 1956 World Championship by handing his car over to title rival and team-mate Juan Manuel Fangio in the final round. In what was a cruel twist of fate, he was denied any subsequent challenge for the crown, suffering a fatal accident during the 1958 German Grand Prix.

Collins was part of a new generation of British talent to emerge from that country's pioneering Formula 500 Championship. After a few promising runs for a variety of British teams from 1954 to 1955, his big chance came when he was signed by Ferrari for 1956. He won the Belgian and French Grand Prix that year and would almost certainly have taken the crown were it not for his act of supreme sportsmanship at Monza in the season finale.

He stayed at Ferrari in company with his close friend Mike Hawthorn for the rest of his time. Two weeks after winning the 1958 British Grand Prix, he was chasing Tony Brooks' race-leading Vanwall at the Nürburgring when his car left the road and overturned.

◄ Collins stayed loyal to Ferrari from 1956 until his demise in 1958. He was a firm favourite of Enzo Ferrari.

Peter Collins	
Nationality	British
Seasons	1952–58
Teams driven for	HWM, Vanwall, Owen, Maserati, Ferrari
Number of major victories	3

◄ Peter Collins was just 20 years old when he made his Grand Prix debut, in 1952, and only 26 when he was killed.

▲ Peter Collins with his Ferrari in 1957. Ferrari were not fully competitive that year, and Collins' best finishes were third in France and Germany.

► Peter Collins in his Mercedes at Targa Florio in 1955. He was beaten by team-mate Stirling Moss after suffering an accident.

David Coulthard

T he Scot's big career break came under the tragic circumstances of Ayrton Senna's death in 1994. As Williams' test driver, Coulthard took over the seat of the legendary Brazilian and established himself as a regular Grand Prix winner. His first victory came in 1995 in Portugal.

After beginning in karting, Coulthard served an apprenticeship in the British junior categories. He was competing in the European Formula 3000 Championship when his Formula One chance came. After taking four consecutive pole positions for Williams at the end of 1995, he switched to McLaren.

Initially, this was a backward step in terms of competitiveness, but he began his winning sequence for his new team with victory in Australia in 1997. The McLarens of 1998 and 1999 were the fastest cars but Coulthard was outshone by team-mate Mika Häkkinen. He mounted a serious title challenge to Michael Schumacher in 2001 but by this time the Ferraris had gained a performance advantage over McLaren. He continued to win races for McLaren through 2002 and 2003 and has served the team for longer than any other driver in its 35-year history.

◀ David Coulthard in his Williams FW17 at the Spanish Grand Prix, Barcelona, in 1995. It was his first full season of Formula One.

David Coulthard	
Nationality	British
Seasons	1994–present
Teams driven for	Williams, McLaren
Number of major victories	13

◀ David Coulthard has spent most of his Formula One career with McLaren after getting his first break with Williams.

▼ Coulthard took a great victory at Monaco in 2002. Here, he is chased by Juan Pablo Montoya and Michael Schumacher, neither of whom could break his defence.

Arthur Duray

Born in New York but a resident of France, Duray was one of the top drivers of the era of the sport before World War I. He enjoyed a long career that stretched from the turn of the 20th century to the late 1920s, though his halcyon days were with de Dietrich in 1905–07.

After establishing the land speed record at 134.31km/h (83.46mph) in 1903 for Gobron-Brille, Duray began racing with that company. De Dietrich then recruited him and they won the 1906 Circuit des Ardennes together.

After de Dietrich withdrew from the sport in 1912, Duray was left without a top drive but, undeterred, he continued in the small car class. He scored a stunning second place in the 1913 Indianapolis 500, having led for much of the distance, in a 3-litre Peugeot that was 2.5 litres down on the rest of the field. After the war, he continued racing in the voiturette and sports car categories, and continued to set speed records before his retirement in 1928.

▲ Arthur Duray in 1908.

◀ Arthur Duray, with de Dietrich emblem, at the 1907 Moscow–St Petersburg race.

Arthur Duray	
Nationality	French
Seasons	1903–14
Teams driven for	Gobron-Brille, de Dietrich, Delage, Peugeot
Number of major victories	1

▼ Arthur Duray in the Alcyon voiturette (small car) in the 1912 French Grand Prix. He continued in this class into the 1920s.

Juan Manuel Fangio

his Argentinian legend was a
five-time World Champion in the
1950s, and was commonly referred to
as "El Maestro". His amazing Grand Prix
career began when he was already in
his late 30s, and he won his final title
at the age of 46.

Hailing from a modest family
background in Balcarce, his early racing
exploits were on dirt roads in saloon
cars, partly financed by whip-rounds
among the people of his village. He
quickly established a huge reputation
in his homeland, but it was not until
the leading European teams and drivers
of the day visited Argentina for an
off-season mini-series in 1948 that the
phenomenon of Fangio was revealed
to the wider world.

Jean-Pierre Wimille was acknowledged as the world's finest driver at
that time. In the Rosario Grand Prix, he
and Fangio were matched in identical
Gordinis. They staged a superb duel.
Wimille won but only after Fangio's
car had begun to lose power. Fangio
took the consolation of fastest lap.
Afterwards, Wimille paid tribute to his
rival and rightly predicted that great
things awaited him.

The Argentinian Motor Club paid
for a national team that included
Fangio to race in European events in
1949. His form in the club's Maserati
proved beyond all doubt his stunning

▲ Fangio (18) starts the 1954 French Grand
Prix in pole position, ahead of Karl Kling (20).

Juan Manuel Fangio

Nationality	Argentinian
Seasons	1949–58
Teams driven for	Alfa Romeo, Maserati, Mercedes, Ferrari
Number of major victories	24

speed, leading to his recruitment by
Alfa-Romeo for the 1950 season.

Only unreliability kept him from
victory in the inaugural World
Championship that year, but he was
a dominant champion in 1951. A neck-
breaking accident kept him out for
most of 1952 but he was back in his
winning stride by 1953. He then won
four successive world titles, a record
that lasted 46 years. He retired in 1958
and returned to his homeland, where
he ran a Mercedes-Benz dealership until
his death in 1995.

◀ Fangio became
a legend through
his exploits in the
1950s, when he
won five world
titles in eight years.

▶ Juan Manuel
Fangio winning
the International
Trophy of 1951
at Silverstone
for Alfa Romeo.

Giuseppe Farina

Farina was already 44 years old when, in 1950, he won the inaugural World Championship. As a highly promising newcomer in the 1930s, his best years were probably lost to the war.

Farina had qualified to become a doctor of political science when at 26 years old he began his racing career. At Maserati he was taken under the wing of Tazio Nuvolari, but he really began to shine in voiturette racing with Alfa Romeo before the war intervened.

After a spell with Ferrari, he moved back to Alfa after the war in the new Formula One category. As a driver in the fastest car, he was well placed when the World Championship was inaugurated. His only competition for the title was team-mate Juan Manuel Fangio, whom he defeated through a superior finishing record. He won races in subsequent seasons with Ferrari, but retired at the end of 1955, having been troubled by leg burns incurred the previous year. He was killed in a road accident in 1966, while driving to the French Grand Prix.

◀ The 1950 World Championship title was the culmination of a long career for Giuseppe Farina.

▼ Farina became the sport's first World Champion with three victories in 1950.

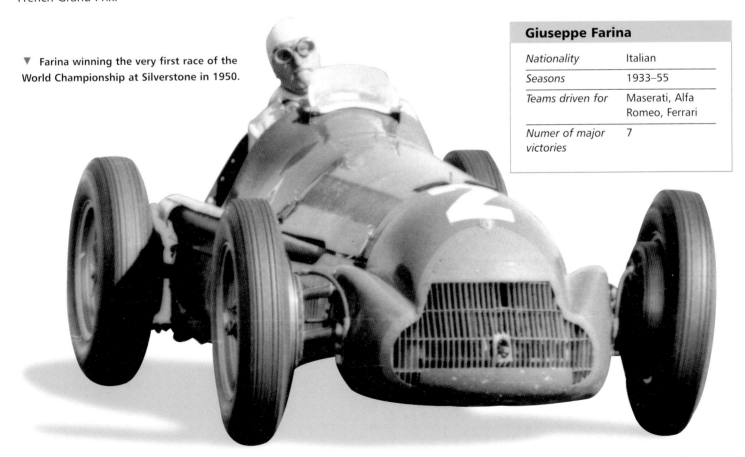

▼ Farina winning the very first race of the World Championship at Silverstone in 1950.

Giuseppe Farina

Nationality	Italian
Seasons	1933–55
Teams driven for	Maserati, Alfa Romeo, Ferrari
Numer of major victories	7

Emerson Fittipaldi

By moving from his native Brazil to race in Europe to further his career, and then becoming World Champion in 1972 and 1974, Emerson Fittipaldi blazed a trail that countless South American drivers have followed ever since.

The son of a sports journalist, Emerson raced karts from an early age, along with his elder brother Wilson. He arrived in Britain in 1968 to race in the junior Formula Ford category, and proved an instant sensation. Lotus' Colin Chapman shrewdly signed him to drive the team's Formula Three and Formula Two cars, and by 1970 he was making his Formula One debut.

In fairy-tale fashion, he won his fifth Grand Prix, this result in America ensuring that Lotus' recently-deceased Jochen Rindt became a posthumous World Champion. After a sequence of victories, he became the sport's youngest-ever World Champion in 1972, aged 25. He joined McLaren for 1974 and promptly won another title.

Surprisingly, he left McLaren at the end of 1975 to drive for the Brazilian Copersucar team that had been founded by his brother Wilson. It proved a frustrating venture, and in five years of trying Emerson never did find success with the cars. He retired for a time before making a glorious comeback in Indycar racing, winning two Indy 500s before his final retirement from motorsport in 1996.

Emerson Fittipaldi	
Nationality	Brazilian
Seasons	1970–80
Teams driven for	Lotus, McLaren, Fittipaldi
Number of major victories	14

▲ Fittipaldi's final podium came with third place in the 1980 USA West Grand Prix – from 24th on the grid.

▼ Fittipaldi's victory at Watkins Glen in 1970 ensured that his late team-mate Jochen Rindt took the world title.

▲ Fittipaldi stands on top of the podium after his fifth Grand Prix, the USA, in 1970.

José Froilán González

The burly Argentinian, known as the "Pampas Bull", won Ferrari's first ever championship-stature Grand Prix, when he beat his friend Fangio's Alfa at Silverstone in 1951.

Fangio was instrumental in getting González an opportunity in Europe in 1950, and his form in a privately-run Maserati brought him his recruitment to Ferrari the following year. After a spell alongside Fangio at Maserati, he returned to Ferrari in 1954, again winning the British Grand Prix and finishing runner-up in the World Championship that season.

At the end of the year, he was injured in a sports car race and niggles from this led to his retirement from regular competition, though he continued to appear at his home Grand Prix until 1960. He concentrated thereafter on his garage business.

Froilan Gonzalez	
Nationality	Argentinian
Seasons	1950–60
Teams driven for	Maserati, Ferrari
Number of major victories	2

◄ Froilián González at the Argentine Grand Prix in 1973, 13 years after his retirement.

▼ *(right)* Froilán González during the 1954 German Grand Prix in his Ferrari.

▼ *(bottom)* Silverstone and the start of the 1951 British Grand Prix, with González (12) racing head to head with Juan Manuel Fangio's Alfa Romeo. González won the race, and Fangio finished in second place.

▼ *(left)* Froilán González on his way to the first Championship-status Grand Prix win for Ferrari at Silverstone in 1951.

Dan Gurney

▼ Gurney took his first Grand Prix victory at Rouen in 1962. It stands as the only such win for the Porsche marque.

In a 12-year Formula One career that spanned spells at Ferrari, BRM, Porsche, Brabham and his own Eagle team, the American Gurney frequently displayed outstanding talent, but was never able to create the right circumstances for a title bid.

The son of an opera singer, he began racing sports cars in California in the early 1950s. The American Ferrari importer Luigi Chinetti was instrumental in getting Gurney a chance with the Ferrari sports car team in Europe in 1958. This opportunity led to his Grand Prix graduation with the team the following year. He made a great impression, running at the front in just his second race.

Uneasy about the politics within Ferrari, he moved to BRM for 1960, but the car proved less competitive than hoped, and this led him to accept an offer to lead Porsche's new Formula One effort for 1961. He gave the team its only Grand Prix victory at France in 1962, having narrowly lost out in the same race in 1961. The disappointing form of the cars led to the German company's withdrawal at the end of 1962, and this left Gurney to hook up with Jack Brabham, who was in the throes of establishing his own team.

Gurney, rather than double World Champion Brabham, proved to be the cutting edge of the driving squad, and in 1964 he gave them their first victory, in France. He won again in Mexico that year, but at the end of a relatively

Dan Gurney	
Nationality	American
Seasons	1959–70
Teams driven for	Ferrari, BRM, Porsche, Brabham, Eagle, McLaren
Number of major victories	4

▼ Two years after his success for Porsche, Gurney gave the Brabham team its first win.

barren 1965, he left to pursue the dream of creating his own team, Eagle. This cost him a real chance of the 1966 World Championship, as Brabhams proved the dominant cars that year.

Gurney won in Belgium in 1967 in the Eagle, but thereafter the car was left behind by the new DFV-powered machines and Gurney's interest in Formula One waned. He drove his last Grand Prix in 1970, as a stand-in at McLaren, and went on to enjoy considerable success as a team owner in Indy car racing.

▲ Dan Gurney celebrates his victory at Rouen in France in 1964.

Mika Häkkinen

The furiously fast Finn came back from near-death in 1995 to win the World Championships of 1998 and 1999 with McLaren-Mercedes.

Managed by former World Champion Keke Rosberg after early years in karting and Formula Ford, he was backed by Marlboro to pursue his career in Britain where he became Formula Three Champion in 1990. Lotus' Peter Collins had a sharp eye for new talent, and he signed Hakkinen for 1991. He performed with much promise, but the team's glory days were over. For 1993, he accepted a role as test driver with McLaren, reasoning that he needed to show his pace in a top car even if it meant not racing in the short term.

When McLaren dropped Michael Andretti near the end of the season,

Mika Häkkinen	
Nationality	Finnish
Seasons	1991–2001
Teams driven for	Lotus, McLaren
Number of major victories	20

after a series of disappointing performances, Häkkinen stepped up to replace him. In a sensational performance, he outqualified his team-mate, the great Ayrton Senna, and his future was seemingly assured.

In qualifying for the 1995 Australian Grand Prix, a puncture-induced accident left him critically injured, and only an

emergency tracheotomy, track-side, saved his life. Remarkably, he seemed to have lost none of his speed when he returned for the start of 1996.

The breakthrough came at the end of 1997 in Jerez, though Häkkinen's victory there was gifted to him by Williams' Jacques Villeneuve, as thanks for McLaren co-operation in not attacking him in the early stages of the race as he fought for the world title with Michael Schumacher.

It was the prelude to a devastating run of victories in the superb McLaren-Mercedes of 1998 and 1999. Häkkinen only narrowly lost out on a third title in 2000. He retired at the end of 2001, though left the door open for a future possible return. In 2002, he announced his retirement was permanent.

▲ *(right)* Mika Häkkinen in the Lotus 102B at the rain-shortened Australian Grand Prix.

▲ *(left)* Häkkinen at the Melbourne Grand Prix in 2001. It was here he made the decision to retire from Formula One.

▶ Häkkinen driving his McLaren MP4-14 to victory in the Brazilian Grand Prix at Interlagos in 1999.

Mike Hawthorn

awthorn became the first British World Champion when he took the title for Ferrari in 1958. He immediately retired from what was then a lethally dangerous sport, but ironically was killed in a road accident just a few months later.

After a lightning quick rise through British club racing in the early 1950s, aided by his former bike-racing father, Hawthorn found himself on the international stage in 1952, when Formula Two was made the World Championship category. Some great performances in a Cooper-Bristol caught the eye of Enzo Ferrari, who signed him for 1953. In the French Grand Prix of that year, Hawthorn scored his first victory after a stirring wheel-to-wheel battle with Juan Manuel Fangio's Maserati.

It would be another five years before Hawthorn was once again in a fully competitive Ferrari, and although he won only the French Grand Prix in 1958, he scored highly everywhere and secured the title in the final round – with some help from team-mate Phil Hill, who moved aside to hand him second place.

After retiring to his garage business, Hawthorn fatally crashed his road car near Guildford in January 1959.

Mike Hawthorn	
Nationality	British
Seasons	1952–58
Teams driven for	Ferrari, Vanwall, BRM
Number of major victories	3

◄ Blonde and dashing, Hawthorn captured the public's imagination.

▼ Mike Hawthorn takes over the car of Ferrari team-mate José Froilán González on lap 16 of the 1954 German Grand Prix.

▲ Hawthorn in the Ferrari model 246 at the Monaco Grand Prix. The car won him the 1958 World Championship title.

▲ Hawthorn and Stirling Moss battled hard over the destiny of the 1958 world title. Hawthorn narrowly won.

Damon Hill

The 1996 World Champion Hill graduated from the role of test driver to racer for the mighty Williams-Renault team, following the departure of Nigel Mansell. It was a gifted opportunity, and it led to a fruitful association for all concerned.

The son of double World Champion Graham Hill, Damon began racing on motorbikes, and did not progress to cars until he was well into his 20s. A front runner in British Formula Ford and Formula Three racing, he was competing in Formula 3000 in 1991 when he was offered the chance by Williams to test-drive for Formula One.

He made his Grand Prix debut with the uncompetitive Brabham team in 1992. It proved useful experience for when he gained his first big break with Williams the following season. Alongside the great Alain Prost, he acquitted himself well, and he won his first Grand Prix in Hungary.

In 1994, he stepped up as team leader following the death of Prost's replacement, Ayrton Senna. His nemesis proved to be Benetton's Michael Schumacher, and the championship battle distilled into a final round shoot-out between the two men. Schumacher and Hill pulled well away from the rest in Adelaide, and Hill pounced when Schumacher was slowed after an off-track moment, but the German turned in on him, damaging Hill's suspension. With both out, Hill had lost the title. He was comfortably beaten by Schumacher in 1995, but put this to rights in 1996. With his new team-mate Jacques Villeneuve as his only serious rival, Hill clinched the title in Japan.

Controversially, Williams dropped Hill for 1997, leaving him to drive for the smaller Arrows team with which he came within an ace of winning the Grand Prix in Hungary. For 1998, he switched to Jordan, winning the team's first – and his 22nd – Grand Prix, at Belgium. He retired after a disappointing 1999 season.

Damon Hill	
Nationality	British
Seasons	1992–99
Teams driven for	Brabham, Williams, Arrows, Jordan
Number of major victories	22

▲ *(Top)* Damon Hill making his Grand Prix debut in the outclassed Brabham BT60B at the 1992 British Grand Prix.

◀ Hill in 1998 when he drove for Jordan and gave them their first Grand Prix win.

▶ Hill taking his Williams FW18 to a dominant victory in the 1996 Brazilian Grand Prix.

Graham Hill

The World Champion of 1962 and 1968 became a folk hero of the sport for his gritty determination and winning public persona. He retired from the driving seat in 1975 to devote himself to running his own team, but was killed piloting his light aircraft in November of that year.

After talking himself into a mechanic's job with Lotus in the mid-1950s, Hill got himself into the driving seat of the team's Formula Two and sports cars. When Lotus graduated to Formula One in 1958, Hill was one of the drivers. It wasn't until he switched to BRM in 1960, though, that he began to show some form; he looked set to win a superb victory in that year's British Grand Prix, but spun it away. For 1962, BRM had produced a powerful new V8 engine, and with this he scored his first race successes, culminating in his first world title at the end of that season.

He stayed at BRM, a regular race winner, until transferring back to Lotus for 1967. In between, he won the 1966 Indianapolis 500. The new Cosworth DFV engine in the Lotus 49 gave Hill a highly competitive but unreliable

▲ Graham Hill in 1973.

▼ Graham Hill in the BRM P48 at the British Grand Prix, Silverstone, 1960. He stormed up the field after stalling on the grid, but retired from the lead late in the race after a spin caused by brake failure.

Graham Hill	
Nationality	British
Seasons	1958–75
Teams driven for	Lotus, BRM, Brabham, Hill
Number of major victories	14

1967 season. When his friend and team-mate Jim Clark was killed early in 1968, Hill pulled the team back together with some great performances, and he clinched his second title in the final round. He won his fifth Monaco Grand Prix in 1969, but badly injured his legs at Watkins Glen. He never regained his Formula One form subsequently, but battled on for a few more years, and won the 1972 Le Mans 24 Hours sports car race for Matra.

He was returning from a test session with his team when he crashed his plane in fog as he attempted to land at Elstree near London. Five team members, including his young driver Tony Brise, died with him.

Phil Hill

America's first World Champion, Hill took the title with Ferrari in 1961. The son of a California postmaster, Hill began racing sports cars in the early 1950s, working on and preparing them himself. Ever-improving form brought him to the attention of Ferrari importer Luigi Chinetti who got Hill a sports car chance with the Ferrari works team. He enjoyed considerable success here, but his constant badgering for a Formula One chance took a long time to be answered.

In his first Formula One drive for the team, at Monza in 1958, he took third place and fastest lap. At the next event in Morocco, he outpaced his team-mate and that year's World Champion, Mike Hawthorn. Such an impressive start ensured a permanent place in the Formula One team.

He took fourth place in the 1959 Championship, but suffered in 1960 through Ferrari's front-engined policy. The following year, the Ferrari 156 was by far the fastest car of the season, and Hill became locked in battle for the title with his team-mate Wolfgang von Trips. Into the penultimate round at Monza

▲ **Race winner Phil Hill (Ferrari) at the Italian Grand Prix, Monza, 1961.**

▼ **Phil Hill in the Ferrari 156 leads team-mate Wolfgang von Trips at the Belgian Grand Prix, 1961. Hill won the race, and Trips came second in a Ferrari 1-2-3-4.**

Phil Hill	
Nationality	American
Seasons	1958–66
Teams driven for	Ferrari, ATS, Cooper, Eagle
Number of major victories	3

there was little to split them, but von Trips crashed to his death. Hill won the race and the title in the most tragic of circumstances.

Hill never approached such heights again in Formula One. Ferrari was overwhelmed by the British teams in 1962, though Hill performed superbly. A move to the new ATS team for 1963 proved disastrous, and his last full season was with Cooper in 1964. He enjoyed further sports car success – having won Le Mans three times – before retirement at the end of 1966. He later devoted himself to his classic car restoration business in California.

Denny Hulme

▼ Denny Hulme took his only pole position at the South Africa Grand Prix in 1973, when he gave the McLaren M23 its debut drive.

New Zealand's first, and to date only, World Drivers' Champion, Denny Hulme took the title for the Brabham team in only his second full Formula One season.

After winning a "Driver To Europe" award in his home country, Hulme served his racing apprenticeship with Brabham, driving their Formula Two cars as well as being the truck driver. He got occasional runs in the Formula One car in 1965, and was promoted to the seat full-time the following year, after Dan Gurney left the team.

His role was one of back up to Jack Brabham in 1967. But frequently "improvements" made to the team leader's car proved unreliable, and Hulme was invariably there to pick up the pieces, and ultimately the title. He moved to fellow countryman Bruce McLaren's team for 1968, where he

remained until the end of his Formula One career in 1974. He challenged for the Championship again in 1968, for McLaren, and was a regular race-winner until he left Formula One. He came out

of retirement to race touring cars in Australia in the 1980s and early 1990s, and it was while competing in the Bathurst race in 1992 that he suffered a fatal heart attack. He was 55.

Denny Hulme

Nationality	New Zealand
Seasons	1965–74
Teams driven for	Brabham, McLaren
Number of major victories	8

▼ Hulme driving the Brabham BT7 in his Grand Prix debut at the 1967 Monaco Grand Prix. He finished in eighth place.

▲ Third place in the 1967 Mexican Grand Prix secured Hulme's world title from his team-mate Jack Brabham.

James Hunt

World Champion of 1976 after a dramatic battle with Niki Lauda, Hunt was a controversial figure from the beginning of his Formula One career in 1973 to the end in 1979. In between he produced some brilliant drives for Hesketh and McLaren.

In the junior categories, he established a reputation as being quick but accident-prone, and was nicknamed "Hunt the Shunt". After being dropped by the March Formula Three team, he was picked up by Lord Hesketh's eccentric new team.

They initially planned to tackle Formula Two together in 1973, but after realizing they could compete

in Formula One for a little more money by buying a car from March, they did just that. Hunt soon began to surprise the Formula One paddock with his speed, and within a few races was running near the front. In the American Grand Prix, he chased victor Ronnie Peterson hard all the way, and crossed the line just fractions of a second behind. The March was replaced by a Hesketh design in 1974, and Hunt won the non-championship International Trophy Formula One race at Silverstone. In 1975, he won the Dutch Grand Prix

in a brilliant drive, during which he held off the faster Ferrari of Niki Lauda.

It was the Austrian with whom Hunt was locked in combat after he moved to McLaren for 1976, with Hunt clinching the title by just one point in the final round at Japan. He won three more times in 1977, but the competitiveness of McLaren was on the wane. He switched to Wolf for 1979, but the car proved no more competitive than the McLaren, and he retired part way through the season. He died in 1993, aged 46, after suffering a heart attack.

◄ James Hunt: daring, dashing, all-British hero of the 1970s.

James Hunt	
Nationality	British
Seasons	1973–79
Teams driven for	Hesketh, McLaren, Wolf
Number of major victories	10

▲ James Hunt winning the 1976 British Grand Prix at Brands Hatch. He was later disqualified from the race.

▼ When the 1979 Wolf WR7 – here, at Argentina – proved uncompetitive, Hunt decided to hang up his helmet.

Jacky Ickx

T wice runner-up in the World Championship, the Belgian Ickx was one of the fastest drivers around in the late 1960s and early 1970s.

He graduated from motorcycle racing to Formula Three and touring cars with Ken Tyrrell. A move to Formula Two followed. At that time the German Grand Prix on the 22.5km (14-mile) Nürburgring circuit allowed for Formula Two cars to join Formula Ones. Ickx caused a sensation by qualifying third-quickest for the 1967 event, faster than Jackie Stewart, John Surtees and Jack Brabham, all of whom were in Formula One cars with engines 1.4 litres bigger than that in Ickx's Formula Two Matra.

This performance brought a Ferrari drive for 1968. He won that year's French Grand Prix in the rain, and his reputation as one of the greatest wet weather drivers took hold. A switch to Brabham for 1969 gave him second place in the World Championship, and then it was back to Ferrari for 1970, where he was the only man to threaten Jochen Rindt's posthumous title.

Ferrari were by then producing ever-less competitive cars, and this allowed Ickx to grab only the occasional victory before leaving the team in 1973. A disappointing spell with Lotus led to him leaving Formula One to concentrate on sports cars, where he continued to be highly successful. He retired in 1985, having won the Le Mans 24 Hours six times.

▼ Ickx at the German Grand Prix and his beloved Nürburgring circuit, on his way to his final Grand Prix victory.

Jacky Ickx	
Nationality	Belgian
Seasons	1967–79
Teams driven for	Cooper, Ferrari, Brabham, Lotus, Wolf, Ensign, Ligier
Major victories	8

▲ Ickx in 1970, when he was in real contention for the world title.

◀ Ickx's Ferrari leads Peterson (March) and team-mate Clay Regazzoni at the German Grand Prix in 1972.

Alan Jones

T he first of many to win a World title with the Williams team, the Australian Jones drove Formula One cars from 1975 to 1981 before a brief retirement. He returned in 1985–86, but without the same level of success.

The son of Melbourne racing star Stan Jones, he moved to Britain in the early 1970s and became a front-runner in the British Formula Three and Formula 5000 categories. He drove for a series of small, underfunded Formula One teams in 1975 and 1976, but despite a race-leading drive for Surtees in the 1976 race of champions he entered 1977 without a drive. It looked as though his Formula One career was over, but after the tragedy of Tom Pryce's death in the South African Grand Prix, Jones was rescued by the Shadow team. He drove several very strong races, culminating in a surprise victory in Austria.

This led to his recruitment by Frank Williams to drive the first Patrick Head-designed Williams for 1978. This proved a highly competitive machine, and Jones was challenging for victory in the 1978 USA West Grand Prix. Head's ground-effect FW07 of 1979 was even better and, in the latter half of that year, Jones took four victories. This was the build-up to his title-winning campaign of 1980. He drove some superb, aggressive races in 1981, still in the FW07, and bowed out with victory in the final race at Las Vegas, having announced his retirement.

He was tempted back by Arrows into a brief comeback in 1983, and a more serious one, by the new Ford-backed Beatrice team, in 1985. Although the Ross Brawn-designed car was good, its Ford V6 lacked horsepower and Jones was never a serious contender. He called it a day – along with the Beatrice team – at the end of 1986.

Alan Jones	
Nationality	Australian
Seasons	1975–86
Teams driven for	Hesketh, Hill, Surtees, Shadow, Williams, Arrows, Beatrice
Number of major victories	12

◄ Alan Jones on top of the podium for the first time at the Osterreichring in 1977.

▲ *(right)* Alan Jones took a surprise win for Shadow in the rain at Austria in 1977. It was this result that attracted him to Williams for 1978.

► Jones bowed out of Formula One for the first time in great style, winning the 1981 Las Vegas Grand Prix.

Niki Lauda

T he three-time World Champion Lauda became one of the all-time legends of the sport when, in 1976, he made a comeback from being given the last rites on his deathbed to fourth place in the Italian Grand Prix in just a matter of weeks.

Lauda was recruited by Ferrari in 1974 as a promising newcomer who had shown well in the outclassed BRM of 1973. His technical adeptness and capacity for testing made him the perfect partner for Ferrari designer Mauro Forghieri, as they spent hour upon hour testing at Ferrari's new Fiorano test track. The hard work paid off as Lauda reeled off a great sequence of nine pole positions and took his first two victories.

In 1975, his Ferrari 312T dominated the Championship, with five wins. After beginning 1976 in similar fashion, he crashed in the early laps of the German Grand Prix, incurring critical lung damage as he lay unconscious in his burning car. After a remarkable comeback, he pulled out of the title-deciding Japanese Grand Prix, unwilling to risk his life in the blinding spray. This lost him the title to James Hunt.

He won back the title in 1977, and then walked out on Ferrari with two races still to go – an act of revenge for the lack of support he felt the team gave him in his 1976 comeback.

▲ Niki Lauda in the BRM P160E of 1973. It was his pace in this car that brought him to the attention of Ferrari.

Niki Lauda	
Nationality	Austrian
Seasons	1971–85
Teams driven for	March, BRM, Ferrari, Brabham, McLaren
Number of major victories	25

▼ Lauda takes the lead from Andrea de Cesaris on his way to victory in the 1982 USA West Grand Prix at Long Beach.

He joined the Brabham team where he scored two victories in 1978, but at the penultimate race of 1979 he promptly retired, saying he was bored with driving round in circles.

After two years building up his airline business, he was tempted to return for 1982 by McLaren's Ron Dennis. He won on his third race back, and went on to victory in the 1984 World Championship. He retired permanently at the end of 1985.

▼ Lauda at Zolder, Belgium, in 1976, five races before his scarring accident, and the prelude to the bravest comeback of all time.

Vincenzo Lancia

◀ Lancia at the French Grand Prix of 1906.

he son of a wealthy country squire who had a soup-manufacturing empire, Lancia was a trainee with the Ceirano car company – which hired its workshop space from Lancia's father – when the company was taken over by Fiat at the turn of the 20th century. He had already made his competition debut in a small-time race with Ceirano, and was used by Fiat for similar events as well as being employed by them as a test driver.

When Fiat progressed to international racing, Lancia went with them. He soon established a reputation as a furiously fast competitor, but often his mechanical sympathy seemed to desert him and he would invariably retire from leading positions – often leaving victory to his team-mate Felice Nazzaro.

Whilst still in the employ of Fiat, he founded his own company, Lancia, to produce sporting road cars. His driving career at Fiat continued until 1910, after which he concentrated on the running of his company. He would preside over this and engineer many innovations until his death in 1937, aged 56. His son Gianni took over the car company which bore the family name and later took it into Grand Prix racing. Just like Vincenzo, the 1954–55 Lancia proved to be very fast but, ultimately, unreliable.

▼ *(left)* Vincenzo Lancia in 1907.

Vincenzo Lancia	
Nationality	Italian
Seasons	1900–10
Teams driven for	Fiat
Number of major victories	0

▼ Lancia winning the Florio Cup in a 75hp Fiat with an average speed of 115.70km/h (71.89mph) in 1904.

Emile Levassor

The winner of the first ever motorcar race, engineer Emile Levassor triumphed in the 1895 Paris–Bordeaux–Paris race in his Panhard-Levassor by over five hours.

As a partner in the former woodworking company, Panhard, he took it into car manufacture when a friend acquired the French commercial rights to the new Daimler engine. The engine was installed in a chassis more advanced than that of the Daimler, and this led to the car being the dominant force in the pioneer sport.

Levassor suffered an accident after hitting a dog during the 1896 Paris–Marseilles race. His car rolled, throwing him out, and although he was able to restart and finish the event in fourth place, the internal injuries he incurred proved fatal. He died the following year, aged 53. Motorsport's first hero had also become its first fatality.

▼ Emile Levassor.

◀ Emile Levassor, winner of the first true motor race, in 1895.

▼ Levassor is commemorated in stone at Porte Mallot near Paris.

Emile Levassor

Nationality	French
Seasons	1895–96
Teams driven for	Panhard
Number of major victories	1

EVASSOR

Nigel Mansell

A dominant World Champion in 1992, Mansell's career was a Wurlitzer ride of high-drama and spine-tingling excitement.

He was a struggling Formula Three driver with a broken bone in his neck from a recent race accident when Lotus boss Colin Chapman invited him to test a Formula One car. Keeping his injury secret, Mansell did the test and performed well enough to be offered a test-driver role for the team in 1980. He made his race debut in Austria that year, sitting bathed in leaking petrol for many laps before the car eventually failed. He was signed as a full-time member of the race team in 1981, but his career received a setback with the death of Chapman in 1982.

Although Mansell was retained by the team, he no longer received the same treatment, and relations became strained with the new management. He was dominating the wet Monaco Grand Prix of 1984 when he made a mistake and crashed out. The following year he was replaced – Lotus signed Ayrton Senna – but Mansell's career was given a lifeline as he was recruited by Williams for 1985. Towards the end of the season, he made a breakthrough victory in front of his home crowd at Brands Hatch. He immediately followed it up with another, in South Africa.

His 1986 season was a fierce battle with new Williams team-mate Nelson Piquet, though both ultimately lost out

▲ Nigel Mansell leading the 1984 Monaco Grand Prix in his Lotus 95T. He later crashed out of the race.

Nigel Mansell	
Nationality	British
Seasons	1980–95
Teams driven for	Lotus, Williams, Ferrari, McLaren
Number of major victories	31

▼ (left) Mansell: determination always saw him through. He was one of the most exciting performers the sport has seen.

▼ (right) Mansell leading the 1990 British Grand Prix. He announced his retirement after the race but later changed his mind.

to Alain Prost. Mansell was on course for the title, with 19 laps to go in the final race, when a rear tyre exploded dramatically. He was again in title contention in 1987, but injured his back in practice for the penultimate race.

He joined Ferrari in 1989, and won his first race for them. He won a total of three races for the team, but left at the end of 1990 to rejoin Williams. After narrowly losing the 1991 title to McLaren's Ayrton Senna, Mansell wiped up in 1992 with the devastatingly fast active-ride Williams FW14B. Unable to agree terms for 1993, he headed for America, where he became CART Champion. He returned to Williams in 1994 as a stand-in, and won the Australian Grand Prix. His full Formula One comeback with McLaren in 1995 was aborted after just a few races as the car proved uncompetitive.

Guy Moll

The Algerian driver Moll looked to have a brilliant career ahead of him after making an instant impact at the highest level of the sport, in the early 1930s.

A protégé of compatriot and Bugatti driver Marcel Lehoux, Moll finished second in the 1933 Pau Grand Prix, his first international competition. This brought him to the attention of Enzo Ferrari, who recruited him to drive Alfa Romeos alongside established stars, Achille Varzi and Louis Chiron.

Guy Moll	
Nationality	Algerian
Seasons	1933–34
Teams driven for	Alfa Romeo
Number of major victories	1

▼ Guy Moll, winner of the Monaco Grand Prix, in 1934. Enzo Ferrari is third from the top on the extreme left of the picture.

He instantly proved their match, and won the 1934 Monaco Grand Prix. For a virtial rookie, such performances bordered on miraculous.

He was fighting Mercedes driver Luigi Fagioli for victory at Pescara, in 1934, when he crashed trying to lap the Mercedes of Ernst Henne. He was thrown out of his car into a tree, suffering fatal injuries. Several decades later, Enzo Ferrari said he believed Moll would have proved himself to be one of the all-time great drivers had he lived.

Juan Pablo Montoya

▼ Montoya *(left)* and Michael Schumacher in one of several wheel-to-wheel battles: here, at Melbourne in 2002.

Since entering Formula One in 2001, the Colombian Montoya has established himself as one of the sport's most exciting performers.

After winning the 1998 European Formula 3000 Championship, Montoya transferred to American CART racing. He won the championship at his first attempt, astounding veterans of the series with his phenomenal car control and an ability to overtake in places never seen before. In 2000, he won the Indianapolis 500 at his first attempt.

The Williams Formula One team had put him on a long-term contract when he was still in Formula 3000, and for 2001 they decided it was time to bring him to Formula One. In Brazil, his third race, he created a sensation by overtaking Michael Schumacher, rubbing tyres, then pulling away to victory. Only the mistake of a lapped backmarker denied him. He finally won at Monza for the Italian Grand Prix. In 2002 he scored seven pole positions, and in 2003 was in contention for the World Championship until the penultimate round.

Juan Pablo Montoya	
Nationality	Colombian
Seasons	2001–present
Teams driven for	Williams
Number of major victories	3

▼ Brazil 2001: Montoya makes his move inside Schumacher to take the lead, rubbing wheels along the way *(inset)*.

▶ Juan Pablo Montoya, a combative performer whose exciting driving style has captured imaginations.

Stirling Moss

From the time of Juan Manuel Fangio's retirement in 1958 to his own injury-induced retirement in 1962, Stirling Moss was widely recognized as the world's greatest driver. That he never won the world title was seen as an indictment of the Championship rather than any slur on his skills.

After establishing a big reputation in the British junior classes, Moss competed in his first Formula One season in 1954 with a privately-owned Maserati 250F. His form in this was so impressive that he was later given a drive with the works team. Only mechanical failure lost him that year's Italian Grand Prix. This led to his recruitment by Mercedes for the 1955 season, when he drove alongside the acknowledged master of Formula One, Fangio. Moss won the British Grand Prix, but to this day he is unsure whether Fangio allowed him to do so.

Following Mercedes' withdrawal, Moss rejoined Maserati, but it was his switch to the British Vanwall team in 1957 that brought him bigger success. Between 1957 and 1958 he won six Grands Prix for the team. His tally of four wins in 1958 compared to one for the World Champion, Mike Hawthorn.

▼ Moss drove one of his greatest races in the under-powered Rob Walker Lotus 18 to win the Monaco Grand Prix in 1961.

◄ Stirling Moss, photographed at Silverstone in 1955.

After Vanwall's withdrawal, Moss spent most of the remainder of his career driving for privateer Rob Walker, first in a Cooper and latterly a Lotus. In 1961, he produced two of his greatest drives to win the Monaco and German Grands Prix against the faster Ferraris. Early in 1962 he suffered a big accident at a non-championship race at Goodwood, and his life hung in the balance for a while. Though he made a full recovery, he felt his incomparable skills had been impaired, and reluctantly retired, still in his early 30s. He remains a household name in retirement.

▼ Stirling Moss beats Mercedes team-mate Juan Manuel Fangio to the chequered flag in the 1955 British Grand Prix.

Stirling Moss

Nationality	British
Seasons	1951–62
Teams driven for	HWM, Connaught, Cooper, Maserati, Mercedes, Vanwall, Walker, BRP, Ferguson
Number of major victories	16

Felice Nazzaro

azzaro was one of the master drivers for a long period from the early-1900s to the early 1920s. His successes came almost exclusively with Fiat, for whom he later became competition director.

Like his compatriot Vincenzo Lancia, he was apprenticed to the Ceirano company at the turn of the century, but was retained when that company was bought out by Fiat. When Fiat moved into big-time international racing, Nazzaro immediately proved his class. His drives were a calculating blend of early race caution and searing speed when the occasion demanded it, and his finishing record was far superior to the more spectacular Lancia's. In 1907, he won all three major races of the season, and was still winning in 1922.

◄ A portrait of Felice Nazzaro in 1907 when he won all three major races of the season. He raced successfully until 1924.

▼ (left) Felice Nazzaro, in the 1913 French Grand Prix at Amiens. This was one of the few races in which he didn't drive for the Fiat marque.

In that year he took victory in the French Grand Prix, the same race in which his nephew, Biagio Nazzaro, was killed in another Fiat. He retired from the driving seat at the end of 1924, but remained with the company until his death in 1940.

Felice Nazzaro	
Nationality	Italian
Seasons	1900–24
Teams driven for	Fiat, Itala
Number of major victories	5

▼ Nazzaro's Fiat came second at the Italian Grand Prix of 1922, on the new Monza track, but here he leads a Bugatti and a Diatto.

Tazio Nuvolari

Still regarded by many as the greatest driver who has ever lived, Nuvolari's reign as a giant of the sport lasted from the late 1920s until the outbreak of World War II. Though his list of victories in Bugattis, Alfa Romeos, Maseratis and Auto Unions was long, it was his frequent giant-killing "impossible" victories against superior machinery that sealed his reputation.

Never interested in taking over the family farms, instead Tazio sold some of the land he had inherited to begin a career in motorcycle racing. He became a hero of that sport in the mid-1920s, his spectacular style in sharp contrast to the cool calculation of his arch rival, Achille Varzi.

The two drivers combined forces to form their own racing stable, in which to begin their car racing careers proper, though Nuvolari had already dabbled with four-wheel competition. Though they were both successful in their team of Bugattis, it was an uneasy relationship, and Varzi left after little more than a year.

▲ Tazio Nuvolari c. 1933.

▼ Nuvolari in action for Alfa Romeo at the Monaco Grand Prix of 1932.

Tazio Nuvolari	
Nationality	Italian
Seasons	1928–46
Teams driven for	Alfa Romeo, Bugatti, Maserati, Auto Union
Number of major victories	18

By the time Nuvolari received his first big break in a works Alfa Romeo, courtesy of Enzo Ferrari, he was already 37 years old. But it made no difference to his form, and he racked up one spectacular victory after another, often after stirring battles with Varzi.

The overwhelming superiority of the German cars from 1934 onwards left Nuvolari in uncompetitive machinery. Varzi, by contrast, had signed with Auto Union, and made it a stipulation that he would not drive alongside Nuvolari. In the 1935 German Grand Prix, Nuvolari drove the old-fashioned Alfa P3 to a staggering victory over a field of cutting-edge Mercedes and Auto-Unions, to the bewilderment of the officiating Nazis. He performed similar miracles with Alfa on several occasions in 1936.

Following the death of Auto Union's Bernd Rosemeyer, and the ill-health of Varzi, Nuvolari was recruited by Auto Union part-way through 1938. Despite never having raced mid-engined machines before, he showed that, at the age of 45, his genius was still intact. He took two victories, including a stirring comeback drive in that year's Donington Grand Prix and the 1939 Czechoslovakian Grand Prix.

Post-war, Nuvolari took up the sport once more but by now he was an ill man, and he frequently had to retire from races coughing up blood. Still he couldn't stop, and still the miraculous performances unfolded. In both the 1947 and 1948 Mille Miglia races, he was robbed of victory after truly staggering drives. He died in 1953.

◄ Nuvolari driving for Auto Union in 1938.

Riccardo Patrese

P atrese is the holder of the record for the greatest number of Grand Prix starts. Between 1977 and 1993 the Italian lined up to do battle on the Formula One grid no less than 256 times. He won on six occasions for the Brabham and Williams teams.

A graduate of karting, he rose to car racing prominence in Formula Three and Formula Two, and made his Formula One debut with the Shadow team at Monaco in 1977. A new team, Arrows, was formed for 1978 from Shadow, and Patrese became their lead driver. In only the team's second race, Patrese was dominating the South African Grand Prix when the car failed. He was the only driver in the team's history to have put an Arrows on pole position – a feat he achieved at Long Beach, in the United States in 1981.

Patrese's first victory didn't come until he transferred to Brabham, for whom he won the 1982 Monaco Grand Prix. After an interlude at Alfa Romeo he stayed with Brabham until Bernie Ecclestone sold it at the end of 1987. Patrese transferred to Williams in 1988, and went on to win four races for the team between 1990 and 1992. After a season with Benetton alongside Michael Schumacher in 1993, Patrese brought his distinguished career to an end.

Riccardo Patrese	
Nationality	Italian
Seasons	1977–93
Teams driven for	Shadow, Arrows, Brabham, Williams, Alfa Romeo, Benetton
Number of major victories	6

◄ Riccardo Patrese in 1988.

▼ (*below*) Patrese in his first Formula One season, finishing sixth for Shadow at the Japanese Grand Prix at Fuji in 1977.

▼ (*bottom*) Patrese in 1993, his final season in Formula One, driving for Benetton at the South African Grand Prix.

Ronnie Peterson

The Swede was known unofficially as "the world's fastest driver" during the peak of his career in the 1970s. Although he never managed to translate this tag into the World Championship title, he was twice runner-up and lit up many races with some electrifying performances and astonishing car control.

Winning the 1969 Monaco Formula Three race proved to be his catapult into Formula One the following year. In 1971, driving for March, he finished runner-up to Jackie Stewart in the World Championship. But it wasn't until his move to Lotus in 1973 that he began winning races. In 1973, he set what was then a record of nine pole positions during the season, and his raw speed comfortably eclipsed that of his reigning World Champion team-mate, Emerson Fittipaldi.

Lotus cars subsequently lost their competitiveness and Peterson left for a couple of barren seasons of his own, before returning in 1978, this time as a contracted number two driver to the incumbent Mario Andretti. Lotus were by now the dominant team once again,

▲ Ronnie Peterson in his Lotus 72E on his way to second place in the British Grand Prix at Silverstone in 1973, the year in which he set nine pole positions.

Ronnie Peterson

Nationality	Swedish
Seasons	1970–78
Teams driven for	Lotus, March, Tyrrell
Number of major victories	10

thanks to their 79 model. Although there were several races where Peterson was quicker than his team-mate, he dutifully fulfilled his contracted role. Two wins, including a superb wet weather performance in Austria, confirmed his speed was very much still there. At the Italian Grand Prix, he was involved in a startline collision, and his car was thrown into the barriers, breaking one of his legs. That night he died from a brain embolism triggered by the broken bone. His second place in the Championship to Andretti was thus taken posthumously.

▲ Ronnie Peterson in 1971. He died following an accident at the start of the Italian Grand Prix in 1978.

◄ Peterson finished a close second in the 1971 Italian Grand Prix after leading for much of the race.

Nelson Piquet

▼ Piquet's Brabham BT49C took third place at Long Beach in 1981, the scene of his first victory 12 months earlier.

The great Brazilian driver won three World Championships in the 1980s, and brought his long Formula One career to a close at the end of 1991, a season during which he proved he was still capable of winning races.

The son of a diplomat, Piquet moved to Europe to pursue the career he had begun in his homeland, inspired by the success of Emerson Fittipaldi. He was recruited by the Brabham team at the end of 1978, after winning that year's British Formula Three Championship and making a few Formula One appearances with a privately-run McLaren. Teamed alongside Niki Lauda at Brabham in 1979 he proved every bit as quick, and following Lauda's retirement, Piquet entered 1980 as the clear team leader. After winning his first Grand Prix at Long Beach, he

Nelson Piquet

Nationality	Brazilian
Seasons	1978–91
Teams driven for	Ensign, Brabham, Williams, Lotus, Benetton
Number of major victories	23

▼ Nelson Piquet, three times World Champion, seen here in 1986.

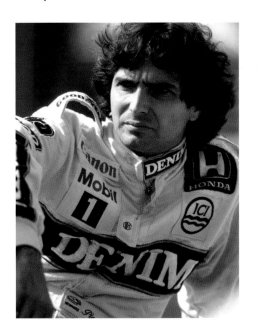

challenged Williams' Alan Jones hard for the title, but ultimately had to wait until 1981 for his first Championship.

He repeated the feat two years later, in the turbocharged Brabham-BMW, after a dramatic late-season comeback to overhaul a big points deficit to rival Alain Prost. The Brabham team's form dwindled subsequently, and Piquet switched to Williams for 1986, only narrowly losing out on the title. He won it in 1987 despite a big shunt at Imola that dulled his speed for some time afterwards. After poor seasons with

Lotus in 1988–89, many believed he was a spent force when Benetton recruited him in 1990. But he proved the doubters wrong with victories in the final two races of the year. He won again in Canada 1991 but retired from Formula One at the end of the season. He subsequently incurred serious leg injuries while practising for the 1992 Indianapolis 500.

▼ Piquet took a great victory in the 1987 Hungarian Grand Prix after passing the Lotus of Ayrton Senna.

Didier Pironi

Frenchman Pironi looked to be on his way to the 1982 World Championship when he suffered a career-ending accident during the warm-up session for the German Grand Prix at Hockenheim.

The son of a wealthy construction company boss, he rose through the Elf-sponsored ranks of French junior racing in the 1970s, before graduating to Formula Two in 1977. There, he finished third in the Championship but earned wider recognition when he stepped back down to Formula Three for a one-off race supporting the 1977 Monaco Grand Prix, and won it. This was the springboard for his Formula One debut with Tyrrell in 1978.

It was not until he joined the more competitive Ligier team in 1980 that Pironi really began to show what he could do. He took his first Grand Prix victory in Belgium and produced some stunningly fast drives, not all of which were rewarded, through no fault of his own. His form in the Ligier led to his recruitment to Ferrari for the following year. Paired alongside Gilles Villeneuve, he struggled initially but with a much improved car for 1982 he began to look strong once more.

He took victory in the San Marino Grand Prix in controversial circumstances, Villeneuve feeling that Pironi had duped

Didier Pironi	
Nationality	French
Seasons	1978–82
Teams driven for	Tyrrell, Ligier, Ferrari
Number of major victories	3

◀ **Didier Pironi celebrates his third victory at the Dutch Grand Prix in 1982. This result put him in the lead for that year's World Championship title.**

▼ **Pironi took his Ligier JS11/15 to his maiden victory at the Belgian Grand Prix at Spa in 1980.**

him and gone against team orders in passing him on the last lap. After Villeneuve's subsequent fatal accident, Pironi assumed leadership of the team. He won again in Holland, and by the time of the German Grand Prix had a comfortable Championship lead.

He crashed in conditions of blinding spray, hitting the back of Alain Prost's Renault at very high speed. The Ferrari reared high in the air before crashing down, and Pironi suffered serious leg injuries. Though he recovered, his right foot was no longer strong enough for the heavy braking required and he quietly retired. He took up power boating, and was killed competing in a race off the Isle of Wight in 1987.

◀ **Pironi in the Ferrari 126C2, the fastest car of 1982.**

Alain Prost

▼ Sparks flew when Prost joined Ferrari in 1990. Here, he takes the *Eau Rouge* corner at Spa, during the Belgian Grand Prix.

Winner of four World Championships and 51 Grands Prix, Frenchman Prost is statistically the second most successful driver in the sport's history, behind Michael Schumacher.

His Formula One career spanned 13 years, during which time he earned a reputation for searing speed disguised beneath silky smoothness. One of the most analytical of drivers, he was nicknamed The Professor.

He made his Formula One debut with McLaren in 1980 after winning the 1979 European Formula Three Championship. Promising form there led to his recruitment by Renault, for whom he won his first Grand Prix in 1981. Tension with team-mate René Arnoux in 1982 led to Prost's clear status as team leader in 1983. He established a big lead early in the Championship that year, but was ultimately thwarted by the late-season pace of Nelson Piquet's Brabham-BMW. He was sensationally sacked by Renault in the aftermath of losing the title, but this worked to his advantage in that he was able to sign for McLaren the following season, and McLaren produced the fastest car of 1984. Prost became locked in battle for the title with his team-mate Niki Lauda, but lost out by half a point in the last round.

But Prost couldn't be denied forever. He took a comfortable championship victory with McLaren in 1985, a feat he repeated in 1986, becoming the first back-to-back title winner since Jack Brabham in 1959–60. He was joined at McLaren in 1988 by Ayrton Senna, and so began one of the most dramatic and long-running feuds in Formula One. He lost out to his team-mate in the 1988 title battle, but won in 1989 after controversially blocking Senna's passing move in Japan. Transferring to Ferrari for 1990, he again battled with Senna's McLaren for the title, this time coming off second when Senna drove into him – again in Japan.

He was sacked from Ferrari after a disappointing 1991 season and sat out the following year. He returned in 1993

▲ Alain Prost, World Drivers' Champion in 1985, 1986, 1989 and 1993.

Alain Prost	
Nationality	French
Seasons	1980–93
Teams driven for	McLaren, Renault, Ferrari, Williams
Number of major victories	51

with Williams, and took his fourth title in the best car in the field. He retired – as the most successful driver in the sport's history – and turned team owner in 1997, after buying Ligier and renaming it Prost. The team went into receivership at the end of 2001.

► Prost won at Monaco in 1984, but was awarded only half points. It cost him the title.

Kimi Raikkonen

R aikkonen took over very big shoes when he stepped in to replace fellow Finn Mika Häkkinen at McLaren at the end of 2001.

Raikkonen was just 21 years old when, in 2001, he made his Grand Prix debut with Sauber. This marked only his second season of car racing. After a successful karting career he had graduated to cars in 2000, winning the British Formula Renault Championship. Inexperience proved to be little handicap in Formula One as he scored several World Championship points and was often quicker than his more experienced team-mate Nick Heidfeld.

Such performances brought Raikkonen to the attention of the McLaren team, where in 2002 he produced several stunning performances. He was within a few laps of winning the French Grand Prix that year when a backmarker's oil spillage cost him dearly. He won the 2003 Malaysian Grand Prix and followed it up with a campaign that took him to the final round with a chance of the World Championship. In the end he had to settle for runner-up to Michael Schumacher, but few would bet against him going one better in the future.

Kimi Raikkonen	
Nationality	Finnish
Seasons	2001–present
Teams driven for	Sauber, McLaren
Number of major victories	1

◀ Kimi Raikkonen in 2002.

▼ (below) In the Sauber-Petronas C20 at the Australian Grand Prix, Melbourne, 2001.

▼ (bottom) In 2003, Raikkonen took victory in Malaysia and scored consistently high places throughout the season.

Marcel Renault

Marcel backed his elder brother Louis in establishing the Renault company at the turn of the 20th century, and together they raced the cars that Louis's factory built. Although both proved to be among the leading drivers of the day, it was Marcel who was particularly brilliant.

With Louis he had owned a repair shop in Billancourt for a steam yacht they both owned. His engineering skills then helped Louis develop an improved gearbox on Louis's de Dion car. When they went into business to produce cars, Marcel helped his brother fund it all. With a voiturette car that was far less powerful than the opposition, Marcel won the 1902 Paris–Vienna race outright. He was charging through the field in the 1903 Paris–Madrid when he tangled with Leon Théry. The Renault

Marcel Renault	
Nationality	French
Seasons	1900–03
Teams driven for	Renault
Number of major victories	1

speared off into a tree and Marcel received injuries from which he later died. His brother Louis – who finished the race second, not knowing of Marcel's accident – retired from race driving with immediate effect.

◀ Marcel Renault in 1903.

▼ Marcel Renault competing in the 1903 Paris–Madrid race in his Renault.

Carlos Reutemann

T he Argentinian driver proved an often inspired performer in a Formula One career that lasted from 1972 to 1982, but losing the 1981 Championship to Nelson Piquet in the final round proved to be as close as he ever got to the world crown.

One of only three men to set pole position on their Grand Prix debuts, Reutemann achieved this feat at the 1972 Argentine Grand Prix, driving for Brabham. It was the beginning of a long love affair for the home fans, and Reutemann was a national hero for the rest of his career.

He took his first Grand Prix victories with the Brabham BT44 of 1974 and 1975 . His performances were occasionally in a class of their own, reducing everyone else to mere support roles, but finding such a level consistently proved to be elusive. Recruited to Ferrari at the end of 1976, he won races for them in 1977 and 1978, finishing third in the Championship in the latter year. A move to Lotus in 1979 proved ill-timed and he moved onto Williams for 1980, winning the Monaco Grand Prix and again finishing third in the title chase.

He began 1981 at the peak of his powers and after disobeying team orders to beat Alan Jones in Brazil,

Carlos Reutemann	
Nationality	Argentinian
Seasons	1972–82
Teams driven for	Brabham, Ferrari, Lotus, Williams
Number of major victories	12

◄ Carlos Reutemann, an enigmatic performer for 10 years. On his day he was unbeatable.

▼ Reutemann won from pole at the USA Grand Prix in 1974 in his Brabham BT44, the third victory of his season.

he went on to lead the Championship by a handsome margin by mid-season. The second half of his year was disappointing and, as Piquet caught up his points tally, they entered the final round in Las Vegas separated by just one point. Despite scoring a brilliant pole position, Reutemann had a disappointing race and finished eighth. With Piquet finishing fifth, Reutemann lost the Championship. He announced his retirement but changed his mind before the beginning of the 1982 season. He took second place in the South African Grand Prix, but after one more race decided that he did want to retire after all, and turned his back on the sport. He has since established himself as a leading politician in Argentina.

◄ Reutemann took a great second place in his non-turbo Williams at the 1982 South African Grand Prix, his penultimate race.

Jochen Rindt

ustrian Jochen Rindt became 1970 World Champion posthumously. He was killed at Monza that season, practising for the Italian Grand Prix. But in the remaining four races no-one was able to overhaul the points score he had built up from five victories earlier in the year.

He funded his early racing by selling the business inherited from parents who were killed in a wartime air-raid. He broke onto the international scene when, as a virtual unknown, he beat Graham Hill to win a Formula Two race at Crystal Palace in 1964. He made his Formula One debut later that year, at his home race with Rob Walker. For the next three years, he drove Cooper's outdated cars, finishing third in the 1966 Championship. A move to Brabham in 1968 underlined his stunning turn of speed, but the cars were unreliable. This led to him taking up an offer to join Lotus for 1969. In Colin Chapman's 49 model, he was devastatingly fast but didn't win until the final race of the year, in the USA.

For 1970, Lotus produced the ground-breaking 72 model. Initially it proved uncompetitive and Rindt gave the old 49 an unbelievable last-lap victory at Monaco. Thereafter, he transferred to the 72 and rattled off four consecutive wins. He had confided to friends that if he won the 1970 title, he would consider retirement. It was an option he was never granted.

▲ Jochen Rindt on his way to victory at the Dutch Grand Prix of 1970. It was one of five wins that season.

Jochen Rindt	
Nationality	Austrian
Seasons	1964–70
Teams driven for	Cooper, Brabham, Lotus
Number of major victories	6

◄ Rindt only hours before his death at the Italian Grand Prix, Monza, September 1970. He was said to be contemplating retirement.

▲ Rindt's Lotus 72 runs without wings. It was perhaps a contributory factor in his fatal accident at Monza, which occured a short while after this picture was taken.

► Rindt's Brabham BT24 – here at South Africa – was fast but unreliable in 1968.

Pedro Rodriguez

▼ Pedro Rodriguez had to settle for second place, at the Dutch Grand Prix at Zandvoort in 1971, after suffering a misfire.

The Mexican Rodriguez was often a spectacular performer in Formula One from the late 1960s until his death in a sports car accident in 1971.

The elder brother of Ferrari driver Ricardo Rodriguez, the pair had caused a sensation in sports car racing in the late 1950s when, as teenagers, they enjoyed success at an international level, funded initially by their wealthy businessman father. When Ricardo was killed practising for the 1962 Mexican Grand Prix, Pedro considered retirement, but returned for more sports car success. He made occasional Formula One appearances, notably with Lotus and Ferrari, but these never led to permanent seats. For the 1967 South African Grand Prix he was offered a drive by Cooper – and he went on to win the race, thus securing his drive for the rest of the season.

At BRM in 1968 he frequently showed great speed, particularly in the wet. He also won the Le Mans 24 Hours sports car race that year for Ford, partnered by Lucien Bianchi. BRM gave him a competitive but unreliable car in 1970, and he won the Belgian Grand

Prix with it. In the wet 1971 Dutch Grand Prix, he fought for the lead with fellow wet-weather maestro Jacky Ickx, but finished second after the car developed a misfire. His sports car drives for Porsche during this time were quite sensational, and he was undoubtedly one of the world's greatest drivers when he crashed to his death in a minor sports car race at the Norisring in Germany in July 1971. Deeply fatalistic he had always said that God chooses when it's your time.

Pedro Rodriguez

Nationality	Mexican
Seasons	1963–71
Teams driven for	Lotus, Ferrari, Cooper, BRM
Number of major victories	2

▼ Pedro Rodriguez at the British Grand Prix, Brands Hatch, in 1970,

◄ Rodriguez was enjoying his strongest season in 1971, with the BRM P160 in Formula One, and with Porsche in sportscar.

Keke Rosberg

The World Champion of 1982, Rosberg was the first Finn to be successful in Formula One, blazing a path that others have since followed.

A tough, shrewd operator, he made his way up the racing ladder through enterprise, hard graft and a lot of talent. But even so, it was a struggle and by the time he made it to Formula One in 1978 he was already 29. In the non-championship International Trophy – his third ever Formula One race – he took the unfancied Theodore car to victory. But even this did not attract him to the top teams, and he served his time with ATS and Fittipaldi.

It was the late-notice retirement of Alan Jones at the end of 1981 that created Rosberg's opportunity with Williams. He responded by winning his first Grand Prix at Dijon 1982 and scoring highly throughout the season to clinch the Championship in the final round. He won a handful of races in his remaining three years with Williams, but he was never a Championship contender. He drove for McLaren in his final season of 1986 and was leading his final race, in Australia, when his car suddenly stopped.

His subsequent activities included racing in touring and sports car, managing the career of Mika Häkkinen and latterly that of son, Niko Rosberg.

Keke Rosberg	
Nationality	Finnish
Seasons	1978–86
Teams driven for	Theodore, ATS, Wolf, Fittipaldi, Williams, McLaren
Number of major victories	5

▲ Rosberg in his McLaren MP4/2C during his final Grand Prix, at Adelaide in 1986. He was leading the race when the car failed.

▼ (left) Rosberg cut a colourful figure in Formula One during the 1980s, and a cigarette was rarely far from his lips.

▼ (right) Rosberg took victory with Theodore in the International Trophy race at Silverstone in 1978.

Bernd Rosemeyer

osemeyer burst onto the Grand Prix scene of the mid-1930s like a meteorite, instantly causing a sensation with his speed for Auto Union, this despite never having raced a car of any description before, his only racing experience being with motorcycles.

The DKW team for which he raced motorcycles was part of the Auto Union group, and he got a trial in the awesome V16, mid-engined machine at the end of 1934, and subsequently made his debut part-way through 1935. He was heading for victory in his second-ever race before a misfire held him back to second. In his first full season of 1936, he became European Champion. His drives left onlookers spellbound, his talent seemingly limitless. He was widely considered to be the world's fastest driver during his brief career.

Bernd Rosemeyer	
Nationality	German
Seasons	1935–37
Teams driven for	Auto Union
Number of major victories	5

It all came to an end in January 1938. Attempting to set a world speed record for Auto Union on a German autobahn, a side wind blew his car out of control at over 400km/h (250mph). He was killed after hitting some trees.

◀ Bernd Rosemeyer.

▼ Rosemeyer in the Auto Union C type at the Donington Grand Prix in 1937.

Jody Scheckter

▼ Jody Scheckter's Wolf WR1 leads John Watson's Brabham at the Monaco Grand Prix of 1977. Scheckter won.

The 1979 World Champion for Ferrari, South African Scheckter, entered Formula One in the early 1970s with a "wild boy" tag, and he left it as a respected elder statesman at the end of 1980.

After winning a "Driver to Europe" scheme in South Africa, Scheckter made his name in British Formula Ford and Formula Three racing. He was picked up by McLaren to drive its Formula Two car and by the end of that season, 1972, he was making his Grand Prix debut for the team.

He was comfortably leading the 1973 French Grand Prix, only his third Formula One race, until hit by Emerson Fittipaldi. In the following race at Silverstone, he created an impact for the wrong reasons, when his spin into the pit wall on the first lap took out much of the field. Despite this, he was chosen by Ken Tyrrell as the lead driver of his team in 1974, in the wake of Jackie Stewart's retirement and the

Jody Scheckter	
Nationality	South African
Seasons	1972–80
Teams driven for	McLaren, Tyrrell, Wolf, Ferrari
Number of major victories	10

death of François Cevert. He justified his selection with a strong third place in the World Championship, winning two Grands Prix along the way. In 1976, he became the only man to win a Grand Prix in a car with other than four wheels, when he took the six-wheel Tyrrell P34 to victory in Sweden. A move to the new Wolf team for 1977 saw Scheckter perform brilliantly, winning

on the team's debut in Argentina and leading the World Championship until mid-season. But it was his move to Ferrari for 1979 that consolidated his status. Three victories and some mature performances clinched him the title comfortably, with two rounds to go.

▼ Jody Scheckter led the 1973 French Grand Prix in this McLaren.

▲ Scheckter in 1980, the year of his retirement from Formula One.

Michael Schumacher

T he most successful driver of all time, six-time champion Schumacher continues to rack up success upon success after over a decade in Formula One.

With his early career subsidized by Mercedes-Benz, he graduated from German Formula Three into the World Sportscar Championship with the Mercedes team. His speed there created a sensation and marked him out as a likely Formula One star. His Grand Prix chance came with Jordan at the 1991 Belgian Grand Prix, where he was quicker than team-mate Andrea de Cesaris. By the next race he had been snapped up by Benetton, and he proceeded to outpace triple World Champion Nelson Piquet.

He won his first Grand Prix at Spa in 1992, the first anniversary of his debut. By 1994, he was ready to push for the Championship and was engaged in battle with his biggest rival, Ayrton Senna, when the Brazilian crashed to his death at Imola. In a controversial duel with the Williams of title rival Damon Hill at the final round in Australia, Schumacher drove his damaged car into Hill's, forcing them both to retire but ensuring the title was Michael's. He repeated the feat in 1995, this time without controversy.

◄ Schumacher caused a sensation by qualifying a Jordan in seventh place on his Formula One debut at Spa in 1991.

▼ (below left) Michael Schumacher, took his fifth world title in 2002.

Michael Schumacher

Nationality	German
Seasons	1991–present
Teams driven for	Jordan, Benetton, Ferrari
Number of major victories	70

He then took up the challenge of turning the troubled Ferrari team back into world beaters. He had a difficult first season with them in 1996 but, aided subsequently by the arrival of his design team from Benetton, Ross Brawn and Rory Byrne, he piloted an ever-faster succession of Ferraris. He lost the 1997 title fight to Jacques Villeneuve, when a similar move to the one he'd pulled on Hill went wrong, leaving him in the gravel trap, with Villeneuve continuing. He again lost out in the last round in 1998, this time to Mika Häkkinen. In 1999, he broke his leg at Silverstone, leaving him out for much of the season.

But in 2000 came the crowning glory of his career, when he won the title, the first Ferrari driver to do so for 21 years. He was a dominant champion in 2001, passing Alain Prost's record of 51 Grand Prix victories along the way, and even more successful in 2002, winning a record 11 races in that season alone. This brought him level with the record held since 1957 by Juan Manuel Fangio, and in 2003 he went on to beat that watermark by clinching championship number six at the final round in Japan.

◄ The Ferrari team celebrate Schumacher's Canadian Grand Prix victory in 2003.

Ralf Schumacher

▼ Ralf Schumacher guides his Williams-BMW FW23 to his first Formula One victory at Imola in 2001.

The younger brother of Michael Schumacher is a highly talented Formula One racer in his own right, and has taken a succession of victories with the Williams-BMW team.

After a karting career, Ralf took up junior car racing in his native Germany, progressing to the German Formula Three Championship in 1995, where he was runner-up. A move to the Japanese Formula Nippon series in 1996 secured him a major championship, and this proved his springboard to Formula One with the Jordan team in 1997.

He was extremely quick from the start, but initially rather accident-prone. This continued until half-way through

◀ (far left) Ralf Schumacher has driven for Williams since 1999.

◀ (left) Ralf was immediately quick in his debut season of 1997 with Jordan.

the 1998 season, after which his performances became notably more mature. He was catching team-mate Damon Hill in the Belgian Grand Prix and looked ready to take the victory, before team orders were imposed, leaving him a frustrated second.

He moved to Williams in 1999, a team that initially couldn't offer him a

Ralf Schumacher	
Nationality	German
Seasons	1997–present
Teams driven for	Jordan, Williams
Number of major victories	6

potentially race-winning car but which promised a future partnership with BMW. This came good in 2001, with Ralf taking his first victory at Imola and following it with two more. He continued his race-winning form into 2002 and 2003, and in due course he could well become the second member of the Schumacher family to win a world title.

▼ Ralf Schumacher took his Jordan-Peugeot to third place in the Argentinian Grand Prix in 1997.

Henry Segrave

Segrave was the first British driver to win a Grand Prix when he took his Sunbeam to victory in France in 1923. In his short time in top flight racing, before he took up the challenge of the landspeed record, he established himself among the elite of drivers.

A British national, he was born in Baltimore in the United States, but raised in Ireland and educated at Eton, England. After serving in World War I, his imagination was captured by motorsport when he spectated at an American race. He took up the sport at Brooklands in Britain, and badgered Sunbeam racing boss Louis Coatalen to be included in Sunbeam's works team in 1921. In the 1922 French Grand Prix, he ran as high as third before retiring,

assuring himself a permanent place on the Sunbeam team. Following his victory of 1923, he was dominating the early stages of the 1924 race when the Sunbeam's electrics played up. He took some consolation with victory in the San Sebastian Grand Prix, in Spain, later in the year. After a further win at Miramas, France in 1926, he retired from racing altogether to concentrate on speed records.

In 1927, he became the first man to exceed 322km/h (200mph) and in 1929, he raised the record to 372.46km/h (231.44mph) in the Irving-Napier Golden Arrow. Later that year, he was killed attempting a water speed record, when his boat hit a log on Lake Windermere. He was 34.

▲ *(left)* Henry Segrave.

◄ Segrave in his Sunbeam at the French Grand Prix at Tours in 1923. He won the race.

▼ The 1921 Grand Prix at Le Mans. Segrave (10) finished ninth, and Jimmy Murphy in the Deusenberg (12) was the winner.

Henry Segrave	
Nationality	British
Seasons	1921–26
Teams driven for	Sunbeam
Number of major victories	3

Ayrton Senna

The World Champion of 1988, 1990 and 1991, Brazilian Senna proved himself one of the greatest exponents of the sport ever seen until his death at the 1994 San Marino Grand Prix.

He came to Britain to make his name after a successful karting career in Brazil that began when he was a child. He dominated in British Formula Ford, Formula 2000 and Formula Three, leading to Formula One tests with Williams, Brabham and McLaren in 1983. He opted, though, to make his debut with the smaller Toleman team for 1984. At a wet Monaco, in only his fifth Grand Prix, he was closing down fast on leader Alain Prost and looked set to pass when the race was stopped short of its allocated distance. Such form led to his recruitment by Lotus for 1985. He took his first victory at Estoril in Portugal, with an astonishing display of virtuosity in the wet conditions.

Further wins followed with Lotus, but it was no longer a World Championship calibre team, and for 1988 he joined McLaren – alongside the great Prost. It was arguably the strongest driver line up of all time and it was inevitable that their relationship became difficult. Amid some incredibly intense battles, Senna emerged on top in 1988, Prost in 1989. Senna's clinching of the 1990 title by aiming his car at Prost's Ferrari and not lifting as they reached the first corner added to the impression that utter ruthlessness backed up his talent. Although the 1992 and 1993 McLarens were outclassed by the cars of Williams, Senna still produced some stunning drives, none more so than at Donington, England, in 1993, when, in wet conditions, he put in one of his greatest ever performances to win.

He transferred to Williams for 1994, setting pole position for the first three races, taking his tally to 65, still an all-time record. He was leading at Imola from his new rival, Michael Schumacher, when he crashed to his death. Motorsport – and the nation of Brazil – went into deep mourning.

► Senna caused a sensation by taking a Toleman to second place at the rain-soaked Monaco Grand Prix in 1984.

▲ Ayrton Senna tragically lost his life in an accident on lap six of the San Marino Grand Prix at Imola, 1 May 1994.

◄ Senna at the Mexican Grand Prix, Mexico City, in 1992.

Ayrton Senna	
Nationality	Brazilian
Seasons	1984–94
Teams driven for	Toleman, Lotus, McLaren, Williams
Number of major victories	41

Raymond Sommer

This French driver was responsible for some of the greatest giant-killing acts seen in Grand Prix racing, from his early years in the 1930s up to the time of his death in 1950.

The son of a pioneer aviator, he was from a sufficiently wealthy background that he was able to indulge his passion for speed. He bought a succession of ex-works Grand Prix cars from Alfa Romeo and Maserati, and prepared and entered them himself. His form frequently embarrassed the works teams with the latest equipment, and he was repeatedly offered factory drives, but invariably turned them down. Fiercely independent, he preferred to race on his own terms.

In the 1932 Marseilles Grand Prix, Sommer sensationally defeated the factory Alfa and Maserati teams with his old Alfa Monza. It was a performance he looked on-course to repeat at Spa in 1950 when, at 43 years of age and with an outclassed Talbot, he pushed the far faster Alfa Romeos. Initially the Alfa pit crew believed he couldn't possibly be on the same lap, but he was. It was to Alfa's great relief

▲ Raymond Sommer racing a Maserati in Jersey in 1947.

that the Talbot broke down and took him out of the race, but those with long memories weren't surprised.

Sommer was killed competing in a minor French hillclimb event at the end of the year, when it is believed a wheelbearing on his Cooper seized.

Raymond Sommer	
Nationality	French
Seasons	1932–50
Teams driven for	Alfa Romeo, Ferrari
Number of major victories	3

▲ Sommer at the Italian Grand Prix in 1950.

◄ Sommer's Alfa Romeo finished second at the 1946 Nice Grand Prix. Here he is leading Chaboud in the Delahaye.

Jackie Stewart

Triple World Champion Jackie Stewart is remembered not only for his masterly performances behind the wheel, but also for initiating and progressing the sport's safety campaign in the late 1960s up to his retirement from racing in 1973.

The Scot began his single-seater career in British Formula Three, where he was a dominant champion in 1964, driving for Ken Tyrrell's team. He moved straight into Formula One in 1965 with BRM, scoring his first Grand Prix win that year and ending up third in the World Championship.

It was an incredible rookie year, but success was harder to come by in the two seasons that followed. In 1966 he suffered a frightening accident in the Belgian Grand Prix and it was this that initiated his safety campaign, something that continued throughout and beyond his driving career.

For 1968, he hooked up once more with Tyrrell who ran a Matra-Ford for him and the winning ways returned. He only narrowly missed out on that year's Championship, and in 1969 the partnership was dominant as Stewart took his first world title.

With the new "Tyrrell" car Stewart dominated in 1971, but a stomach ulcer compromised his 1972 season. He began 1973 having decided he would retire at the end of the year, though this was a secret shared by only his inner circle. He won five Grands Prix that year, and clinched his third title with a stunning recovery drive at Monza that showed he was every bit as fast as he'd ever been.

He subsequently continued his long relationship with Ford, and in 1996 became a Formula One team owner as he established Stewart Grand Prix, with Ford backing. The team won the 1999 European Grand Prix with Johnny Herbert, but Ford subsequently bought out Stewart and rebranded the team as Jaguar.

▲ Jackie Stewart was restricted to fifth place in the USA Grand Prix in 1971 because of chunking tyres on his Tyrrell 003.

◄ Stewart in 1971, the year of his second World Drivers' Championship title. This was his first season in the new Tyrrell car.

Jackie Stewart

Nationality	British
Seasons	1965–73
Teams driven for	BRM, Tyrrell
Number of major victories	27

► Stewart outran BRM team-mate Graham Hill to win his first Grand Prix in his debut year, at Italy in 1965.

John Surtees

This Englishman is the only person to have won World Championships in both motorcycle racing and Formula One. He was one of the greatest drivers of the 1960s, and could conceivably have been even more successful had he made different career choices.

Between 1956 and 1960, Surtees won seven world titles in various motorcycle classes. He made his Grand Prix debut with Lotus in 1960, and his enormous potential on four wheels was made clear when he scored pole position at Portugal in only his third Grand Prix.

After two seasons in privateer teams, he was recruited by Ferrari for 1963. He won in Germany that year, and his analytical approach was fundamental in improving the team's competitiveness. This progressed into 1964 when, after a particularly strong second half of the season, he clinched the Championship at the final round. At the end of 1965, he suffered a serious accident in a Can-Am sports car, in which he was lucky to survive.

Impressively, he recovered in time for the start of the 1966 season. He and Ferrari were favourites for the title, and he took a superb victory in the wet

▲ Pole sitter John Surtees retired on lap 36 of the 1960 Portuguese Grand Prix.

John Surtees

Nationality	British
Seasons	1960–72
Teams driven for	Lotus, Ferrari, Cooper, Honda, BRM, Surtees
Number of major victories	6

Belgian Grand Prix. Following a row with the Ferrari team manager, he left and drove the rest of the season for Cooper, winning the Mexican Grand Prix.

Thereafter, he was involved with the Honda Formula One project – giving the team victory in the 1967 Italian Grand Prix – and with BRM, before going off to form his own Formula One team. His last full season in the driving seat was 1971, after which he concentrated on running the team. In eight years of toil, Team Surtees was never able to succeed in the same way as Surtees the driver.

▲ John Surtees in 1968.

◀ Surtees in the Honda RA300 (car 14) leads Chris Amon's Ferrari 312 at the Italian Grand Prix, Monza, in 1967.

Leon Théry

Recognized as the greatest driver of his era, Théry won the Gordon Bennett Cup races – the equivalent of a World Championship today – in 1904 and 1905, driving Richard-Brasier cars.

Known as "The Chronometer" for his incredibly consistent speed, he won in machinery that was no better than that of his leading rivals, who would invariably make mistakes as they tried in vain to keep up. He was also noted for his very thorough preparation, and would spend weeks testing his cars before the races.

He left Richard-Brasier along with co-founder Georges Richard in 1906, to set up a new car company, though this was unsuccessful. He returned to Brasier for the 1908 French Grand Prix and ran third until the car failed. He died a year later from tuberculosis.

▲ A portrait of Leon Théry in 1904 after winning the Gordon Bennett cup.

▶ Théry in the 1905 Gordon Bennett trophy race in a Brasier. He won this race just as he had won the 1904 event.

Leon Théry	
Nationality	French
Seasons	1903–08
Teams driven for	Richard-Braiser
Number of major victories	4

Wolfgang von Trips

▼ Wolfgang von Trips during the 1960 Argentine Grand Prix in his Ferrari.

The German count was leading the World Championship for Ferrari, in 1961, when he crashed to his death during the Italian Grand Prix at Monza.

After beginning his career in sports car racing in the 1950s, von Trips was taken on by Ferrari, driving his first Grand Prix for the team at Monza in 1956. He was retained as an occasional driver by the team for the next three years, but got his chance as a full-time member in 1960 after the departures of Tony Brooks and Dan Gurney.

In between racing that season, he conducted much development work on the new mid-engined Ferrari, and this put him in good stead for the 1961

Wolfgang von Trips	
Nationality	German
Seasons	1956–61
Teams driven for	Ferrari
Number of major victories	2

season, when the 156 "sharknose" model was the fastest car in the field. He battled with his team-mate Phil Hill for the destiny of the crown, winning both the Dutch and British Grand Prix, and had a narrow points lead over the American as they began the penultimate round of the championship at Monza.

After a poor start, he was making his way towards the front. On lap three, he passed Jim Clark, but Clark's Lotus then slipstreamed him down the

following straight, and under braking for the Parabolica turn, moved to von Trips' inside to repass. Probably not realizing the Lotus was still there, von Trips moved the same way as Clark. Their wheels interlocked and the Ferrari was thrown up the banking and along the fence, killing 14 spectators along the way. Von Trips was thrown out on to the track, and killed upon impact. Germany would have to wait another 33 years for its first World Champion.

▲ Wolfgang von Trips after winning the 1961 British Grand Prix. It was a brave performance on a rain-soaked track.

◄ Von Trips (Ferrari 156) won the British Grand Prix at Aintree in 1961. He led the World Championship at this point.

Achille Varzi

One of the greatest drivers of the 1930s, Milanese Varzi won Grands Prix for Alfa Romeo, Maserati, Bugatti and Auto Union after a successful career as a motorcycle racer.

Known as "The Ice Man" for his unnatural calm and cool, his clinical but stunningly fast driving reflected his temperament. This formed an elemental contrast with the style of his great adversary, the flamboyant Tazio Nuvolari. The two were rivals in motorcycle racing and moved into car racing together, forming their own team to run a pair of Bugattis.

Although successful, Varzi was uneasy being in the same team as his biggest rival, and moved on to works drives with much success over the years. Many of his victories came after stirring battles with Nuvolari. For 1935, he was recruited by Auto Union and began well, but early in 1936, he became addicted to morphine and his form dropped off alarmingly. He was

▲ Achille Varzi at Monaco in 1933.

Achille Varzi	
Nationality	Italian
Seasons	1928–48
Teams driven for	Alfa Romeo, Maserati, Bugatti, Auto Union
Number of major victories	18

dismissed by the team and did not reappear in racing until after the war, by which time he had kicked the habit and was back in good health.

He immediately began winning races again for Alfa Romeo, but was killed in practice for the 1948 Swiss Grand Prix, when his car overturned as he was attempting to wrest pole position from his team-mate Jean-Pierre Wimille.

▼ Varzi in a Bugatti leads two similar models on the Monaco circuit in 1933.

Gilles Villeneuve

The French-Canadian was one of the fastest, most spectacular drivers the sport has ever seen. He looked set for a glittering future, but was killed after crashing his Ferrari, while qualifying for the Belgian Grand Prix at Zolder in 1982.

Villeneuve started out by racing snowmobiles in Canada, becoming World Champion in the discipline before moving into car racing. A dominant North American Formula Atlantic Champion in 1976, he gained big international recognition when World Champion-elect James Hunt took part in a round of the Atlantic series, as Villeneuve's team-mate, and was beaten by him. Hunt reported back to his Formula One team, McLaren, who entered a third car for Villeneuve in the 1977 British Grand Prix.

His debut in an obsolete model was sensational, and he was set to finish fourth when a faulty temperature gauge sent him to the pits. When Niki Lauda walked out on Ferrari before the season was over, the Italian team recruited Villeneuve as his replacement. At the end of 1978 he won his first Grand Prix – fittingly at his home track of Montreal. For 1979, he was

Gilles Villeneuve	
Nationality	Canadian
Seasons	1977–82
Teams driven for	McLaren, Ferrari
Number of major victories	6

◀ Gilles Villeneuve in 1978, his first full season in Formula One. He took victory in the final race of the season.

▼ Villeneuve made his Grand Prix debut at Silverstone in 1977. He was on course for fourth place. Until a faulty temperature gauge sent him to the pits.

contracted in a support role to the experienced Jody Scheckter, but initially was clearly quicker. He won three Grands Prix that year but stood by team instructions, following Scheckter home at Monza and finishing the season as runner-up in the Championship.

He took two remarkable victories in 1981, with an uncompetitive Ferrari, but began 1982 as title favourite with a much-improved car. He was duped by team-mate Didier Pironi into losing the San Marino Grand Prix and was afterwards furious. Still angry two weeks later in Belgium, he was attempting to beat Pironi's qualifying time when a slower car moved into his path. The Ferrari flew high in the air before crashing down nose-first. Villeneuve was fatally injured.

◀ Villeneuve suffered a very uncompetitive Ferrari in 1980. He finished in fifth place in the Monaco Grand Prix that season.

Jacques Villeneuve

Villeneuve in characteristic hard-charging mode in his BAR 003 at Monza in 2000.

By winning the 1997 World Drivers' Championship, Jacques Villeneuve established himself as a Formula One star in his own right, rather than merely the son of Gilles.

He took up racing in the late 1980s, some years after the death of his father. With no karting experience, he initially struggled in the Italian Formula Three series, but subsequently made quick progress. With sponsorship backing from Players Tobacco, he moved to the United States, won the Formula Atlantic Championship and progressed to Indycars. In 1995, his second season there, he won the Championship as well as the prestigious Indianapolis 500.

This was his springboard to Formula One with the mighty Williams team. In Australia in 1996, he became only the third man to set pole position on his Grand Prix debut. He took his first victory at the Nürburgring a few months later and took the Championship battle

Jacques Villeneuve	
Nationality	Canadian
Seasons	1996–present
Teams driven for	Williams, BAR
Number of major victories	11

with team-mate Damon Hill all the way to the final round, but ultimately finished runner-up.

He clinched the 1997 title at the final round in Jerez, Spain, after his only rival, Ferrari's Michael Schumacher, attempted to drive him off the track. The outcome left Schumacher in the gravel trap and Villeneuve still running.

The Williams team lost its form in 1998, and for 1999 Jacques became part of the new BAR team. In five years of struggle, Villeneuve never came close to winning another race. He and BAR parted company at the end of 2003.

Villeneuve's BAR-Honda 002 comes to a fiery end at the Spanish Grand Prix in 2000.

Jacques Villeneuve has had a tough time, with little success, since winning the World Championship title in 1997.

John Watson

The popular Ulsterman was a leading light of Formula One from the mid-1970s to the early 1980s, and only narrowly lost out on the 1982 World Championship.

After a promising but under-funded career in the junior categories, Watson was given his Formula One chance by Bernie Ecclestone's Brabham team in 1973. Unfortunately, he broke his leg on his debut as a result of a sticking throttle. He came back and, in 1974, showed good speed in a privately-entered Brabham. After a half-season in the uncompetitive Surtees for 1975, Watson was recruited by the Penske team at the end of 1975. He gave the team its only Formula One victory with a great drive at Austria in 1976, but even that wasn't enough to prevent the team withdrawing at the season's end.

Back at Brabham for 1977, Watson drove superbly and only appalling luck kept him from winning at least two

Grands Prix. He left at the end of 1978 to join McLaren – unfortunately, just as the team was beginning a downward plunge. It took until 1981 to climb out of the rut, but Watson hung on and took an emotional victory in the British Grand Prix. In 1982, he won at Zolder and Detroit, and took the title battle with Keke Rosberg to the wire in Las

John Watson	
Nationality	British
Seasons	1973–84
Teams driven for	Brabham, Surtees, Lotus, Penske, McLaren
Number of major victories	5

◄ Watson with the beard he wore until he won his first Grand Prix in Austria in 1976.

Vegas, but finished second. In his last season in 1983, he took a remarkable victory at Long Beach from 22nd on the grid. He was replaced at McLaren by Alain Prost in 1984.

▼ John Watson in the Penske PC4 at the Austrian Grand Prix in 1976. It was his first Grand Prix win.

Jean-Pierre Wimille

At the time of his death, while practising for a race in Argentina in 1949, Wimille was recognized as the world's number one driver.

After a series of remarkable drives in less than fully competitive cars in the 1930s, Wimille spent World War II as a member of the French Resistance. Returning to racing after the war, he finally got his hands on machinery worthy of his abilities in the early post-war years, when he was recruited by the dominant Alfa Romeo team.

In 1947 and 1948, he was clearly the quickest man in a squad that included the legendary Achille Varzi. He won the French and Italian Grand Prix in 1948 and, had there been a World Championship at that time, there is no doubt that Wimille would have taken the crown.

He crashed his Simca-Gordini into a tree on his third lap of practice for the 1949 Perón Grand Prix in Argentina,

Jean-Pierre Wimille	
Nationality	French
Seasons	1930–48
Teams driven for	Bugatti, Alfa Romeo
Number of major victories	4

with fatal consequences. It was believed that the early morning sun had blinded him. Bizarrely, it was the first time Wimille had ever worn a crash helmet.

◀ Jean-Pierre Wimille. The Frenchman was widely regarded as the world's greatest driver during the late 1940s.

▼ Wimille in the Alfa 158 at the Grand Prix of the Nations, Geneva, Switzerland, in 1946.

The Circuits

There are 17 battlegrounds in 15 countries and five continents on which the Formula One World Championship is fought. The demands of each track are very different, placing varying strains on both man and machine. But, like Formula One itself, the venues and tracks are constantly altering, evolving with the technology of the cars, circuit safety and the commercial packaging of the sport. It is this latter demand that is leading to a changing geography of the championship, as the sport spreads its tentacles to new countries. As from 2004, the series no longer visits Austria but instead will pay its first visit to Bahrain and China. In the longer-term future, countries such as India, Turkey and Dubai are expected to host Grands Prix, illustrating its global appeal.

Key to Circuits

	Direction of race
	Start grid
	Finishing line
10	Bend number
`6   289`	Gear engaged/ speed km/h
(T2)	Timing point

◀ The Hockenheim track in 2000.

Australia *Albert Park*

Australia hosted its first World Championship Grand Prix in 1985, around a street circuit in Adelaide. It was here in 1986 that Nigel Mansell suffered his famous 300km/h (190mph) tyre blow-out that lost him the World Championship. This circuit continued to host the event until 1995, but two years earlier Melbourne – which has traditionally been in competitive opposition with Adelaide – secured a deal with Formula One boss Bernie Ecclestone to host the Grand Prix from 1996. It is now the traditional season-opening race, where the form of the new cars and car/driver combinations is revealed for the first time, setting the tone of the season to come.

The track chosen for the Melbourne race was, like Adelaide, a street circuit, albeit one constructed around the roads of a public park in the seaside district of St Kilda. There had been motor racing at Albert Park in the 1950s, but only for national-level events.

There was some local opposition against the Grand Prix, but this has melted away since the event has proved such a prestigious commercial success for the city. Albert Park is now one of the most successful Grands Prix in terms of attendance and financial return for the city and its restaurants and hotels.

The circuit follows quite closely the outline of the park's boating lake. Its sequence of fast bends, punctuated by three tight corners demands a tricky aerodynamic compromise between straightline speed and downforce. Braking and traction are especially important here, though its smooth,

▲ *(top)* Second place finisher Juan Pablo Montoya fends off Michael Schumacher's winning Ferrari, having earlier passed his rival round the outside.

▲ *(above)* Montoya's Melbourne form in the Williams FW24 raised hopes of a strong season in 2002. It was not to be.

▲ Martin Brundle gets airbourne in his Jordan 196 after a first corner accident at the Australian Grand Prix, 1996.

◄ David Coulthard moves over to let Häkkinen through to win the Australian Grand Prix in 1998.

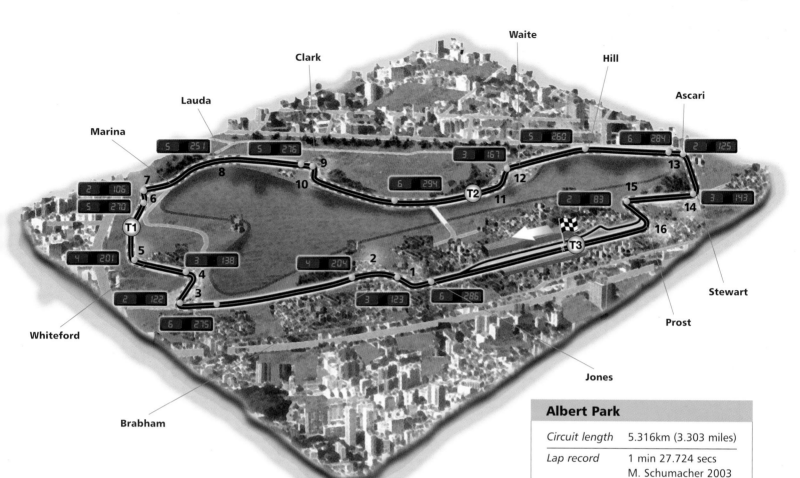

Clark
Waite
Hill
Lauda
Ascari
Marina

5 251
5 276
3 167
5 260
6 284
2 125

2 106
6 294
2 83
3 143

5 270

4 201
3 138
4 204

2 122

3 123
6 286

6 275

7
8
9
10
11
12
13
14
15
16
6
T1
5
4
3
2
1
T2
T3

Whiteford
Stewart
Prost
Jones
Brabham

Albert Park

Circuit length	5.316km (3.303 miles)
Lap record	1 min 27.724 secs M. Schumacher 2003
Previous winners	2003 D. Coulthard 2002 M. Schumacher 2001 M. Schumacher

▼ **Michael Schumacher's Ferrari F1-2001 races past the Albert Park Marina in practice for the 2002 Australian Grand Prix.**

dusty surface means that tyre wear tends to be low. This has ramifications on strategy, as it usually proves quicker over a race distance to pit only once, as the tyres degrade slowly.

On the fast approach to the tight first corner in the opening seconds of Melbourne's first Grand Prix in 1996, Martin Brundle's Jordan got airborne after clipping a rival's car. He barrel-rolled through the air in spectacular fashion but, remarkably, stepped out completely unhurt. A day earlier Jacques Villeneuve had made a great Formula One debut by qualifying his Williams on pole position.

There was controversy in 1998 when, after mishearing an instruction on the radio, McLaren's Mika Häkkinen pitted from the lead when the team were not ready for him. His delay allowed team-mate David Coulthard to take over at the front, but Coulthard then acceded to a team request that he back off and allow Häkkinen back in front.

Tragically, a track marshal was killed in 2001 after being hit by a wheel from Jacques Villeneuve's crashing BAR. Improvements to the protective fencing were made in time for the 2002 event. Michael Schumacher won this race for Ferrari after a thrilling early battle with Juan Pablo Montoya. Australia's Mark Webber made a great Grand Prix debut by bringing his Minardi home in fifth place in front of a crowd of adoring countrymen.

Austria *A1-ring*

The rapid success of Austrian driver Jochen Rindt in the early 1960s created such a whirlwind of interest that it sparked a campaign to have an Austrian Grand Prix as part of the World Championship.

Austria's only race venue at the time was in rural Zeltweg, where two runways of a still-used military airfield, nestling within a valley of the Styrian mountains, formed a temporary circuit. The first races were held there in 1958. Later, Rindt's sensational success in Formula Two – where as a novice he beat established Formula One stars such as Graham Hill – gained Zeltweg a World Championship Grand Prix for 1964. It was at this race that Rindt made his Formula One debut, although the event was won by Lorenzo Bandini's Ferrari after more favoured runners such as Jim Clark, Graham Hill and John Surtees retired with suspensions broken on the airfield's appallingly rough surface.

The governing body demanded changes to the track if the race were to continue as a championship event, but its continued use as an airfield made this impractical. Rindt's success helped raise finance for a circuit to be built on the other side of the valley, near the village of Spielberg. It was named the Osterreichring and opened in July 1969.

◀ Jacques Villeneuve's Williams leads Eddie Irvine for Ferrari and David Coulthard for McLaren in 1997.

▼ Barrichello (*right*), after leading all the way, controversially moved aside for Schumacher on the line in 2002.

▼ Allan McNish's Toyota set against the Tyrolean backdrop in 2002. The track's sharp contours can be seen clearly.

It was a magnificent racing circuit, following the varying contours of the land through beautiful forests, with a sequence of supremely challenging fast bends. It held its first Grand Prix in 1970 and, fittingly, Rindt arrived there as the runaway leader of the championship. He retired from the race and, a few weeks later, was killed while practising for the Italian Grand Prix. The Austrian Grand Prix and the Osterreichring nonetheless continued to prosper, even more so after another Austrian driver – Niki Lauda – began to be successful.

The event was part of the calendar until 1987. In that year, television schedules were badly disrupted after it took three attempts to get the race underway, following a series of startline collisions on the narrow grid. At a time when there were already increasing safety concerns about the lack of run-off areas, it led to the race being dropped from the calendar once again. After some years, a new group of businessmen took over the circuit and,

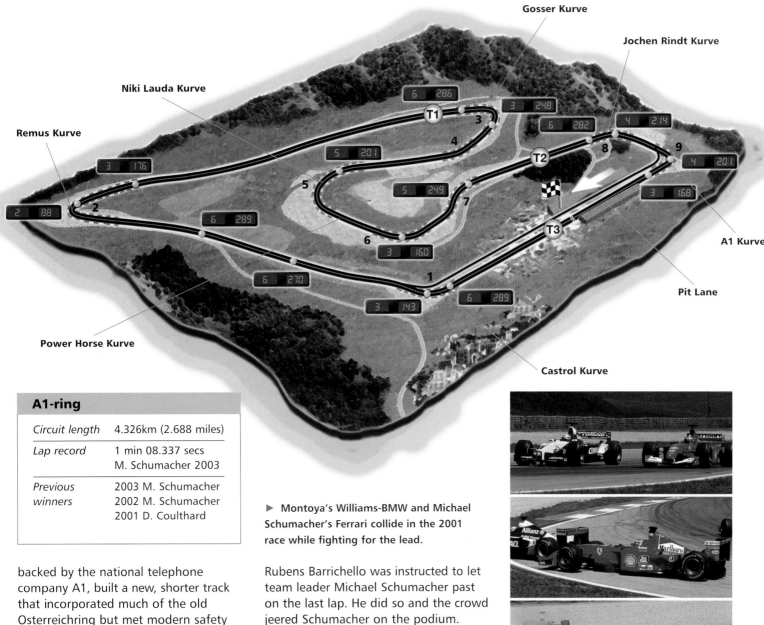

Gosser Kurve

Jochen Rindt Kurve

Niki Lauda Kurve

Remus Kurve

Power Horse Kurve

A1 Kurve

Pit Lane

Castrol Kurve

A1-ring	
Circuit length	4.326km (2.688 miles)
Lap record	1 min 08.337 secs M. Schumacher 2003
Previous winners	2003 M. Schumacher 2002 M. Schumacher 2001 D. Coulthard

▶ Montoya's Williams-BMW and Michael Schumacher's Ferrari collide in the 2001 race while fighting for the lead.

backed by the national telephone company A1, built a new, shorter track that incorporated much of the old Osterreichring but met modern safety standards. Named the A1-ring, it hosted its first Grand Prix in 1997.

One of the shortest tracks on the calendar, the A1-ring features two longish straights, including a couple of steep uphill sections. Engines are on full throttle for 60 per cent of the lap, and reach peak revs in top gear at three parts of the track. Interspersed by tight corners, it places a premium on power, braking and traction. Similar lap times can be achieved using very different aerodynamic set ups, so varied are the track's demands. Its low-grip, smooth surface makes it easy on tyre wear, and this makes one-stop race strategies the most common choice.

There was controversy here in 2002. After leading for the entire race, Ferrari's

Rubens Barrichello was instructed to let team leader Michael Schumacher past on the last lap. He did so and the crowd jeered Schumacher on the podium.

The circuit's contract ended in 2003 and was not renewed. The final race saw Michael Schumacher coming back from a pit lane fire to win. It was a fittingly dramatic end to the era.

▶ Giancarlo Fisichella's pole-winning Benetton leads the 1998 Austrian Grand Prix.

Belgium *Spa-Francorchamps*

T here have been two circuits within this spectacular wooded Ardennes valley, the first of which hosted Grands Prix between 1925 and 1970. Thereafter, it was deemed too dangerous for Formula One. A second, shorter track was built using part of the original public road circuit but then veering into a specially constructed downhill section. This first hosted a Grand Prix in 1983, and has been used ever since.

What both circuits had in common was their incredibly challenging nature. The original featured flat-out sweeps that followed the dramatically changing contours of the valley through villages, within inches of stone walls, trees and houses through its 12.8km (8 mile) length. In the final Grand Prix there, Chris Amon set the fastest lap at an average 244.74km/h (152.08mph). It was also dangerous, and had a horrific record of fatalities. Jackie Stewart's accident there in the 1966 Belgian Grand Prix initiated his long-running Formula One safety campaign.

The 1983 track used the same downhill section of public road to begin the lap, leading into the dramatic Eau Rouge bend, still considered the greatest challenge of all by most

▲ Two competitors pass under a bridge as residents of a local hotel watch the action.

▼ The Jordan team took its first victory in fine style with a 1-2 in the wet 1998 Belgian Grand Prix, with Damon Hill leading team-mate Ralf Schumacher.

Formula One drivers. In a good car with a brave driver, this left-right sweep, with a downhill approach and an uphill exit, can be taken foot-to-the-floor in top gear. A long, steep hill then leads to Les Combes, a tight second-gear right-hander, and the point where the new track parts with the old public road. A series of daunting, downhill bends takes the track to the valley's floor, where it rejoins the tail-end of the old circuit at Stavelot. A flat-out kink and short straight precede the "Bus Stop" chicane, so called because of its extreme tightness. The exit of this leads to La Source hairpin and the beginning of another lap.

The altitude variations and large area of forest lead to highly changeable weather conditions, and sudden heavy rain is always a possibility. Frequently, it can be raining on one side of the circuit and dry on the other.

One of the most dramatic Grands Prix of the modern era took place in 2000, with a wheel-to-wheel battle between title rivals Michael Schumacher and Mika Häkkinen. Schumacher had made a remarkable Formula One debut here in 1991 and, with four victories, had a special affinity with the place. For the 2000 race he had gambled on there being rain, and had set up his car with lots of downforce. But the rain held off,

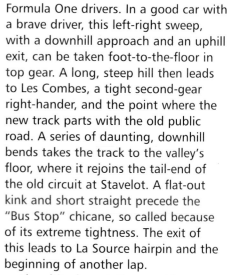

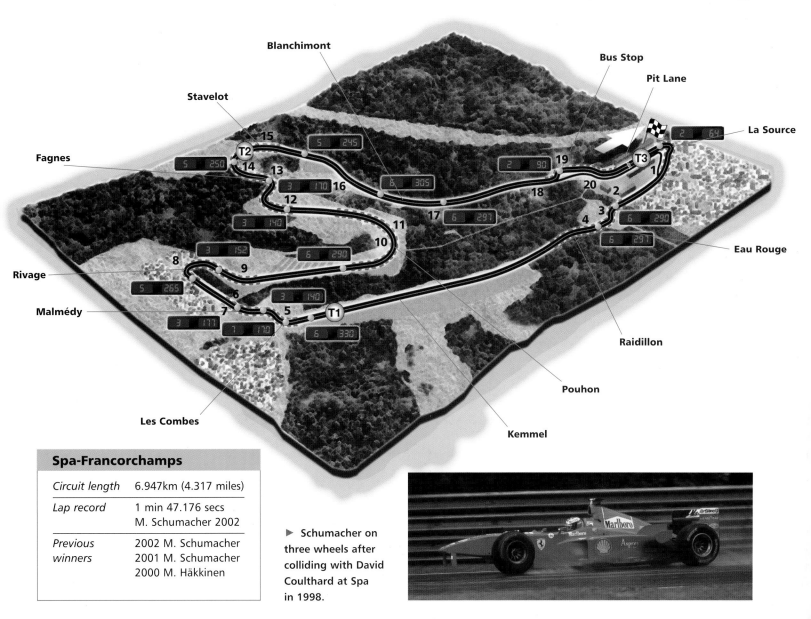

Blanchimont

Bus Stop

Pit Lane

Stavelot

La Source

Fagnes

Rivage

Malmédy

Les Combes

Kemmel

Pouhon

Raidillon

Eau Rouge

Spa-Francorchamps

Circuit length	6.947km (4.317 miles)
Lap record	1 min 47.176 secs M. Schumacher 2002
Previous winners	2002 M. Schumacher 2001 M. Schumacher 2000 M. Häkkinen

▶ Schumacher on three wheels after colliding with David Coulthard at Spa in 1998.

allowing Häkkinen to close down Schumacher's lead. Much quicker up the hill to Les Combes, Häkkinen moved to the Ferrari's inside but, at almost 320km/h (200mph), Schumacher edged the McLaren towards the grass, forcing Häkkinen to back off. The Finn was now angry. On the next lap, at exactly the same place, Schumacher and Häkkinen came up to lap the BAR of Ricardo Zonta. Schumacher passed him on the left, Häkkinen on the right. A startled Zonta watched in amazement as Häkkinen took the lead, on his way to a great gladiatorial victory.

A row over tobacco advertising saw Spa removed from the 2003 calendar, but its planned return for 2004 has brought a sigh of relief from aficionados of the sport.

▶ Race winner Ayrton Senna leads McLaren team-mate Gerhard Berger in 1990.

Brazil *Interlagos*

ituated on shifting land between two underground lakes – hence its name – the Interlagos track first hosted local-level motor racing in the 1930s. Back then it was an open site within an unpopulated area south of the city of São Paulo. The subsequent population explosion of that city saw the site enveloped by shanty town *favellas*.

Nonetheless, with Emerson Fittipaldi giving Brazil her first World Champion in 1972, Interlagos hosted a round of the series the following year. In fairytale fashion, Fittipaldi won in his JPS Lotus, a feat he repeated the following year in a McLaren. In that race he could hear the screaming cheers of the crowd as he passed race leader, Ronnie Peterson. In 1975, another Brazilian, Carlos Pace, won the race for Brabham. It was to be his only Formula One victory before being killed in a plane crash two years later. The circuit was subsequently renamed in his memory.

The track used between 1973 and 1980 was wonderfully demanding, with a banked, almost flat-out first corner. Unusually, the track ran in an anti-clockwise direction. Concerns about lack of run-off areas for the ever-faster cars, and the intolerance of

ground-effect cars for the notoriously bumpy surface were the reasons given for moving the Brazilian Grand Prix to Rio de Janeiro in 1981, to a track that first hosted the race in 1978. Perhaps significantly, Brazil's new racing hero Nelson Piquet hailed from Rio.

But the later success of São Paulo's Ayrton Senna helped bring the impetus back to Interlagos. The mayor of the city struck a deal with Formula One supremo Bernie Ecclestone for the race to return there for 1990, on a new circuit within the same grounds.

Senna himself contributed to the design, which used some of the original

track but which by-passed the fast but dangerous former Turn One. The outer part of this track largely comprised part of the old circuit, and was very quick, with a fast uphill kink on to the pit straight. A downhill left-right S-bend (later named the Senna Esses) signalled the start of the new section, with an infield comprising mainly tight bends, though with one hugely challenging downhill fifth-gear left-hander, Turn 11.

Yet the bumps of the old track remained a problem, and no matter how much resurfacing work is done, new bumps always seem to appear. The shifting land beneath is the culprit,

▲ *(top)* Nigel Mansell got his Ferrari career off to a great start with a win at Brazil in 1989.

▲ *(above)* Alain Prost spun his Williams-Renault out of the lead in the 1993 event, handing victory to arch-rival Ayrton Senna.

◄ Race winner Ayrton Senna leads the field in the 1991 race; Mansell follows.

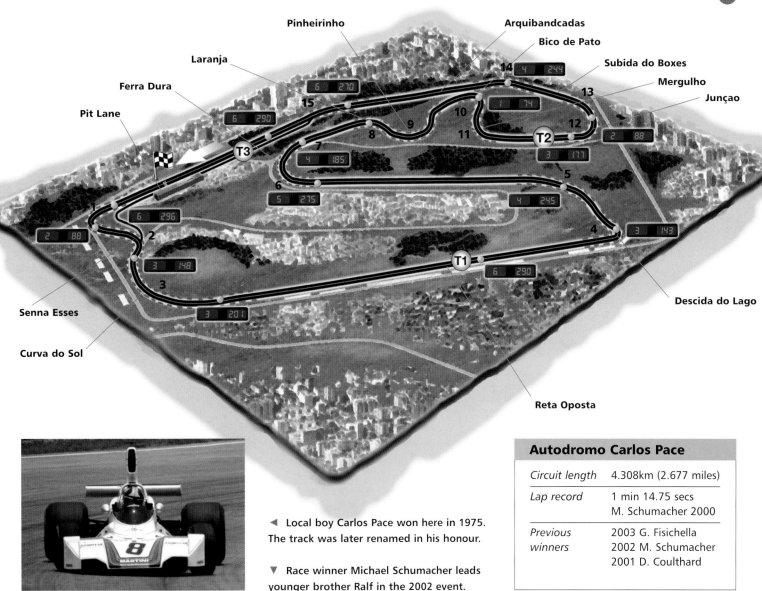

Pinheirinho

Arquibandcadas

Bico de Pato

Laranja

Subida do Boxes

Ferra Dura

Mergulho

Junçao

Pit Line

Senna Esses

Curva do Sol

Descida do Lago

Reta Oposta

◄ Local boy Carlos Pace won here in 1975. The track was later renamed in his honour.

▼ Race winner Michael Schumacher leads younger brother Ralf in the 2002 event.

Autodromo Carlos Pace

Circuit length	4.308km (2.677 miles)
Lap record	1 min 14.75 secs M. Schumacher 2000
Previous winners	2003 G. Fisichella 2002 M. Schumacher 2001 D. Coulthard

and it brings an extra dimension to the problems faced by drivers and engineers as they try to set up the cars. Ride heights have to be bigger than at any other track on the calendar, reducing the aerodynamic efficiency and grip of the cars. Furthermore, the changeable weather can wreak havoc – as was seen in 2003 when a huge storm 30 minutes before the start created conditions that caused a chaotic, accident-infested race.

In 2001, Juan Pablo Montoya, in only his third Grand Prix, made himself a hero to millions, when he took the lead from Michael Schumacher with a daring wheel-rubbing move at the end of the straight into the Senna Esses. He pulled away quickly, and looked set for victory, but was later hit by the lapped car of Jos Verstappen. Despite his Colombian nationality, Montoya is a favourite with the wildly enthusiastic Interlagos fans. São Paulo native, Rubens Barrichello, closely follows him in their affections.

Canada *Montreal*

ituated on the Ile Notre Dame, a man-made island between the St Lawrence River and the St Lawrence Seaway, the Montreal track first hosted the Canadian Grand Prix in 1978, after the old Mosport circuit was deemed too dangerous.

The island had been built to house the world trade fair of 1967, and it hosted the Olympic Games of 1976, but more usually was parkland. The park roads were joined to form a circuit of long, fast straights and tight chicanes and hairpins. The fans went home very happy after the 1978 race, when local hero Gilles Villeneuve won for the first time in his Ferrari.

Villeneuve featured heavily in 1979 too, finishing second after a thrilling lead battle with the faster Williams of Alan Jones. In the wet 1981 race, he finished third despite running for much of the distance with no front wing.

But the month before he was due to take part in the 1982 event, he was killed during qualifying for the Belgian Grand Prix. The circuit was renamed in his memory.

The 1982 race saw further tragedy when Ricardo Paletti was killed in a startline accident, when his Osella rammed into the back of the stalled

pole position Ferrari of Villeneuve's former team-mate, Didier Pironi.

The circuit has changed little over the years, and it invariably produces an exciting race. The combination of high speeds on the long straights, followed by tight second-gear bends, means that it is the most punishing circuit of all for brakes. The carbon-fibre brake discs of

◀ Gilles Villeneuve celebrates his first Formula One win with Quebec Premier Pierre Trudeau, on the Montreal podium in 1978.

▼ Mika Häkkinen's McLaren leading a lapped Arrows at the hairpin during the 2000 event.

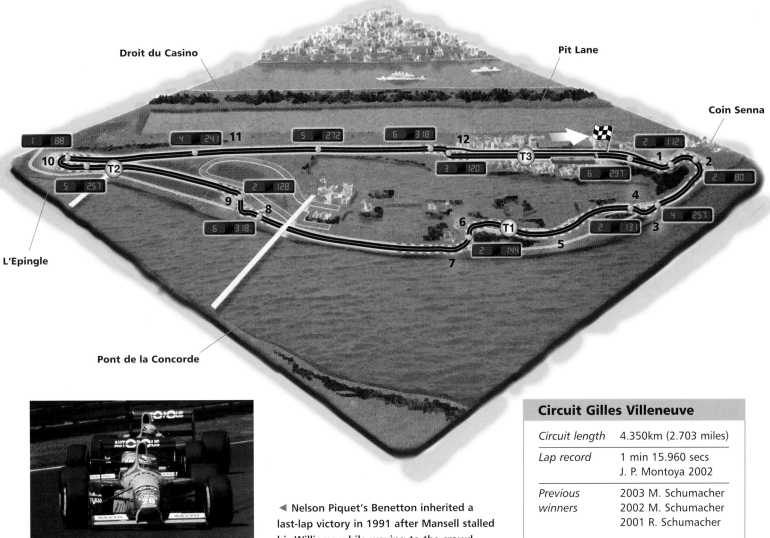

Droit du Casino

Pit Lane

Coin Senna

1 88
4 241
11
5 272
6 318
12
2 112
1
2 80
10
T2
5 257
2 128
3 120
T3
6 297
4
4 257
9
8
6 318
9
8
6
T1
2 13
3
L'Epingle
7
2 144
5

Pont de la Concorde

Circuit Gilles Villeneuve	
Circuit length	4.350km (2.703 miles)
Lap record	1 min 15.960 secs J. P. Montoya 2002
Previous winners	2003 M. Schumacher 2002 M. Schumacher 2001 R. Schumacher

◄ Nelson Piquet's Benetton inherited a last-lap victory in 1991 after Mansell stalled his Williams while waving to the crowd.

modern Formula One cars begin to oxidize at temperatures over 600°C (1112°F). Here, they reach over 800°C (1472°F) repeatedly and are rarely allowed to drop below 500°C (932°F) before they are needed again. Brake wear is extreme, and lack of brakes is a frequent cause of retirement.

But it was the pressure of rival, Mika Häkkinen, rather than the lack of brakes that caused Michael Schumacher to crash out of the race in 1999. The two had engaged in a fierce duel that took them clear of the rest of the field. Finally, Michael took a little too much speed into the final corner and smashed hard into the unforgiving wall at its exit. Häkkinen duly took the win, a vital part of his successful campaign that year.

In 2001, the battle for victory was an all-Schumacher affair as Michael's Ferrari led early from brother Ralf's Williams-BMW. For lap after lap, Ralf would edge alongside in the final chicane, only to be discouraged as Michael veered toward him. The race's

turning point came when the Ferrari had to pit for fuel. Ralf's fuel tanks were bigger, and with little tyre wear from the dusty track, he was able to reel off four super-quick laps with clear air ahead of him. This enabled him to make his pitstop and rejoin the race in the lead for a comfortable victory.

Rows over tobacco advertising have threatened the future of this event (the 2004 event was initially cancelled) but its popularity with teams and fans has helped maintain its place on the calendar.

▼ Jean Alesi takes the flag for the only Formula One win of his career, in 1995.

Europe *Nürburgring*

The European Grand Prix used to be a title bestowed in turn on a different European race each year, but fell into disuse in the mid-1970s. It was revived in 1983, when Brands Hatch hosted a Grand Prix just a few months after Silverstone's British Grand Prix. The title was subsequently used to cover any doubling-up of races in the same country: the new Nürburgring held the European Grand Prix in 1984 (Hockenheim held the German Grand Prix); in 1985, Brands Hatch featured the European race, while Silverstone's event bore the "British" tag. Then, in 1993, Donington Park was granted a Grand Prix of Europe, and Silverstone retained its regular British Grand Prix slot on the Formula One calendar.

More recently, the popularity of Formula One in Germany, following the success of Michael Schumacher, has made it viable for that country to host two Grands Prix per season. One of them, that held at the Nürburgring, now holds the full-time claim to the European Grand Prix title.

The "new" Nürburgring was first used in 1984. It was built as a modern venue to attract Formula One back to

▲ An aerial view of the new Nürburgring. The new circuit was built because of serious safety concerns about the original track.

▼ Ralf Schumacher (*right*) fights out the first corner of the 2002 European Grand Prix with Williams-BMW team-mate Juan Pablo Montoya. Rubens Barrichello's Ferrari (*directly behind Montoya*) won the race.

the region after the original track – a 22.5km (14 mile) section of road running through forested valleys – was deemed too dangerous, following Niki Lauda's near-fatal accident in 1976.

It is a relatively flat and featureless circuit, with constant radius bends and plenty of run-off area. Its surface is quite abrasive, demanding a fairly hard tyre compound. After a series of first corner incidents – where out-of-control cars going through the gravel trap had a tendency to come back on to the track on the exit as other cars filed past – the layout was changed for 2002. A double bend now takes the racing line out of reach of first corner spinners.

One of the most exciting races of modern Formula One took place at this track in 1995. It began in wet but drying conditions. Most chose to start on wet tyres, but not Jean Alesi in the Ferrari. As David Coulthard's Williams led from Michael Schumacher's Benetton and Damon Hill's Williams, Alesi was able to use his fantastic car control to hang on to them.

As the track began to dry, so the wet-tyred leaders had to pit – leaving Alesi with a 20-second lead and no

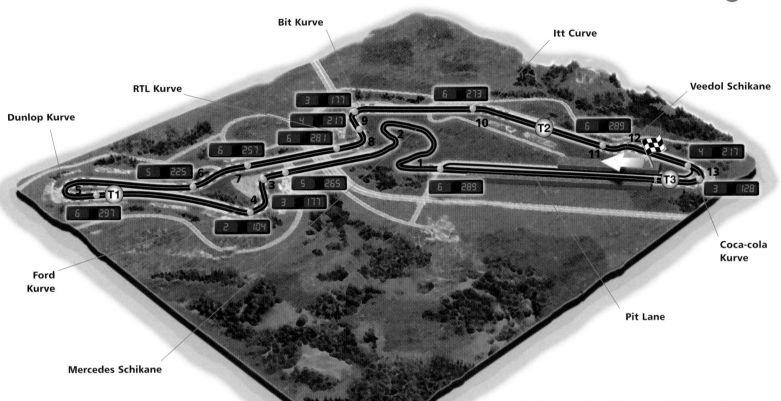

Bit Kurve

Itt Curve

RTL Kurve

Veedol Schikane

Dunlop Kurve

3	177
4	217
6	281
6	257
5	225

| 6 | 273 |
| 6 | 289 |

| 6 | 289 |

5	265
3	177
2	104

| 4 | 217 |
| 3 | 128 |

T1 | 6 | 297 |

Ford Kurve

Coca-cola Kurve

Pit Lane

Mercedes Schikane

need to stop. With Coulthard now second, Schumacher and Hill were engaged in a furious battle over third place, and the German gave the Brit a chop on one occasion that almost took the Williams off the circuit. Eventually Hill succeeded in getting by, but then threw away the move by getting off line at the next corner, allowing Schumacher to retake the place. Michael then began to pull away.

Coulthard began to suffer handling difficulties, and was passed by both Schumacher and Hill, but still Alesi was

leading comfortably, even after a routine refuelling stop. But Schumacher began his relentless chase of the Ferrari. Alesi and his team took a long time to wake up to the threat of the closing Benetton. By the time Jean tried to respond, it was too late; Schumacher was now on his tail. With seven laps to go, Schumacher made an aggressive move down the inside into the chicane. It gave Alesi the option of making way or taking them both off. He chose the former, allowing Schumacher his seventh win of the season, on his way to the world title.

Nürburgring

Circuit length	5.144 km (3.196 miles)
Lap record	1 min 32.2265 secs M. Schumacher 2002
Previous winners	2003 R. Schumacher 2002 R. Barrichello 2001 M. Schumacher

▲ Johnny Herbert's Stewart took victory in the 1999 European Grand Prix.

▶ Jacques Villeneuve withstood pressure from Michael Schumacher to take his first Formula One win, at the Nürburgring, 1996.

▲ (top) Alain Prost's McLaren-Porsche won the first race held at the new Nürburgring for the 1984 European Grand Prix.

▲ (above) Niki Lauda's BRM in 1973: airborne action at the old Nürburgring.

France *Magny-Cours*

A race enthusiast farmer, Jean Bernigaud, built the original track on this site in 1960. Situated a few miles away from the town of Nevers, in the Loire Valley, it still nestles between green farmland and traditional French châteaux.

It was not until 1991 that the circuit played host to the French Grand Prix, by which time it was very different from the original. The current format was built in 1988, with the help of government grants. The Ligier team, later renamed Prost, was based here until Alain Prost moved it to Paris in 2000. Magny-Cours was also the base for the Winfield Racing School that established a whole generation of Elf-backed French racing drivers in the 1970s and 1980s. François Cevert, Patrick Depailler, Jacques Laffite and René Arnoux, among others, all started their careers here as raw novices. Laffite and Arnoux were consultants for the layout of the current track.

The most notable characteristic of this circuit is its incredibly smooth, bump-free surface. Teams can set the ride height of their cars lower here than at any other track, bringing big benefits in aerodynamic grip. Many of the corners are long and flowing, meaning the tyres are under lateral load for

◄ David Coulthard scythes down the inside of Michael Schumacher in 2000.

◄ Nigel Mansell (Williams) leads Alain Prost (Ferrari) in 1991.

▼ *(below left)* Ralf Schumacher's Williams-BMW leads brother Michael's Ferrari in 2001.

a long time. Combined with the soft compounds allowed by the surface, this makes tyre wear a critical factor.

The 1999 French Grand Prix at Magny-Cours was a fascinating struggle between several teams and drivers,

with changeable weather making the outcome uncertain right to the end.

The sky was threatening but the track dry as the race started, and Rubens Barrichello's Stewart led from pole position ahead of Jean Alesi's Sauber and David Coulthard's McLaren. At the end of the first lap, Heinz-Harald Frentzen's Jordan and Michael Schumacher's Ferrari followed in fourth and fifth place. Coulthard quickly passed both Alesi and Barrichello to take the lead. He pulled out a big gap over the rest before pulling to the side of the track with electrical failure on the 10th lap.

As Barrichello retook the lead, the rain began falling. But then stopped again after a couple of laps. Alesi was coming under pressure from Frentzen, and behind them was Mika Häkkinen, who had passed Schumacher. Häkkinen then passed Frentzen, Alesi and Barrichello in quick succession to take the lead in his McLaren.

On the 21st lap, the rain arrived properly, and everyone pitted for wet weather tyres. The Stewart team gave Barrichello a very quick stop, enabling

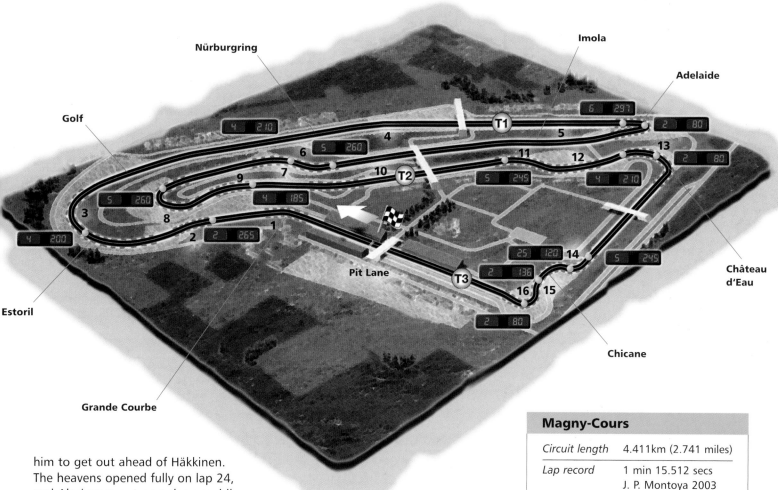

Nürburgring

Imola

Adelaide

Golf

4	210
6	297
2	80

T1

4

5

6 | 5 | 260

11

12

13

2 | 80

9

7

10

T2

| 5 | 245 |
| 4 | 210 |

3 | 5 | 260

8

| 4 | 185 |

4 | 200

2

2 | 265

1

Pit Lane

| 25 | 120 |
| 2 | 136 |

14

| 5 | 245 |

T3

Château d'Eau

Estoril

16 | 15

| 2 | 80 |

Chicane

Grande Courbe

him to get out ahead of Häkkinen. The heavens opened fully on lap 24, and Alesi spun out on a deep puddle, bringing Frentzen up to third. The rain was now so heavy that the safety car came out, neutralizing the race for the next 11 laps. With the race back on, Häkkinen attempted to wrest the lead back from Barrichello but spun, dropping to seventh. At around the same time, Schumacher – who had lost radio contact with his pit – had passed Frentzen and was in now second place.

After one failed attempt, Schumacher succeeded in passing Barrichello on lap 42. But soon after, he slowed due to electrical glitches in his car. He came in early for his second fuel stop to have the problem attended to. Barrichello thus led again but by now Häkkinen was carving back through the field and, after passing Frentzen, he took the lead from Barrichello for a second time. He began pulling away at the rate of three seconds per lap. Häkkinen and Barrichello made their second planned fuel stops, putting Frentzen in front.

Frentzen's Jordan had bigger fuel tanks than the other cars and, with the slower pace forced by the rain and the safety car, he now had enough fuel in reserve not to make his originally planned second stop. The McLaren and

Stewart teams waited for Frentzen to come in – and waited, and waited. At the end of 72 laps, Frentzen crossed the line to give Jordan an unexpected victory from Häkkinen and Barrichello.

Magny-Cours

Circuit length	4.411km (2.741 miles)
Lap record	1 min 15.512 secs J. P. Montoya 2003
Previous winners	2003 R. Schumacher 2002 M. Schumacher 2001 M. Schumacher

▼ Schumacher leads into turn one at the start of the French Grand Prix, 2 July 2000.

Germany *Hockenheim*

Hockenheim has been the venue of the German Grand Prix since 1977 (with the exception of 1985, when the new Nürburgring hosted its second Grand Prix), though it hosted the event on one occasion before that, in 1970. For many years, it was the fastest Grand Prix track on the calendar, due to two very long straights. Even since being interrupted by chicanes in the 1980s, these stretches still allowed the Formula One cars of the 1990s to reach over 360km/h (224mph) in top gear. The straights – which ran through a wood – featured no spectating areas and were linked by a stadium section, where the crowds gather and where the pit lane is situated. This layout was used for the last time in 2001. For the 2002 race, a new section of track cut out much of the length of the straights, turning right through the former wood around half way down the first straight into a new infield section that then links back up with the truncated second straight just before the stadium. The new layout enables the cars to be seen by spectators for a greater proportion of the lap.

Situated around 112km (70 miles) south of Frankfurt, the original Hockenheim circuit was built as a test track by Mercedes in the late 1930s. When a new autobahn was built in the 1960s, it split the original track in two,

▲ *(top)* Jacky Ickx's Ferrari leads Jochen Rindt's Lotus in the first Grand Prix to be held at Hockenheim in 1970. Rindt won.

▲ *(above)* Niki Lauda on his way to an emotional Ferrari win in 1977.

▼ Jarno Trulli's Jordan leads Olivier Panis' BAR during a midfield battle in the last Grand Prix to be held on the unfettered Hockenheim track, in 2001.

but, using compensation money from the government, the circuit owners planned a new layout using only the far side of the former site. Racing began on this new track in 1966. Two years later, it gained notoriety when the great Jim Clark was killed here in a Formula Two race. His Lotus went out of control through a left-hand kink on the first straight, probably as the result of a slow puncture, and came to rest against a tree.

Safety standards were improved by the erection of barriers to protect cars from the trees. In 1970, under pressure from the Grand Prix Drivers' Association, the Nürburgring was being altered to improve safety, and so the German Grand Prix of that year was held at Hockenheim for the first time. The race was won by Jochen Rindt's Lotus. It would be another seven years before the event returned there, this time permanently, after the Nürburgring was finally dismissed as intrinsically too dangerous for Formula One. This had become clear through Niki Lauda's near-fatal accident there in 1976. It was therefore fitting that Lauda won the 1977 race at Hockenheim.

In 1980, Patrick Depailler was killed during a test session, when a suspected suspension failure put his Alfa Romeo head-on into the barriers at around 240km/h (150mph) at the Ost-Kurve. Another chicane was added to slow the cars through this section. Two years later, Didier Pironi's career came to an end after an accident caused by the

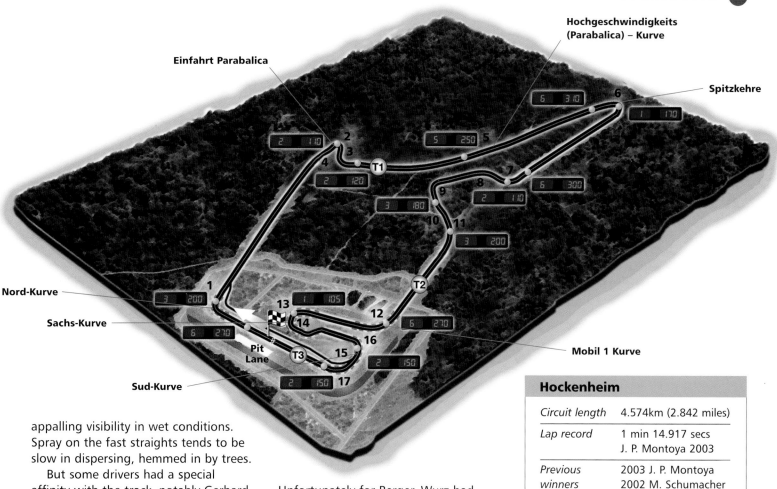

Hochgeschwindigkeits
(Parabalica) – Kurve

Einfahrt Parabalica

Spitzkehre

Nord-Kurve

Sachs-Kurve

Sud-Kurve

Pit Lane

Mobil 1 Kurve

appalling visibility in wet conditions. Spray on the fast straights tends to be slow in dispersing, hemmed in by trees.

But some drivers had a special affinity with the track, notably Gerhard Berger. He won here for Ferrari in 1994, his only victory in his three-year second stint with the team. He was on-course to win the event in 1996 for Benetton until his engine blew on the last lap, handing victory to Damon Hill. But his greatest race here was his last one, in 1997. He had missed the previous three races because of a sinus problem, and been replaced by stand-in Alex Wurz.

Unfortunately for Berger, Wurz had performed superbly, and questions were being asked about whether Berger was needed. But worse, much worse, in the days leading up to his comeback, Berger learned that his father had been killed in a plane crash. It was somehow fitting that Berger should dominate the weekend. He started from pole position and led the race from beginning to end. At the end of the season he retired.

Hockenheim

Circuit length	4.574km (2.842 miles)
Lap record	1 min 14.917 secs J. P. Montoya 2003
Previous winners	2003 J. P. Montoya 2002 M. Schumacher 2001 R. Schumacher

▼ *(left)* Michael Schumacher in the Ferrari 310B on his way to second place in 1997.

▼ *(right)* A Toyota TF102 approaches the new hairpin at the heavily remodelled Hockenheim track during the German Grand Prix in 2002.

Great Britain *Silverstone*

In late-1940s Britain, the search was on for a major new race venue. Brooklands was no more, with half of its speed bowl destroyed to make room for aircraft production facilities. But as the war took away, so it created. In the heart of rural Northamptonshire, near the sleepy little village of Silverstone, there was a wartime airfield that was no longer needed. The perimeter roads of the runways made for a perfect high speed challenge. In 1948, it hosted the British Grand Prix. It has held it, on and off, ever since.

Initially, the country's governing body, the RAC, wished to spread its favours, and for a time the race alternated between Silverstone and Aintree near Liverpool. Subsequently – until 1986 – Brands Hatch in Kent took over the Aintree slot. But when Brands was deemed no longer suitable for Formula One, Silverstone monopolized the event.

It was a fast, flat and featureless track, very demanding and exacting, but for some drivers slightly disorienting. The early straw-bale markers soon gave way, first to oil drums, then concrete posts, and finally proper kerbs. But the farm remained in the track's infield – with the wheat usually high by the time

▲ *(top)* **Jack Brabham took his Cooper to victory at Silverstone in 1960, on his way to a second World Championship.**

▲ *(above)* **Michael Schumacher (Ferrari) celebrates victory in the 2002 race at the same Silverstone venue at which he broke his leg in 1999.**

of mid-July, the British Grand Prix slot – and the "Silverstone hare" still does invariably appear on-track during the weekend. Until the late 1980s, the layout remained much the same, once the original incorporation of the airfield runway was abandoned after 1948.

The corners were fast, and demanded a lot of commitment and precision on the way in. After Jody Scheckter crashed at the quick Woodcote corner, at the end of the first lap of the 1973 race, taking much of the field out with him, a chicane was incorporated there to slow things down. But it was still a fast track, and vied with the Osterreichring from the mid-1970s to mid-80s as the fastest on the calendar. In 1985, Keke Rosberg's turbocharged Williams-Honda set a qualifying lap speed of 258.97km/h (160.924mph), a Formula One record that stood until 2002.

This was rather too fast, in fact. The run-off areas demanded by these sort of speeds would have moved the spectators impossibly far back from the action. For the 1992 race, a complete redesign was in place. There was a new infield section before Woodcote, entered via the awesome Bridge Corner, a slightly banked top-gear right-hander. The right-left sweep of Becketts on to the Hangar Straight became more sharply defined, and there was a new section – Vale – between the Stowe and Club corners, which slowed things down further. Essentially, this remains the layout of the track today.

50

◄ **Felippe Massa (Sauber) spinning at the first corner of the 2002 British Grand Prix.**

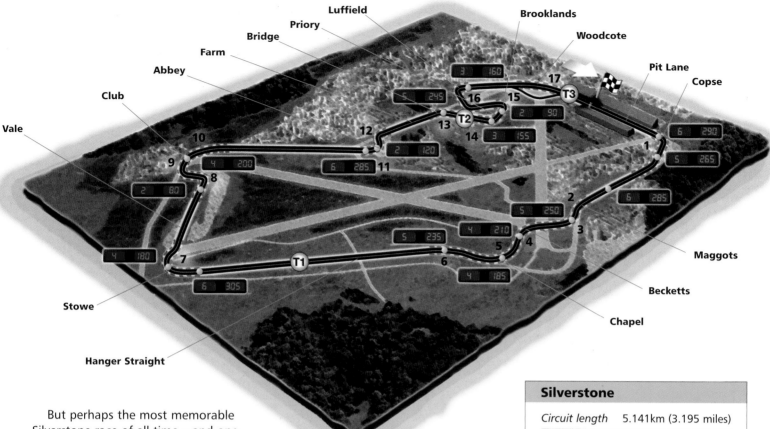

Luffield
Priory
Bridge
Farm
Abbey
Club
Vale
Brooklands
Woodcote
Pit Lane
Copse
Maggots
Becketts
Chapel
Stowe
Hanger Straight

| 10 | 9 | 8 | 12 | 11 | 7 | T1 | 6 |

Track data boxes: 3 160 · 5 245 · 16 · 15 · 2 90 · 17 · T3 · 13 · T2 · 14 · 3 155 · 4 200 · 2 120 · 6 285 · 6 290 · 5 265 · 1 · 2 80 · 5 235 · 5 210 · 5 250 · 2 · 3 · 4 · 5 · 4 180 · 6 305 · 4 185 · 6

But perhaps the most memorable Silverstone race of all time – and one of the greatest races in Formula One history – came on the old track, in 1987. The Williams-Hondas were the dominant machines of the time and no one other than their drivers, Nelson Piquet and Nigel Mansell, really had a chance. Piquet led the early going with Mansell chasing.

Then Mansell began to sense a vibration – a wheel weight had fallen off. It forced him to make an unplanned pit stop on lap 36 of the 65-lap race. With new tyres, he rejoined and with nothing to lose he turned up his turbo boost and set about catching his team-mate, now 28-seconds ahead.

He closed down at a rapid rate and the partisan crowd sensed something big was about to happen. With two laps to go, approaching Stowe corner at the end of the 305km/h (190mph) Hangar Straight, Mansell feigned for the outside. Piquet covered him and Mansell immediately darted to the inside and passed. Entering the last lap, Mansell's fuel read-out was telling him he had nothing left, but there was just enough to get him home. He ran out on the slowing down lap – and was mobbed.

Silverstone

Circuit length	5.141km (3.195 miles)
Lap record	1 min 22.236 secs R. Barrichello 2003
Previous winners	2003 R. Barrichello 2002 M. Schumacher 2001 M. Häkkinen

▼ *(left)* Ayrton Senna's McLaren leads Gerhard Berger's Ferrari in the 1988 race. Senna won; team-mate Prost withdrew.

▼ *(right)* Mansell-mania: the crowd invade the track after homegrown hero Nigel Mansell dominated the 1992 race in his Williams-Renault FW14B. Mansell's successes attracted a new breed of race fan to Silverstone.

Hungary *Hungaroring*

It was Formula One supremo Bernie Ecclestone who pushed hardest for a Grand Prix behind the old Iron Curtain. For several years there was talk of a Moscow Grand Prix, but discussions always broke down at an early stage. It was then suggested to Ecclestone that he look at Hungary, where the regime might be more accommodating.

There was already a history of motor racing in the country as it had hosted a pre-war Grand Prix around the streets of Budapest, and even as late as the 1960 the city had been host to other European touring car events. The government was sold on the idea of a Grand Prix but, after looking at feasibility studies, decided that a new purpose-built track should be created. Work began in 1985, ready for the inaugural Grand Prix of 1986. The circuit was to be built in a rural valley some miles outside the city. Situated in a natural amphitheatre, it allowed for superb viewing for spectators.

However, as the allocated land area was fairly small, the track had to turn in on itself several times. Consequently it is very tight, offering no real chance for the cars to stretch their legs and there is only one possible overtaking spot. In terms of the set-up required of the

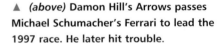

▲ *(top)* Nigel Mansell pulls off after a rear wheel came adrift while he was leading the late stages of the 1987 race.

▲ *(above)* Damon Hill's Arrows passes Michael Schumacher's Ferrari to lead the 1997 race. He later hit trouble.

cars, it needs maximum wing settings, just like at Monaco. For 2003, a new section of track was built in an effort to encourage more overtaking.

Nelson Piquet won the first race on the new Hungarian track, in August 1986, in his Williams-Honda. He had earlier taken the lead with a stunning round-the-outside pass of Ayrton Senna's Lotus at the first corner, the Williams on full opposite lock as it completed the manoeuvre. Piquet won again the following year, but only after his team-mate Nigel Mansell's wheel nut came off while leading.

The 1989 race was perhaps the most exciting Hungarian race. After early-leader Riccardo Patrese retired

◄ Fernando Alonso won at the Hungaroring in 2003. At 22 years and 26 days he became the youngest ever Grand Prix winner.

Hungaroring

Circuit length	4.384km (2.724 miles)
Lap record	1 min 22.095 secs J. P. Montoya 2003
Previous winners	2003 F. Alonso 2002 R. Barrichello 2001 M. Schumacher

▶ **Mika Häkkinen (McLaren-Mercedes) took a dominant win at Hungary in 1999 in the absence of injured rival Michael Schumacher.**

his Williams with a punctured radiator, Ayrton Senna was leading in the McLaren and looked set for victory. But that was to reckon without Nigel Mansell, who had qualified his Ferrari in only 12th place. In the race his car was handling superbly, and he had quickly fought his way through the pack. He was on Senna's tail as they came up to lap the Onyx of Stefan Johansson, who kept well over to the left of the track, aware that the leaders were bearing down on him. Senna seemed caught momentarily off-guard and boxed himself in behind. Mansell, anticipating this superbly, swung across the back of Senna's gearbox with just millimetres to spare and passed both cars in one move, on his way to victory. It gave the lie to the track's no-passing reputation.

▶ **The scenic Hungaroring in August 2000.**

Italy *Monza*

S ituated in a former royal park in suburbs around 24km (15 miles) north of Milan, Monza is the oldest track on which the World Championship is still fought. It held its first Grand Prix in September 1922, and has hosted it almost every year since.

Monza was not the first purpose-built racing circuit in Europe – that honour belonged to Brooklands in Britain – but it was the first to be used for a Grand Prix. The 1922 Italian race, in fact, marked the first time that spectators were charged an entrance fee to watch a Grand Prix.

Comprising two circuits in one, the "speed bowl" was in essence an American-style oval track, with two long straights joined by two heavily banked corners. Within this was a "road circuit" designed to replicate the demands of public road racing that had comprised Grands Prix up until this time. The two tracks criss-crossed one another via a bridge, and shared the same pit straight. The speed bowl was demolished in 1938, but part of the banking was incorporated into the road course. In 1955, a new banked circuit was built to replace the pre-war one, and the layout allowed for a combination of banked and road circuit to be used. This combined track hosted the Grands Prix of 1955 and 1956, but

▲ *(top)* **The closest finish. Only 0.1seconds separated the first five finishers in the 1971 race. Peter Gethin got the verdict, from Peterson, Cevert, Hailwood and Ganley.**

▲ *(above)* **The first lap crash which claimed the life of Ronnie Peterson at the Italian Grand Prix on 10 September 1978.**

there were concerns about the stresses tyres and suspensions were subject to by the banking, and from 1957 the road course was reverted to once more. Even this was an extremely fast track, with much flat-out running and high speed bends, such as the Lesmos and Parabolica, making the races fantastically gripping slip-streaming battles where, typically, the outcome would be in doubt right up to the finish line.

There was one last Grand Prix held on the banking in 1960, but subsequently that section fell into disuse – though it still remains, an impressive weed-infested monument to a bygone era.

The high speeds meant the Monza circuit bore witness to many tragedies, and, initially, poor spectator protection meant they, too, were often involved. In 1928, Emilio Materassi crashed into the spectator enclosure on the main straight, killing 27 people and himself. As late as 1961, the Ferrari of Wolfgang von Trips reared along the spectator

◄ **The safety car leads the cars past the old banked circuit at the Italian Grand Prix in 2000.**

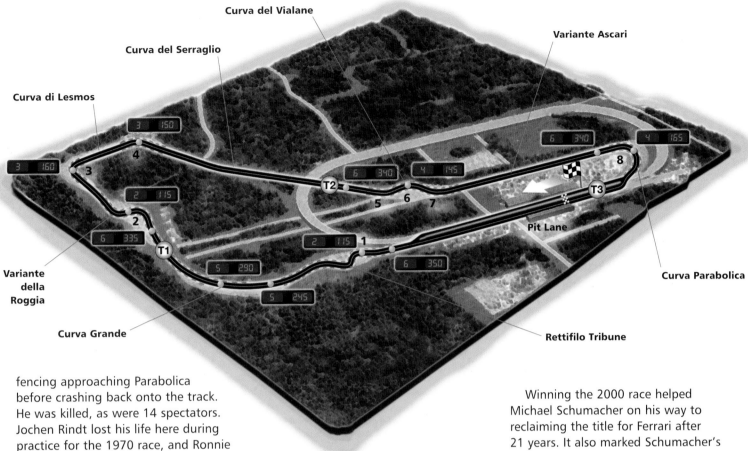

Curva del Vialane

Curva del Serraglio

Variante Ascari

Curva di Lesmos

3 150

3 160

4

3

2 115

6 340

4 145

6 340

4 165

8

T2

2

5 6 7

T3

6 335

T1

2 115

1

Pit Lane

Variante della Roggia

5 290

6 350

Curva Parabolica

5 245

Curva Grande

Rettifilo Tribune

fencing approaching Parabolica before crashing back onto the track. He was killed, as were 14 spectators. Jochen Rindt lost his life here during practice for the 1970 race, and Ronnie Peterson died as a result of a first-lap start-line crash in the 1978 event.

Amid the fanatical Ferrari fans, Peter Gethin won for BRM in 1971, and his average speed of 242.62km/h (150.76mph) still stands as the fastest Grand Prix race average of all time. Subsequently, chicanes were installed to slow the cars down, and whilst making it safer it also brought about the end of the classic slipstreaming battles.

Monza	
Circuit length	5.793km (3.600 miles)
Lap record	1 min 21.832 secs M. Schumacher 2003
Previous winners	2003 M. Schumacher 2002 R. Barrichello 2001 J. P. Montoya

Winning the 2000 race helped Michael Schumacher on his way to reclaiming the title for Ferrari after 21 years. It also marked Schumacher's 41st Grand Prix victory, which brought him level to the record of Ayrton Senna. Schumacher – who had been racing against Senna at Imola in 1994, when the Brazilian crashed to his death – broke down in tears in the press conference.

▼ *(below)* Schumacher wins in 2000.

▼ *(bottom)* Italian fans celebrate the World Championship title won by Ferrari in 2001.

◄ *Tifosi* shout for Scuderia Ferrari at the Italian Grand Prix in 2001.

Japan *Suzuka*

H osting the Japanese Grand Prix since 1987, Suzuka is renowned as one of the greatest challenges an Formula One driver can face. Its sequence of super-fast bends demand ultimate commitment and many rank its 290km/h (180mph) corner, 130R, as the ultimate test of nerve and skill.

Owned by Japanese manufacturer Honda, the circuit was built as a test track by the company in the early 1960s. Subsequent races were held there, though the newly-inaugurated but short-lived Japanese Grand Prix of 1976 and 1977 ran at the rival Fuji track.

It was not until the time of Honda's prominence as a Formula One engine supplier, in the mid-1980s, that it was able to exert its influence and have a Japanese Grand Prix reinstated to the calendar, this time at Suzuka.

As the Japanese race has usually been either the penultimate or final race of the year, it has frequently been host to championship deciders. In 1989, title rivals Alain Prost and Ayrton Senna collided at the chicane. Prost retired but Senna rejoined from the escape road and went on to win the race. He was then disqualified for rejoining the track

▲ Gerhard Berger took his first Ferrari win at Suzuka, 1987, with the F1/87. It was Formula One's fastest car by the end of the year.

in a dangerous manner, leaving him unable to overhaul Prost's points advantage in the one race remaining. A year later, Senna took his revenge as he again fought out the destiny of the crown with Prost. Using his points advantage in his favour, as Prost had done the previous year, Senna simply drove his rival off the track at the first corner. Both retired into the gravel trap,

▼ Mika Häkkinen leads Michael Schumacher in the 2000 Japanese Grand Prix, as they fight for the World Championship title.

but Senna became World Champion. In 2000, Michael Schumacher clinched the first World Championship for a Ferrari driver in 21 years after a supremely tense battle with his only rival, McLaren's Mika Häkkinen. The Finn led the first part of the race, with Schumacher following in his tracks as both pulled well clear of the rest of the field. The McLaren was the first to make

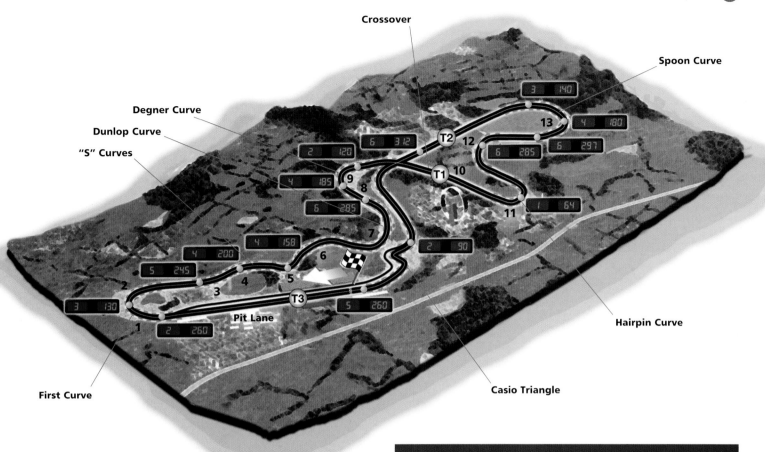

Crossover

Spoon Curve

Degner Curve

Dunlop Curve

"S" Curves

First Curve

Pit Lane

Hairpin Curve

Casio Triangle

Suzuka	
Circuit length	5.859km (3.641 miles)
Lap record	1 min 33.408 secs R. Schumacher 2003
Previous winners	2003 R. Barrichello 2002 M. Schumacher 2001 M. Schumacher

▶ Damon Hill took a superb victory in the 1994 Japanese Grand Prix. Rival Michael Schumacher got stuck behind Mika Häkkinen, losing vital time.

its routine fuel and tyre stop, but just as Häkkinen was rejoining, spots of rain began to fall. Critically, this meant Häkkinen was unable to generate sufficient heat into his new tyres and, for a couple of laps, he was slow. Schumacher, yet to stop and on tyres already up to temperature, was able to lap quickly enough to build sufficient gap to allow him to pit and rejoin without losing the lead. Häkkinen gave chase, but it was to no avail. In bringing the world title back to Italy, Schumacher had succeeded in doing what no one had managed since Jody Scheckter in 1979.

▶ Michael Schumacher sealed a record-breaking sixth World Championship title in Japan at the final round of the 2003 world championship series.

Malaysia *Sepang*

T he Malaysian government sought to host a globally prestigious annual event as part of its programme of economic expansion, and Formula One fitted the bill perfectly. To this end, a brand new circuit was constructed on the outskirts of Kuala Lumpur, with facilities that rendered other Formula One venues previous-generation. It hosted its first Grand Prix in 1999.

The track is situated on a former stretch of derelict land adjacent to Kuala Lumpur airport. It was designed by German Hermann Tilke to incorporate a wide variation of corners. Two 0.9km (0.56-mile) straights are joined by a hairpin, but perhaps the most spectacular part of the track is an unusually wide and gradual chicane, where the Formula One cars sweep left-right at around 200km/h (125mph). Further around the lap, Turn 12 is a highly dramatic fourth gear downhill left-hander, leading into the loop that takes the cars down the first of the long straights.

Grand Prix spectators are housed in grandstands beneath spectacular sun-sensitive leaf-design roofing, with blinds that open and close according to the light. From there they can see much of the circuit, thanks to the land's contours and the site's relatively compact area.

▲ Eddie Irvine was helped to victory by second-placed team-mate Michael Schumacher in 1999.

◀ Schumacher drove his Ferrari F1-2000 to victory at Sepang in 2000.

The inaugural race, the penultimate round of the 1999 championship, got the event off to a great start. Michael Schumacher, after breaking his leg at Silverstone, had missed much of the season, leaving his Ferrari team-mate Eddie Irvine to battle McLaren's Mika Häkkinen for the championship. Schumacher was finally fit to race again for Malaysia, and his brief was to aid Irvine in the Championship fight.

After setting pole position by over a second, Schumacher took off into the lead ahead of Irvine, whom he allowed past after four laps. As Irvine pushed on, intent on building up his lead, Schumacher endeavoured to slow the

◀ Alex Yoong (Minardi PS02) in his home Grand Prix was meant to pack the Sepang grandstands in 2002.

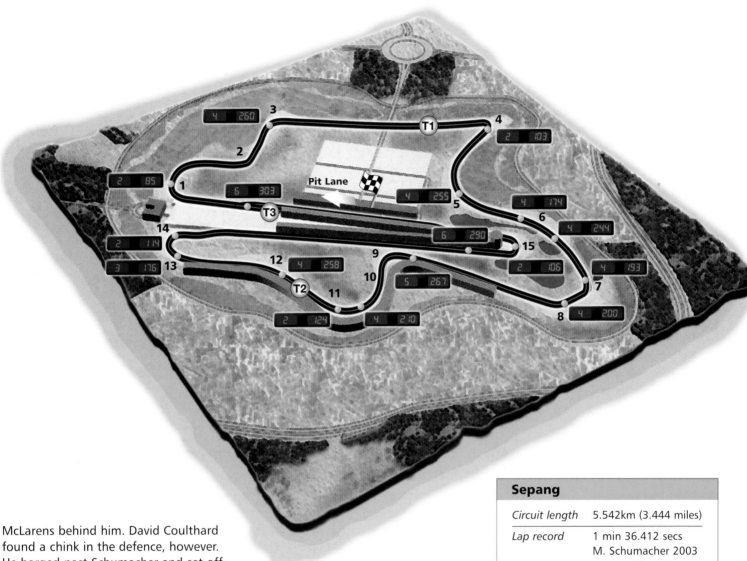

Pit Lane

McLarens behind him. David Coulthard found a chink in the defence, however. He barged past Schumacher and set off after Irvine, but on lap 15, Coulthard's car lost its fuel pressure and retired.

As Schumacher repeatedly prevented Häkkinen from making progress, Irvine built up enough of a lead that he was comfortably back in front after all had made their first fuel stops. Irvine then did a short second stint, increasing his lead even further, before a second and final fuel stop. He rejoined just behind Häkkinen, who then made his second stop. This left Schumacher – who wasn't making a second stop – in the lead from Irvine. Schumacher allowed Irvine through for a second time, and the Ferraris finished 1-2, with Häkkinen a frustrated third, allowing the title fight to go to the final round in Japan. It was a superb demonstration of team work from the Italian team.

Post-race, it was announced that the aerodynamic barge boards on the side of the Ferraris were of a shape not permitted by the regulations. They were initially disqualified, but reinstated on appeal a few days later.

▼ **The beautiful Malaysian paddock by night, illuminated by lasers.**

Sepang	
Circuit length	5.542km (3.444 miles)
Lap record	1 min 36.412 secs M. Schumacher 2003
Previous winners	2003 K. Raikkonen 2002 R. Schumacher 2001 M. Schumacher

Monaco *Monte Carlo*

T he race around the streets of the tiny principality, home of the jet-set crowd and super-rich, has become synonymous with the image of Grand Prix racing. Since 1929, cars have raced past the yachts in the Mediterranean harbour, around tortuous bends more usually clogged with traffic. The slowest Grand Prix track on the calendar, it is also the most exacting. Unlike other tracks, there are no run-off areas and no margin for error. One slip and the car is in the barriers, its race over.

The idea for the race came from Anthony Noghes, president of the Monegasque car club and close friend of the ruling Grimaldi family. The town was already host to the Monte Carlo rally, but Noghes conceived cars racing wheel-to-wheel through the streets. Even in the 1920s, the course was considered very narrow for such an event, but the inaugural race of 1929 – won by William Grover-Williams in a Bugatti – was considered a big success in attracting custom and prestige to

the area, and it has continued, on and off, to this day. It is the venue of choice for team sponsors to attend.

The course traces its way up a hill cut out of the cliff face and via the blind exit of Massenet corner into Casino Square. There, with the Casino on one side and the Hôtel de Paris on the other, the cars weave their way to the top of the hill that leads them down to Mirabeau, a very tight right-hander leading on to an even tighter left-hander, Loews. Taken in first gear at no more than 48km/h (30mph), this is the slowest corner in Grand Prix racing. Drivers have to be very careful to allow themselves enough room to get round, and cars frequently have extra steering lock made available to prevent the embarrassment of not being able to manage it. After a couple of successively quicker right-handers, the cars enter the famous tunnel, cut through solid rock beneath the Hôtel de Paris. After a flat-out kink in the middle, the cars exit the dim light at around 290km/h (180mph) before extreme braking for a first-gear chicane. The track then follows the harbour

◀ **The start of the race: eventual winner Michael Schumacher (Ferrari) leads the field towards Massenet in 2001.**

▼ **Chris Amon (Ferrari 312), in third, passes the fatal accident of Lorenzo Bandini at the 1967 Monaco Grand Prix.**

▲ **Ayrton Senna (McLaren) fends off Nigel Mansell's Williams during the closing stages to win at Monaco in 1992. Mansell had earlier been forced to pit while leading.**

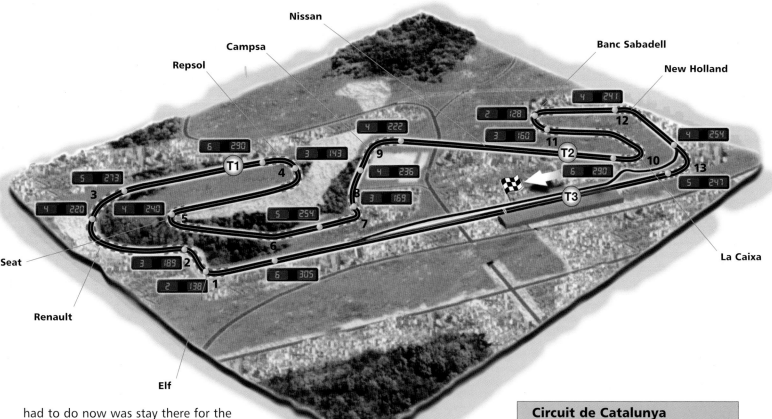

Nissan

Campsa

Repsol

Banc Sabadell

New Holland

T1

T2

T3

Seat

Renault

Elf

La Caixa

had to do now was stay there for the final 15 laps. It looked a relatively easy task for the Finn, who was notoriously cool under pressure.

The laps duly ticked away and, with Schumacher slowing even more, Häkkinen built up his lead to over half a minute. As he went past the pits for the last time, the McLaren's engine could be heard to be running rough. A few corners later, Mika pulled off to the side of the track. Michael couldn't believe his luck as he was handed victory on the last lap of the race.

On his slow-down lap, he stopped to give his disconsolate rival a lift back to the pits. Even Schumacher felt sorry for Häkkinen on that day.

▼ (left) Winner Mika Häkkinen (McLaren MP4-13) leads David Coulthard in the Spanish Grand Prix in 1998.

Circuit de Catalunya	
Circuit length	4.730km (2.939 miles)
Lap record	1 min 20.143 secs R. Barrichello 2003
Previous winners	2003 M. Schumacher 2002 M. Schumacher 2001 M. Schumacher

▼ Gerhard Berger leads McLaren team-mate Ayrton Senna into the first corner of the 1991 race. Winner Nigel Mansell is here in third, with Michael Schumacher fourth.

USA *Indianapolis*

Formula One's biggest challenge in the modern era has always been how to open up the American market. Hosting a race in the world's biggest economy would naturally make the sport more attractive to sponsors and television companies looking for advertising revenue. Yet America has always had its own domestic race series, namely NASCAR stock cars and ChampCar single-seaters. Formula One meant little, if anything, to the average American television viewer.

There had been American Grands Prix at Watkins Glen in New York State through the 1960s and 1970s, but in the end they became economically unviable. In the 1970s and 1980s, Formula One dallied with street circuits in Long Beach, Detroit, Phoenix and Las Vegas. But part of the problem was the slow average speeds to which the cars were limited. To race fans brought up on a diet of lap speeds in excess of 320km/h (200mph) from both NASCAR saloons and ChampCar single-seaters on their super-fast oval tracks, Formula One hardly captured the imagination.

Using Indianapolis as a venue for a new American Grand Prix from 2000 was an inspired idea. Virtually every

American knew about Indianapolis, home of "the world's greatest race", the Indy 500. This ChampCar race had run since 1911 and was part of the very fabric of American life, one of the great sporting classics. By holding a Formula One race here, Grand Prix racing would benefit from the fame of the venue.

However, the famous banked speed bowl was not a suitable circuit for a Formula One machine. Instead, a new circuit was constructed that used part of the traditional track, but which then veered off into an infield of more or

▲ Michael Schumacher spins his Ferrari F1-2000, but still goes on to win the USA Grand Prix at Indianapolis in 2000.

▼ *(left)* Juan Pablo Montoya's Williams-BMW FW23 leads the field around the famous Indy banking in 2001.

▼ *(right)* Mika Häkkinen celebrates what would turn out to be his final Grand Prix victory before retirement in 2001. He is flanked by Michael Schumacher *(left)* and McLaren team-mate David Coulthard.

Indianapolis	
Circuit length	4.192km (2.605 miles)
Lap record	1 min 11.473 secs M. Schumacher 2003
Previous winners	2003 M. Schumacher 2002 R. Barrichello 2001 M. Häkkinen

less conventional Formula One track configuration. After 12 corners this rejoined the existing track on the banking of what is "Turn One" in ChampCar parlance, but which became Turn 13 of the Formula One track, given that the cars were travelling clockwise, the opposite way to the Champcars.

The Formula One circuit covered only a fraction of the area of the speedway, leaving the huge grandstands of three-quarters of the oval deserted. Yet even this made for over 200,000 spectators, well up on most European venues. Since 2000, the event has begun the slow task of turning America on to Formula One.

▼ Jarno Trulli (*left*) and Jenson Button about to clash in the early laps of the USA Grand Prix at Indianapolis. This was their second tangle in three races. The pair later became team-mates at Renault.

Statistics

Who was the fastest, the greatest, the best qualifier, the top racer? Who made the best car? These are questions to which there are no definitive answers. Comparison between eras of motor racing is not strictly possible; in the pioneer days of the sport there was one major race per year, at the inauguration of the World Drivers' Championship in 1950 there were seven major Grands Prix. Today the season comprises 17 races. Statistics therefore can be misleading, over-emphasizing modern achievements at the expense of earlier ones. But all have been recorded and heralded.

◄ Japanese Grand Prix, Suzuka, 2002.

World Champion Drivers

1950 Giuseppe Farina (Italy)
1951 Juan Manuel Fangio (Argentina)
1952 Alberto Ascari (Italy)
1953 Alberto Ascari (Italy)
1954 Juan Manuel Fangio (Argentina)
1955 Juan Manuel Fangio (Argentina)
1956 Juan Manuel Fangio (Argentina)
1957 Juan Manuel Fangio (Argentina)
1958 Mike Hawthorn (Britain)
1959 Jack Brabham (Australia)
1960 Jack Brabham (Australia)
1961 Phil Hill (USA)
1962 Graham Hill (Britain)
1963 Jim Clark (Britain)
1964 John Surtees (Britain)
1965 Jim Clark (Britain)
1966 Jack Brabham (Australia)
1967 Denny Hulme (New Zealand)
1968 Graham Hill (Britain)
1969 Jackie Stewart (Britain)
1970 Jochen Rindt (Austria)
1971 Jackie Stewart (Britain)
1972 Emerson Fittipaldi (Brazil)
1973 Jackie Stewart (Britain)
1974 Emerson Fittipaldi (Brazil)
1975 Niki Lauda (Austria)
1976 James Hunt (Britain)
1977 Niki Lauda (Austria)
1978 Mario Andretti (USA)
1979 Jody Scheckter (South Africa)
1980 Alan Jones (Australia)
1981 Nelson Piquet (Brazil)
1982 Keke Rosberg (Finland)
1983 Nelson Piquet (Brazil)
1984 Niki Lauda (Austria)
1985 Alain Prost (France)
1986 Alain Prost (France)
1987 Nelson Piquet (Brazil)
1988 Ayrton Senna (Brazil)
1989 Alain Prost (France)
1990 Ayrton Senna (Brazil)
1991 Ayrton Senna (Brazil)
1992 Nigel Mansell (Britain)
1993 Alain Prost (France)
1994 Michael Schumacher (Germany)
1995 Michael Schumacher (Germany)
1996 Damon Hill (Britain)
1997 Jacques Villeneuve (Canada)
1998 Mika Häkkinen (Finland)
1999 Mika Häkkinen (Finland)
2000 Michael Schumacher (Germany)
2001 Michael Schumacher (Germany)
2002 Michael Schumacher (Germany)
2003 Michael Schumacher (Germany)

World Champion Constructors

1958 Vanwall
1959 Cooper

▲ Riccardo Patrese's Arrows A3 claimed pole position but failed to finish the USA Grand Prix (West), Long Beach, in 1981.

1960 Cooper
1961 Ferrari
1962 BRM
1963 Lotus
1964 Ferrari
1965 Lotus
1966 Brabham
1967 Brabham
1968 Lotus
1969 Matra
1970 Lotus
1971 Tyrrell
1972 Lotus
1973 Lotus
1974 McLaren
1975 Ferrari
1976 Ferrari
1977 Ferrari
1978 Lotus
1979 Ferrari
1980 Williams
1981 Williams
1982 Ferrari
1983 Ferrari
1984 McLaren
1985 McLaren
1986 Williams
1987 Williams
1988 McLaren
1989 McLaren
1990 McLaren
1991 McLaren
1992 Williams
1993 Williams
1994 Williams
1995 Benetton
1996 Williams
1997 Williams
1998 McLaren
1999 Ferrari
2000 Ferrari
2001 Ferrari
2002 Ferrari
2003 Ferrari

Grands Prix Formulae

1906 Max weight 1000kg
1907 Max weight 1000kg
      Fuel consumption:
        30 litres/100km (9.4mpg)
1908 Max weight 1150kg
      Max cylinder bore:
        4-cylinder engines: 155mm
        6-cylinder engines: 127mm
1912 Max width 175cm
1913 Min weight 800kg
      Max weight 1100kg
      Fuel consumption:
        20 litres/100km (14.1mpg)
1914 4.5-litre max
      Max weight 1100kg
1921 3-litre max
      Min weight 800kg
1922–25 2-litre max
         Min weight 650kg
1926–27 1.5-litre max
(1926)   Min weight 600kg
(1927)   Min weight 700kg
1928   Min weight 500kg
         Max weight 750kg
1929–30 Min weight 900kg
         Fuel consumption:
           14 litres/100km (20.1mpg)
1931–33 No stipulation
1934–37 Max weight 750kg
1938–39 3-litre forced induction
         4.5-litre normally aspirated
1947–51 1.5-litre forced induction
         4.5-litre normally aspirated
1952–53 2-litre normally aspirated
         0.5-litre forced induction
1954–60 2.5-litre normally aspirated
         0.75-litre forced induction
1961–65 1.5-litre norm.aspirated only
         Min weight 450kg
1966–85 3-litre normally-aspirated
         1.5-litre forced induction
(1966–68) Min weight 500kg
(1969–81) Min weight 530kg
(1982)   Min weight 580kg
(1983)   Min weight 540kg
         Forced induction fuel max
         250 litres
(1984–85) Min weight 540kg
         Forced induction fuel max
         220 litres. No fuel stops
1986   1.5-litre forced induction
         Min weight 540kg. Fuel
         max 195 litres. No fuel stops
1987   1.5-litre forced induction

	3.5-litre normally aspirated Forced induction fuel max 195 litres. Forced induction boost 4-bar max. No fuel stops. Min weight 540kg
1988	1.5-litre forced induction 3.5-litre normally aspirated Forced induction fuel max 150 litres. Forced induction boost 2.5-bar max. No fuel stops. Forced induction 540kg Normally aspirated 500kg
1989–94	3.5-litre normally-aspirated only. Min weight 500kg
(1994)	Fuel stops allowed
1995–present)	3-litre normally aspirated only Fuel stops allowed Min weight 600kg including driver
(1999–present)	10-cylinder engines only

Championship Race Wins (Drivers)

Michael Schumacher	70
Alain Prost	51
Ayrton Senna	41
Nigel Mansell	31
Jackie Stewart	27
Jim Clark	25
Niki Lauda	25
Juan Manuel Fangio	24
Nelson Piquet	23
Damon Hill	22
Mika Häkkinen	20
Stirling Moss	16
Jack Brabham	14
Emerson Fittipaldi	14
Graham Hill	14
Alberto Ascari	13
David Coulthard	13
Mario Andretti	12
Alan Jones	12
Carlos Reutemann	12
Jacques Villeneuve	11
Gerhard Berger	10
James Hunt	10
Ronnie Peterson	10
Jody Scheckter	10
Denny Hulme	8
Jacky Ickx	8
René Arnoux	7
Rubens Barrichello	7
Tony Brooks	6
Jacques Laffite	6
Riccardo Patrese	6
Jochen Rindt	6
Ralf Schumacher	6
John Surtees	6
Gilles Villeneuve	6

Michele Alboreto	5
Giuseppe Farina	5
Clay Regazzoni	5
Keke Rosberg	5
John Watson	5
Dan Gurney	4
Eddie Irvine	4
Bruce McLaren	4
Thierry Boutsen	3
Peter Collins	3
Heinz-Harald Frentzen	3
Mike Hawthorn	3
Johnny Herbert	3
Phil Hill	3
Juan Pablo Montoya	3
Didier Pironi	3
Elio de Angelis	2
Patrick Depailler	2
José Froilán González	2
Jean-Pierre Jabouille	2
Peter Revson	2
Pedro Rodriguez	2
Jo Siffert	2
Patrick Tambay	2
Maurice Trintignant	2
Wolfgang von Trips	2
Jean Alesi	1
Fernando Alonso	1
Giancarlo Baghetti	1
Lorenzo Bandini	1
Jean-Pierre Beltoise	1
Jo Bonnier	1
Vittorio Brambilla	1
François Cevert	1
Luigi Fagioli	1
Peter Gethin	1
Richie Ginther	1
Innes Ireland	1
Jochen Mass	1
Fernando Alonso	1
Giancarlo Fisichella	1
Luigi Musso	1

▲ Kimi Raikkonen's McLaren-Mercedes MP4/17 lost time when a tyre exploded at the German Grand Prix, Hockenheim, 2002.

Alessandro Nannini	1
Gunnar Nilsson	1
Carlos Pace	1
Olivier Panis	1
Kimi Raikkonen	1
Ludovico Scarfiotti	1
Piero Taruffi	1

Championship Race Wins (Teams)

Ferrari	166
McLaren	137
Williams	112
Lotus	79
Brabham	35
Benetton	27
Tyrrell	23
BRM	17
Cooper	16
Renault	16
Alfa Romeo	10
Ligier	9
Maserati	9
Matra	9
Mercedes	9
Vanwall	9
Jordan	4
March	3
Wolf	3
Honda	2
Eagle	1
Hesketh	1
Penske	1
Porsche	1
Shadow	1
Stewart	1

Championship Pole Positions (Drivers)

Ayrton Senna	65
Michael Schumacher	55
Jim Clark	33
Alain Prost	33
Nigel Mansell	32
Juan-Manuel Fangio	28
Mika Häkkinen	26
Niki Lauda	24
Nelson Piquet	24
Damon Hill	20
Mario Andretti	18
René Arnoux	18
Jackie Stewart	17
Stirling Moss	16
Alberto Ascari	14
James Hunt	14
Ronnie Peterson	14
Jack Brabham	13
Graham Hill	13
Jacky Ickx	13
Jacques Villeneuve	13

Gerhard Berger	12
David Coulthard	12
Juan Pablo Montoya	11
Jochen Rindt	10
Rubens Barrichello	9
Riccardo Patrese	8
John Surtees	8
Jacques Laffite	7
Emerson Fittipaldi	6
Phil Hill	6
Jean-Pierre Jabouille	6
Alan Jones	6
Carlos Reutemann	6
Chris Amon	5
Giuseppe Farina	5
Clay Regazzoni	5
Keke Rosberg	5
Patrick Tambay	5
Mike Hawthorn	4
Didier Pironi	4
Ralf Schumacher	4
Elio de Angelis	3
Tony Brooks	3
Teo Fabi	3
José Froilán González	3
Dan Gurney	3
Jean-Pierre Jarier	3
Jody Scheckter	3
Michele Alboreto	2
Jean Alesi	2
Fernando Alonso	2
Heinz-Harald Frentzen	2
Stuart Lewis Evans	2
Kimi Raikkonen	2
Jo Siffert	2
Gilles Villeneuve	2
John Watson	2
Lorenzo Bandini	1
Jo Bonnier	1
Thierry Boutsen	1
Vittorio Brambilla	1
Eugenio Castellotti	1
Peter Collins	1
Andrea de Cesaris	1
Giancarlo Fisichella	1
Bruno Giacomelli	1
Denny Hulme	1
Carlos Pace	1
Mike Parkes	1
Tom Pryce	1
Peter Revson	1
Wolfgang von Trips	1

Championship Pole Positions (Teams)

Ferrari	166
Williams	123
McLaren	115
Lotus	107

Brabham	39
Renault	33
Benetton	16
Tyrrell	14
Alfa Romeo	12
BRM	11
Cooper	11
Maserati	10
Ligier	9
Mercedes	8
Vanwall	7
March	5
Matra	4
Shadow	3
Jordan	2
Lancia	2
Arrows	1
Honda	1
Lola	1
Porsche	1
Stewart	1
Toleman	1
Wolf	1

Engine Championship Race Wins

Ford Cosworth DFV	155	(1967–83)
Renault V10	75	(1989–97)
Ferrari Martinelli V10	47	(1996–03)
Honda turbo V6	40	(1984–88)
Ferrari Forghieri flat-12	37	(1970–79)
Mercedes Ilmor V10	32	(1997–03)
Porsche TAG turbo V6	25	(1984–87)
Coventry Climax V8	23	(1961–65)
Renault turbo V6	20	(1979–86)
Ford Cosworth HB	19	(1989–94)
Coventry Climax 4	17	(1958–61)
Ferrari Lampredi straight-4	16	(1952–55)
Honda Goto V10	16	(1989–90)
Ferrari Forghieri turbo V6	15	(1981–88)
Honda Goto V12	13	(1991–92)
Alfa Romeo straight-8	12	(1950–51)
BRM V8	12	(1962–66)
Ferrari Lombardi V12	11	(1989–95)
Maserati straight-6	9	(1953–57)
BMW turbo 4	9	(1982–86)
BMW V10	9	(2001–03)
Mercedes straight-8	9	(1954–55)
Vanwall straight-4	9	(1957–58)
Repco V8	8	(1966–67)
Ferrari Chiti V6	6	(1961–63)
Ferrari Jano V6	5	(1958–60)
Lancia V8	5	(1956)
BRM V12	4	(1970–72)
Mugen Honda V10	4	(1996–99)
Ferrari Lampredi V12	3	(1951)
Ferrari Bellai V8	3	(1964)
Ferrari Colombo V12	3	(1966–68)
Matra V12	3	(1977–81)
Ford Cosworth CR V10	2	(1995–03)

Maserati V12	2	(1966–67)
BRM straight 4	1	(1959)
BRM H16	1	(1966)
Honda Nakamura V12	1	(1965)
Honda Irimagiri V12	1	(1967)
Porsche flat-8	1	(1962)
Weslake V12	1	(1967)
Renault 111-deg V10	1	(2003)

Engine Championship Race Wins by Manufacturer

Ford	176
Ferrari	161
Renault	96
Honda	75
Mercedes	42
Coventry Climax	40
Porsche	26
BMW	18
BRM	18
Alfa Romeo	12
Maserati	11
Vanwall	9
Repco	8
Lancia	5
Matra	3
Weslake	1

Fastest Race Laps in Championship Grands Prix (Drivers)

Michael Schumacher	56
Alain Prost	41
Nigel Mansell	30
Jim Clark	28
Mika Häkkinen	25
Niki Lauda	25
Juan Manuel Fangio	23
Nelson Piquet	23
Gerhard Berger	21
Stirling Moss	20
Damon Hill	19

▲ Jarno Trulli's Renault R202 leads David Coulthard's McLaren-Mercedes MP4/17 at the German Grand Prix, 2002.

Ayrton Senna	19	Thierry Boutsen	1
David Coulthard	18	Andrea de Cesaris	1
Clay Regazzoni	15	Giancarlo Fisichella	1
Jackie Stewart	15	Bertrand Gachot	1
Jacky Ickx	14	Mauricio Gugelmin	1
Alan Jones	13	Mike Hailwood	1
Riccardo Patrese	13	Brian Henton	1
René Arnoux	12	Hans Herrmann	1
Alberto Ascari	11	Innes Ireland	1
Rubens Barrichello	11	Eddie Irvine	1
John Surtees	11	Karl Kling	1
Mario Andretti	10	Onofré Marimon	1
Jack Brabham	10	Roberto Mieres	1
Graham Hill	10	Roberto Moreno	1
Denny Hulme	9	Luigi Musso	1
Juan Pablo Montoya	9	Sataru Nakajima	1
Ronnie Peterson	9	Jackie Oliver	1
Jacques Villeneuve	9	Jonathan Palmer	1
James Hunt	8	Henri Pescarolo	1
Jacques Laffite	7	Pedro Rodriguez	1
Ralf Schumacher	7	Lodovico Scarfiotti	1
Gilles Villeneuve	7	Marc Surer	1
Giuseppe Farina	6	Piero Taruffi	1
Emerson Fittipaldi	6	Maurice Trintignant	1
Heinz-Harald Frentzen	6	Luigi Villoresi	1
José Froilán González	6	Alex Wurz	1
Dan Gurney	6		
Mike Hawthorn	6		
Phil Hill	6		

Fastest Race Laps in Championship Grands Prix (Teams)

Didier Pironi	6	Ferrari	167
Jody Scheckter	6	Williams	125
Carlos Pace	5	McLaren	112
John Watson	5	Lotus	70
Michele Alboreto	4	Brabham	41
Jean Alesi	4	Benetton	36
Jean-Pierre Beltoise	4	Tyrrell	20
Patrick Depailler	4	Renault	19
Kimi Raikkonen	4	BRM	15
Carlos Reutemann	4	Maserati	15
Jo Siffert	4	Alfa Romeo	14
Chris Amon	3	Cooper	13
Tony Brooks	3	Matra	12
Richie Ginther	3	Ligier	11
Jean-Pierre Jarier	3	Mercedes	11
Bruce McLaren	3	March	7
Jochen Rindt	3	Vanwall	6
Keke Rosberg	3	Surtees	4
Lorenzo Bandini	2	Eagle	2
Vittorio Brambilla	2	Honda	2
François Cevert	2	Jordan	2
Teo Fabi	2	Shadow	2
Jochen Mass	2	Wolf	2
Alessandro Nannini	2	Ensign	1
Patrick Tambay	2	Gordini	1
Derek Warwick	2	Hesketh	1
Fernando Alonso	1	Lancia	1
Richard Attwood	1	Parnelli	1
Giancarlo Baghetti	1		
Jean Behra	1		

▲ Giancarlo Fisichella (Jordan) leads team-mate Takuma Sato, Enrique Bernoldi (Arrows) and Jacques Villeneuve (BAR) in the Spanish Grand Prix, Barcelona, 2002.

Age of World Champions

1950	Farina	44 years
1951	Fangio	40
1952	Ascari	34
1953	Ascari	35
1954	Fangio	43
1955	Fangio	44
1956	Fangio	45
1957	Fangio	46
1958	Hawthorn	29
1959	Brabham	33
1960	Brabham	34
1961	P.Hill	34
1962	G.Hill	33
1963	Clark	27
1964	Surtees	30
1965	Clark	29
1966	Brabham	40
1967	Hulme	31
1968	G.Hill	39
1969	Stewart	30
1970	Rindt	28
1971	Stewart	32
1972	Fittipaldi	25
1973	Stewart	33
1974	Fittipaldi	27
1975	Lauda	26
1976	Hunt	29
1977	Lauda	28
1978	Andretti	38
1979	Scheckter	29
1980	Jones	34
1981	Piquet	29
1982	Rosberg	34
1983	Piquet	31
1984	Lauda	35
1985	Prost	30
1986	Prost	31
1987	Piquet	35
1988	Senna	28

1989	Prost	34
1990	Senna	30
1991	Senna	31
1992	Mansell	39
1993	Prost	38
1994	M.Schumacher	25
1995	M.Schumacher	26
1996	D.Hill	36
1997	Villeneuve	26
1998	Häkkinen	30
1999	Häkkinen	31
2000	M.Schumacher	31
2001	M.Schumacher	32
2002	M.Schumacher	33
2003	M.Schumacher	34

Average age of World Champion:
34 years
Youngest World Champion when
title sealed: Emerson Fittipaldi (1972)
25 years, 298 days
Oldest World Champion when title
sealed: Juan Manuel Fangio (1957)
46 years, 41 days

Top 10 Youngest Championship Grand Prix winners

Fernando Alonso
22 years, 26 days (2003)
Bruce McLaren
22 years, 80 days (1958)
Jacky Ickx
22 years, 104 days (1968)
Michael Schumacher
23 years, 188 days (1992)
Emerson Fittipaldi
23 years, 296 days (1970)
Mike Hawthorn
24 years, 86 days (1953)
Jody Scheckter
24 years, 131 days (1974)
Elio de Angelis

▲ Fourth-placed Jenson Button (Renault)
lost his first podium finish on the final lap
with an anti-roll bar malady, Sepang, 2002.

24 years, 148 days (1982)
David Coulthard
24 years, 181 days (1995)
Peter Collins
24 years, 208 days (1956)

Top 10 Oldest Championship Grand Prix Winners

Luigi Fagioli
53 years, 22 days (1951)
Giuseppe Farina
46 years, 276 days (1955)
Juan Manuel Fangio
46 years, 41 days (1957)
Piero Taruffi
45 years, 219 days (1952)
Jack Brabham
43 years, 339 days (1970)
Nigel Mansell
41 years, 97 days (1994)
Maurice Trintignant
40 years, 200 days (1958)
Graham Hill
40 years, 90 days (1969)
Clay Regazzoni
39 years, 312 days (1979)
Carlos Reutemann
39 years, 35 days (1981)

Top 10 Youngest Championship Grand Prix Participants

Mike Thackwell
19 years, 82 days (1980)
Ricardo Rodriguez
19 years, 209 days (1961)
Fernando Alonso
19 years, 261 days (2001)
Esteban Tuero
19 years, 320 days (1998)
Chris Amon
19 years, 326 days (1963)
Jenson Button
20 years, 52 days (2000)
Eddie Cheever
20 years, 54 days (1978)
Tarso Marques
20 years, 71 days (1996)
Peter Collins
20 years, 94 days (1952)
Rubens Barrichello
20 years, 295 days (1993)

Laps in the Lead of Championship Grands Prix

Michael Schumacher	3,909
Ayrton Senna	2,982
Alain Prost	2,705
Nigel Mansell	2,099
Jim Clark	2,039

Jackie Stewart	1,893
Niki Lauda	1,620
Nelson Piquet	1,572
Mika Häkkinen	1,490
Damon Hill	1,352
Graham Hill	1,073
David Coulthard	891
Jack Brabham	827
Mario Andretti	799
Ronnie Peterson	706
Gerhard Berger	695
Jody Scheckter	671
Carlos Reutemann	648
James Hunt	634
Jacques Villeneuve	628
Alan Jones	594
Rubens Barrichello	590
Riccardo Patrese	570
Gilles Villeneuve	533
Jacky Ickx	529
René Arnoux	506
Keke Rosberg	506
Emerson Fittipaldi	478
Denny Hulme	436
Jochen Rindt	387

Number of Championship Grands Prix Contested (Drivers)

Riccardo Patrese	256	(1977–93)
Gerhard Berger	210	(1984–97)
Andrea de Cesaris	208	(1980–93)
Nelson Piquet	204	(1978–91)
Jean Alesi	201	(1989–2001)
Alain Prost	199	(1980–93)
Michael Schumacher	195	(1991–2003)
Michele Alboreto	194	(1981–94)
Nigel Mansell	187	(1980–95)
Rubens Barrichello	180	(1993–2003)
Graham Hill	176	(1958–75)
Jacques Laffite	176	(1974–86)
Niki Lauda	171	(1971–85)
Thierry Boutsen	163	(1983–93)
Mika Häkkinen	162	(1991–2001)
Ayrton Senna	161	(1984–94)
Martin Brundle	158	(1984–96)
David Coulthard	157	(1994–2003)
Heinz-Harald Frentzen	157	(1994–2003)
John Watson	152	(1973–85)
Olivier Panis	141	(1994–2003)
René Arnoux	149	(1978–89)
Derek Warwick	147	(1981–93)
Carlos Reutemann	146	(1972–82)
Eddie Irvine	146	(1993–2002)
Emerson Fittipaldi	144	(1970–80)
Johnny Herbert	144	(1989–2000)
Jean-Pierre Jarier	135	(1971–83)
Eddie Cheever	132	(1978–89)
Clay Regazzoni	132	(1970–80)

Number of Championship Grands Prix Contested (Teams)

Ferrari	686	(1950–2003)
McLaren	559	(1966–2003)
Lotus	490	(1958–94)
Williams	478	(1975–2003)
Tyrrell	418	(1970–98)
Brabham	399	(1963–92)
Arrows	382	(1978–2002)
Ligier	326	(1976–96)
Benetton	317	(1986–2001)
Minardi	303	(1985–2003)
March	230	(1970–92)
Jordan	213	(1991–2003)
BRM	197	(1951–77)
Sauber	179	(1993–2003)
Renault	156	(1977–2003)
Lola	139	(1962–93)
Osella	132	(1980–90)
Cooper	129	(1955–68)
Surtees	118	(1970–78)
Alfa Romeo	112	(1950–85)
Fittipaldi	104	(1976–82)
Shadow	104	(1973–80)
ATS	99	(1977–84)
Ensign	99	(1973–82)
BAR	83	(1999–2003)
Dallara	78	(1988–92)
Maserati	69	(1950–58)
Jaguar	67	(2000–2003)
Matra	60	(1968–72)
Zakspeed	54	(1985–89)

Greatest Number of Championship Points Scored (Drivers)

Michael Schumacher	1038
Alain Prost	798.5
Ayrton Senna	614
Nelson Piquet	485.5
Nigel Mansell	482
David Coulthard	451
Niki Lauda	420.5
Mika Häkkinen	420
Gerhard Berger	386
Damon Hill	360
Jackie Stewart	360
Rubens Barrichello	337
Carlos Reutemann	310
Graham Hill	289
Emerson Fittipaldi	281
Riccardo Patrese	281
Juan Manuel Fangio	277.5
Jim Clark	274
Jack Brabham	261
Jody Scheckter	255
Denny Hulme	248
Jean Alesi	240
Ralf Schumacher	235
Jacques Laffite	228
Jacques Villeneuve	219
Clay Regazzoni	212
Alan Jones	206
Ronnie Peterson	206
Bruce McLaren	196.5
Eddie Irvine	191

Greatest Number of Championship Points Scored (Teams)

Ferrari	3082.5
McLaren	2,790.5
Williams	2,341.5
Lotus	1,370
Brabham	865
Benetton	851.5
Tyrrell	621
BRM	433
Renault	415
Ligier	390
Cooper	333
Jordan	274
March	180.5
Arrows	167
Matra	155
Sauber	141
Wolf	79
BAR	70
Shadow	67.5
Vanwall	57

World Championship Points Systems

1950–59:	8-6-4-3-2 for first five places in race. 1 point for fastest lap.
1959–90:	9-6-4-3-2-1 for first six places.
1991–2002:	10-6-4-3-2-1 for first six places.
2003–on:	10-8-6-5-4-3-2-1 for first eight places.

(shortened races awarded half-points)

Closest Grand Prix finishes

Italy 1971	0.010 secs	(Peter Gethin/ Ronnie Peterson)
USA 2002	0.011 secs	(Rubens Barrichello/ Michael Schumacher)
Spain 1986	0.050 secs	(Ayrton Senna/ Nigel Mansell)
Austria 1982	0.080 secs	(Elio de Angelis/ Keke Rosberg)
France 1954	0.100 secs	(Juan Manuel Fangio/ Karl Kling)

▲ Winner Mika Häkkinen's Mclaren MP4-13 at the Spanish Grand Prix, Barcelona, 1998.

France 1961	0.100 secs	(Giancarlo Baghetti/ Dan Gurney)
Austria 2002	0.182 secs	(Michael Schumacher/ Rubens Barrichello)
Britain 1955	0.200 secs	(Stirling Moss/ Juan Manuel Fangio)
Holland 1955	0.200 secs	(Juan Manuel Fangio/ Stirling Moss)
Italy 1967	0.200 secs	(John Surtees/ Jack Brabham)
Spain 1981	0.210 secs	(Gilles Villeneuve/ Jacques Laffite)
Monaco 1992	0.215 secs	(Ayrton Senna/ Nigel Mansell)
Holland 1985	0.232 secs	(Niki Lauda/Alain Prost)
Hungary 1990	0.288 secs	(Thierry Boutsen/ Ayrton Senna)
Switzerland 1950	0.300 secs	(Giuseppe Farina/ Luigi Fagioli)
France 1956	0.300 secs	(Peter Collins/ Eugenio Castellotti)
Austria 1999	0.313 secs	(Eddie Irvine/ David Coulthard)
Holland 1978	0.320 secs	(Mario Andretti/ Ronnie Peterson)
France 1993	0.342 secs	(Alain Prost/ Damon Hill)
Japan 1991	0.344 secs	(Gerhard Berger/Ayrton Senna)

Index

▲ Race winner Michael Schumacher in the Ferrari F2002 at the German Grand Prix, Hockenheim, in 2002.

▲ Nelson Piquet (Brabham BMW BT52)
retired but was classified 13th at the 1983
German Grand Prix at Hockenheim.

▲ Stuart Lewis-Evans (Vanwall), 1957.

PICTURE CREDITS
All photographs supplied by
Sutton Motorsport Images
except for the following.
t = top; b = bottom; l = left;
r = right; c = centre
Malcolm Jeal 146br; 154bl; 176t, tr, b.
Ludvigsen Library 24bl, br; 25t, b; 96t; 98t, b, c; 103b; 105t; 106t, c, b; 114t; 117t, b; 119br; 122b; 147cl, b; 149tl, tr; 154t; 155t, c; 166t, c, br; 175t, b; 178; 181b; 194b; 198c; 200t, bl, br; 209b.